DULWICH PICTURE GALLERY

BRITISH

John Ingamells

UNICORN PRESS

First published 2008 for Dulwich Picture Gallery by
Unicorn Press, 76 Great Suffolk Street, London SE1 0BL
www.unicornpress.org

Paperback edition available from Dulwich Picture Gallery: ISBN 978 1 906509 02 6
Hardback edition available from Unicorn Press: ISBN 978 1 906509 01 9

A catalogue record for this book is available from the British Library.

Designed by Guilland Sutherland
Typeset in Adobe Garamond
Printed in Great Britain by Saxon Print Group

CONTENTS

PREFACE

Dulwich Picture Gallery's British School holdings offer a fascinating insight into the history of collecting. This is arguably true of all our collections; but unlike, say, the Dutch, Flemish, Italian, or French Schools, the British paintings did not for the most part arrive in the Gallery via the famous Bourgeois bequest of 1811 (although there are some fine British paintings in that bequest also). A significant group of them considerably predate Francis Bourgeois, originating in the bequests of Edward Alleyn and William Cartwright, actors both, in the 17th century (1626 and 1686 respectively). Until 1994, when the Gallery became an independent charitable trust, Dulwich Picture Gallery was in fact known as Dulwich *College* Picture Gallery; we were governed by the College – and Dulwich College was founded by Alleyn. Our joint history with that famous public school means that there have been paintings on display on this site for nearly four hundred years, not just the two hundred we usually brag about (and we are right to brag; our foundation in 1811 means that we are the oldest public art gallery in England). There are no outright masterpieces in the two actors' collections; their interest lies in the simple fact of their existence – two aspirational collections put together by non-aristocrats in the entertainment business intent on bettering their perceived standing in the world.

It is arguable that the paintings that belonged to Edward Alleyn were always intended for educational purposes. It was a school he had founded, after all – his paintings of kings, queens, sybils and worthies were almost certainly intended as teaching aids and inspirers of young minds. They are crude productions, but nonetheless fascinating for that, revealing a market for art that flew well beneath the radar of the era's more magnificent collectors such as the Earl of Arundel and Charles I. Cartwright's pictures, however, give evidence of a relatively well-off 'ordinary' man buying the best he can afford in a rather more developed market place – not Lely, but Lely's talented if all too often inebriated pupil John Greenhill; not Van Dyck, but Isaac Fuller; and from the Dutch School – not Rembrandt, but Colonia. In espousing the cause of Greenhill, Cartwright did us all a favour. The artist's early death (a cautionary tale: he fell downstairs in Covent Garden, drunk) could have meant that he tumbled just as entirely from the annals of art history in this country; Cartwright's six pictures by him reveal a genuine, if variable, talent, including a self-portrait of considerable ambition.

Another extraordinary element in Cartwright's collection is the remarkable group of actor portraits, including two friends and colleagues of Shakespeare: Nathan Field, who took Shakespeare's place on the Board of the Globe, and – the only known portrait, if it is indeed him – Richard Burbage, Shakespeare's particular friend, the first Hamlet, the first Lear. Cartwright's father, also William and also an actor, would have known these two – and presumably Shakespeare – personally. It really is one of the most intriguing things about Dulwich, that if there were any justice, searchers for that elusive portrait of the Bard would surely find it here. Sadly, that holy grail has eluded us; but the presence of these actor portraits may well have been one of the defining factors in the Gallery's history. John Philip Kemble, the leading actor of his generation, knew of them; and Kemble was a great friend of Francis Bourgeois. Did the spark of the idea to bequeath the collection to the College come from the actor?

Genuinely fascinating as these collections undoubtedly are in historical terms, the fact remains that, when Horace Walpole visited the College, he recorded only 'a hundred mouldy portraits among apostles sibyls and kings of England.' These were then housed in the first floor gallery of the west wing of the Jacobean college. They were soon to be comprehensively eclipsed. Bourgeois' magnificent bequest in 1811 of the collection he had put together with friend and fellow art-dealer Noel Desenfans created the nation's first public art gallery, and of course required a new building – Sir John Soane's great design, the blueprint of so many institutions worldwide (and very nearly not built at all: this is where our third Founder, Margaret Desenfans, Noel's wife, achieved her particular immortality – she provided the necessary funds to allow the building to go ahead). But although the bequest included works by Van Dyck, Reynolds and Gainsborough, and one or two other British artists, it did not have a great showing of British painting. The reasons for this are, like everything to do with our founders, rather interesting and personal. Their thriving art dealership had taken a particular turn in the 1790s, when Stanislaus Augusutus, king of Poland, commissioned them to put together a 'national collection' for Poland. Although the whole deal fell through in 1795 with that country's partition, the notion of a collection 'for the inspection of the public' (as Bourgeois was to put it in his will) seems to have taken root. The two dealers, in particular Bourgeois, who seems to have gradually transformed from dealer into collector over the next 15 years, clearly saw their house in Charlotte (now Hallam) Street – lined, as it was, with paintings from floor to ceiling of every room – as a proto-'National Gallery'. Indeed, Desenfans tried and failed to interest the British Government in taking the collection on as such. Meanwhile, they were generous with their hospitality, always happy to show people round, and with a particular interest in providing inspiration for artists. The collection was carefully shaped to represent the best in art as it was then perceived – so, heavy on Bolognese classical and Dutch Italianate, rich in Poussin, Rembrandt and Rubens, but virtually no Renaissance Italian art (still characterised as 'primitive') and – significantly – poor in British art, which they presumably felt (with the obvious exception of the Flemish Van Dyck) did not deserve its place in the pantheon quite yet. It is entirely characteristic that the most high-profile contemporary British picture was a studio version of Reynolds's *Mrs Siddons* – that ostentatiously Michelangelesque gauntlet thrown down before European artistic prejudice. Gainsborough is amongst their paintings simply as the portraitist of Philippe de Loutherbourg, who for a couple of years had been Bourgeois's teacher in the 1770s, and who, for no doubt similarly personal reasons, joins Richard Wilson as the sole representatives of British landscape. Beechey is represented by portraits of John Philip Kemble and Charles Small Pybus, both friends of the founders. And so it goes. The collection also included over twenty works by Bourgeois himself – the rags and tags of his studio, one suspects, and not doing even his modest talent justice.

This situation was rectified later, firstly with the magnificent Linley bequest of 1835, which provided a sequence of gorgeous images by Gainsborough (and others, including the young Thomas Lawrence) of possibly the best-looking and certainly one of the most talented musical families in England, Thomas Linley and his sons and daughters – including the famous Gainsborough of the beautiful Linley sisters, Elizabeth and Mary. Their brothers fared equally well at Gainsborough's hands – young Tom and Samuel, both of whom died tragically young, cutting short, in Tom's case, the career of a musician hailed as 'England's Mozart'; Samuel died even before the artist could finish his portrait, which nonetheless stands now as a miraculous testimony to Gainsborough's genius, the product, so family sources claimed, of a mere 48 minutes' work. William, the youngest, was fortunate to be portrayed – all lustrous hair and sensitive profile – by another prodigiously talented teenager, Thomas Lawrence, at the beginning of his brilliant career. All in all, this gift (the link to the Gallery being another brother, Ozias, who was organist at the College chapel) finally provided Dulwich Picture Gallery with British masterpieces that were the equal of the Old Masters. Their glamorous presence encouraged other gifts and bequests, the most important of which was undoubtedly that of Charles Fairfax Murray in 1911, persuaded by the formidable chair of the Board of Governors responsible for the Gallery, Henry Yates Thompson.

Murray was an artist, of the pre-Raphaelite persuasion, himself; but he became most notable as a collector (if you discount his colourful lifestyle from the equation: he had one family in Italy, another in England). His gift, in 1911, of over fifty spectacular paintings, mostly British, is one of the transforming moments in the Gallery's history. From Murray came the Gallery's beautiful early Gainsborough, *An Unknown Couple in a Landscape*, its two Hogarths, its Hudsons, its George Knapton – the beauteous *Lucy Ebberton* – its Kneller, and its great Lelys; and much more besides. The gap left by the prejudices of the Founders was, by the Linley gift and the generosity of Murray, spectacularly filled.

We could not have asked for a more distinguished scholar for this project than John Ingamells, who, funded by the Paul Mellon Centre for Studies in British Art, endured a couple of years of working in the most impossibly cramped conditions, maintaining his formidable concentration against continuous interruption. We are most grateful to him, and to the Mellon Centre, for their support in achieving this long-overdue volume, which will be the first of three, and the first full scholarly catalogues ever to be published of Dulwich's famous collection. Thanks in particular should go to Professor Brian Allen for his steadfast support, and to Guilland Sutherland, who is responsible for the clarity and beauty of the design. Margaret Reid, Curator of the Gallery from 2004–06, facilitated John Ingamells' work; her successor, Xavier F. Salomon, saw the project through its final stages towards publication; and Fulvio Rubesa helped arrange the necessary photographic campaign, funded again by a generous grant from the Paul Mellon Centre.

IAN A.C. DEJARDIN
DIRECTOR

ACKNOWLEDGMENTS

My first acknowledgment must be to the Paul Mellon Centre, the sponsor of this catalogue, and to its Director, Brian Allen. Responding in 1996 to an appeal from Desmond Shawe-Taylor, then Director of the Dulwich Picture Gallery, he invited me to undertake this catalogue as other commitments allowed. My second acknowledgment is to the Director of the National Portrait Gallery for allowing me to retain a desk in the Heinz archive and to continue enjoying the vast resources of the NPG.

At Dulwich Ian Dejardin (who succeeded Desmond Shawe-Taylor as Director in 2005), Margaret Reid and Jack Kettlewell have been very patient and extremely helpful, while a busy Gallery staff has shown great forebearance; I am most grateful to them all. I have profited immeasurably from research already undertaken on the Dulwich collection by, or under the direction of, Giles Waterfield (Director 1979–96). He organised a series of exhibitions exploring aspects of the collection, each accompanied by an exemplary catalogue: *A Nest of Nightingales* 1988 described the Linley gift, *Mr Cartwright's Pictures* 1987-88 and *Edward Alleyn* 1994 published extensive research and documentation; *Death, Passion and Politics* 1995 examined Van Dyck's *Venetia, Lady Digby*, and *Conserving Old Masters* 1995 published detailed analyses of Gainsborough's *Misses Linley* and *Mrs Moody*. Nor must I omit the other important contributors to those catalogues, principally the late Geoffrey Ashton, Susan Foister, Nicola Kalinsky, Anne Sumner and the late Richard Jeffree. I further profited from the extensive researches of the late Peter Murray and of Richard Beresford, compilers, respectively, of the 1980 and 1998 Dulwich catalogues.

At Dulwich College I was generously helped by the former Keeper of Archives, Jan Piggott, and by his successor Calista Lucy.

For their help over specific questions I am deeply grateful to Hugh Belsey, Marijke Booth, Margie Christian, Tarnya Cooper, Elizabeth Einberg, Alastair Laing, Emma Lauze, Paul Matthews, Sophie Plender, Aileen Ribeiro, Nicole Ryder, Jacob Simon and Carolyn Stewart. Further important acknowledgments to the published works of others will be found in footnotes.

I must finally acknowledge the vast resources of the London Library, the Courtauld Institute Library, the Witt Library and the National Art Library.

JOHN INGAMELLS

EXPLANATION

This catalogue of British paintings describes forty per cent of the pictures in the Dulwich Picture Gallery. Their divergent and remarkable character results from the original donors: two successful seventeenth-century actors with modest ambitions as virtuosi (Edward Alleyn and William Cartwright), an ambitious late eighteenth-century dealer (Noel Desenfans) with his protégé, an untalented painter (Sir Francis Bourgeois), and a serious connoisseur-dealer of the late nineteenth-early twentieth century (Charles Fairfax Murray). These five, who may not have had much to say to each other, gave nearly 70% of the works here catalogued. The remainder came from separate donors, of whom William and Ozias Linley stand pre-eminent. Only four paintings are known to have been purchased or commissioned (DPG440, DPG491, DPG304 and DPG627).

To emphasise this curious history, the catalogue has been arranged in sections, the first four devoted to the individual donors, the last two to further acquisitions and to the portraits included in previous Dulwich catalogues which presently hang in Dulwich College.

Deciding what makes a picture British has not always been easy. Works by Van Dyck and Canaletto painted in England are included, leaving the Flemish and Italian works by these masters to appear in later volumes (this breaks with National Gallery practice, for example). Some unattributed paintings are hesitantly catalogued as British (as DPG365, p.56; DPG385, p.64; and DPG151, p.125).

While pictures are arranged alphabetically by artist within the Bourgeois, Linley, Fairfax Murray and Acquisitions sections, different systems have had to be applied to the Alleyn, Cartwright and Dulwich College sections, as explained in the relevant introductions.

At the beginning of an entry the artist's name is sometimes qualified, as follows: *attributed* implies a degree of doubt; *studio of* produced under the artist's guidance; *manner of* suggestive of the artist's style; *circle of* by a contemporary artist influenced by; *after* a copy. The initial paragraph describing the condition names the earliest conservators but otherwise only the enigmatic Johannes Hell, whose extensive treatment of the collection between 1945 and 1970 remains undocumented save for the approximate dates as given. Subsequent anonymity is not, of course, to denigrate in any way the continuing fine work being undertaken for Dulwich, principally by Sophie Plender and Nicole Ryder. All the pictures were examined by Patrick Lindsay in 1989 as part of a conservation programme funded by the Getty Institute and his reports proved invaluable.

Lastly it is emphasized that exhibition catalogues included under EXH. will often add to the published accounts cited under REF. under which heading only the most immediately relevant books and articles are cited. Further references are contained in the footnotes. The Concordance identifies each picture in previous Dulwich catalogues.

ABBREVIATIONS

including abbreviated titles of books

Aberystwyth 1945
An exhibition of sixty pictures from the Royal, Gregynog, and Dulwich Collections, National Library of Wales, Aberystwyth, 1945

Aberystwyth 1946
An exhibition of seventy- two pictures from the Gregynog, Dulwich College and other Collections, National Library of Wales, Aberystwyth, 1946

Aberystwyth 1947
An exhibition of fifty-one pictures from the Gregynog, Dulwich College and other Collections, National Library of Wales, Aberystwyth, 1947

AC
Arts Council

AG
Art Gallery

Alleyn's Diary
Alleyn MSS in the Dulwich College Library, MS IX; transcribed in Young 1889, ii, pp.51-255; part transcribed in Warner 1881, pp.165-87

Ashton 1997
G. Ashton, *Pictures in the Garrick Club*, ed. K.A. Burnim & A. Wilton, 1997

Aubrey 1718
J. Aubrey, *Natural History and Antiquities of the County of Surrey*, i, 1718

Aubrey 1719
J. Aubrey, *Natural History and Antiquities of the County of Surrey*, v, 1719, appendix

(Aubrey undertook his 'perambulation' through Surrey in July-October 1673,but continued to revise his material; unfinished at his death in 1692, it was edited and published by Richard Rawlinson)

Becket 1951
R.B. Becket, *Lely*, 1951

Beresford 1998
R.B. Beresford, *Dulwich Picture Gallery, Complete Illustrated Catalogue*, 1998 see Concordance

BPG
British Portrait Gallery (within the Manchester *Art Treasures* exhibition, 1857)

Brayley 1850
E.W. Brayley, *History of Surrey*, 1850

Britton 1813
J. Britton, 'A Brief Catalogue of Pictures, Late the property of Sir Francis Bourgeois, R.A., with the sizes and proportions of the Pictures, 24 May 1813' (Dulwich College Library, MS XVII) [*measurements in feet and inches including frames; the pictures were removed from Charlotte Street to Dulwich in September 1814*]

Brown Ledger
Robert Brown's Ledger (National Art Library, MSL/1993/3/1; unfoliated), an account with Mr Allen, Warden of Dulwich College, 11 October 1810 to 15 March 1817, for the repair of pictures. Ninety-seven are listed of which forty-four are identified here as British. Some entries, as *'two seapieces by Castoro'* or *'a Portrait of a Lady on Panel'* remain unidentified.

Burl. Mag.
The Burlington Magazine

Capital Collection 2002
L. Dukelskaya & A. Moore, *A Capital Collection, Houghton Hall and The Hermitage*, 2002

Mr Cartwright's Pictures 1987
Mr Cartwright's Pictures, a seventeenth-century collection, exhibition catalogue by G.A. Waterfield and N. Kalinsky, with contributions from various hands, Dulwich Picture Gallery, 1987-88

Cartwright Inventory
Cartwright's Inventory c.1680, Dulwich College Library, MS XIV; transcribed in Young 1889, i, pp.472-80, and *Mr Cartwright's Pictures* 1987, pp.20-27; part transcript in Warner 1881, pp.204-08

Collection for a King, Washington DC, Los Angeles, 1985-86
Collection for a King, Old Master Paintings from the Dulwich Picture Gallery, 1985, exhibition catalogue by G.A. Waterfield with contributions from various hands, National Gallery of Art, Washington DC; Los Angeles County Museum of Art, 1985-86

Collins Baker 1912
C.H. Collins Baker, *Lely and the Stuart Portrait Painters*, 2 vols., 1912

Collins Baker 1915
C.H. Collins Baker, 'Nederlandsche Portretten de Dulwich Gallery', *Onze Kunst*, 1915, pp.101-107

Collins Baker 1933
C.H. Collins Baker, *British Painting*, 1933

Conserving Old Masters 1995
Conserving Old Masters, Paintings recently restored at Dulwich Picture Gallery, exhibition catalogue with introduction by G.A. Waterfield, entries from various hands, Dulwich Picture Gallery, 1995

Cook 1914
Sir Edward Cook , *Catalogue of the Pictures in the gallery of Alleyn's College of God's Gift at Dulwich*, 1914 (nos. 1-593 listed in order of accession number); see Concordance

Cook 1926
Sir Edward Cook , *Catalogue of the Pictures in the gallery of Alleyn's College of God's Gift at Dulwich*, 1914, revised 1926 (nos. 1-608 listed in order of accession number); see Concordance

Croft-Murray 1962
E. Croft-Murray, *Decorative Painting in England 1537-1837*, i *Early Tudor to Sir James Thornhill*, 1962

Croft-Murray & Hulton 1960
E. Croft-Murray & P. Hulton, *British Museum Catalogue of British Drawings ... XVI & XVII centuries*, 2 vols., 1960

CS
J. Chaloner Smith, *British Mezzotinto Portraits*, 4 vols., 1878-83

Death, Passion and Politics 1995
Paintings in their Context V: Death, Passion and Politics, Van Dyck's Portraits of Venetia Stanley and George Digby, exhibition catalogue ed. A. Sumner, Dulwich Picture Gallery, 1995-96

Denning 1858
S.P. Denning assisted by his son the Rev Stephen Denning, 'Catalogue of Pictures' (MS, Dulwich Picture Gallery archive; listed in order of the old picture numbers up to no.366 only); see Concordance

Denning 1859
S.P. Denning, 'Catalogue of Pictures' (MS, Dulwich Picture Gallery archive; listed in order of the old picture numbers up to no.202 only); essentially a neater version of Denning 1858; see Concordance

Desenfans 1790-91
Evening Mail, 31 December 1790-7 January 1791 (Mr Desenfans Collection, a list in three instalments of 338 pictures disposed in 15 rooms at Charlotte Street)

Desenfans 1802
A Descriptive Catalogue... of some Pictures ... purchased ... for the Late King of Poland Which will be exhibited early in 1802, At the Great Room, No.3, Berners Street ... by Noel Desenfans Esq. Late Consul General of Poland in Great Britain. 2 vols., 2nd ed.,1802 [sold by Skinner & Dyke, March 24-29, 1802,; see Whitley 1928b, pp.31-34]

Desenfans 1804
'List of Pictures to be Insured, 6 July 1804', by Desenfans (Dulwich College Library, MS XVI.16; printed in Warner 1881, pp.224-27)

DNB
Dictionary of National Biography, 1885-
See also *ODNB*

Duleep Singh
F. Duleep Singh, *Portraits in Norfolk Houses*, ed. E. Farrar, 2 vols. [1927-28]

Edward Alleyn 1994
Edward Alleyn, Elizabethan Actor, Jacobean Gentleman, exhibition catalogue ed. A. Reid & R. Maniura, with contributions from various hands, Dulwich Picture Gallery, 1994

ENG.:
engraved

EXH.:
exhibited

Farington
The Diary of Joseph Farington 1793-1821, 16 vols., 1978-1984, + index 1998; vols. i-vi ed. K. Garlick & A. Macintyre, vii-xvi ed. K. Cave

Garlick 1954
K. Garlick, *Sir Thomas Lawrence*, 1954

Garlick 1964
K. Garlick, 'A catalogue of the paintings, drawings and pastels of Sir Thomas Lawrence', *Wal. Soc.*, XXXIX, 1964

Garlick 1989
K. Garlick, *Sir Thomas Lawrence, a complete catalogue of oil paintings*, 1989

GC 1901
A. Graves & W.V. Cronin, *A History of the Works of Sir Joshua Reynolds*, 4 vols., 1899-1901

GEC
G. E. Cockayne, *The Complete Peerage*, 2nd ed., revised by V. Gibbs *et al.*, 1910-59

GM
Gentleman's Magazine

Graham
R. Graham, *A Short Account of the most eminent Painters, both ancient and modern, down to the present times*, 2nd ed., 1716 (printed as a supplement to Dryden's translation of Du Fresnoy's *Art of Painting*)

Gwynn 1898
S. Gwynn, *Memorials of an Eighteenth Century Painter*, 1898

Highfill
P.H. Highfill, K.A. Burnim & E.A. Laughans, *A Biographical Dictionary of Actors, Actresses ... 1660-1800*, 16 vols., 1973-93

Hind 1955
A.M. Hind, *Engraving in England in the sixteenth & seventeenth centuries*, ii, *The Reign of James* I, 1955

Ingamells 2004
J. Ingamells, *National Portrait Gallery, Mid-Georgian Portraits 1760-90*, 2004

Jameson 1842
Mrs Jameson, *Handbook to the Public Galleries of Art in and near London*, ii, 1842 [Dulwich Gallery, pp.435-506]

Kerslake 1977
J. Kerslake, *National Portrait Gallery, Early Georgian Portraits*, 2 vols., 1977

Kolekcja dla Króla, Warsaw, 1992
Kolekcja dla Króla [Collection for a King], Royal Castle, Warsaw, 1992 (catalogue numbers in two parts: I the paintings; II archival including graphics)

Leeds 1947-53
54 Dulwich paintings lent to the City Art Gallery, Leeds, while the Dulwich Gallery was being rebuilt after the war; the pictures were first shown for a few months in 1947 at the National Gallery, London. Additional loans, *hors catalogue*, were made to Leeds in 1949 and 1952.

Leslie & Taylor 1865
C.R. Taylor & T. Taylor, *Life and Letters of Sir Joshua Reynolds*, 2 vols., 1865

Lewis 1979
A.S. Lewis, *Joseph Highmore*, Harvard Univ. Ph.D. thesis, University Microfilms International, 2 vols., 1979

Lysons 1792
D. Lysons, *The Environs of London*, i, 1792 (Dulwich Gallery, pp. 108-12); 2nd ed., i, 2, 1811, pp.80-83

Mag.
Magazine

Manning & Bray
O. Manning & W. Bray, *History and Antiquities of the county of Surrey*, i, 1804; ii, 1809; iii, 1814

Mannings 2000
D. Mannings, *Sir Joshua Reynolds, a Complete Catalogue of his Paintings, the subject pictures catalogued by M. Postle*, 2 vols., 2000

Mannings (Postle) 2000
refers to a subject picture in Mannings 2000; see above

Memoirs of the late Noel Desenfans, 1810
Memoirs of the late Noel Desenfans Esq., containing also A Plan for preserving the portraits of Distinguished Characters; Poems and Letters, 1810 [the *Memoirs* are sometimes credited to John Taylor who wrote 'Lines addressed to Noel Desenfans …', f.p.180]

Millar 1963
O. Millar, *The Tudor, Stuart and early Georgian Pictures in the Collection of Her Majesty The Queen*, 2 vols., 1963

Millar 1969
O. Millar, *The later Georgian Pictures in the Collection of Her Majesty The Queen*, 2 vols., 1969

Millar 1992
O. Millar, *The Victorian Pictures in the Collection of Her Majesty The Queen*, 2 vols., 1992

Millar, D., 1995
D. Millar, *The Victorian Watercolours in the Collection of Her Majesty The Queen*, 2 vols., 1995

Milner 1927
J.D. Milner, 'Tilly Kettle', *Wal. Soc.,* XV, 1927, pp.47-103

Murray 1980
P. Murray, *The Dulwich Picture Gallery, A Catalogue*, 1980 (listed alphabetically by artist, divided into Exhibited and Non-Exhibited Paintings, the latter summarily listed pp.299-305); see Concordance

National Gallery 1947
see Leeds 1947-53

Nest of Nightingales 1988
Paintings and their Context II: A Nest of Nightingales, Thomas Gainsborough The Linley Sisters, exhibition catalogue by G.A. Waterfield, with contributions from various hands, Dulwich Picture Gallery, 1988
The exhibition, confined to the Dulwich pictures, was restaged at the Holburne Museum, Bath, 1995, using the same catalogue.

NPE
National Portrait Exhibitions held at the South Kensington Museum:
1866 *National Portraits ending with the reign of King James the second*
1868 *National Portraits commencing with the fortieth year of the Reign of George the third*

NPG
National Portrait Gallery, London

Obras Maestras, Madrid, Bilbao, 1999
Obras Maetras de la Dulwich Picture Gallery; exhibition catalogue by D. Shawe-Taylor and I.A.C. Dejardin; Banco Bilbao Vizcaya, Madrid, and Museo de Bellas Artes, Bilbao, 1999

ODNB
Oxford Dictionary of National Biography, 2004
See also *DNB*

Old Master Paintings, Japan, 2000
Old Master Paintings from the Dulwich Picture Gallery, exhibition catalogue by D. Shawe-Taylor and I.A.C. Dejardin; Isetan Museum of Art, Tokyo; Hiroshima Museum of Art; Koriyama City Museum of Art, Fukushima; Daimaru Museum, Umeda-Osaka; Prefectural Museum of Art, Yamanashi; Okazaki City Museum, Aichi, and the Prefectural Museum of Art, Kumamoto, 2000

Ormond 1973
R. Ormond, *National Portrait Gallery, Early Victorian Portraits*, 2 vols., 1973

os
old-style (Julian calendar)

Passavant 1836
J.D. Passavant, *Tour of a German Artist in England*, i, 1836 (Dulwich Gallery, pp.60-70); a translation of Passavant's *Kunstreise durch England und Belgien*, 1833

Pearman 1876
Rev A.J. Pearman, 'The Kentish Family of Lovelace', *Archaeologia Cantiana*, x, 1876, pp.184-220

Pearman 1893
Rev A.J. Pearman, 'The Kentish Family of Lovelace', *Archaeologia Cantiana*, xx, 1893, pp.54-63

Piper 1963
D. Piper, *Catalogue of the seventeenth-century Portraits in the National Portrait Gallery*, 1963

Pleasants 1919
J. Hall Pleasants, 'The Lovelace Family and its Connections', *Virginia Mag.*, xxvii, 1919, pp.393-403

Pleasants 1920
J. Hall Pleasants, 'The Lovelace Family and its Connections', *Virginia Mag.*, xxviii, 1920, pp.83-90, 176-87, 285-95, 375-81

Poole
R.L. Poole, *Catalogue of Portraits in the possession of the University, Colleges, City, and County of Oxford*, 3 vols., 1912–25

PROV.:
provenance

RA schools
pictures lent to the RA schools for copying

REF.:
selected references

Rembrandt to Gainsborough, Houston TX, Louisville KY, 1999-2000
Rembrandt to Gainsborough, Masterpieces from Dulwich Picture Gallery, exhibition catalogue by I.A.C. Dejardin, D. Shawe-Taylor and G. A. Waterfield, Museum of Fine Arts, Houston TX; Speed Art Museum, Louisville KY, 1999-2000

Roberts 1907
W. Roberts, *Beechey*, 1907

Seymour 1733
R. Seymour, *A Survey of the Cities of London and Westminster and Parts adjacent*, i, 1733 (Dulwich Gallery, p.209)

Smith 1831
J. Smith, *A Catalogue raisonné of the works of the most eminent Dutch, Flemish and French Painters*, iii, 1831

Soane and After 1987
Soane and After, The Architecture of Dulwich Picture Gallery, exhibition catalogue by G.A. Waterfield, Dulwich Picture Gallery, 1987

Sparkes 1876
J.C.L. Sparkes, *A Descriptive Catalogue of the Pictures in the Dulwich College Gallery*, 1876 'the first printed catalogue to be more than a list of names' (Bourgeois Bequest alone; alphabetically by artist) see Concordance

Sparkes & Carver 1890
J.C.L. Sparkes and A.J. Carver, *Catalogue of the Cartwright Collection and other Pictures and Portraits at Dulwich College*, 1890 (numbered consecutively by groups – portraits, subject pictures, landscapes and sea-pieces, animals etc., Kings and Queens, Sibyls and Virtues) see Concordance

Sparkes & Richter 1880
J.P. Richter & J.C.L. Sparkes, *Catalogue of the Pictures in the Dulwich College Gallery*, 1880 (a revision of Sparkes 1876; Bourgeois Bequest alone, alphabetically by artist) see Concordance

Sparkes & Richter 1892
J.P. Richter & J.C.L. Sparkes, *Catalogue of the Pictures in the Gallery of Alleyn's College of God's Gift at Dulwich*, 1892 (combining the 1880 and 1890 catalogues; the pictures renumbered, a separate sequence listing pictures not exhibited) see Concordance

Sparkes & Richter 1905
J.P. Richter & J.C.L. Sparkes, *Catalogue of the Pictures in the Gallery of Alleyn's College of God's Gift at Dulwich*, 1905 (a revision of the 1892 catalogue with the addition of five pictures) see Concordance

Stewart 1983
J.D. Stewart, *Kneller*, 1983

Strong 1969a
R. Strong, *National Portrait Gallery, Tudor and Jacobean Portraits*, 2 vols., 1969

Strong 1969b
R. Strong, *The Elizabethan Icon: Elizabethan & Jacobean Portraiture*, 1969

VAM
Victoria and Albert Museum

Van Dyck 2004
S.J. Barnes, N. de Poorter, O. Millar & H. Vey, *Van Dyck, A Complete Catalogue of the Paintings*, 2004

Vertue
G. Vertue, Notebooks i–vi, *Wal. Soc.*, XVIII, 1930; XX, 1932; XXII, 1934; XXIV, 1936; XXVI, 1938; XXIX, 1947 (index volume); XXX, 1955

Waagen 1854
G.F. Waagen, *Treasures of Art in Great Britain*, ii, 1854 (Dulwich Gallery, pp.341-49)

Wal. Corr.
W.S. Lewis ed., *Horace Walpole's Correspondence*, 43 vols. + 5 vols index, 1937-83

Wal. Soc.
Walpole Society

Walker 1985
R. Walker, *National Portrait Gallery, Regency Portraits*, 2 vols., 1985

Walpole *Visits*
'Horace Walpole's Journals of Visits to Country Seats &c', *Wal. Soc.*, XVI, 1928, pp.11-80

Ward & Roberts 1904
H. Ward and W. Roberts, *Romney*, 2 vols., 1904

Warner 1881
G. Warner, *Catalogue of the Manuscripts and Muniments of Alleyn's College of God's Gift, at Dulwich*, 1881

Waterfield 1989
G.A. Waterfield, " 'That White-faced Man': Sir Francis Bourgeois", *Turner Studies*, 1989, ix, 2, pp.36-48

Waterhouse 1941
E.K. Waterhouse, *Reynolds*, 1941

Waterhouse 1953
E.K. Waterhouse, 'Preliminary check list of Portraits by Thomas Gainsborough', *Wal. Soc.*, XXXIII, 1953

Waterhouse 1958
E.K. Waterhouse, *Gainsborough*, 1958

Waterhouse 1994
E.K. Waterhouse, *Painting in Britain 1530-1790*, 5th ed., 1994

Whinney & Millar 1957
M. Whinney & O. Millar, *English Art 1625-1714*, 1957

Whitley 1928a
W.T. Whitley, *Artists and their Friends in England 1700-1799*, 2 vols., 1928

Whitley 1928b
W.T. Whitley, *Art in England 1800-1820*, 1928

Whitley 1930
W.T. Whitley, *Art in England 1821-1837*, 1930

Young 1889
W. Young, *A History of Dulwich College*, 2 vols., 1889

LIST OF PAINTINGS

THE ALLEYN BEQUEST 1626

ALLEYN PORTRAITS

443 *Edward Alleyn*
444 *Mrs Joan Alleyn*

ROYAL PORTRAITS

521 *William I*
522 *William II*
523 *Henry I*
524 *Henry II*
525 *Richard I*
526 *King John*
527 *Edward I*
528 *Henry IV*
530 *Henry V*
529 *Henry VI*
531 *Richard III*
532 *Henry VII*
533 *Henry VIII*
534 *Anne Boleyn*
535 *Edward VI*
536 *Queen Mary*
384 *James VI and I*
417 *Henry, Prince of Wales*

SIBYLS

537 *Egyptian Sibyl*
538 *Samian Sibyl*
539 *Cumanan Sibyl*
540 *Cumaean Sibyl*
541 *Delphic Sibyl*
542 *European Sibyl*
543 *Hellespontic Sibyl*
544 *Persian Sibyl*
545 *Tiburtine Sibyl*

VIRTUES

546 *Piety*
547 *Liberality*

PROTESTANT REFORMERS

368 *Théodore De Beza*
369 *William Perkins*
370 *John Calvin*
419 *Alexander Nowell*
421 *Martin Luther*

POET

427 *Dante*

THE CARTWRIGHT BEQUEST 1686

393 *William Cartwright*, Greenhill
387 *'Mrs Cartwright'*, Greenhill
399 *A Lady as a Shepherdess*, Greenhill
400 *'Old Mr Cartwright'*
388 *'Mrs Cartwright's Sister'*
411 *'Young Mr Cartwright'*

LOVELACE PORTRAITS

372 *Serjeant William Lovelace*
364 *Thomas Lovelace*
367 *Sir William Lovelace of Bethersden*
365 *Sir William Lovelace of Woolwich*
363 *Richard Lovelace*, Dobson
378 *'Althea Cartwright'*
373 *John, 3rd Baron Lovelace*

ROYAL PORTRAITS

392 *Elizabeth, Queen of Bohemia*
414 *Charles I*, after Van Dyck
426 *Queen Henrietta Maria*, after Van Dyck
381 *Queen Henrietta Maria*, after Van Dyck
424 *Charles II*, after Wright
416 *James II as Duke of York*, Greenhill

THEATRICAL PORTRAITS

385 *called Nathan Field*
390 *called Thomas Bond*
391 *Portrait of a Man*
395 *called Richard Burbage*
423 *called Richard Perkins*

MISCELLANEOUS PORTRAITS

420 *Archbishop Laud*, after van Dyck
379 *Head of a Girl*, Fuller
389 *Portrait of a Lady*, Gheeraerts the younger
374 *Head of a Bearded Man*, Greenhill
418 *Self Portrait*, Greenhill
362 *Portrait of a Lady*, Huysmans
354 *The Judde Memorial*
375 *called Sir Martin Frobisher*
377 *Mrs Dirge*
430 *Michael Drayton*

LANDSCAPE, HISTORY, STILL LIFE

360 *The Thames from Somerset House*, Cornelis Bol
359 *A Galley of Malta*, Castro
361 *Ships in Rough Water off a Mediterranean Port*, Castro
428 *A Sea Fight with Barbary Corsairs*, Castro
436 *A Calm*, Castro
437 *A Dutch East-Indiaman off Hoorn*, Castro
517 *Dutch Levanters in a Rough Sea*, Castro
518 *A Storm at Sea*, Castro
371 *Sheep Shearing*, Colonia
431 *The Flight into Egypt*, Colonia
352 *The Infants Christ and St John*, after Van Dyck
408 *Susannah and the Elders*, after Lely
376 *Landscape*, Streeter
429 *Still Life*, Parry Walton

THE BOURGEOIS BEQUEST 1811

111 *John Philip Kemble*, Beechey
169 *Charles Small Pybus*, Beechey
6 *Tiger Hunt*, Bourgeois
100 *Cupid*, Bourgeois
135 *Landscape with Cattle (A Young Shepherd with his Flock)*, Bourgeois
149 *Helena brought before the Altar to be Sacrificed*, Bourgeois
294 *Landscape with Cattle (Cows by a Lake)*, Bourgeois
301 *Funeral Procession of a White Friar*, Bourgeois
308 *Sea Shore with Horse and Cart*, Bourgeois
310 *Friar in Prayer*, Bourgeois
311 *Soldiers*, Bourgeois
325 *Landscape with Cattle (Cows on a Hillock by a Stream)*, Bourgeois
335 *Sea Shore with Rearing Horse*, Bourgeois
342 *A Man holding a Horse*, Bourgeois
344 *Tobias and the Angel*, Bourgeois
459 *Religion in the Desert*, Bourgeois
460 *Landscape with Soldiers*, Bourgeois
461 *Figures in a Landscape*, Bourgeois
462 *Landscape with Cattle (A Cow Resting)*, Bourgeois
463 *Cavalry in a Landscape*, Bourgeois
465 *Self Portrait, after Beechey*, Bourgeois
466 *Self Portrait, after Beechey*, Bourgeois
467 *William Tell*, Bourgeois
488 *called Noel Desenfans on Horseback*, attributed to Bourgeois
194 *Venetia, Lady Digby, on her Deathbed*, Van Dyck
170 *George Digby, 2nd Earl of Bristol*, Van Dyck
201 *Portrait of a Lady*, manner of Van Dyck
66 *Philippe-Jacques De Loutherbourg*, Gainsborough
80 *Portrait of a Lady in White*, Johnson
89 *Portrait of a Lady in Blue*, Johnson
297 *Landscape with Cattle*, De Loutherbourg
339 *Landscape with Cattle and Figures*, De Loutherbourg
298 *A Calm*, studio of Monamy
28 *Noel Desenfans*, Northcote
172 *Sir Francis Bourgeois*, Northcote
94 *Self Portrait*, Opie
102 *Recovery from Sickness*, Reynolds
223 *The Calling of Samuel*, Reynolds
333 *An Officer on Horseback*, Reynolds
104 *Self Portrait*, studio of Reynolds
318 *Mrs Siddons as the Tragic Muse*, studio of Reynolds
171 *View of Tivoli*, Richard Wilson
150 *Landscape in imitation of Jacob Ruisdael*, Woodburn
151 *Portrait of a Man*
200 *Portrait of a Lady*
486 *Landscape with Horses*
503 *Noel Desenfans*

THE LINLEY BEQUEST 1835

140 *Thomas Linley the elder*, Gainsborough
302 *Samuel Linley*, Gainsborough
320 *Elizabeth and Mary Linley*, Gainsborough
331 *Thomas Linley the younger*, Gainsborough
178 *William Linley*, Lawrence
475 *Maria Linley*, Lawrence
474 *called The Rev Ozias Thurston Linley*, attributed to Lawrence
456 *Mrs Thomas Linley*, Lonsdale
476 *The Rev Ozias Thurston Linley*, Oliver

THE FAIRFAX MURRAY GIFT 1911-17

591 *Portrait of a Man*, Beach
574 *Portrait of a Youth*, Beale
575 *Portrait of a Lady*, Dahl
576 *Portrait of a Man*, Dahl
584 *Sir William Jones*, Dubois
585 *Elizabeth, Lady Jones*, Dubois
569 *Portrait of a Man*, attributed to Fuller
588 *A Couple in a Landscape*, Gainsborough
595 *Richard Haines the younger*, attributed to Grignion the younger
566 *Portrait of a Lady*, Highmore
562 *A Fishing Party*, Hogarth
580 *Portrait of a Man*, Hogarth
578 *Portrait of a Lady*, Hudson
579 *Portrait of a Man*, Hudson
604 *John Dive*, circle of Hysing
567 *Dorothy, Viscountess Townshend*, Jervas
582 *Eliza and Mary Davidson*, Kettle
583 *Portrait of a Lady*, Kettle
606 *Lucy Ebberton*, Knapton
596 *Portrait of a Man*, attributed to Knapton
570 *called The Howard Children*, Kneller
555 *Nymphs by a Fountain*, Lely
559 *Portrait of a Lady with a Blue Drape*, Lely
560 *Portrait of a Lady in Blue holding a Flower*, Lely
563 *A Boy as a Shepherd*, Lely
587 *Mrs George Morland*, Muller
565 *John, Baron Somers*, Riley
568 *William Chiffinch*, Riley
590 *William Hayley*, Romney
573 *called Aubrey de Vere, 20th Earl of Oxford*, Soest
592 *Sir Henry Vane the younger*, Soest
603 *Louis-François Roubiliac*, Soldi
581 *Portrait of a Lady*, Vanderbank
589 *Portrait of a Man*, attributed to Henry Walton
586 *Mrs Benjamin West II with her son Benjamin West III*, West
593 *Portrait of a Lady with Mask and Cherries*, Benjamin Wilson
561 *Portrait of a Baron*

ACQUISITIONS 1831-1961

611 *Portrait of a Physician*, attributed to Beale
17 *Sir Francis Bourgeois*, Beechey
464 *Self Portrait*, Bourgeois
291 *Charles Kemble*, Briggs
632 *Landscape (Four Figures in a Wood)*, Brodie
600 *A View of Walton Bridge*, Canaletto
519 *Mallards on a Pond*, attributed to Cradock
548 *James VI and I*, attributed to de Critz the elder
304 *Princess Victoria aged Four*, Denning
655 *A Woodman*, Denning
405 *Portrait of a Man*, after Van Dyck
316 *Mrs Elizabeth Moody with her sons Samuel and Thomas*, Gainsborough
618 *Self Portrait*, Green
446 *The Tribute Money*, Hodgkins
492 *Samson and the Lion*, Hodgkins
493 *Samson and the Philistines*, Hodgkins
607 *Old-time Tuition at Dulwich College*, Horsley
449 *George Bartley*, Lane
500 *Mrs Sarah Bartley*, Lane

THE ALLEYN BEQUEST 1626

The pictures in this section are all by Unknown Artists and are catalogued as follows

Edward Alleyn [1]

Edward Alleyn (1566–1626), founder of the College of God's Gift at Dulwich, actor, theatre owner, courtier and philanthropist, was born on 1 September 1566 and baptized at St Botolph's, Bishopsgate. By 1583 he was acting with the Earl of Worcester's Men before touring with Lord Strange's Men. By 1593 he had joined the Lord Admiral's Men with whom he established himself in the Marlovian role of Tamburlaine (1594). In 1592 he had married Joan Woodward (c.1573–1623), stepdaughter of Philip Henslowe, who owned the Rose Playhouse. Alleyn went into partnership with him and they eventually owned, besides the Rose, the First Fortune Playhouse and the particularly profitable Bear Garden; in 1604 they were appointed joint Masters of Bulls, Bears and Mastiff Dogs (a position Alleyn later held on his own). By 1597 Alleyn was performing far less frequently on the stage, being increasingly engaged in management. After Henslowe's death in 1616 he added the Second Fortune Playhouse to his investments and he also owned at least three London public houses[2] whose income was to be inherited by his second wife, Constance (b. 1603, d. before 1636), daughter of the poet and divine John Donne, whom he married in 1623 (she later remarried the Rev Samuel Harvey of Abury Hatch). Both Alleyn's marriages were childless.

In 1605 Alleyn had purchased the manor of Dulwich and was living there with his first wife in 1613 when he began to build on Dulwich Green 'a chapel, a schoolhouse and twelve almshouses', obtaining the Royal patent for its incorporation in 1619. Alleyn also built almshouses in Finsbury and directed in his will that further almshouses for ten people should be built in the parishes of St Botolph without Bishopsgate, and St Saviour's, Southwark.

Alleyn died on 25 November 1626 and was buried the following day in the College Chapel.

1 For detailed accounts of Alleyn see Young 1889, ii, pp.1–50, and Alleyn's Diary. Concise accounts by J.R. Piggott, *Dulwich College*, 1990, pp.5–12; S.P. Cerasano in *Edward Alleyn* 1994, pp.11–33, and in *Shakespeare Survey*, 47, 1994, pp.171–79.

2 Sometimes described as bordellos (Piggott, 1990, p.6), cf. 'A catalogue of pictures was taken among Alleyn's effects to Dulwich; the items of the catalogue cannot be quoted, the pictures were destroyed. These had probably been used as decorations of the stew-houses, Alleyn's property' (W. Rendle, 'The Stews on Bankside', *Antiquarian Mag.*, 1882, p.76).

The Bequest [1]

In his Will Alleyn left to the Corporation of God's Gift College, all his 'hangings [and] pictures' in the 'said College'.[2] No inventory survives, but Alleyn's diary itemizes his purchase between 1618 and 1620 of three sets of heads – 26 Monarchs, 14 Heads of Christ, Our Lady and the Apostles,[3] and 12 Sibyls. Twenty-six of these fifty-two pictures survive at Dulwich today. They are very modest workshop productions, approximately uniform in size, and were acquired as the College was being completed, doubtless as moral and historical exemplars. The portraits of Alleyn himself and his first wife must surely have been his, but there is a slight element of doubt concerning the other pictures here catalogued. A pair of Virtues, now set into a Jacobean chimneypiece, and the set of five Protestant reformers fit into the Alleyn pattern and it seems likely that the portrait of Dante (perhaps originally with some literary companions) was also his – but the existence of a second seventeenth-century Bequest, from William Cartwright (with an incomplete inventory), makes certainty impossible. All thirty-seven Alleyn pictures (as identified below) are by unidentified British artists. See also DPG392, p.60, and DPG354, p.72.

Alleyn's Diary also conveys his concern with the decorative arts, of which no visual evidence survives (some of this work may have been for Alleyn's house, as apart from the new school). There were Flemish tapestries,[4] carved, painted and gilded chimneypieces, a painting of the Four Seasons, a painted and gilded staircase, a painted and gilded bed, and a great clock dial.[5] Of the painters named, Toby, Gregory Carman, Goodman Gardyner and Buckett, only the last may be identified as Rowland Buckett (d.1639) of the Painter-Stainers' Company. On two occasions we find Alleyn dining with Goodman Gardyner and on another with 'ye painter',[6] suggesting he enjoyed the company of artists.

On 17 April 1618 Alleyn had visited 'arundell Howse wher my Lord showld me all His statues & picktures that came from Italy'. There was, of course, a distance between Mytens and Buckett, and Dulwich could not begin to match Arundel House, but Alleyn's visit suggests he aspired to be a man of taste.

1 For a more detailed survey of Alleyn's collection, see S. Foister in *Edward Alleyn* 1994, pp.33–61.

2 Young 1889, i, p.93; Alleyn's will is PRO PROB 11/148 and is printed in Young 1889, i, pp.92–95.

3 Alleyn's Diary, 10 November 1620 ('*bought of mr gibkin 14 Heads of Christ ou La: & ye 12 apostles att noble a peec – 4.13.4*'), last mentioned at Dulwich by Seymour 1733, p.209.

4 Alleyn's Diary, 22 November 1619, when he paid £8 for Flemish tapestries.

5 Alleyn's Diary, 18 December 1617, 17 March 1617 (os), 9 & 28 May 1618, 21 & 23 November 1618, July 1619, and 4 September 1619.

6 Alleyn's Diary, 9 September and 25 November 1621; 8 March 1617 (os).

Display of the Alleyn and Cartwright Pictures [1]

Alleyn's pictures are not in good condition; they are much repainted and the panels were clearly unstable for many years. A glance at how they have been displayed (along with the Cartwright pictures) goes some way to explain this. The picture gallery in the west wing of the old College (not mentioned in the Founder's plans) fell down in June 1661 and was repaired in 1667. A rare impression of Norden's engraved view of London (presented by Cartwright), drawn from near Dulwich and with the 'Representation of the City Cavalcade on the Lord-Mayor's Day' was quickly ruined by damp. In 1733 the pictures hung in a dining room adjoining the picture gallery, but by 1745 they were back in the gallery (in 1734 described as a long room, 80 x 15 feet, which was 'seldom made any use of'). In 1791 the gallery was partially rebuilt and the pictures were dispersed throughout the College. It appears that the imminence of the Bourgeois gift in 1811 prompted some reassessment and between 1810 and 1817 many pictures from the College were cleaned and repaired by Robert Brown.[2] In 1870 they were placed in the Master's house in the New College, but in 1884 and 1886 two wings of Soane's Gallery previously allotted to 'Poor Sisters' as almshouses were converted for the display of the Cartwright and other pictures (as galleries VI and VII). The first printed catalogue of the Alleyn and Cartwright pictures appeared in 1890 (Sparkes & Carver 1890). The Alleyn pictures were last displayed together in 1994 in the *Edward Alleyn* exhibition at Dulwich, and the Cartwright pictures in the *Mr Cartwright's Pictures* in 1987–88. They are currently dispersed between Tredegar House, Dulwich College and the Dulwich Picture Gallery.

1 This note is based on Aubrey 1718; Aubrey 1719; Seymour 1733, p.209; *GM*, xv, 1745, p.426; *European Mag.*, xx, 1791, p.88, Young 1889, i, pp.462–63, 465, 471, 472, 492; *Wal. Corr.*, xi, p.289.

2 Brown Ledger, describing his work for Dulwich.

ALLEYN PORTRAITS

DPG443 *Edward Alleyn*

Canvas 203.8 x 114 lined; repaired by G. Paterson 1790;[1] restored by an attendant who added a coat of arms 1876;[2] 'frizzelled' in 1911; a line of filler along bottom edge; in the top left corner earlier photographs show a fringed curtain draped round the pillar, the pediment of which remains visible; a damage in the face has been overpainted; pentimento at the bottom of the gown on his right side; the darkest areas of the costume have been much re-worked, the fur trim of the gown showing a thick, distinctive craquelure; an area between the feet and beneath the gown was scraped down; cleaned 1994.

Inscribed upper left: *1626*; brown eyes, sandy coloured hair and beard; wearing a black hat and a black gown trimmed with black fur over a black suit with grey stockings, holding his tan gloves in his left hand; on the little finger of his right hand a red sardonyx signet ring bearing his arms;[3] black buckled shoes with brown soles sewn on with white cord (this is probably a restoration). Details of his fur-trimmed gown appear more clearly in the copy by W.B. Morris (DPG551, p.235) and the drawing by Sylvester Harding (D4, p.247).

PROV.: Probably Alleyn Bequest 1626; at Dulwich by 1692.

EXH.: *Edward Alleyn* 1994 (1); College Board Room 1980–.

ENG.: J. Wooding 1789 (bust-length oval), showing a square-cut rather longer beard, dark moustache, the face looking almost straight at the spectator;[4] T. Nugent 1792 (*Biographical Mirrour*, i, 1795) from the drawing by S. Harding (see D4, p.247) based on DPG443, but showing differences in the gloves, cuffs, position of the ring, angle of the head, and position of his right foot, and clearly showing a pillar and drape in the background;[5] later etchings by E. Bocourt, and anon. (reversed); anon. three-quarter-length, and anon. half-length (reversed; Smeaton's *The Unique*, 1830); anon. vignette (*Dramatic Mag.*, 1830).

REF.: Aubrey 1718, p.195; Seymour 1733, p.209; Lysons 1792, p.112; S. Foister in *Edward Alleyn* 1994, pp.57–58, 61n50–51.

Unrecorded in his diary, this is the only known image of Edward Alleyn (1566–1626), the identification being confirmed by provenance and by the signet ring with the sitter's arms.[6] The inscribed date may refer to the date of his death and not necessarily of the picture, although it may well date from 1620–30. Vertue c.1726 listed at Dulwich a half-length portrait of the founder and another 'done after his death'.[7] Young remarked in 1889 that DPG443 was 'probably painted some years after his death; it certainly appears to be that of a man rather under than over fifty years of age' (as suggested by his hair)[8] and in 1791 it was alleged that 'the resemblance of his face is said to have been drawn when he lay dead in his coffin'[9] – in which case the portrait was not part of the Alleyn Bequest. But it is more likely, as Foister believed, that it had belonged to the sitter. It was first recorded at Dulwich by Aubrey, i.e. before 1692.

The figure bulks uncomfortably within the canvas and may be over life size. From an examination of the ring (and the use of regression predictions) Alleyn's height has been estimated as approximately 180cms. and his weight at 130–150 lbs. – perhaps not the monstrous figure of Marlowe's Tamburlaine, but imposing enough at the time.[10]

For a three-quarter length copy by W.B. Morris, c.1900 (clearly showing the fur trim to Alleyn's gown), see DPG551, p.235, and the half-length drawing by Sylvester Harding engraved by Nugent, see D4, p.247. The portrait was adapted for a memorial window in St Giles, Cripplegate, 1996, showing Alleyn cradling in his left arm a model of the almshouses he built in that parish.[11]

A bust-length oval engraving by Lawrance [Laurence] Johnson first published in 1603 (in the *The Generall Historie of the Turkes*) has been doubtfully identified as Alleyn.[12]

1 Young 1889, i, p.471: 'a large framed tablet' formerly suspended beneath the picture read 'With a view to hand down to posterity the pious memory of Edward Alleyn, Esq., founder of the College of God's Gift, Dulwich, A.D.1626, this original Portrait was repaired by Mr George Paterson, of St Botolph, Bishopsgate, London, and these frames given by Mr Henry Stent and Mr Richard Woodyer, churchwardens of the said parish, A.D.1790'. Young suggested that Paterson had 'considerably altered the picture. The face seems to have been largely "assisted", and the beard trimmed, although the linen frill appears to be untouched. The hands seem genuine, except probably the ring; but the right shoe is "false" and out of drawing'. The churchwardens of St Botolph were amongst the executors of Alleyn's Will as inspectors of the School and assistants to the Warden and Fellows (see Young 1889, i, pp.30, 34, 49, 66, 85, 90).

2 The coat of arms now just visible, upper left; it appears in none of the early photographs of DPG443, nor in the copy by W.B. Morris of c.1900, see DPG551, p.235.

3 *Ar. a chevron betw. three cinquefoils gu.*

4 Described by Young 1889, i, p.471. Unlettered example in NPG archive.

5 Illus. Young 1889, ii, front.; Murray 1980 supposed these differences might indicate the extent of the 1790 'repairs', but Harding's drawing seems an evocation rather than a copy (S. Foister, *Edward Alleyn* 1994, p.61 n51; S.P. Cerasano, *Shakespeare Survey*, 47, 1994, p.174n6). See also Brayley 1850, iii, p.235: 'engraved about sixty years ago by Mr Sylvester Harding; but [the portrait] has since been retouched and injudiciously altered'.

6 But see note 1 above. The ring is preserved by the College, see S.P. Cerasano, *Shakespeare Survey*, 47, 1994, p.175, and *Edward Alleyn* 1994, pp.66–68.

7 Vertue, ii, p.13; was his reference to a half-length a confusion with the Cartwright portrait by Greenhill, DPG393, or did it refer to the half length engraved by Johnson, see note 12?

8 Young 1889, i, p.470.

9 *European Mag.*, xx, 1791, p.88.

10 See Cerasano, at note 5, pp.174–79, and in *Edward Alleyn* 1994, p.67.

11 As illus. *Edward Alleyn* 1994, p.28; the almshouses were destroyed in the 1939–45 war.

12 M. Holmes, *Theatre Notebook*, 5, 1950, pp.11–13, and P. Thomson, *Shakespeare's Professional Career*, 1993, p.65 (illus.). But J.H. Astington, 'The 'Unrecorded Portrait' of Edward Alleyn', *Shakespeare Quarterly*, 44, 1993, pp.73–86, effectively undermined the identity, which was also doubted by Foister, *Edward Alleyn* 1994, p.61 n50.

1626

DPG444 *Mrs Joan Alleyn*

Oak panel 79.1 x 63.2 of three vertical members, from the left 24, 12 and 27.3 wide, supported by two horizontal battens and three vertical strips of canvas partly covering centre joins and the right-hand edge; repaired by Holder 1912; Hell 1945–51; conserved 1993 when it was noted that the black dress had 'a high degree of damage, the face and hands are the least damaged; glove and book certainly reworked to disguise damage; detailing of the ruff had been reconstructed; the hat damaged in the band round the rim';[1] the brim on the spectator's right may have been widened; the panel joins show signs of movement.

Inscribed upper right: *AETS 22/ 1596*; fair hair, blue eyes; wearing a black capotain hat over a white linen cap with a black ribbon; black panelled dress with a stomacher embroidered with floral motifs; a red book in her right hand and in her left a pair of brown gloves, their backs bearing a decorative blue and white horseshoe motif and their red gauntlets white roses.

PROV.: Alleyn Bequest 1626.

EXH.: *Coronation Exhibition*, Manchester, 1953 (26); *Edward Alleyn* 1994(2); *Obras Maestras*, Madrid, Bilbao, 1999(35).

REF.: Aubrey 1718, p.195; S. Foister in *Edward Alleyn* 1994, p.58.

The identification is traditional. Joan Woodward (c.1573–1623), step daughter of the theatrical manager Philip Henslowe, married in 1592 Edward Alleyn as his first wife; she was illiterate; she was buried in the old Chapel at Dulwich with a stone inscribed: *Here lyeth in Hope of Resurrection, the Body of* Joane, *the religious and loving Wife of* Edward Alleyn *Esqr. Founder of this Colledge, who departed this mortal Life the 28th of* June *1623, being in the 51 year of Her Age.*[2]

The costume indicates the dress of a citizen's wife[3] but, having been extensively retouched, some details might be regarded with caution.[4]

1 'Broadly it is my impression that the obvious reworking is restoration that disguises a great deal of damage, rather than changes that make the image more acceptable to a later period' (Jim Dimond, Area Museums Service for South Eastern England, letter of 4 January 1994 on file).

2 Aubrey 1718, p.197, quoted two memorial inscriptions, a free stone in the chancel and a painted inscription on the south wall; Young 1889, i, p.463 said both 'have long disappeared'.

3 It compares, for example, with that worn by Mrs Esther Kello in her portrait of 1595 in the Scottish National Portrait Gallery (PGL18) illus. R.K. Marshall, *Costume in Scottish Portraits 1560–1830*, 1986, p.35, or that in two miniatures of unidentified ladies by Isaac Oliver of c.1587 (see G. Reynolds, *British Portrait Miniatures*, Fitzwilliam Museum Handbook, 1998, pp.28–29; S. Lloyd, *Portrait Miniatures from the collection of the Duke of Buccleuch*, 1996, p.75, no.21).

4 E.g. an undated letter from Janet Thomas (on file) suggesting the shoulder puffs and sleeve banding are exaggerated, and see also note 1 above.

ROYAL PORTRAITS c.1618–20

In 1618 and 1620 Edward Alleyn bought portraits of 26 English Monarchs at 6s 8d each,[1] perhaps from Gipkyn (see p.34), being a complete sequence from William I to James I with, in addition, Anne Boleyn and the Black Prince, as follows:

29 September 1618: *Bought 6 pictures of K:J: q E: q m: K E: K: H: ye 8th & K:H: ye 5th.* £2.0s.0d. [viz. James I, Elizabeth I, Queen Mary, King Edward VI, Henry VIII and Henry V]

8 October 1618: *Bought 8 pictuers off E ye 3rd R ye 2 H ye 4: H ye 6: E ye 4: E ye 5: R ye 3 H ye 7* £2.13s.4d. [viz. Edward III, Richard II, Henry IV, Henry VI, Edward IV, Edward V, Richard III and Henry VII]

25 September 1620: *bought 6 Head of E ye 2/E ye I/ H ye 3/Jo: Ri: ye 1/ H:ye 2/ pd 6s 8d a peec* £2.0s.0d. [viz. Edward II, Edward I, Henry III, John, Richard I, Henry II]

30 September 1620: *pd for 6 Heds of H: ye 1st: Steuen: W: rufus: W: conquer: black princ: an of bullen* £2.0s.0d. [viz. Henry I, Stephen, William II, William I, The Black Prince (*Edward 1330–76, son of Edward III*) and Anne Boleyn]

Alleyn bought his monarchs in approximately reverse chronological order; in 1618 buying Edward III to James I, and in 1620 William I to Edward II (and adding Ann Boleyn and the Black Prince). Of these 26 portraits nine remain untraced today: Stephen (reigned 1135–54), Henry III (1216–72), Edward II (1307–27), Edward III (1327–77), Richard II (1377–99), Edward IV (1461–83), Edward V (1483) and Elizabeth I (1558–1603), with Edward the Black Prince (elder son of Edward II).

They present a series of crudely painted derivative images painted on rough-hewn oak panels. With the exception of the living monarch, James I, each has a black 'curtain wall' in the background on which is (or was, one may assume) inscribed the monarch's name; three have the same 'folded' background hanging (Henry IV, Richard III and Henry VIII), where the others show a hanging drape (which has a coloured lining in three instances: Henry VII, Edward VI and Mary). They were probably not all produced in the same workshop, and Foister has suggested differences 'in the facial modelling between the Tudor portraits of 1618 and the earlier monarchs bought in 1620';[2] nevertheless Alleyn acquired them to complete a set and perhaps, as Gibson suggested, they were painted to order.[3]

Such sets had become relatively common with the advent of the Long Gallery in Tudor and Jacobean mansions.[4] Several groups of English monarchs survive (none historically complete and all ending in the later sixteenth century), for example in the Royal Collection, the National Portrait Gallery (from Hornby Castle), at Hardwick, Albury Park, Hatfield and the Deanery at Ripon, while a less uniform collection belongs to the Society of Antiquaries. Nearly all are painted on oak panels and measure approximately 56 x 43. Alleyn's monarchs hold particular interest as being the largest of such sequences to survive, and the only ones which may be firmly dated.

Fanciful sequences of English kings had previously appeared in medieval sculpture (e.g. at the cathedrals of Canterbury, Lincoln, Winchester and York, and at Westminster Hall and Richmond Palace), but the earliest graphic sequence appears to be that included in John Rastell's *The Pastyme of People*, 1529, a set of 18 'rough, bold' woodcuts, from William I to Richard III.[5] In 1597 appeared the *Booke containing the True Portraiture of the Kings of England* illustrated with oval woodcuts, many of which were used as sources for the engravings in Holland's far more sophisticated *Baziliwologia* of 1618, with portraits of English Kings from William I to James I.[6]

1 Alleyn's Diary; Young 1889, ii, pp.108, 109, 188; S. Foister in *Edward Alleyn* 1994, pp.39–51.
2 Foister in *Edward Alleyn* 1994, p.42.
3 Gibson 1975, p.82, and 1995, p.10 (see note 4).
4 See Strong 1969b, pp.47–50; P. Tudor-Craig, *Richard III*, NPG, 1973, p.80; R. Gibson, *National Trust Yearbook*, 1975, pp.81–87, and *Folio*, Spring 1995, pp.9–16; Foister in *Edward Alleyn* 1994, pp.39–52. In Scotland George Jamesone painted 109 Scottish Kings for a triumphal arch celebrating the visit of Charles I to Edinburgh in 1633 (see D. Thomson, *George Jamesone*, 1974, pp.95–101); later, in 1684–88, Jacob de Wet was to paint a set of 110 for Holyrood Palace, where they remain.
5 H.C. Leavis, *Engraved British Royal Portraits from 1521*, 1917, pp.13–23; see Vertue, iv, pp.103, 146.
6 See Hind 1955, pp.115–39, pls.54–66.

DPG521 *William I*

Oak panel 57.2 x 42.5 of two vertical members, the left 27 wide; a knot in the centre of the top edge and old worm holes along the right-hand panel, which is chamfered; charcoal(?) underdrawing visible in helmet and shoulder; Hell 1965; conserved 1980.

Inscribed centre left: *WILLIAM / CONQVEROR*; dark blue eyes, greying moustache and brownish hair; on his helmet balances a coronet with red and yellow plumes and on the breastplate the Royal arms (*gu. 2 lions passant regardant or*); a red curtain behind.

PROV.: Bt. by Alleyn, 30 September 1620; Alleyn Bequest 1626.

EXH.: *Autumn Festival*, Bromsgrove, 1966(1); *Edward Alleyn* 1994(79).

REF.: S. Foister in *Edward Alleyn* 1994, pp.42, 44.

William I (1027–87), reigned 1066–87.

The image resembles the engraving in the *Baziliwlogia* 1618,[1] itself derived from an engraving of Manfred (King of Sicily 1258–66) in the *Regum Neapolitanorum*, 1605,[2] (cf. Richard I below). Vertue also noted this derivation for the head of William I in Martyn's *Historie of the Kings of England* (1618).[3]

1 Hind 1955, pl.55b.
2 Strong 1969b, p.48, figs.43, 44.
3 Vertue, v, p.103.

DPG522 *William II*

Chamfered oak panel 57.2 x 42.4 of two vertical members, the left 8.6 wide; dead wormholes along vertical join; large knot showing below the chain and a smaller one at the top; raised grain; the sky and face retouched; consolidated 1990.

Inscribed centre left: *WILLIAM / RVFVS*; brown eyes and hair; wearing a red velvet gold crown with ermine trim, a collar of rubies and blackstones and a golden cloak over a red tunic; a green curtain behind.

PROV.: Bt. by Alleyn, 30 September 1620; Alleyn Bequest 1626.

EXH.: *Autumn Festival*, Bromsgrove, 1966(4); *Edward Alleyn* 1994(80); Tredegar House 1995–.

William II (c.1056–1100), reigned 1087–1100.

The image resembles the engraving by Renold Elstrack in the *Baziliwologia* 1618 (Hind 1955, pl.55c).

DPG523 *Henry I*

Chamfered oak panel 56.8 x 42.5 of two vertical members, the left 9 wide; damage by his right shoulder; raised grain; the face, sky and right half of the cloak retouched; Hell 1965; consolidated 1990.

Inscribed centre left: *HENRY.I.*; blue grey eyes, white hair; wearing a jewelled red silver crown, a gilt brocade cape with a jewelled trim over a blue tunic; a green curtain behind.

PROV.: Bt. by Alleyn, 30 September 1620; Alleyn Bequest 1626.

EXH.: *Edward Alleyn* 1994(81); Tredegar House 1995–.

Henry I (1068–1135), reigned 1100–35.

The image resembles the engraving by Renold Elstrack in the *Baziliwologia* 1618 (Hind 1955, pl.55d).

DPG524 *Henry II*

Oak panel 57.5 x 41.9 of two vertical members, the left 26.4 wide; a batten over the join removed; a knot on the lower left edge; chip on top right corner; scattered losses with large retouchings in the forehead, where the chain goes under the ermine, and in the sky; craquelure particularly prominent in the white of the ermine; Hell 1965; consolidated 1990.

Inscribed centre left: *HENRY.II.*; brown eyes, dark brown hair; wearing a blue velvet gold crown, a jewelled collar beneath a falling ermine collar and a red tunic; a green curtain behind.

PROV.: Bt. by Alleyn, 25 September 1620; Alleyn Bequest 1626.

EXH.: *Autumn Festival*, Bromsgrove, 1966(7); *Edward Alleyn* 1994(82); Tredegar House 1995–.

REF.: S. Foister in *Edward Alleyn* 1994, pp.45–46.

Henry II (1133–89), reigned 1154–89.

The image resembles the engraving in the *Baziliwologia* 1618 (Hind 1955, pl.56b; *Edward Alleyn* 1994, p.45).

DPG525 *Richard I*

Oak panel 57.5 x 41.9 of three vertical members, from the left 8.1, 25.6 and 8.2 wide, with cross battens removed; a canvas support with three small horizontal battens on left-hand join; uneven top edge; scattered retouchings; lifting paint in the curtain; Hell 1965; consolidated 1990.

Inscribed centre right: *RICHARD.I.*; blue eyes, fairish hair; wearing a crown of pink and red velvet with gold trefoils and pearls, and a red tunic beneath silver armour with gilt decoration; the sword in his right hand has a gilded hilt; a green curtain to the left.

PROV.: Bt. by Alleyn, 25 September 1620; Alleyn Bequest 1626.

EXH.: *Autumn Festival*, Bromsgrove, 1966(9); *Edward Alleyn* 1994(83); Tredegar House 1995–.

Richard I (1157–99), reigned 1189–99.

The image resembles the engraving in the *Baziliwologia* 1618,[1] which was taken from the engraving of René of Anjou (titular King of Sicily 1417–80) in the *Regum Neapolitanorum*, 1605 (cf. William I above).[2]

1 Hind 1955, pl.56c.
2 Vertue, v, p.103; Strong 1969b, p.48.

DPG526 King John

Chamfered oak panel 57.5 x 41.9 of two vertical members, the left 22 wide, with two butterfly wedges in the centre; flat chamfered fixing blocks top and bottom and another behind a knot on the left edge by the inscription; the surface abraded and retouched; Hell 1965; consolidated 1990.

Inscribed centre left: *K.JOHN.*; brown eyes, light brown hair; wearing a red velvet crown and an ermine-lined red cape over a richly figured golden suit; a green curtain behind.

PROV.: Bt. by Alleyn, 25 September 1620; Alleyn Bequest 1626.

EXH.: *Autumn Festival*, Bromsgrove, 1966(10); *Edward Alleyn* 1994(84); Tredegar House 1995–.

King John (c.1167–1216), reigned 1199–1216.

The image resembles the engraving by Renold Elstrack in the *Baziliwologia* 1618 (Hind 1955, pl.56d).

DPG527 Edward I

Chamfered oak panel 57.5 x 41.9 of three vertical members, from the left 7.8, 24.7 and 9.4 wide; cross battens removed from the joins which are not flush *verso*; the shoulders repainted; widespread retouchings; a wooden dowel in the bottom left corner; Hell 1965; consolidated 1990.

Inscribed centre right: *EDWARD.I.*; brown eyes, dark brown hair; wearing a green velvet crown with purple flowers and ermine lining, a black cape with pink lining worn over a richly-figured green costume; in his black-gloved right hand a sword with gilded hilt; a golden chain hangs across his right shoulder; a scarlet curtain behind.

PROV.: Bt. by Alleyn, 25 September 1620; Alleyn Bequest 1626.

EXH.: *Autumn Festival*, Bromsgrove, 1966(13); *Edward Alleyn* 1994(85); Tredegar House 1995–.

Edward I (1239–1307), reigned 1272–1307.

The image resembles the engraving by Renold Elstrack in the *Baziliwologia* 1618 (Hind 1955, pl.57b).

DPG528 Henry IV

Chamfered oak panel 58.1 x 45.4 of three vertical members, from the left 16.4, 16 and 13 wide; worm holes at the left join; three vertical splits, two in centre panel running from top edge to the face; battens on the joins removed; scattered retouchings; Hell 1965; revarnished 1990.

Inscribed centre right: *HENRIE.4*; brown eyes, black hair; wearing a red chaperon with gold trim and a turquoise jewel set in the side; a red shirt beneath a dark green jacket with rich gold filigree edging and a fur collar; round his neck a light blue ribbon with a blackstone set in gold; a deep scarlet curtain behind.

PROV.: Bt. by Alleyn, 8 October 1618; Alleyn Bequest 1626.

EXH.: *Edward Alleyn* 1994(86); Tredegar House 1995–.

REF.: S. Foister in *Edward Alleyn* 1994, p.45.

Henry IV (1367–1413) reigned 1399–1413.

The image resembles the engraving in the *Baziliwologia* 1618[1] which ultimately derived from an engraving of Charles VI of France in the *Cronique abregee des faits, gestes et vies illustres des Rois de France*, 1555.[2]

1 Hind 1955, pl.59a.
2 Strong 1969a, ii, pl.276.

DPG530 Henry V

Oak panel 58.1 x 45.6 of three vertical members, from the left 11.8, 17 and 16.8 wide, secured by blocks top and bottom and with two butterfly wedges along each join; a crack in the right-hand panel is secured by three blocks; a triangular inset at top of the centre panel, another at the top-left corner; dead worm holes in left-hand panel; scattered retouchings and scratches across the collar and forefinger; Hell 1965; blisters in curtain behind the neck treated and surface cleaned 1990.

Brown eyes and tonsured hair; wearing a green coat with black fur trim over a red shirt; richly jewelled collar with rubies and blackstones with a red pendant, and a blackstone ring on his right forefinger; a deep red drape behind.

PROV.: Bt. by Alleyn, 29 September 1618; Alleyn Bequest 1626.

EXH.: *Autumn Festival*, Bromsgrove 1966(23 as Edward V); *Edward Alleyn* 1994 (87 as Henry V); Tredegar House 1995–.

REF.: S. Foister in *Edward Alleyn* 1994, p.51.

Henry V (1387–1422), reigned 1413–22.

Wrongly identified as Edward V until 1994 (and therefore numbered out of sequence).The image reverses the standard portrait of Henry V as seen in the Royal Collection and the National Portrait Gallery (545),[1] and in the engraving by Renold Elstrack in the *Baziwlogia* 1618.[2]

1 Millar 1963, i, no.6; ii, pl.2; Strong 1969a, i, p.144; ii, pls.281, 282.
2 Hind 1955, pl.59b.

DPG529 *Henry VI*

Chamfered oak panel 57.2 x 43.8 of three vertical members, from the left 16.2, 15.6 and 12 wide; a split runs down the centre panel from the top, another bottom left; scattered retouchings, including an old scratch on the cheek; Hell 1965; consolidated 1990.

Inscribed centre left: *HENRIE.6.*; greyish eyes, grey hair; wearing a black hat and a deep green tunic trimmed with ermine (the black spots with exaggerated tails, cf. DPG531 and DPG532) over a red tunic with brown fur cuffs and a gold-trimmed collar; round his neck a golden S chain with blackstones set in gold; a red curtain behind.

PROV.: Bt. by Alleyn, 8 October 1618; Alleyn Bequest 1626.

EXH.: *Autumn Festival*, Bromsgrove, 1966(20); *Edward Alleyn* 1994(88); Tredegar House 1995–.

REF.: S. Foister in *Edward Alleyn* 1994, pp.45, 47–49.

Henry VI (1421–71), reigned 1422–61.

The image resembles anonymous portraits in the Royal Collection and the National Portrait Gallery (2457)[1] and relates to Renold Elstrack's engraving in the *Baziliwlogia* 1618.[2]

1 Millar 1963, i, nos.8, 9; ii, pl.4; Strong 1969a, i, pp.146–47; ii, pls.283, 284.
2 Hind 1955, pl.59c; *Edward Alleyn* 1994, p.47.

DPG531 *Richard III*

Chamfered oak panel 57.8 x 44.8 of three vertical members, from the left 15.5, 15 and 14.3 wide; small vertical splits upper left and right and a knot in the middle panel below centre; retouchings in the face and left hand; Hell 1965; surface cleaned 1990.

Inscribed centre right: *RICHARD.3.*; blue eyes, dark hair; wearing an ermine-lined black cap, a scarlet cape trimmed with ermine (see DPG529) over a green suit with gold figuring; an ill-fitting ring on the little finger of his right hand; a black curtain behind.

PROV.: Bt. by Alleyn, 8 October 1618; Alleyn Bequest 1626.

EXH.: *Richard III*, NPG, 1973(P24); *Edward Alleyn* 1994(89); Tredegar House 1995–.

REF.: S. Cerasano, *Shakespeare Quarterly*, 33, 1982, pp.342–44; S. Foister in *Edward Alleyn* 1994, pp.52, 60n40.

Richard III (1452–85), reigned 1483–85.

Of many surviving portraits of Richard III,[1] DPG531 most closely resembles a portrait at Charlecote;[2] a fine version in the Royal Collection probably dates from the early sixteenth century[3] and another is in the National Portrait Gallery (148).[4] Foister emphasized how DPG531 agrees with the standard image of the King, ignoring the Shakespearian construction of the hump-backed villain.

1 See P. Tudor-Craig, *Richard III*, NPG, 1973, pls.25–39.
2 Exh. *Richard III*, NPG, 1973(P2, illus.).
3 Millar 1963, i, no.14; ii, pl.5.
4 Strong 1969a, i, p.263; ii, pls.515, 516.

DPG532 *Henry VII*

Chamfered oak panel 55.2 x 41.3 of three vertical panels, from the left 8.2, 13.8 and 19.3 wide; supporting cross battens removed on the left; a number of vertical splits; chipped at top right corner; retouchings on the forehead, bridge of nose, chin and neck; Hell 1965; revarnished 1990.

Inscribed, centre right: *HENRIE.7*; blue-grey eyes, white hair; wearing a black cap and, over a red tunic, a gold-figured brown robe trimmed with ermine (see DPG529), a fur scarf and a richly jewelled collar; a scarlet curtain with green lining behind.

PROV.: Bt. by Alleyn, 8 October 1618; Alleyn Bequest 1626.

EXH.: *Autumn Festival*, Bromsgrove, 1966(26); *Edward Alleyn* 1994(90); Tredegar House 1995–.

Henry VII (1457–1509), reigned 1485–1509.

The image ultimately derives from the contemporary Holbein drawing in the National Portrait Gallery of Henry VIII with Henry VII (4027) and particularly resembles the later head seen in the Remigius van Leemput copy in the Royal Collection (Strong 1969a, i, pp.153–54; ii, pls.305, 306; Millar 1963, i, no.216, ii, pl.26).

DPG533 *Henry VIII*

Chamfered oak panel 58.4 x 45.7 of three vertical members, from the left 14, 17.1 and 14.6 wide; vertical splits upper right and left; a prominent surface flaw in his right cheek; Hell 1965; surface cleaned 1990.

Blue-grey eyes, greying light brown beard; wearing a black jewelled hat with white plume, a red jacket with sable fur trim over a silver suit with white figuring, and the dark blue collar with red Garter badge; a deep red curtain behind.

PROV.: Bt. by Alleyn, 29 September 1618; Alleyn Bequest 1626.

EXH.: *Autumn Festival*, Bromsgrove, 1966(28); *Dulwich College – a School and its Art*, South London AG, 1981; *Edward Alleyn* 1994(91); Tredegar House 1995–.

REF.: S. Foister in *Edward Alleyn* 1994, pp.40, 43.

Henry VIII (1491–1547), reigned 1509–47.

The image ultimately derives from the *ad vivum* Holbein drawing in the National Portrait Gallery (4027) and resembles the later head seen in the Remigius van Leemput copy in the Royal Collection (Strong 1969a, i, pp.153–54; ii, pls.305, 306; Millar 1963, i, no.216, ii, pl.26).

DPG534 *Anne Boleyn*

Chamfered oak panel 56.8 x 42.2 of three uneven vertical members, from the left approximately 6.6, 30.6 and 5 wide; knots top and lower left; scattered losses and numerous retouchings; the flesh areas much reworked and void of colour; Hell 1965; consolidated 1990.

Inscribed, centre left: *ANN.BOLEYN*; blue-grey eyes, dark brown hair; wearing black jewelled headdress, a pearl necklace with a B pendant (for Boleyn), and a black dress with a collar of rubies; a green curtain behind.

PROV.: Bt. by Alleyn, 30 September 1620; Alleyn Bequest 1626.

EXH.: *Edward Alleyn* 1994(92); Tredegar House 1995–.

REF.: S. Foister in *Edward Alleyn* 1994, pp.40, 50, 51.

Anne Boleyn (1507–36) married Henry VIII in 1533 as his second Queen.

The image resembles that in the National Portrait Gallery (668), which has been described as a mechanical version of the standard portrait of Anne (Strong 1969a, i, pp.5–6; ii, pl.8; Millar 1963, i, under no. 42).

DPG535 *Edward VI*

Chamfered oak panel 57.2 x 45 of three vertical members, from the left 16, 15 and 14 wide; two small vertical splits bottom right, a horizontal damage below his left shoulder and an old damage across his left eye; the top right edge has several notches; retouched throughout; Hell 1965; surface cleaned 1990.

Blue eyes, fair hair; wearing a black jewelled cap, a white collar and black jacket set with blackstones in gold; a green curtain with red lining behind.

PROV.: Bt. by Alleyn, 29 September 1618; Alleyn Bequest 1626.

EXH.: *Autumn Festival*, Bromsgrove, 1966(31); *Edward Alleyn* 1994(93); Tredegar House 1995–.

REF.: S. Foister in *Edward Alleyn* 1994, pp.40–42.

Edward VI (1537–1553), reigned 1547–53.

Formerly identified as Edward V, according to labels, *verso*. The image ultimately derives from the portrait attributed to William Scrots in the Royal Collection,[1] engraved by Simon van de Passe for the *Baziliwologia* 1618.[2]

1 Millar 1963, i, no.49; ii, pl.33. Cf. Strong 1969a, ii, pls.171, 172.
2 Hind 1955, pl.62b; *Edward Alleyn* 1994, p.42.

DPG536 Queen Mary

Chamfered oak panel 58.1 x 41.9 of four vertical members, from the left 19, 13 and 3.4 wide, with a later panel 6.5 wide added on right-hand side; vertical cracks run through the centre and up from the bottom edge; a retouched diagonal damage from the left eye to the lower jaw; Hell 1965; surface cleaned 1990.

Grey eyes, light brown hair; wearing a French hood adorned with pearls and rubies, a white embroidered collar and a dark brown dress with a large pendant jewel; a green curtain with red lining behind.

PROV.: Bt. by Alleyn, 29 September 1618; Alleyn Bequest 1626.

EXH.: *Edward Alleyn* 1994(94); Tredegar House 1995–.

REF.: S. Foister in *Edward Alleyn* 1994, p.40.

Queen Mary (1516–58), reigned 1553–58.

The image ultimately derives from the contemporary portrait by Anthonis Mor of which there are autograph versions at Compton Wynyates dated 1554, the Escorial and the Isabella Stewart Gardner Museum, Boston MA.[1] The type was engraved by Francis Delaram for the *Baziliwlogia* 1618.[2]

1 See *Treasure Houses of Britain*, NG Washington, 1985, no.19; Strong 1969a, ii, pl.415.
2 Hind 1955, pl.62d; illus. *Edward Alleyn* 1994, p.40.

DPG384 James VI and I

Oak panel 57.8 x 38.1, of three vertical members, from the left 14.5, 14.5 and 9 wide; the centre panel is chamfered on all four sides; the left-hand panel along the vertical edge; the chamfering is shorter at the top than the bottom; there are two butterfly keys across each member and two square keys top and bottom with another in the bottom left corner; the joins are crudely filled and the surface is heavily retouched.

Grey eyes, sandy hair; wearing a hat with a black plume and the Feather jewel, a silver jacket, and the Great George.

PROV.: Bt. by Alleyn, 29 September 1618; Alleyn Bequest 1626.[1]

REF.: S. Foister in *Edward Alleyn* 1994, pp.51, 52.

James I (1566–1625), reigned as James VI in Scotland 1567–1625 and as James I in England 1603–1625; see DPG548, p.200.

Although of somewhat better quality than the other Monarchs, as befitted the reigning King under whom Alleyn held minor court office, DPG384 remains a pedestrian derivation from the de Critz pattern (see DPG548, p.200); it was presumably the James I which Alleyn bought in 1618 as part of his bulk purchase of Kings and Queens. The construction of the panel and the position of the head and collar within the composition strongly suggest it was cut along the top and right-hand edges to make it conform with the rest of the set.

1 S. Foister, in *Edward Alleyn* 1994, p.51, considered the Alleyn provenance uncertain.

DPG417 Henry, Prince of Wales

Canvas 141 x 126.8 including two vertical strips, each approximately 11 wide, left and right edges; lined and cleaned by Brown 1814;[1] 'not in good condition' in 1931; tacking edges show the canvas has not been cut down, but refilled tacking holes indicate it had once been folded over along the left and bottom edges; X-radiography shows a horse's head in the upper-left background; cleaned and relined 2000.

Blue eyes, light-brown hair; wearing a gilded corslet and arm armour, a pink-brown doublet with pearls and white stockings with the Garter.

PROV.: Probably Alleyn Bequest 1626; at Dulwich by 1697.

EXH.: Alleyn's Boys School 1910; Dulwich College 1914–31; *Edward Alleyn* 1994 (47); Dulwich College 2004–.

REF.: Aubrey 1718, p.195; S. Foister in *Edward Alleyn* 1994, pp.51, 52.

'Of an amiable Majestick Countenance, his hair of an Auborne Collour, long faced and broad forehead',[2] Henry Frederick, Prince of Wales (1594–1612), eldest son of James I (see above), Prince of Wales 1610, died prematurely of typhoid fever; he was Patron of the Prince's Players, a company with which Edward Alleyn was closely involved.

The execution of armour and costume shows some of the same crudity as the other Royal portraits in the Alleyn collection, although the face mask is somewhat better. The composition derives from the whole-length engravings of 1612 by W. Hole and S. van de Passe,[3] 'deliberately project[ing] the Prince *à l'antique* profile as a man of war, skilled in arms'.[4] Both engravings were taken from a now untraced drawing 'in little' by Isaac Oliver produced as a pattern for engraving and later given to Charles I by Inigo Jones.[5] Oliver also produced a large drawing of Prince Henry, once at Whitehall and now untraced.[6] Perhaps the erased horse's head in the background of DPG417 was going to refer to military exercises.

1 Brown Ledger, 28 November 1814, '*a Portrait of Prince Henery*'.
2 Sir Charles Cornwallis, *Life of Henry Prince of Wales*, 1641, p.93, as quoted by Strong 1969a, p.162.
3 Hind 1955, pp.258, 321, pls.152, 199. Both plates show the Prince's plumed helmet on the ground to the left; Hole shows a plain background, van de Passe a distant parade ground with tilting in progress (cf. note 6 below). The Hole plate was used as the front. for Drayton's *Polyolbion*, 1612, and was adapted for the *Herwologia* 1620 (Hind 1955, pl.71d). See also R. Strong, *Artists of the Tudor Court*, VAM, 1983 (259).
4 R. Strong, *Henry, Prince of Wales, and England's Lost Renaissance*, 1986, p.130.
5 Hind 1955, pp.258, 405; 'Abraham van der Doort's Catalogue of the collections of Charles I', *Wal. Soc.*, XXXVII, 1960, p.153, no.23 ('a drawing in little of Prince Henry where hee is playing wth a lance being side faced ...'). Hind 1955, p.405, cites an annotation by van der Dort (Bodleian MS. Ashmole 1514, f.193) saying the drawing was done as a pattern for engraving.
6 Hind 1955, *loc.cit.*; van der Doort, *op.cit.*, p.107, no.17 ('the biggest lim'd Picture that was made by Prince Henry being lim'd in a sett laced Roofe [*Ruff*] in a gilded Armo^{r} and a Landskip by wherein some Souldiers and Tents are made ...').

W. Hole, *Henry, Prince of Wales*, engraving, 1612 (National Portrait Gallery, London)

IAL·Y·P

SIBYLS c.1618–20

The twelve legendary sibyls, pagan virgins distinguished by their geographical names, prophesied specific episodes in the life of Christ. Their history and iconography, as well as their prophecies, are variously described.[1] Alleyn's sibyls have no identifiable visual source, but each is approximately characterized by origin; only the European sibyl displays a separate attribute. They are crude images to an extent that led Lysons to comment how 'the taste for sybils must be much altered, or Mr Alleyn had a very dear bargain; it would be difficult to meet with a broker that would give fourpence a piece for them now'.[2] As with the Monarchs described above, however, this incomplete set remains of interest as being dated and having a complete provenance. The three missing sibyls are the *Eritrean*, the *Libyan* and the *Phrygian*.

On 3 November 1620 Alleyn *Chayngd my 12 owld sybyles for 12 new & gaue 40d a peec to boot to mr gibbkin so pd* £2.0s.0d,[3] an exchange price ('*to boot*'); at 3s 4d each, they were half the price of the monarchs. Nothing is known of the earlier set (also, presumably, from 'Gibbkin'). Of the nine now at Dulwich, four are on canvas and five on panel, suggesting they may have been a job lot rather than a set. Perhaps one may distinguish a slight difference in quality between canvases and panels, the former showing greater individuality, the latter a more monotonous characterization (save the apprehensive and elderly *Hellespontic Sibyl*). The identity of 'Gibbkin' is not completely clear, but he was probably related to (or even was) the painter John Gipkyn;[4] a week later, on 10 November 1620, Alleyn bought from him a set of fourteen heads of Jesus, Mary and the twelve Disciples (see p.19), and on 14 November Alleyn paid 'm[r] gibkin' for gilding unspecified pictures.

Comparable painted sets of sibyls are recorded in English collections[5] and in Bradninch church, Devon, the early-sixteenth-century screens to the chancel and choir aisles are painted with fifty-two figures of Old and New Testament subjects, prophets, sibyls and saints.[6]

1 See, for example, L. Réau, *L'Iconographie de l'art chrétien*, 1956, ii, pp.420–30 – whence the following defining notes have been taken; E. Wind, 'Michelangelo's Prophets and Sibyls', *Proceedings of the British Academy*, li, 1960, pp.57–73, and S. Foister in *Edward Alleyn* 1994, pp.53–54, 60–61nn41, 43.
2 Lysons 1792, p.116.
3 Alleyn's Diary; Young 1889, ii, p.193.
4 John Gipkyn (fl. 1594–1629), member of the Painter-Stainers' Company; official artist for many of the Lord Mayor's shows between 1604 and 1618; painter of the *Old St Paul's Diptych* 1616 (Society of Antiquaries, London), see P. Tudor-Craig, *Old St Paul's*, 2004, pp.18–25, 38n75.
5 E.g. a set of panels of heads of Sibyls, Prophets and Sages set into the panelling as a frieze at Chastleton House, Oxon., and another set formerly at Cheyney Court, Herefords., dated 1611; see Foister in *Edward Alleyn* 1994, pp.60–61n41.
6 Croft-Murray 1962, p.169b.

DPG537 *Egyptian Sibyl*

Canvas 61 x 44.4 lined by Morrill; Brown 1812?[1] heavily retouched; surface cleaned 1990.

Inscribed above: *SIBILLA AEGIPTIA*; brown eyes, dark hair, brown skin; wearing a white headdress and tunic with red-patterned fringe and a pale blue drape with clasp on her right shoulder.

PROV.: Bt. by Alleyn from Gibbkin, 3 November 1620; Alleyn Bequest 1626.

EXH.: *Edward Alleyn* 1994(95); Tredegar House 1995–.

REF.: S. Foister in *Edward Alleyn* 1994, pp.52–54.

The Egyptian sibyl [*Sibylla Agrippa, Aggripina*] foretold the Flagellation and was sometimes shown with a whip or standing by a column.

1 Brown Ledger, '*Lining cleaning Repairing Stipling &c: twelve Picrs.*', 4 November 1812, may have referred to the set of twelve Sibyls.

DPG538 *Samian Sibyl*

Canvas 58.7 x 44.1 lined by Morrill; Brown 1812?[1] heavily retouched; surface cleaned 1990.

Inscribed above: *SIBILLA SAMIA*; brown eyes, fair hair; wearing a pale, striped turban with a blue rosette and black plume and a white tunic trimmed in brown and gold with rubies and pearls.

PROV.: Bt. by Alleyn from Gibbkin, 3 November 1620; Alleyn Bequest 1626.

EXH.: *Edward Alleyn* 1994(96); Tredegar House 1995–.

REF.: S. Foister in *Edward Alleyn* 1994, pp.52–54.

From Samos in southern Greece, the Samian sibyl foretold the Nativity and was sometimes shown with a cradle or a rose.

1 Brown Ledger, see DPG537 note 1.

DPG539 *Cumanan Sibyl*

Oak panel 57.2 x 40.9 of two vertical members, the left 15 wide, crudely planed and primed, with many prominent retouchings; Brown 1812?[1] surface cleaned 1990.

Inscribed above: *SIBILLA CVMANA*; blue eyes, light brown hair; wearing a golden diadem, a golden brown cloak with jewelled clasp on her right shoulder, a red tunic with gold figuring and a gold collar set with precious stones.

PROV.: Bt. by Alleyn from Gibbkin, 3 November 1620; Alleyn Bequest 1626.

EXH.: *Edward Alleyn* 1994(97); Tredegar House 1995–.

REF.: S. Foister in *Edward Alleyn* 1994, pp.52–54.

The Cumanan sibyl [*Sibylla Cimmera*, *Ciemeria*, *Emeria*] from the Bosphorus, foretold how Christ would live in poverty on earth (or how the Virgin would feed the infant Christ) and was sometimes shown with a crown or cornucopia.

The distinction between the Cumanan and Cumaean Sibyls is often obscured.

1 Brown Ledger, see DPG537 note 1..

DPG540 *Cumaean Sibyl*

Canvas 63.5 x 45.1 lined by Morrill; Brown 1812?[1] heavily retouched; consolidated 1990.

Inscribed above: SIBILLA CVMEA; brown eyes, light brown hair with white bands; wearing a pink tunic and a dark drape (originally probably dark green).

PROV.: Bt. by Alleyn from Gibbkin, 3 November 1620; Alleyn Bequest 1626.

EXH.: *Edward Alleyn* 1994(98); Tredegar House 1995–.

REF.: S. Foister in *Edward Alleyn* 1994, pp.52–54.

The Cumaean sibyl [*Sibylla Amalthea*] from Italy, foretold the Nativity in Bethlehem and was sometimes shown with a cradle.

The profile head and upswept hair, exceptional in this series of sibyls, provide a distant mannerist echo.

See DPG539 above.

1 Brown Ledger, see DPG537 note 1.

DPG541 *Delphic Sibyl*

Oak panel 57.2 x 41 of three vertical members, from the left 11.5, 25 and 4.5 wide; Brown 1812?[1] splinters missing from the top corners and from the top of the central member; heavily retouched; consolidated 1990.

Inscribed above: SIBILLA DELPHICA; blue eyes, light brown hair dressed with a golden clasp and pearls; wearing a pearl earring, a green tunic with gold collar, and a red drape with a jewelled shoulder clasp.

PROV.: Bt. by Alleyn from Gibbkin, 3 November 1620; Alleyn Bequest 1626.

EXH.: *Edward Alleyn* 1994(99); Tredegar House 1995–.

REF.: S. Foister in *Edward Alleyn* 1994, pp.52–54.

The Delphic sibyl from central Greece foretold the Mocking of Christ and was sometimes shown with a crown of thorns.

1 Brown Ledger, see DPG537 note 1.

DPG542 *European Sibyl*

Oak panel 57.2 x 41 of three vertical members, from the left 11.4, 25.3 and 4.3 wide, the joins supported with canvas; Brown 1812?[1] heavily retouched; surface cleaned 1990.

Inscribed above: SIBILLA EVROPEA; brown eyes and brown hair with a gold clasp; wearing a white tunic and holding an open book, a gold sceptre in her left hand.

PROV.: Bt. by Alleyn from Gibbkin, 3 November 1620; Alleyn Bequest 1626.

EXH.: *Edward Alleyn* 1994(100); Tredegar House 1995–.

REF.: S. Foister in *Edward Alleyn* 1994, pp.52–54.

The European sibyl foretold the Flight into Egypt and was sometimes shown with a sword indicating the Massacre of the Innocents.

1 Brown Ledger, see DPG537 note 1.

DPG543 *Hellespontic Sibyl*

Oak panel 57.2 x 42.4 of two vertical members, the left averaging 17 wide, the join not aligned; Brown 1812?[1] heavily retouched with vertical scratching lower left; revarnished 1990.

Inscribed above: SIBILLA HELESPONTICA; brown eyes; wearing a black hood with pink lining, a white wimple and a dark green tunic.

PROV.: Bt. by Alleyn from Gibbkin, 3 November 1620; Alleyn Bequest 1626.

EXH.: *Edward Alleyn* 1994(101); Tredegar House 1995–.

REF.: S. Foister in *Edward Alleyn* 1994, pp.52–54.

The Hellespontic sibyl [*Sibylla Elepontia*, *Aspontia*, *Aegea*] from near Troy, foretold the Crucifixion and was sometimes shown with a cross or nails. With the Phrygian Sibyl, she was regarded as being much older than the other Sibyls.

1 Brown Ledger, see DPG537 note 1.

DPG544 *Persian Sibyl*

Oak panel 57.2 x 42.3 of three vertical members, from the left 8.7, 25.9 and 7.7 wide, the joins, which are not flush, supported with canvas; Brown 1812?[1] heavily retouched; surface cleaned 1990.

Inscribed above: SIBILLA PERSICA; brown eyes and hair; wearing a pearl earring, a dark blue-green tunic with black veil and a red drape with shoulder clasp.

PROV.: Bt. by Alleyn from Gibbkin, 3 November 1620; Alleyn Bequest 1626.

EXH.: *Edward Alleyn* 1994(102); Tredegar House 1995–.

REF.: S. Foister in *Edward Alleyn* 1994, pp.52–54.

The Persian sibyl foretold the Temptation in the Wilderness and was sometimes shown with a dragon beneath her feet and a lantern.

1 Brown Ledger, see DPG537 note 1.

DPG545 *Tiburtine Sibyl*

Canvas 57.2 x 42.5 lined by Morrill; Brown 1812?[1] a prominent scratch on the surface runs from top left to bottom right; revarnished 1990.

Inscribed above: SIBILLA TIBVRTINA; brown eyes, her dark brown hair coiled over her ears dressed with a striped white turban; wearing a red tunic with a green drape.

PROV.: Bt. by Alleyn from Gibbkin, 3 November 1620; Alleyn Bequest 1626.

EXH.: *Edward Alleyn* 1994(103); Tredegar House 1995–.

REF.: S. Foister in *Edward Alleyn* 1994, pp.52–54.

The Tiburtine sibyl [*Sibylla Albumana*, *Albuna*], the Roman sibyl from the Tiber or Tivoli, foretold the Immaculate Conception and was sometimes shown with a dove, or showing the Emperor Augustus the site of S. Maria in Aracoeli in Rome.

1 Brown Ledger, see DPG537 note 1.

DPG546 *Piety*

Oak panel 152.3 x 61 of seven rough-hewn horizontal members with butterfly insets; there are several subsequent splits; heavily overpainted, with areas of lifting paint, some retouchings now discoloured; see below.

Inscribed above: *PIETAS*; wearing a pink dress with a yellow girdle and white wimple; a black book at her waist, her right hand round the neck of a stork (a symbol of piety), her left holding up a flaming stone altar.

PROV.: See DPG547.

EXH.: *Edward Alleyn* 1994(104).

REF. see DPG547.

DPG547 *Liberality*

Oak panel 152.3 x 61 of seven rough-hewn horizontal members, with butterfly insets; there are several subsequent splits; heavily overpainted, with areas of lifting paint; see below.

Inscribed above: *LIBERALITAS*; a fair haired figure wearing a green dress with a golden drape; emptying two bronze cornucopia: from that in her left hand flow fruit and flowers, from the other, various articles of dress and ornament with coins, books, pens and spoons.

PROV.: Alleyn Bequest 1626; Masters' Library, Dulwich College.

EXH.: *Edward Alleyn* 1994(105).

REF.: Brayley 1850, iii, p.236; Young 1889, ii, p.116; Croft-Murray 1962, p.194b; S. Foister in *Edward Alleyn* 1994, pp.37–38.

The figure ultimately derives from *Liberalita* in Ripa's *Iconologia* (1593).

Since at least the mid-19th century these two panels have been incorporated within a Jacobean-style wooden chimneypiece, now in the Masters' Library in Dulwich College.[1] It is assumed they were taken there from Alleyn's old College building, where Canon Carver is said to have found them about to be demolished in 1858 during the rebuilding.[2] In 1994, when they were removed for the *Edward Alleyn* exhibition, they were found to have been unduly restrained with screws at the corners; after the exhibition they were reinstalled without the screws.

The inscribed titles suggest they may have been part of a series of Virtues.[3] They appear to be contemporary with the Monarchs and Sibyls described above and are similarly inept, if more ambitious. Croft-Murray considered the handling characteristic of [Rowland] Buckett (fl. 1600, d. 1639) who was paid for painting a heavily gilded chimneypiece at Dulwich (see p.19), but Foister found no more than 'a superficial resemblance' to his work.[4]

In 1850 Brayley proposed they were from 'the Queen's barge',[5] part of which Edward Alleyn had bought on 19 December 1618: *bought off mathewes* [Master of the Queen's Barge] *all ye upp pt off ye quens owld barge* £2.2s.6d,[6] and in July 1619 Alleyn had paid a further £2.9s.5d *for Joyners work about ye chimney peces of ye barge for stuff to add to ye barge stuff*,[7] i.e. Alleyn adapted panelling from the Queen's barge for a chimneypiece.[8] Croft-Murray doubted that the Virtues were from the Queen's barge and Foister considered their origin mysterious, but the unusual construction of the panels, with their very rough horizontal (rather than vertical) members, may indicate they were taken from a larger structure .

1 Illus. J.R. Piggott, *Dulwich College*, 1990, pp.54–55.
2 S. Hodges, *God's Gift*, 1981, p.118.
3 The Virtues were variously listed but, for example, Crispin de Passe the elder included Liberalitas and Pietas in different engraved sets of Virtues (Hollstein, *Dutch & Flemish Etchings, Engravings & Woodcuts c.1450–1700*, xv, 1964, pp.179, 183).
4 See Croft-Murray 1962, p.194b, and Foister in *Edward Alleyn* 1994, p.37.
5 Brayley 1850, iii, p.236; repeated by Young 1889, i, p.470, and in previous editions of this Catalogue. Anne of Denmark, consort of James I, was to die within three months of Alleyn's purchase; from September 1618 she was confined to Hampton Court by illness.
6 Alleyn Diary; Young 1889, ii, p.116. (In 1574 William Herne had painted Queen Elizabeth's barge with 'five stories of poetry'; Croft Murray 1962, p.181a).
7 *Ibid.*; Young 1889, ii, p.143.
8 *Ibid.*; Young 1889, ii, pp.148, 157. Foister in *Edward Alleyn* 1994, p.37. In September 1619 payments were made to Goodman Gardyner for painting two chimney pieces and '*4 figuers of ye seasons*'.

PROTESTANT REFORMERS

These five portraits of sixteenth-century Protestant reformers were probably acquired by Alleyn to supplement his apostles, sibyls and monarchs. They were not, however, produced as a set (the sizes vary slightly) and evidently did not come from the same workshop. Perkins and Nowell, both derived from engravings in the *Herwologia*, show a comparable format; Calvin, Beza and Luther, each with a book in his hand, derive from Continental engravings, and appear to come from a second workshop.[1]

The depiction of the Protestant reformers from the reigns of Henry VIII to Queen Elizabeth was one of the themes of Henry Holland's second book of engraved portraits, the *Herwologia* of 1620,[2] regarded as the natural sequel to his *Baziliwlogia*, or book of Kings from William I to James I, of 1618.

1 See S. Foister, *Edward Alleyn* 1994, pp.55–56.
2 Hind 1955, pp.145–58, pls. 68–85.

DPG368 Théodore De Beza

Canvas 33.3 x 25.8 lined and cleaned by Brown 1815;[1] relined with new stretcher by Morrill; crudely retouched with many old losses; an old tear down the right side of beard.

Inscribed upper right below brim of hat: *DE Beza 1605*; white beard, grey eyes, wearing a black hat and gown with brown fur trim.

PROV.: Probably Alleyn Bequest 1626.

EXH.: *Edward Alleyn* 1994(108).

REF.: S. Foister in *Edward Alleyn* 1994, pp.54–56, 61n47.

Théodore De Beza (or de Bèze; 1519–1605), French scholar and reformer, succeeded Calvin at Geneva in 1564; he published the *Confessions de la foi chrétienne* in 1559.

The image may ultimately derive (with the addition of a broad-brimmed hat) from one of the half-length engravings in Beza's *Icones* (1580).

1 Brown Ledger, 13 October 1815, '*Two portraits de beza & companion*'.

DPG369 *William Perkins*

Canvas 30.8 x 25.4 lined and repaired by Brown 1815;[1] damage lower right; discoloured varnish; probably cut down.

Inscribed upper left: *Perkins. / 1602*; dark hair, brown eyes; wearing a white collar, grey coat with black stripes, a red-bound book stands on the table.

PROV.: Probably Alleyn Bequest 1626.

EXH.: *Edward Alleyn* 1994(106).

REF.: S. Foister in *Edward Alleyn* 1994, pp.54–56, 61n46.

William Perkins (1558–1602), puritan theologian whose writings were held in high repute by Calvinist sympathizers; 'lame' in his right hand, he wrote with his left.

The image is taken from the engraving by Willem or Magdalena van de Passe in the *Herwologia* 1620 which Hind noted was taken from a painting 'in a kinsmans custody';[2] the *Herwologia* plate was itself taken from either an engraving by Elstrack[3] or from the original portrait in Christ's College, Cambridge.[4]

1 Brown Ledger, 28 June 1815, '*Lining Cleaning & three picrs. of Luther Calvin & Pirkens*'.
2 Hind 1955, p.158, pl.84c; *Edward Alleyn* 1994, p.57.
3 Hind 1955, p.188, pl.103c.
4 J.W. Goodison, *Portraits in Christ's, Clare and Sidney Sussex Colleges*, 1985, p.32(66); a version at Sidney Sussex, *ibid.*, p.84(176).

DPG370 *John Calvin*

Canvas 34 x 27 lined and repaired by Brown 1815;[1] relined with new stretcher by Morrill; old vertical tear below right; blisters treated 1989.

Inscribed upper right: *Calvin / 1564* (now obscure); wearing black.

PROV.: Probably Alleyn Bequest 1626.

EXH.: *Edward Alleyn* 1994(109).

REF.: S. Foister in *Edward Alleyn* 1994, pp.54–56, 61n47.

John Calvin (1509–64), French reformer and theologian; left Paris in 1533, settled in Geneva 1541; the most influential writer of the Protestant reformers, first publishing the *Institutiones* 1536 (Alleyn owned a copy of Norton's 1562 translation).[2]

The image derives from one of the many engraved profile portraits, of which one, without the hand, appeared in Beza's *Icones* (1580).

1 Brown Ledger, see DPG369 note 1.
2 *Edward Alleyn* 1994 (121).

DPG419 *Alexander Nowell*

Canvas 33.7 x 26 lined and cleaned by Brown 1815;[1] relined with new stretcher by Morrill; numerous retouchings in face and garments; discoloured varnish; lifting craquelure, mainly in lower area, consolidated 1989.

Inscribed in yellow top right: *A. Nowell / 16*[01?]; grey eyes; wearing a black cap and a brown fur-trimmed cloak over his black buttoned tunic.

PROV.: Probably Alleyn Bequest 1626.

EXH.: *Edward Alleyn* 1994(107).

REF.: S. Foister in *Edward Alleyn* 1994, pp.54–56.

Alexander Nowell (1507?–1602) eminent puritan, Dean of St Paul's 1560 (where he preceded John Donne, Alleyn's father-in-law).

The image is taken from the engraving by Willem or Magdalena van de Passe in the *Herwologia* 1620, which Hind noticed was taken from a picture 'from a shop by Poules'.[2] Other portraits of him at Oxford show a wide-brimmed black hat and a fishing rod in the background (referring to his reputation as a *piscator hominum*).[3]

1 Brown Ledger, see DPG368 note 1.
2 Hind 1955, p.158, pl.84b; *Edward Alleyn* 1994, p.57.
3 In the Bodleian Library and at Brasenose College (Poole, i, p.23, no.55, and ii, p.249, no.14).

DPG421 *Martin Luther*

Canvas 34 x 26.9 lined and repaired by Brown 1815;[1] relined with new stretcher by Morrill; disfigured by blistering, scratches, craquelure and very discoloured varnish; blisters treated 1989.

Inscribed upper right: *Luther / 15*[4]*6*; brownish hair and eyes; wearing a red vest, white collar and a black cloak with a brown fur collar; a yellow-bound book in his right hand.

PROV.: Probably Alleyn Bequest 1626.

EXH.: *Edward Alleyn* 1994(110).

REF.: S. Foister in *Edward Alleyn* 1994, pp.54–56, 61n47.

Martin Luther (1483–1546), founder of the German Reformation, excommunicated from the Catholic church in 1521.

The head recalls the last of the Luther portraits by Cranach,[2] but the image may derive more particularly from one of the many related engravings, for example the half-length, without the hand, in Beza's *Icones* (1580).

1 Brown Ledger, see DPG369 note 1.
2 M.J. Friedlander & J. Rosenberg, *Lucas Cranach*, 1978 ed., no.423.

POET

DPG427 *Dante*

Canvas 61.9 x 49.5 lined and cleaned by Brown 1813;[1] scratched surface; an old T-shaped tear lower right, an indent by his left cheek and an old damage centre right repaired with paper lining; a pentiment of leaves behind the shoulders; the jaw and neck overpainted; much discoloured varnish; stabilised 1994.

Inscribed above: *DANTES ALDIGERIV*; grey eyes, white ear flaps; wearing red over a black fur-lined jerkin; the laurel leaves now appear yellow.

PROV.: Probably Alleyn Bequest 1626.

EXH.: *Edward Alleyn* 1994(111).

REF.: S. Foister in *Edward Alleyn* 1994, p.56.

Dante Alighieri (1265–1321), author of the *Divina Commedia.*

The precise source of this coarse painting remains unidentified, but it may be compared, in reverse, with the half-length portraits of Dante in the Uffizi (P1563, pendant to a Petrarch, P1562)[2] and the Yale University Art Gallery.[3] Size and format compare with Alleyn's sets of monarchs and sibyls and Foister has suggested DPG427 may have belonged to a set of poets[4] otherwise including perhaps Ariosto, Tasso and Petrarch.

1 Brown Ledger, 24 August 1813, '*Portrait of a Gentleman with Lorels on his head*', although this entry might also refer to DPG430, p.75.
2 Gli Uffizi, *Catalogo Generale*, 1980, p.508.
3 Both Uffizi and Yale portraits illus. R.T. Holbrook, *Portraits of Dante*, 1911, f.pp.182, 184.
4 *Edward Alleyn* 1994, p.56. To quote a single example of many, a painted frieze in the Bodleian Library, Oxford, c.1618, includes the heads of Dante, Boccaccio and Aretino.

THE CARTWRIGHT BEQUEST 1686

The paintings in this section are catalogued as follows

William Cartwright [1]

William Cartwright (1607–86), actor, collector and benefactor of Dulwich College was the son of the actor William Cartwright who was a friend of Edward Alleyn, the founder of Dulwich College (see p.19). Both father and son were listed in 1635 among players from the King's Revels banned from performing at Norwich; in 1637 he played with Queen Henrietta's Men at Salisbury Court (where he met Perkins and Bond, see DPG444 and DPG455) and Aubrey called him an 'excellent player'. While the theatres were closed 1642–60 Cartwright became a bookseller and he was almost certainly responsible for a new edition of Heywood's *Apology for Actors* which appeared in 1658 as *The Actor's Vindication* by 'G.E. for W.C.' with a panegyric of Edward Alleyn. In 1660 he was one of the original members and a share holder of the King's Company, then under the management of Thomas Killigrew. From at least 1666 he lived in a comfortable house in Great Turnstile (where the painters John Greenhill and Parry Walton were near neighbours) and he had interests in three other London properties. He died on 9 December 1686 and was buried in St Paul's, Covent Garden. He appears to have been at least three times married, but was described at his death as having spent the last seventeen years of his life alone, 'having neither wife nor childe.'[2]

Perhaps it was his father's friendship with Edward Alleyn that led him to make Dulwich the major beneficiary of his estate, £400 and significant collections of books and pictures. But it was some years before any part of this legacy came to the College, the balance having apparently been taken by unscrupulous servants.

1 For whom, see E. Boswell, *Modern Languages Review*, xxiv, 2, 1929, pp.125–42; G.A. Waterfield & N. Kalinsky, *Mr Cartwright's Pictures* 1987, pp.5–8.
2 See DPG387 nn.4,5.

The Bequest [1]

The Cartwright Inventory, compiled by the aging William Cartwright in the 1680s,[2] lists 239 pictures. Forty-six were later taken by his servants[3] and only 77 are identifiable at Dulwich today;[4] of these forty-eight are here described as by British artists. The Inventory reflects an unsophisticated taste, the profane mixed freely with the religious,[5] with each kind of painting indiscriminately represented. The average valuation for each picture is a little over £3, the most expensive being a huge seapiece by Castro (no longer in the collection; see p.258) at £34. It is impossible to deduce an overall pattern of acquisition, but perhaps the seven Lovelace portraits were bought in the later 1660s from a relation; the still life by Walton and the family portraits by Greenhill (Cartwright's neighbours) were surely commissioned, and the large landscape by Streeter and the twelve seascapes by Castro were evidently purchased in the 1670s as furnishing pieces for the Great Turnstile house. The size of the Inventory suggests that the rooms eventually were quite densely hung.

Overall it seems easy to identify the existing Cartwright pictures within the Inventory. But there are two difficulties; one, that a leaf from the Inventory, containing nos.186–209, is missing, and two, the method of identification from the Inventory. Some of the pictures still bear an 18th-century paper label inscribed in ink (the neat writing not that of the Inventory) giving Inventory number and title (not a literal transcription from the Inventory). These labels must have been affixed after the pictures were received at Dulwich, i.e. each picture was identified from the Inventory. It was not necessarily a fool-proof system, and may be the reason for the difficulties we now have, for example, with the Cartwright family portraits, at least one of which is now missing (see under DPG411).

See also DPG519, p.200 and DPG405, p.205.

1 See G.A. Waterfield & N. Kalinsky in *Mr Cartwright's Pictures* 1987, pp.8–11.
2 Inasmuch as James II is listed as the Duke of York (DPG416) perhaps it was compiled before 1685.
3 Young 1889, ii, p.187.
4 According to Young (1889, i, p.472) Cartwright 'gave away some, his servants stole others after (and perhaps before) his death, and probably some have since been lost or destroyed in various ways'.
5 E.g. 33, *a Soulder & a wench at it, on a bourd in a gilt frame a closit pece* £7, and 34, *a pictur of our Sauiour & his disipells at his last Supper, on a bord, in black & whit in a guilt frame.* £6.

Display

See p.19.

CARTWRIGHT FAMILY PORTRAITS

The Cartwright Inventory is incomprehensible concerning portraits of the Cartwright wives and relations. Only Greenhill's portrait of the donor can be identified without hesitation.

JOHN GREENHILL (1642–76)

DPG393 *William Cartwright*

Canvas 102.8 x 84.9 lined and varnished by Holder 1914; a pentimento behind his right shoulder; the black cloak is painted in resinous paint over a very worn black original; a diagonal damage upper left and numerous scattered retouchings; Hell 1949; restored and revarnished 1987.

Pale brown eyes, dark hair; wearing a black Indian gown; the dog collar embossed with the sitter's initials *W.C.*

PROV.: Cartwright Bequest 1686; Inventory 234 *my pictur in a black dress, with a great doge.*

EXH.: NPE 1866(667); *Samuel Pepys Esq*, NPG, 1970(67); *Mr Cartwright's Pictures* 1987(19); *Man's Best Friend, 400 years of Dog Collars*, Guernsey, 1993(n.n.).

ENG.: R. Clamp 1794 after S. Harding (*Shakspearean Miscellany* 1802).

REF.: Aubrey 1718; Vertue, ii, p.13; Lysons 1792, p.111; Collins Baker 1912, ii, pp.8, 12, 13, 157; R.T. Jeffree in *Mr Cartwright's Pictures* 1987, pp.13, 40–41.

Securely identified from the Cartwright Inventory, this is the only known portrait of William Cartwright (1607-86, see p.45) painted c.1665 when he was already some fifty-eight years old.

Although unattributed in the Inventory, DPG 393 may confidently be given to Greenhill, as Lysons had first stated in 1792.[1] The head leans back, the characterization is strong, but the dog and right hand are weak. It shows Cartwright as a satisfied private gentleman (quite without theatrical allure), the pose reminiscent of Lely's *Duke of Lauderdale* of c.1665 and of Van Dyck's *Thomas Killigrew*.[2] From 1662 Killigrew was the (not particularly successful) manager of the King's Company of which Cartwright was a member.

Vertue recorded that Greenhill had copied Van Dyck's *Killigrew* 'at the age of 20 or 21 [i.e. 1662–63]... so near resembling the original that it was very hard for the most discerning judges of Vandyks works to know which was the Original',[3] and the Greenhill drawing in the Cartwright Album at Dulwich College suggests how he was adapting the composition.[4] In DPG393 the position of the hands is changed so that they both rest on the (rather awful) dog, providing a less elegant pose (they more resemble those of Dobson's *Sir Thomas Chicheley*).[5] The sitter's initials on the dog collar retain the Van Dyck device.

A half-length portrait at Knole in the manner of Lely, inscribed *Wm. Cartwright Obt 1643*, is not of the Dulwich William Cartwright.[6]

1 Waterhouse 1994, p.111, doubted the attribution since the artist was unnamed in the Cartwright Inventory and Vertue (i, p.13) recorded at Dulwich 'W. Cartwright after Lilly his hand on a great dog'.
2 Respectively, Scottish NPG (exh. *Lely*, NPG 1978, no. 37) and Weston Park (*Van Dyck* 2004, p.541, IV.144).
3 Vertue i, p.30.
4 *Mr Cartwright's Pictures* 1987, pp.15, 27, 41n3.
5 Private collection; exh. *Dobson*, NPG, 1983, no.17, illus. Dobson's composition also ultimately derived from the Van Dyck's *Killigrew*.
6 Indeed the inscription indicates the dramatist the Rev. William Cartwright (1611–43), but the portrait dates from much later. Vertue (iv, p.165) recorded the Duke of Dorset buying a portrait of 'Cartwright' at the Halifax sale in 1739; Knole Inventory 1799.

John Greenhill, *Study for the portrait of William Cartwright*, pen and ink (Dulwich College)

John Greenhill (1642–76)

DPG387 'Mrs Cartwright'

Canvas 74.5 x 60 lined; X-radiography and pentimenti show she was first painted with a pearl head-dress and ear-rings, wearing a blue décolleté dress with red sleeves, a pearl brooch at the corsage, and a rather flowing veil round her head; old damages in the right background and the bottom right corner; the black over-painting of two veils and the dress now very uneven and abraded; a black 'roll' of material rests (unconvincingly) over her forearm; her head veil hangs straight down from her head, another spreads out behind; the background area is very thin and heavily retouched; Hell 1952–53.

Blue eyes, fair hair, with very long curls visible by the edge of the veil.

PROV.: Cartwright Bequest 1686; Inventory 116 *my Last wifes pictur, with a black vaile on her head in a gilt frame 3 quarters Clouth* £3.[1]

EXH.: *Mr Cartwright's Pictures* 1987(23); *The Art of Death*, VAM, 1992.

REF.: Collins Baker 1912, ii, pp.8, 157 f.p.8; R.T. Jeffree in *Mr Cartwright's Pictures* 1987, pp.43–44; N. Llewellyn, *The Art of Death*, 1992, p.96.

Although unattributed in the Cartwright Inventory, there seems no reason to doubt that DPG387 was painted by Greenhill, perhaps in the mid-1660s, contemporary with DPG393.[2] Murray 1980 and Jeffree proposed that '*my Last wifes pictur*' shows Jane Hodgson who married a William Cartwright on 19 November 1654 at St James, Clerkenwell (a Hodgson coat of arms is no.160 in the Cartwright Inventory). Cartwright's marriages are something of a mystery, but the registers of St Giles, Cripplegate, record three marriages of a William Cartwright, player;[3] was Jane Hodgson his fourth wife? When Cartwright died in 1686 a childless widower[4] he had probably lived alone for his last seventeen years (if we choose to believe his devious housekeeper Mrs Johnson),[5] implying that his last wife died c.1669. Why was the portrait overpainted with a black mourning veil?[6] According to the Inventory the overpainting was done while the portrait was in Cartwright's possession so that, as Llewellyn surprisingly proposed, the veil might refer to the widower's grief.

See also DPG399 and DPG388 below.

1 An old label *verso* has No 116 *Mrs Cartwright*.
2 Jeffrey suggested early 1660s; Collins Baker 1912 had proposed c.1668–70. Waterhouse 1994, p.111, doubted the attribution since the artist was unnamed in the Cartwright Inventory. Oliver Millar recalled (letter on file) having seen the signature *J. G.* soon after the War.
3 Tomazine Kendall married William Cartwright January 1637; buried as wife of 'William Cartwright player', July 1637; Katherine, wife of William Cartwright player, buried May 1642; Anne, wife of William Cartwright player, buried March 1651. See also note 6.
4 Boswell 1929, p.128, quoting PRO Chancery Proc., *Dulwich v Johnson et al.*, C.7.102/66.
5 Young 1889, i, p.185, quoting Dulwich MSS vi.39, the joint and several answers by Francis and Jane Johnson to the bill preferred against them in Chancery; she explained that she had lived with him for near seventeen years, giving him constant and diligent attendance since he was infirm and would trust no one else in his house when he was out.
6 Seven Cartwrights, possibly children, were buried in St Giles-in-the Fields during the plague of 1665–66, but three William Cartwright marriages recorded in that parish – to Elizabeth Cooke in May 1633 (she d. 1665); to Andria Robins in April 1636 (she d.1652), and to Anne Dober in February 1643 – were evidently of different Cartwrights.

John Greenhill (1642–76)

DPG399 *A Lady as a Shepherdess*

Canvas 94.3 x 73 lined;[1] there remain traces of a palm held in her left hand; retouchings in her cheek and in the sky, and a marked craquelure on the left of the landscape; the bottom of her left hand very rubbed; X-radiography suggests that the foreground well on the right was at first a rocky outcrop; Hell 1953; cleaned 1987.

Signed bottom centre right, on stone ledge: *J.G.*; brown eyes, light brown hair dressed with pearls; wearing a golden-yellow drape with a jewelled clasp over a white shift and a purple skirt; a jewel suspended from pearls hangs at her waist (although the suspension defies comprehension); a sheep stands by her to the left and there is a well to the right.

PROV.: Cartwright Bequest 1686; Inventory 186 or 78 (see below).[2]

EXH.: *Mr Cartwright's Pictures* 1987(22).

REF.: Collins Baker 1912, ii, pp.8, 157, f.p.6; Whinney & Millar 1957, p.179; R.T. Jeffree in *Mr Cartwright's Pictures* 1987, p.43; Waterhouse 1994, p.111.

Dated c.1665 by Waterhouse, this is an early and ambitious work by Greenhill. The discreetly bejewelled shepherdess clearly once carried a palm of martyrdom in her left hand which, with the lamb and the prominent, distant tower, suggests she was first painted as St Agnes,[3] the patroness of those about to be married. The lamb's head is painted in some detail, but the body is obscure.

Previously associated with Cartwright Inventory 78 *my first wifes pictur Like a Sheppardess on 3 quarters Clouth* [i.e. 76 x 63] *in a gilte frame,* £3, but the proposed date and the identification of DPG387 (above) seem to eliminate any possibility of the sitter being one of Cartwright's wives.

1 Probably the '*Portrait of Mrs Cartwright*' lined and cleaned by Brown, 2 November 1813 (Brown Ledger).

2 An old label, *verso*, appears to read *No.186*, a number from the missing pages of the Cartwright Inventory.

3 Cf., for example, Van Dyck's *Lady Barbara Villiers, later Duchess of Lennox and Richmond*, Royal Collection (O. Millar in *Van Dyck* 2004, pp.589–90, IV.205, as c.1640) or the *Nell Gwyn* from the studio of Lely in the National Portrait Gallery (NPG 3976).

Harding, *William Cartwright, Original Picture in Dulwich College*, engraving, 1800 (National Portrait Gallery, London)

Unknown Artist

DPG400 *'Old Mr Cartwright'*

Bevelled oak panel 78.5 x 62.5 of three vertical members, from the left 20, 25.5 and 17 wide; 22 butterfly wedges on joins and 2 on a split top right; two horizontal battens have been removed; a pentimento above his left hand; blisters repaired by Holder 1912; Hell 1945–49 and 1968–69; consolidated 1991.

Inscribed upper left: *AETATIS SV* [AE]/ 59; white hair, blue eyes, a wart above his left eye; wearing a pale blue jerkin with red slashes and blue and black trim, and a black cape; the signet ring on the third finger of his left hand bears arms (apparently *gu. a lion passant regardant or, with in chief gu. four ermines or*; unidentified); his silver sword pommel below right.

PROV.: Cartwright's Bequest 1686; Inventory 168 *oul mr Cartwright Actour in a gilt frame 15s.*

EXH.: *Mr Cartwright's Pictures* 1987(20); *Edward Alleyn* 1994 (42).

REF.: Lysons, 1792, p.111 ('very bad'); R.T. Jeffree in *Mr Cartwright's Pictures* 1987, pp.41, 42.

A flat, lifeless image, presumably a copy. Dateable c.1615 by costume, the inscribed age therefore suggesting the sitter was born c.1555. If the identity of '*oul mr Cartwright Actour*' is correct, and if the sitter was directly related to the donor, he could at best have been his grandfather. He was *possibly* the Cartwright who belonged to the Lord Admiral's Men 1598–1602 and a part-lessee of the Fortune Theatre from Edward Alleyn, with whom he dined between 1618 and 1622. Later references to the actor William Cartwright may refer to another William Cartwright, probably the donor's father: acting with the King and Queen of Bohemia's Men, and an original member of the King's Revels in 1629, whose son was said to have joined him at Norwich in 1635 (see p.45); last mentioned in 1640 in the cast of Nathaniel Richards' *Messalina*, but probably still living in 1647.[1]

A half-length engraving of 'Willm Cartwright' by 'Harding', published by Edward Harding in 1800, from an 'Original Picture in Dulwich College' (no longer in the collection), shows an elderly clean-shaven man c.1615, with greying hair, his right hand at his breast, *possibly* the same sitter as in DPG400.[2]

1 See Boswell 1929, p.126, and Jeffree.

2 The NPG copy is in the collated *Extra Portraits and Views*, bound as Lyson's *Environs of London*, ix.

Unknown Artist

DPG388 *'Mrs Cartwright's Sister'*

Canvas 80.3 x 60 lined and cleaned by Brown 1814;[1] the painted oval ornamental frame is poorly executed; discoloured varnish, retouchings round hat and over the face; consolidated c.1980.

Inscribed upper left: *AET. S. 65/ ANNO DO/ 1644*; brown eyes, red hair; wearing a broad felt hat over a white cap with a plain black gown and white neckerchief; a painted oval.

PROV.: Cartwright Bequest 1686; Inventory 120 *my Last wifes sister in a black frame 3 quarts Clouth, a book in hand & in a hatt,* 10s.[2]

EXH.: *Mr Cartwright's Pictures* 1987(24).

REF.: R.T. Jeffree in *Mr Cartwright's Pictures* 1987, p.44.

An unattributed, mediocre mid seventeeth-century portrait.

The sitter's identity is a mystery. The inscribed age and date seem not to agree with the identification from the Inventory, *my Last wifes sister*. The sitter was 28 years older than Cartwright who in 1644 was 38 years old (it might also be observed that she hardly appears to be 65 years old). Jeffree pointed out that she may have been a half-sister or step-sister, or even a previous sister-in-law of the sitter in DPG387.

1 Brown Ledger, 28 November 1814, '*a Portrait of Mr Cartwrights last wifes Sister*'.
2 An old label *verso* reads ...*120* ....

Unknown Artist

DPG411 *'Young Mr Cartwright'*

Canvas 66.7 x 58.1 lined and cleaned by Brown 1813;[1] given a new stretcher (when, apparently, reduced from 76 x 63) and blistering repaired by Holder 1911; the hair much rubbed above his right shoulder; Hell 1949; cleaned 2005.

Grey-brown eyes, dark hair; wearing a grey suit with falling white lace collar; painted oval.

PROV.: Cartwright Bequest 1686; possibly Inventory 169 *young mr Cartwright Actour in a gilt frame,* 15s.

EXH.: *Mr Cartwright's Pictures* 1987(21).

REF.: Lysons 1792, p.111 (Cartwright the Younger, in Vandyke dress); Boswell 1929, p.139; R.T. Jeffree in *Mr Cartwright's Pictures* 1987, pp.42–43.

The fine falling collar and slashed sleeve suggest a date in the later 1630s. The sitter appears to be about thirty years old, indicating that he was approximately the same age as the donor, but it seems impossible to identify him. Sparkes & Carver 1890 believed he was the son of old Mr Cartwright (DPG400); Boswell believed there could be no reasonable doubt that young Mr Cartwright and the Greenhill (DPG393) showed the same person; Murray 1980 suggested he might have been the brother, cousin or even uncle of the donor; Jeffree, with Sparkes & Carver, saw no resemblance between the sitter and the Greenhill portrait (DPG393). Could the sitter have been 115 in the Cartwright Inventory, *my Last wifes sisters husband in a black frame, 3 quarters Clouth,* or *113 mr wessons picturing a black frame studed with gould 3 quarters Clouth* or *114 mr brutnalls pictur in a black frame filited with gould 3 quarters clouth*, all otherwise untraced?

A closely related portrait was sold in Vienna in 1928 as by Cornelius Jonson, an attribution rejected by Jeffree.[2]

1 Brown Ledger, 2 November 1813, *'Mr Cartwright an Actor'*.
2 According to Jeffree, citing Witt Library, under Cornelius Jonson (not found 2004). E.K. Waterhouse (letter on file of 5 November 1977) believed DPG411 was not by Jonson but 'by a hand one periodically encounters, cf. those by Cornelis de Neve at the Ashmolean' (presumably indicating the De Neve *Self Portrait*, F 657).

See also DPG378 *'Althea Cartwright', p.58*

LOVELACE PORTRAITS

Of the seven Lovelace portraits in the Cartwright Bequest, six show members of the Kentish branch of the family from Lovelace Place, Bethersden, and one shows a member of the Berkshire branch from Lady Place, Hurley, created Barons in 1627. The genealogical connection between the two branches has not been established,[1] but in 1649 Richard Lovelace dedicated his poems to Lady Anne Lovelace, wife of the 2nd Baron Lovelace, while her son, John Lovelace (later 3rd Baron Lovelace), was the dedicatee of his posthumous poems published in 1659.

There were three possible links between William Cartwright and the Lovelace family; he would have known the poet Richard Lovelace whose comedy *The Scholars* was performed c.1637–40 by Queen Henrietta's Men, of whom he was one; the second wife of the 1st Baron Lovelace was the daughter of a Margaret Cartwright,[2] and lastly 'Althea' (see DPG378, p.58) was, it seems, buried in 1665 in St Giles-in-the Fields (i.e. living close to Cartwright) as *Althea Cartwright als Lovelace*, suggesting kinship.

In 1633 Richard Lovelace's mother had left him 'the pictures of his father and myself, and his grandfather',[3] presumably those of Sir William Lovelace the younger (DPG365) and older (DPG367) and probably no.182 in the Cartwright Inventory, *my Lady Loulass with a Littl monkey in her armes on a clouth to ye knees* (now untraced). Richard Lovelace may have sold his family portraits, including those of himself (DPG363) [and Althea (DPG378)?], when he sold Bethersden in 1649 (it is said he died in 1657 in mean circumstances). But the portrait of the 3rd Baron Lovelace (DPG373) must date later, from the 1660s. Or perhaps the portraits came via Althea (d.1665) who may have been a neighbour of William Cartwright's; this seems a more likely provenance than the Barons Lovelace, even though their estates were frequently in jeopardy.[4]

Five of the seven portraits are inscribed in a cursive yellow script.[5] These inscriptions clearly date from the eighteenth century and must have been added by the College authorities. One other picture at Dulwich has a similar inscription, the so-called Queen Elizabeth by Gheeraerts (DPG389, see p.68).

1 Pearman 1876, pp.184–85, Pleasants 1919, pp.394–95, failed to establish a connection but quoted T. Philipot (*Villare Cantianum*, 1659, p.73) who asserted that the three families from Lovelace Place (Bethersden), Bayford and Kingsdown in Berkshire (i.e. Lovelace of Hurley) were shoots from the same stock. See also GEC, viii, p.229, note a.

2 Lord Lovelace [Sir John Lovelace 1599; cr. 1627] m. 2) 1608 Margaret Dodsworth (c.1588–1652), dau. of William Dodsworth, merchant tailor of London, and Margaret Cartwright [who m. 2) Leonard White]; she brought him property in Oxfordshire and a considerable income, said to be worth £50.000; she was the mother of John, 2nd Baron Lovelace (GEC, viii, p.230 and note f; *Commons 1558–1603*, ii, 1981, p.491). Portraits of the 1st Lord Lovelace and of his second wife Margaret by John De Critz were sold Sotheby's, 8 March 1989, lot 19.

3 Pearman 1876, p.209; Pleasants 1920, p.181; will proved 22 May 1633. She left him, besides, 'all the furniture those goods and implements of household which are standing and remaining in [Lovelace Place] at Bethersden'. Jeffree, *Mr Cartwright's Pictures* 1987, p.35, supposed that these would have included the portraits of the poet's great-grandfather (DPG372) and his great-uncle (DPG364).

4 The 2nd Baron 'suffered much in his estates' in the service of Charles I and d. much impoverished (GEC, viii, p.232 note d); in March 1694 a sale of the contents of Lady Place included 20 pictures (cf. GEC, viii, p.233 note d). Were these portraits of other Barons and Baronesses of Hurley?

5 Those that don't being DPG372 and DPG373.

UNKNOWN ARTIST

DPG372 Serjeant William Lovelace

Oak panel 66 x 52.4 of two vertical members, the right 15.8/14.6 wide, with canvas covering the join; a second canvas patch behind the left edge; chamfered on three edges, but not on the left-hand side, suggesting it may have been cut down; widespread retouching; Hell 1945–68; revarnished 1987.

Inscribed upper right: *ANO DNI.1576*; brown eyes, fair beard; wearing a black cap, red legal robes and silver/grey gloves with gold trim; on the index finger of his left hand a ring with the Lovelace arms (see below); a legal document in his right hand; upper left a coat of arms, Lovelace (*gu. on a chief indented arg. three martlets sa.*) quartered with Eynsham (*az. on a saltire engrailed arg. five martlets sa.*),[1] with crest (*on a staff raguly vert an eagle*[2] *displayed arg.*) with below the Lovelace motto *VIRTVTE DVCE*.

PROV.: Cartwright Bequest 1686; Inventory 181 *Sargant Loulass in his red Robes, with his cot of armes in a black frame filted with gould*, 10s.[3]

EXH.: *Mr Cartwright's Pictures* 1987(10).

REF.: Lysons, 1792, p.109; Pleasants 1920, p.84; R. T. Jeffree in *Mr Cartwright's Pictures* 1987, pp.35–36.

William Lovelace (c.1525/30–1577) of Lovelace Place, Bethersden, near Ashford, Kent; eminent lawyer; MP for Canterbury 1563, 1571 and 1572; serjeant-at-law 1567 and justice of Assize 1571; he was twice married, to Anne Lewes (d.1569) and Mary White (d.1578; widow of Thomas Carrell); father of William (DPG367) and Thomas (DPG364); he died on 23 March 1577 and was buried in Canterbury cathedral with a tomb bearing his effigy 'in long robes', alongside his first wife (destroyed early in the 19th century). He acquired additional property in Kent at Chartham, Smarden, Newnham and Grey Friars, Canterbury.

The coat of arms appears a 17th-century addition; the inscribed date might be read as the date of death (23 March 1577, i.e. 1576 OS), and not necessarily of the portrait which appears, nonetheless, to be a late sixteenth-century panel.

A copy on canvas, formerly the property of the Rev. C.A.C. Streatfield, Bridport, was sold Christie's, 6 April 1956, lot 105; an early 20th-century copy was made by Mrs Strother-Stewart for Walter de Curzon Poultney of Baltimore (a Lovelace descendant).[4]

1 See Pleasants 1919, pp.395–96. A fifteenth-century ancestor, Richard Lovelace of Bethersden, had m. an heiress of Eynsham who was endowed with a considerable fortune.

2 But DPG372 seems to show the eagle with a wounded breast like a pelican.

3 An old label formerly *verso* reads: *no 181 Serj. Lovelace.*

4 Pleasants 1920, p.84n.

Unknown Artist

DPG364 *Thomas Lovelace*

Oak panel 76.8 x 59.5 of two vertical members, the right 30/31 wide, with two canvas patches on the join; two vertical splits top right; repaired by Brown 1813[1] and Holder 1911; the surface is abraded and there is widespread retouching; Hell 1945–55; surface cleaned, cross-battens removed, consolidated but not restored 1991.

Inscribed top left in yellow: *AETATITS. SVAE.26./Thomas. lovelace Anno Domini/.1588.* and bottom left: *M. Thos. Lovelace*; fair hair, blue-grey eyes, a harelip; wearing a black hat with a gold-trimmed black band and a floral badge, white ruff, black cloak, yellow waistcoat with red buttons and grey gloves.

PROV.: Cartwright Bequest 1686; Inventory 180 *Thomas Loulass his pictur with a harelip on a bourd in a black frame* 10s.[2]

EXH.: *Mr Cartwright's Pictures* 1987(12).

REF.: R.T. Jeffree in *Mr Cartwright's Pictures* 1987, pp.36–37.

Thomas Lovelace (1563–91), second surviving son of Serjeant Lovelace (DPG372);[3] he inherited the manor and parsonage of Newenham from his father and died without issue; he was buried at St Margaret's, Bethersden.

A flat, unsophisticated portrait.

1 Brown Ledger, 24 August 1813, '*Portrait of Thos. Lovelaces*'.
2 A torn old label *verso* reads … *180* …
3 Pearman 1876, p.208, and Pleasants 1920, p.87, said he was perhaps a pilgrim to Rome in 1583; but Pearman 1893, p.62, later asserted that the pilgrim was Thomas, son of Thomas Lovelace of Kingsdown (d.1605).

Unknown Artist

DPG367 *Sir William Lovelace Kt. of Bethersden*

Oak panel 106.7 x 80.6 of six slightly tapering vertical members of approximately equal width but varying thickness, with an overall convex warp; repaired by Brown 1813;[1] two horizontal supporting battens added by Holder 1911; losses along panel joins; in the lower right area the costume (apparently a cape with ringed decoration) is painted over; scattered retouchings in the left hand, face and background; surface cleaned 1987; the panel treated 1991 when supporting battens were removed.

Inscribed top right: *Ano Dom:1600* and bottom right, in a later hand, *Sir W Lovelace*; fair hair, pale eyes; wearing black with a rich brooch in his hat.

PROV.: Bequeathed 1633 by Lady Anne Lovelace to her son Richard Lovelace; Cartwright Bequest 1686; Inventory 165 *Sr will Loulass on a bord to ye knees with a Chan of gould a bout his neck in a Ruffe & trunke hous in a black frame* £2.[2]

EXH.: *Mr Cartwright's Pictures* 1987(11).

REF.: R. Poole, *Wal.Soc.*, III, 1914, p.36 as by Marcus Gheeraerts; R.T. Jeffree in *Mr Cartwright's Pictures* 1987, p.36.

Sir William Lovelace of Lovelace Place, Bethersden (1561–1629), eldest surviving son of Serjeant Lovelace (DPG372); Gray's Inn 1580, but thereafter 'wholly addicted to martial affairs'; he married c.1580–81 Elizabeth Aucher (d.1627); Kt. 30 July 1599 by the Earl of Essex (Lord Lieutenant of Ireland) for his part in the battle of Offaly; member of the Virginia Company; he lived latterly at Gray Friars, Canterbury, and was buried at Bethersden. He survived his wife, son (see DPG365) and daughter and his executrix was his son's widow.[3]

Jeffree suggested DPG367 was probably painted in London on Lovelace's return from Ireland on the occasion of his knighthood in 1599. An early 20th-century copy was made by Mrs Strother-Stewart for Walter de Curzon Poultney of Baltimore (a Lovelace descendant).[4]

1 Brown Ledger, 24 August 1813, '*Joining Panel … Cleaning … a Portrait of Sir Wm. Lovelace*'.
2 An old label formerly *verso* reads *No.165 Sir Wm. Lovelace.*
3 Pleasants 1920, pp.87–90, 380–81. The only pictures mentioned in his will were those bequeathed to James Collimore 'his [i.e. Collimore's] Father's and Mother's pictures wch hang up in my chamber in the Gray Friars [Canterbury]' (Pleasants 1920, p.89).
4 Pleasants 1920, p.84n.

An Doni. 1600.

Unknown Artist

DPG365 Sir William Lovelace Kt of Woolwich

Bevelled oak panel 64.7 x 54.6 of two vertical members, the left 23.5 wide, a canvas strip supporting the join; convex right member, concave left member; repaired by Brown 1813;[1] splits top and bottom 6.5 from the right-hand edge; retouched on join in the cheek; much abrasion and discoloured varnish.

Inscribed bottom left: *Old Mr Lovelace*; brown eyes, brown beard and upturned moustache; wearing armour with a golden sash with a lace trim.

PROV.: Bequeathed 1633 by Lady Anne Lovelace to her son Richard Lovelace; Cartwright Bequest 1686; Inventory 179 *Loullass his father in black Armor & a red Scarfe on a bourd, in an ould black frame.*[2]

EXH.: *Mr Cartwright's Pictures* 1987(13).

REF.: R.T. Jeffree in *Mr Cartwright's Pictures* 1987, p.37 as Dutch early 17th century.

Sir William Lovelace(1584–1627), soldier, called of Woolwich (where his eldest son was born and his wife's family owned property), but in his will named Sir William Lovelace the younger of Bethersden, only son of Sir William Lovelace (DPG367); Kt. by James I at Theobalds 1609, he married in 1610 Anne Barne (d. 1633) of Woolwich;[3] member of the Virginia Company; he served many years in the Netherlands, where he was killed at the siege of Groll on 12 August 1627; he was the father of Richard Lovelace (DPG363) and of four other sons and three daughters.

Perhaps painted in Holland, as Jeffree suggested, but of indifferent quality and probably a copy. An early 20th-century copy was made by Mrs Strother-Stewart for Walter de Curzon Poultney of Baltimore (a Lovelace descendant);[4] a photograph of another copy in a private collection is in the NPG archive.

A whole-length by Mytens of 1621 was at Courteenhall, Northants, in 1962.[5]

1 Brown Ledger, 24 August 1813, '*Mr Lovelaces Father*'.
2 An old label *verso* reads *No 179 Mr Lovellace's Father.*
3 Dau. of Sir William Barne of Woolwich; she remarried 1630 Jonathan Browne DL.
4 Pleasants 1920, p.84n.
5 Inscribed with identity; indistinctly illus. *CL*, lxxxvi, 1939, p.174; ex-Townshend sale, Christie's, 5 March 1904, lot 39.

William Dobson (1611–46)

DPG363 Richard Lovelace

Canvas 74.9 x 63.5 lined; overpainted background; a fine craquelure on the thinly painted face; cleaned 1987.

Inscribed bottom right: *Col. Lovelace*; brown eyes, black hair, slight moustache; wearing black armour with a fringed red sash and a leather sword belt.

PROV.: Cartwright Bequest 1686; Inventory 100 *Colonell Louliss his pictur in armor in a great gilt frame. 3 quarters clouth.* £3.

EXH.: *Art Treasures*, Manchester, 1857 (BPG 146 unattributed); NPE 1866(630 unattributed); *Marvell and his Contemporaries*, Hull, 1978 (38); *Mr Cartwright's Pictures* 1987(14).

ENG.: R. Clamp 1794 (*Biographical Mirrour*, i, 1795); C. Pye 1824 from a drawing by W. Green; W.C. Edwards 1835 (as after Dobson).

REF.: Collins Baker 1912, i, pp.99, 102, 103; R.T. Jeffree in *Mr Cartwright's Pictures* 1987, pp.37–38 (attributed to Dobson).

Richard Lovelace (1617–c.1657), eldest surviving son of Sir William Lovelace (DPG365), cavalier soldier and poet; he was educated at Charterhouse and Gloucester Hall, Oxford; MA 1636 in which year he wrote a comedy, *The Scholars*; he served as captain in the Scottish expeditions of 1639, on his return taking possession of Lovelace Place at Bethersden and 'his other estates'; he presented the Kentish petition demanding the King's restoration and was consequently imprisoned in April 1642; from prison he wrote the celebrated *To Althea from Prison* ('Stone Walls do not a Prison make'); released on bail in June, he generously supported the King; by 1645 he was in Holland raising troops for the King and serving with the French against Spain; wounded at Dunkirk in 1646, he returned to England in 1647 and met Lely, with whom he was made free of the Painter-Stainers' Company on 26 October 1647, and to whom he dedicated two poems;[1] he was again imprisoned in 1648–49 when he edited his poems published in 1649 (*Lucasta*) with a dedication to Lady Anne Lovelace, wife of his distant kinsman, the 2nd Baron Lovelace of Hurley; he sold Lovelace Place 1649 and, without patrimony, remained unmarried and increasingly destitute; he died in a London lodging house and was buried in St Bride's, Fleet Street. He had been described in his youth as 'the most amiable and beautiful person … of innate modesty, virtue and courtly deportment …' (a Wood).

DPG363 shows Lovelace as a sensitive (even apprehensive) cavalier officer, probably when he was with the King at Oxford in 1645; Jeffree thought it 'one of the most haunting images of its time and entirely worthy of Dobson'. Dobson was also at Oxford, his portraiture then turning toward more wistful, thinly-painted faces in a modest half-length format.[2] Unattributed in the Cartwright Inventory, the portrait was engraved in 1835 as by Dobson, but in 1912 Collins Baker had considered it the work of a close follower, the suppositious F. How.[3] An early 20th-century copy was made for Walter de Curzon Poultney of Baltimore (a Lovelace descendant).[4]

The iconography of Lovelace is otherwise unsatisfactory.[5] An unattributed three-quarter length at Worcester College, Oxford, of a young Oxford graduate with the motto *PRODESSE NON PRAEESSE* shows either Lovelace or Thomas Coke.[6] A bust-length oval etching by Hollar previously called Lovelace[7] may have provided the pattern for the weak engraved bust devised by Francis Lovelace, the poet's brother, as the frontispiece for the *Posthume Poems* of 1659, *in memoriam fratris desideratissimi* (the plate reissued 1795).[8] An engraving by R. Gaywood purporting to show Lovelace as Orpheus is pure fantasy.[9]

1 See N.K. Farmer, *Poets and the Visual Arts in Renaissance England*, 1984, pp.57–60.
2 See M. Rogers in *Dobson*, NPG, 1983-84, p.18, and particularly no.44 in that exhibition, *Unknown Lady*, signed and dated 1645, Birmingham AG. Rogers subsequently agreed that DPG363 was by Dobson (*Mr Cartwright's Pictures* 1987, p.38).
3 Whom he called an *amico di Gugliemo* or *Alunno di Dobson*; there is a signed half-length cleric by How at Holkham (illus. Collins Baker 1912, i, f.p.104).
4 Pleasants 1920, p.178.
5 It has been discussed by C.H. Wilkinson, *The Poems of Richard Lovelace*, 1925, i, pp.lxxvii–lxxxviii.
6 See C.F. Bell, in Wilkinson, 1925 (see note 5 above), i, pp.iii–vi; illus. as the front. Exh. *Treasures of Oxford*, Goldsmiths' Hall, London, 1953, no.376 as attributed to De Critz. The motto is associated with the Cox, Cocks and Cookesey families, which suggests the portrait may show Lovelace's Oxford contemporary, Thomas Coke (c.1613–1656; MP for Leicester 1640) who received an hon. degree in 1635–36 (Wilkinson 1925, i, p.lxxviii, see note 5 above).
7 R. Pennington, *Cat. of the Etched Work of Hollar*, 1982, no.1692 as an unknown sitter; illus. Wilkinson 1925 (see note 5 above), i, f.p.xlii.
8 Illus. C.H. Hartmann, *The Cavalier Spirit*, 1925, f.p.128.
9 *GM*, lxii, 1792, p.166; Wilkinson 1925 (see note 5 above), i, pp.vi, lxxxi, illus. f.p.lxxxviii.

W. Faithorne, *Lucasta*, engraving after 'P.Lilly', 1649 (National Portrait Gallery, London)

UNKNOWN ARTIST

DPG378 *'Althea Cartwright'*

Canvas 76.2 x 63.8 lined and cleaned by Brown 1814;[1] a photogravure of 1923 shows more detail in the flesh areas, the background curtain and the hair;[2] incipient blistering, a patched hole upper right and discoloured varnish; surface cleaned 1986.

Inscribed lower left, by her right wrist: *Althea*; auburn-red undressed hair, blue-grey eyes; wearing a pearl necklace, yellow blouse and a grey cape with a jewel brooch; her right cuff is white.

PROV.: Cartwright Bequest 1686; Inventory 77 *Altheas pictur her hare descheuell on 3 quarters Clouth in a gilt frame.* £2.

EXH.: *Mr Cartwright's Pictures* 1987(15).

REF.: Lysons 1792, p.110 ('Althea, with her hair disheveled, said to be Lucy Sacheverell; though Lovelace always called her Lucasta in his Poems'); R.T. Jeffree in *Mr Cartwright's Pictures* 1987, pp.7, 38.

Of indifferent quality, perhaps c.1645–50. The figure verges on the fanciful, the title given in the Cartwright Inventory conflating those of two Lovelace poems, 'To Althea, from Prison' and 'To Amarantha, That she would dishevel her haire'.[3] But an *Althea Cartwright als Lovelace* was buried at St Giles-in-the-Fields on 11 June 1666, suggesting DPG378 might, for all its informality, be a portrait (see p.53).

'Portraits' of another Richard Lovelace muse, *Lucasta*, are more obviously wishful: a half-length oval engraving by Hollar after Samuel Cooper[4] and an engraved frontispiece by Faithorne for the 1649 poems, lettered *Lucasta* and *P. Lilly Inv*: of a whole-length figure seated in a landscape.

1 Brown Ledger, 28 November 1814, '*Portrait of Althea*'.
2 Illus. C.H. Hartmann, *The Cavalier Spirit*, 1925, f.p.48.
3 Undressed hair in the earlier 17th century could imply an unmarried woman, but by mid-century it could simply indicate a member of a provincial family, as opposed to a lady of fashion (cf. *The McDonald Collection*, Leggatts, 1970, p.31), and see p.82n16 for reference to a miniature of the unmarried Venetia, Lady Stanley, with her hair undressed.
4 Illus. C.H. Wilkinson ed., *The Poems of Richard Lovelace*, 1925, i, f.p.xlii. R. Pennington, *Cat. of the Etched Work of Hollar*, 1982, no.1532 notes that the Cooper may have been the miniature in the Hawkins sale, Christie's, 5th day, 16 May 1904, lot 1020.

Unknown Artist

DPG373 *John, 3rd Baron Lovelace*

Canvas 75 x 63.2 lined; generally abraded; retouchings in chin, jaw and lower lip; discoloured varnish; surface cleaned 1987.

Grey-blue eyes, brown hair; wearing a white shirt, a red-lined black gown with a red tie.

PROV.: Cartwright Bequest 1686; Inventory 121 *my Lord Louless in a red mantell, in a black frame 3 quarters Clouth.* £1.[1]

EXH.: *Mr Cartwright's Pictures* 1987(16).

REF.: Lysons 1792, p.109; R.T. Jeffree in *Mr Cartwright's Pictures* 1987, p.39.

John Lovelace (c.1640–93), succeeded as 3rd Baron Lovelace in 1670; MP for Berkshire 1661–70; by 1677 his extravagance had placed him in serious financial difficulties; he was actively engaged in the Revolution of 1688, being briefly imprisoned at Gloucester in November before occupying Oxford for William in December; he married in 1662 Martha Pye (1642–c.1704) and was survived by three daughters; 'a Man of good natural Parts, but of very ill and very loose principles' (Hearne).

DPG373 may be dated in the early 1660s around the time of his coming of age, his marriage and his election to Parliament. Jeffree has suggested general similarities with the style of Soest, but it has no great quality.

Other portraits of the 3rd Baron include the whole length by Lauron, signed and dated 1689, at Wadham College, Oxford,[2] and a seated three-quarter length at Attingham probably c.1690 and possibly also by Lauron (replica at Dynevor Castle).

1 An old label formerly *verso* reads: *No 121 Lord Lovelace.*
2 Poole, iii, p.219, no.32.

Unknown Artist

DPG392 Elizabeth, Queen of Bohemia

Canvas 183 x 94.3 of four horizontal sections, from the top 16.5, 86, 73 and 7.5 deep; probably lined and cleaned by Brown 1814;[1] repaired and varnished by Reeve 1923; the surface flattened, much retouched and with faded glazes, the background worn; discoloured varnish; Hell 1948–53.

Blue-grey eyes, brown hair; wearing a double layer lace collar, pearl necklace, a gold embroidered dress (the gold embroidery not invariably following the folds of the dress) with a white belt, bows and cuffs; her left little finger has an inset ring on a black string turned round her wrist and on her right hand a blackstone set in gold; on her right arm a double bracelet with blackstones set in gold; a jeweled pendant in her right hand and a fob on a pink ribbon lies on the table which is covered with a gold-fringed purple cloth; in the background a purple chair and a brown arch.

PROV.: Possibly Cartwright Bequest 1686 (but see below).

EXH.: *Edward Alleyn* 1994(47a).

REF.: S. Foister in *Edward Alleyn* 1994, pp.51, 53.

Elizabeth, Queen of Bohemia (1596–1662), daughter of James I, married in 1613 Frederick V (1596–1632), Elector Palatine and King of Bohemia 1619–20.

The identity is probably correct but has been contested due to the crudity of the portrait.[2] Costume suggests a Continental pattern of c.1625-35, and there is some generic resemblance to portraits of Elizabeth by Honthorst of 1622-34[3] but, if correctly identified, DPG392 must date from before 1632 when the Queen assumed mourning.

The provenance is not established. The date implied above would indicate a very late Alleyn acquisition,[4] although the Queen of Bohemia would have complemented his collection of Royal portraits; Alleyn also had some very tenuous connections with the Queen – on 8 September 1620 his wife gave '*to ye queen of Bohemes ayd 3*', and the King of Bohemia's Men performed at Alleyn's theatre, the Fortune, at the same time.[5] DPG392 is not listed in the extant pages of the Cartwright Inventory and in 1814 it appears to have been called simply 'a Lady of Quality' (see note 1).

1 Brown Ledger, 28 November 1814, '*a Whole length portrait of a Lady of Quality*'.
2 A. Laing (*Burl. Mag.*, cxli, 1999, p.549) commented that the sitter was not the Winter Queen, 'but some altogether humbler lady, without her swagger jewellery'.
3 Cf. *Der Winterkönig*, exh. cat. Hamburg, Heidelberg, Prague, The Hague, 2003, cat. nos. 2.1 (of c.1622) and 6.56 (1634), illus. pp.35, 103.
4 Sparkes & Carver 1890, p.10, thought it was 'probably' given by Alleyn (repeated in Dulwich catalogues –1926), and Foister (see REF. above) considered the Alleyn provenance uncertain (although DPG392 was included in the *Edward Alleyn* exhibition in 1994).
5 Sparkes & Carver 1890, p.11 (repeated in Dulwich catalogues –1926).

after SIR ANTHONY VAN DYCK (1599–1641)

DPG414 *Charles I*

Canvas 98.7 x 81.6 lined and cleaned by Brown 1813;[1] relined and nine holes filled by Reeve 1931; scattered retouchings and scumbled overpainting on the curtain; cracked filling on left of the sleeve; discoloured varnish; surface cleaned c.1985.

Light brown beard, brown hair, blue-grey eyes; wearing a black slashed doublet over a white shirt; wearing the lesser George (undetailed) with a very pale blue ribbon; the star of the Garter on his cape, the crown in the right background.

PROV.: Cartwright Bequest 1686; Inventory 94 *Kinge Charles ye ~~Second~~ first in a ~~Sla~~ Slashed dublet, & a ruffe a Larg pece in a gilt frame To ye knees.* £2.

EXH.: *Mr Cartwright's Pictures* 1987(5).

REF.: R.T. Jeffree in *Mr Cartwright's Pictures* 1987, pp.31–32; O. Millar in *Van Dyck* 2004, p.630 (under IV.A.7)

Charles I (1600–49), second son of James I and VI, reigned from 1625; executed 1649.

An early copy of a lost portrait, probably the first Van Dyck painted of the King after his arrival in England in 1632. A studio replica is in the Kunsthistorisches Museum, Vienna, and a version was sold Christie's, 27 June 1980, lot 137. Millar records other variations of the composition, both half and whole length (the latter including a variant exh. *Suffolk Collection*, Ranger's House, 1974, no.34 as by Cornelius Johnson).

1 Brown Ledger, 2 November 1813, '*a Portrait of King Charles I*'.

after SIR ANTHONY VAN DYCK (1599–1641)

DPG426 *Queen Henrietta Maria*

Canvas 104.8 x 84.7 lined and cleaned by Brown 1813;[1] relined with new stretcher by Morrill 1931; much overpainting in the darks and widespread retouchings; much discoloured varnish; consolidated 1990.

Brown eyes and brown hair dressed with a pink ribbon and pearls; wearing a pearl necklace and earrings, a silver skirt and bodice with pink lacing, a pink flower at her breast; a jewelled bracelet on her left arm and a pearl bracelet on her right arm; her right hand rests by her crown; behind her a dark, gold-fringed canopy.

PROV.: Cartwright Bequest 1686; Inventory 93 *Quenne mary in a whit Sattin goun a Larg pece in a gilt frame, To ye knees.* £5.

EXH.: *Mr Cartwright's Pictures* 1987(6); Alleyn's School –1931; Tredegar House 1991–.

REF.: R.T. Jeffree in *Mr Cartwright's Pictures* 1987, pp.32–33; O. Millar in *Van Dyck* 2004, p.520 (under IV.114).

Henrietta Maria (1606–69), youngest daughter of Henri IV of France; a catholic, she married Charles I of England in 1625.

One of many copies of the Van Dyck of portrait of 1632 in the Royal Collection.[2]

Apart from DPG381 below, Cartwright also owned a portrait of the Queen '*in oring coluard bodes, after van dik, coped by oul Reme*'.[3]

1 Brown Ledger, 2 November 1813, '*King Charles's Queen*', (the pair, presumably, to DPG414).
2 Millar 1963, i, no.147; ii, pl.67, and *Van Dyck* 2004, p.519(IV.114). Other copies include those at Drumlanrig Castle, Kilkenny Castle, Burghley and Welbeck.
3 Cartwright Inventory, no.5. Perhaps, as Jeffree suggested, copied from the portrait now in the Wrightsman Collection (*Van Dyck* 2004, p.526, IV.123).

after SIR ANTHONY VAN DYCK (1599–1641)

DPG381 *Queen Henrietta Maria*

Canvas 67 x 54.6 lined with new stretcher by Morrill; the surface abraded; discoloured retouchings and pronounced craquelure; surface cleaned 1987.

Brown eyes and brown hair dressed with pearls; wearing a pearl earring and necklace, a dark blue dress, the sleeves with gold clasps.

PROV.: Cartwright Bequest 1686; Inventory 118 *quenne mary in blue in a gilt frame, 3 quarter clouth.* £2.

EXH.: *Mr Cartwright's Pictures* 1987(9 attributed to Remegius van Leemput after Van Dyck); Tredegar House 1991–.

REF.: R.T. Jeffree, in *Mr Cartwright's Pictures* 1987, p.34; O. Millar in *Van Dyck* 2004, p.635 (under IV.A.19).

See DPG426 above.

A version of Van Dyck's three-quarter length Queen in blue (c.1636?), of which no original has been identified. The best surviving versions are at the Fine Arts Gallery of San Diego and the Bomann-Museum, Celle.[1] Jeffree supposed it may have been a copy by Remegius van Leemput (cf. under DPG426).

If DPG381 has been correctly identified and described in the Cartwright Inventory, it was subsequently cut down. Until 1998 called Princess Mary of Orange (1631–60), daughter of Charles I, in Dulwich catalogues.

1 See *Van Dyck* 2004, p.635(IV.A.19). Another of the many versions is in the Wallace Collection (P118; *Catalogue of Paintings*, iv, 1992, p.115).

after JOHN MICHAEL WRIGHT (1617–94)

DPG424 *Charles II*

Canvas 76.2 x 63.5 lined; an old horizontal tear along the lower edge and an old damage to the left; the face is unevenly cleaned and the wig heavily retouched; discoloured varnish; Hell 1952–53.

Brown eyes, black eyebrows and wig; wearing Garter robes over a red gown; in a painted oval.

PROV.: Cartwright Bequest 1686; Inventory 76 *King Charles ye Second on 3 quarters Clouth in a gilt frame.* £2.[1]

EXH.: NPE 1866(874 as by Greenhill); *Mr Cartwright's Pictures* 1987(7).

REF.: Collins Baker 1912, i, pp.189–90, ii, p.151; R.T. Jeffree in *Mr Cartwright's Pictures* 1987, p.33.

Charles II (1630–85), son of Charles I, whom he succeeded in 1660.

No autograph version of this type, which must date from c.1660–65, has been identified, but a good three-quarter length (the orb in his right hand) is in the National Portrait Gallery (531)[2] and another was sold Christie's, 30 January 1987, lot 132; a copy is in the Judges' Lodgings, Warwick. Before 1980 DPG424 was attributed to Greenhill in all Dulwich catalogues, but it had been correctly identified as Wright by Collins Baker in 1912.

A closely comparable crayon drawing of the King's head attributed to Luttrell is in the Ashmolean Museum.[3]

1 An old ink label *verso* reads *No 76 Charles 2d.*
2 Piper 1963, p.67, pl.9b.
3 Sutherland collection (Burnet i 165); C.F. Bell, *Wal. Soc.*, v, 1917, p.17, illus. f.p.16, pl.2b.

JOHN GREENHILL (1642–76)

DPG416 James II as Duke of York

Canvas 74.9 x 62.2 lined and cleaned by Brown 1813;[1] relined by Holder 1914; widespread retouchings; Hell 1952–53.

Blue-grey eyes, long brown hair; wearing a cuirass and a gold-figured cape with a scarlet sash; in a painted oval.

PROV.: Cartwright Bequest 1686; Inventory 68 *ye Duke of ~~york~~ yorke*[2] *in a gilt frame, on 3 quarters cloth. £2. Grinhill.*

EXH.: *Mr Cartwright's Pictures* 1987(8).

REF.: Collins Baker 1912, ii, p.8; Millar 1963, i, p.121 (under no.240); Piper 1963, p.178 as c.1664; R.T. Jeffree in *Mr Cartwright's Pictures* 1987, pp.33–34.

James, Duke of York (1633–1701), second surviving son of Charles I and Henrietta Maria, succeeded his brother Charles II as King in 1685 but his catholic prejudice led to his downfall in 1688 and he died in exile in France.

A vigorous study, loosely resembling in pose and exactly in dress Lely's seated three-quarter length of the Duke now in the Scottish National Portrait Gallery (901),[3] and his double portrait showing the Duke with his first wife in the National Portrait Gallery (5077). The fall and curls of the hair agree with another three-quarter length by Lely in the Royal Collection showing the Duke in armour.[4] These patterns may be dated between late 1660, when the Duke married, and 1664 when the Duke 'first put on a periwigg'[5] and Greenhill, who was in Lely's studio c.1663-65, may have been working from a Lely original, although Jeffree proposed it was painted *ad vivum*.[6]

1 Brown Ledger, 2 November 1813, '*Portrait of the Duke of York by Greenhill*'.
2 Fragment of an old ink label *verso*: …*ye Duke of York* … .
3 Exh. *Lely*, NPG, 1978, no.32.
4 Millar 1963, i, no.240; ii, pl.100, as by Lely completed by studio assistants.
5 Pepys *Diary*, 15 February 1664.
6 Collins Baker 1912, ii, p.8, had criticised the clumsy brushwork, loose drawing and poor colouring.

UNKNOWN ARTIST

DPG385 called Nathan Field

Oak panel 56.5 x 42 of two vertical members, the right 18 wide, each member slightly bowed and the edges slightly bevelled; a painted border defines a picture size of 54.2 x 40.3; probably the '*Portrait of a Gentleman in white dress*' conserved by Brown in 1813;[1] a vertical split runs to the right of the join and there is a damage in the upper-right area, where the panel appears to have been broken; the panel is supported by 16 mahogany butterfly wedges (and was previously supported by four horizontal battens secured by screws, some of which had penetrated the surface); there are small insets top left and lower right; the painted surface is very worn with widespread losses, particularly in the left background, along the join and split and in the hair; the ear was redrawn; conserved 1991–92.

Slate-grey eyes, dark hair, moustache and tuft; wearing a pearl earring and a shirt with elaborate black cross-stitch decoration; set within a stone arch.

PROV.: Cartwright Bequest 1686; Inventory 167 *master feilds pictur in his Shurt on a bourd in a black frame filited with gould an Actour* 10s.

EXH.: *Art Treasures*, Manchester 1857(BPG 88); NPE 1866(534); *Mr Cartwright's Pictures* 1987(27); *Edward Alleyn* 1994(40); *Searching for Shakespeare*, NPG/New Haven, 2006(52) as probably Nathan Field c.1615.

ENG.: W.N. Gardiner after S. Harding 1790 (*Shakspeare Illustrated* 1793); J. Rogers (early 19th century); anon.

REF.: Lysons 1792, p.110 ('in a shirt trimmed with black lace'); G. Ashton in *Mr Cartwright's Pictures* 1987, pp.46–47; T. Cooper in *Searching for Shakespeare*, NPG/New Haven, 2006, p.136.

Despite the Cartwright Inventory, the identity is not completely certain (see p.45). Nathan Field (1587–1619/20), actor and playwright, son of a Puritan minister, brother of the Bishop of Llandaff, was with the Blackfriar's boy company 1600–08, the King's Revels 1609–11, Lady Elizabeth's Men 1611–15 and the King's Men from 1616 until 1619, when he left following a scandal over fathering a child on the Countess of Argyll; he was recorded as an actor in the first folio of Shakespeare 1623; he wrote at least eight plays, including *A Woman is a Weathercock* and *Amends for Ladies*, and collaborated with both Massinger and Fletcher.

This is easily the most impressive of Cartwright's theatrical portraits. Gesture, costume and hairstyle confirm an early 17th-century date, and Tarnya Cooper considers it the work of an Anglo-Netherlandish painter c.1615. Ashton had previously suggested that, if the sitter is Field, DPG385 may have been one of the first British portraits to show an actor in costume, but for Cooper the informality of the embroidered shirt with its delicate 'blackwork' design suggests rather a private image painted for a friend.[2]

A modern copy by Charles Fullwood is with the Shakespeare Birthplace Trust, Stratford-upon-Avon.

1 Brown Ledger, 2 July 1813.
2 Cf. Hilliard's well-known miniature of a young man against a background of flames showing comparable hair style, an open necked shirt and an ear-ring (VAM, P.5–1917).

Unknown Artist

DPG390 *called Thomas Bond*

Oak panel 39 x 31 with slight, rough bevelling; the painted surface does not reach the bottom edge of the panel; cleaned by Brown 1813;[1] widespread retouchings; a scratch across his right cheek; the right-hand side of the face and the mouth altered; the varnish much discoloured; Hell 1949.

Green-brown eyes, brown hair; wearing a dark brown jacket with gold figuring and a white collar with blue-grey ornament (perhaps birds or leaves).

PROV.: Cartwright Bequest 1686; Inventory 148 *Tom bonds pictur, an Actour, in a band Rought with Imbrodery bared neck, on a bourd in a black frame, very ould.* 2s.[2]

EXH.: *Mr Cartwright's Pictures* 1987(29).

ENG.: R. Clamp 1794 (*Shakspearean Miscellany* 1802), showing less pattern on the collar, a simplified pattern on the dark coat, the hair curled, apparently light in colour, and a slight beard; anon, three-quarter length with his right hand at his breast holding collar string, a belted coat, white hair moustache and hair beneath lower lip.

REF.: Lysons 1792, p.111; G. Ashton in *Mr Cartwright's Pictures* 1987, pp.48–49; T. Cooper in *Searching for Shakespeare*, NPG/New Haven, 2006, p.134 as called Bond, by an Unknown English artist.

The identity depends entirely upon the Cartwright Inventory (see p.45). Tom Bond (d.1635) performed as a minor member of the Red Bull Revels from 1617; he married in 1627 and was with Prince Charles's Company from 1631.

Costume suggests a late 16th-century date which militates against the Bond identity. The cramming of the head and cutting of the shoulders within the panel is uncomfortable and suggested to Ashton the possibility of a copy from an earlier miniature. A small half-length canvas, 'traditionally called Tom Bond', with Christie's in January 1997, showed no particular resemblance to DPG390.

1 Bond Ledger, 24 August 1813, '*Portrait of Tom Bond an Actor on Panel*'.
2 Inscribed *verso*: *Tom Bond actor* and *148*.

Unknown Artist

DPG391 *Portrait of a Man*

Canvas 38.8 x 27.9 stretched over an oak (?) panel with a slight convex warp and some old wormholes, the bottom right-hand corner chipped; the canvas has a horizontal join 10 above the bottom edge, the weaves not aligned and the join much repainted; no traces of tacking edges; both flesh and hair are heavily retouched and the background has many old losses; very thinly painted below the head.

Blue-grey eyes, brown curly hair, with slight moustache and tuft; wearing a black tunic with a white collar;

PROV.: Cartwright Bequest 1686; Inventory either 109 *mr Slys pictur ye Actour in a gilt frame.* £1, or 196 (according to the inscription on the back of the canvas; this number is from the missing part of the inventory).[1]

EXH.: *Mr Cartwright's Pictures* 1987(26); *Edward Alleyn* 1994(11).

REF.: Lysons 1792, p.111; G. Ashton in *Mr Cartwright's Pictures* 1987, pp.45–46; T. Cooper in *Searching for Shakespeare*, NPG/New Haven, 2006, p.134 as called Sly, by an Unknown English artist.

Previously catalogued as *William Sly* or *called William Sly*, but there is little point in retaining this association; he died in 1608 while DPG391 appears to date from c.1635–40. Lysons seems first to have listed a portrait of Sly at Dulwich and no.109 in the Cartwright Inventory is *mr Slys pictur ye Actour in a gilt frame* £1. But, according to the label on the *verso* (see note 1), DPG391 appears to have been identified as no.196 in the Inventory.

DPG391 shows a bluff, strongly-characterised head (remotely in the Dobson mould, as the old label suggested) and the intense, angled stare and open mouth might even suggest a self portrait (or a deliberate *tête d'expression*). The use of a joined canvas (studio detritus?)[2] hardly indicates a commissioned work.

A modern copy by Charles Fullwood is with the Shakespeare Birthplace Trust, Stratford-upon-Avon.

1 An old label *verso* reads: *vi 196 /by Dobson.*
2 The 'second' canvas, although extremely weakly painted, seems hardly an addition for without it the chin remains incomplete.

Unknown Artist

DPG395 *called Richard Burbage*

Canvas 29.8 x 25.8/25.3 lined and cleaned by Brown 1813,[1] the original canvas unevenly cut; the face very worn, with many small losses reflecting the raised canvas weave; a large loss in the left part of the collar; Hell 1949; cleaned and relined 2002.

Grey eyes, brown hair; wearing white collar and black coat; an earthy-red background.

PROV.: Cartwright Bequest 1686; Inventory 105 *mr burbig his head in a gilt frame a small closit pece.* 5s.[2]

EXH.: *Art Treasures*, Manchester, 1857 (BPG 87); NPE 1866(337 'Mr Burbage by himself'); *Mr Cartwright's Pictures* 1987(25); *Edward Alleyn* 1994(23); *Searching for Shakespeare*, NPG/New Haven, 2006–07(51) as probably Burbage.

ENG.: S. Harding 1790 (*Shakspeare Illustrated* 1793)[3] extended to a half length with tightly buttoned coat; two later anon. plates similarly extended.

REF.: Lysons 1792, p.110; S. Foister in *Edward Alleyn* 1994, p.60n11; G. Ashton in *Mr Cartwright's Pictures* 1987, pp.44–45; T. Cooper in *Searching for Shakespeare*, NPG/New Haven, 2006, pp.133–34.

The identity depends entirely upon the Cartwright Inventory (see p.45). Richard Burbage (1569–1619), son of the actor James Burbage (c.1531–97), was the leading player of his day; he inherited an interest in the Blackfriars and Shoreditch theatres, demolishing the latter to build the Globe; he played in the Lord Chamberlain's Company (later the King's Men), excelling in tragedy; he was closely associated with Shakespeare and was a legatee of his Will; he was also a painter,[4] the Chandos portrait of Shakespeare once being associated with him[5] and a picture by *mr burbige ye Actor* was listed in the Cartwright Inventory.[6] Since 1867 DPG395 has been described as 'traditionally attributed to Burbage himself' and the supposition persists.[7]

A slight but freely-painted head, now very much abraded. The uneven edges of the original canvas suggest it was cut down at the right and top (or, as Ashton and Cooper have supposed, intended for sewing into a larger canvas).

A modern copy by Charles Fullwood is with the Shakespeare Birthplace Trust, Stratford-upon-Avon.

1 Brown Ledger, 24 August 1813, '*a head of Mr Burbadge an Actor*'.
2 An old label *verso* reads *No 105 Mr Burbage/An Actor*
3 Harding exhibiting a drawing of a *Master J Burbadge,* RA 1800(774).
4 See *HMC Rutland*, iv, 1894, p.494 under 1613: 'Item 31, Martii, to Mr Shakespeare in gold about my Lorde's impreso, xliiijs.; to Richard Burbage for paynting and making yt, in gold xliiij*s*.. – iiij*li*. viij*s*.'; p.508, under 25 March 1616: 'Paid given to Richard Burbidg for my Lorde's shielde and for the embleance, 4*l*.18*s*'.
5 National Portrait Gallery (1), see Strong 1969a, i, p.279, ii, pls. 545, 546; exh. *Searching for Shakespeare*, NPG/New Haven, 2006(3).
6 No.103 *a womans head on a bord* once thought to be DPG380, see *Mr Cartwright's Pictures* 1987, no.38 (as North Italian school). Lysons 1792, p.112, described at Dulwich 'the head of a woman by Burbadge the actor, in chiaro-oscuro'; on 28 June 1815 Brown lined and cleaned for Dulwich '*two heads one of a Girl & woman by Burbridge*' (Brown Ledger). Cook 1914 and 1926 believed DPG380 to be by Burbage; Murray 1980, p.302, listed it as attributed to Burbage and Beresford 1998, pp.306–07, as Unknown.
7 E.g. P. Thomson, *Shakespeare's Professional Career*, 1992, p.107 (illus.)

Unknown Artist

DPG423 *called Richard Perkins*

Canvas 69.8 x 61.9 lined and cleaned by Brown 1813;[1] thinly painted and much worn in the face and round the head; extensive losses and retouching in the column and plinth; Hell 1949.

Blue-grey eyes, white hair; wearing a black gown with white cuffs and collar.

PROV.: Cartwright Bequest 1686; Inventory 166 *mr pirkines ye Actour in a 3 quarts clouth in a gilt frame.* £2.[2]

EXH.: *Mr Cartwright's Pictures* 1987(28).

ENG.: R. Clamp 1794 (*Shakspearean Miscellany* 1802).

REF.: Lysons 1792, p.110; G. Ashton in *Mr Cartwright's Pictures* 1987, pp.47–48.

The identity depends entirely upon the Cartwright Inventory (see p.45). Richard Perkins (1585?–1650) was a member of the Queen Anne's Company 1602–19, the Red Bull Company 1619–23 and the King's Men 1623/4; he moved to Queen Henrietta's Company (as a colleague of Cartwright) in 1626, becoming the best-known actor in that company; his first wife died in March 1621 and he remarried in November; he retired to Clerkenwell in 1647.

To judge by his sober dress (described by Ashton as that of a gentleman-scholar) DPG423 was probably painted after the closure of the theatres in 1642. Although head and hand are painted with some vigour, the shoulders are poorly proportioned.

1 Brown Ledger, 24 August 1813, '*a Portrait of Mr Perkens an Actor*'.
2 An old label *verso* reads *No 166 Mr Perkins/An Actor*

MISCELLANEOUS PORTRAITS

after SIR ANTHONY VAN DYCK (1599–1641)

DPG420 *Archbishop Laud*

Oak panel 21.6 x 15.9 unevenly bevelled; a fine crack to left of the head and a prominent damage above; discoloured varnish; extensive flaking consolidated in 1988.

Grisaille; wearing a Bishop's rochet and chimere; a painted oval.

PROV.: Cartwright Bequest 1686; Inventory 56 *buship Lauds pictur in black & whit, in a gilte frame a small Closit pece. £1 in ye Library.*[1]

EXH.: *Mr Cartwright's Pictures* 1987(17).

Archbishop Laud (1573–1645), successively Bishop of St David's 1621, Bath and Wells 1626 and London 1628 and Archbishop of Canterbury 1633, was devoted to the King; a stringent administrator of the high Anglican Church, he suffered in the Royalist cause and was executed 1645.

One of many copies and derivations from the three-quarter length portrait by Van Dyck of c.1638 in the Fitzwilliam Museum, Cambridge (2043).[2]

1 An old ink label *verso* reads *Archbishop Laud.*
2 O. Millar in *Van Dyck* 2004, pp.549–50 (iv.153); many versions are there listed.

ISAAC FULLER (1606?–1672)

DPG379 *Head of a Girl*

Canvas 39 x 35.8 lined, the top and right-hand tacking edges turned back; pentimenti on the shoulders; the surface is abraded; an old tear lower right and a damage on the lower right side of the face; losses in the curtain and retouching along the lower edge (making up the original canvas to the lining canvas); surface cleaned 1986; cleaned and relined 2006-7.

Blue eyes, fair hair with green ribbons; wearing a pearl necklace and a blue dress with white collar and bodice; a reddish-brown curtain behind.

PROV.: Cartwright Bequest 1686; Inventory 110 *a girles head doun by fuller in a blue bodys in a black frame filited with gould. £5.*

EXH.: *Mr Cartwright's Pictures* 1987(39).

REF.: Collins Baker 1912, i, pp.97n, 127–28; R.T. Jeffree in *Mr Cartwright's Pictures* 1987, pp.54–55; Waterhouse 1994, p.342n27.

A freshly painted, intimate sketch (conceivably one of Fuller's children?); costume hints at a date in the early 1660s but, as Collins Baker remarked, the work is so slight 'as to give no clue to date, and but little as to style'.

MARCUS GHEERAERTS the younger (1561/2–1636)

DPG389 Portrait of a Lady

Chamfered oak panel 114 x 83.5 of three vertical members, from the left 28.5, 27 and 28 wide, formerly supported with three battens; convex warp; repaired by Brown 1813;[1] the right-hand panel has three splits in the lower area (as reported in 1911), formerly supported with thin ply strips; a chip on the right-hand edge; pentimenti on the hand, bodice, pendant and neckline; the shawl and flesh extensively retouched; the green curtains have darkened, the overdress faded and the red on the lower part of the chair blackened; surface cleaned and varnished c.1980; battens and ply supports removed and the main panel rejoined, retouched and revarnished 1987.

Inscribed bottom left, in yellow: [*Q*]*n Elizabet*[*h*]; pale eyes, brownish hair; wearing a ring round her neck (another would have been attached to the cord around her left wrist), a white dress embroidered with red, black and green flowers, leaves and birds, with red bows, a gold lace collar and cuffs, and a richly woven overdress of a faded puce with black figuring; in the background a red chair and green curtain.

PROV.: Cartwright Bequest 1686; Inventory 97 *a pictur of a woman in an Imbrodred gown & in a Ruff, To ye knee.* £8.

EXH.: *Mr Cartwright's Pictures* 1987(34).

REF.: R.T. Jeffree in *Mr Cartwright's Pictures* 1987, pp.51–52.

One of Cartwright's finest portraits, as Jeffree observed. In 1813 called '*Queen Elizabeth by Zuccera*' (see note 1) but the *Qn Elizabeth* inscription was evidently added in the eighteenth century (see p.53). The pose is matched, in reverse, by the Gheeraerts portrait of Lady Scudamore dated 1615 in the National Portrait Gallery (64).[2]

1 Brown Ledger, 2 November 1813, '*Queen Elizabeth by Zuccera*'.
2 K. Hearn, *Marcus Gheeraerts II*, Tate Gallery, 2002, p.38; Strong 1969a, i, p.243 as *Countess of Pembroke*; Strong 1969b, pl.279 as *Lady Scudamore*.

John Greenhill, *Study of an Old Man's Head*, black chalk (Dulwich College)

John Greenhill (1642–76)

DPG374 *Head of a Bearded Man*

Canvas 75.5 x 62.8 lined and cleaned by Brown 1813;[1] a pentimento on the right shoulder; matt retouchings and much abraded in background areas; a large mended tear in the upper-left background; light wearing on the beard, lip and lower corner beneath signature; the black gown continues beneath the oval to the bottom edge, but not the left arm; probably unfinished.

Reinforced signature, lower left in spandrel: *J.G.*; brown eyes, white and grey beard; his buttoned black dress now illegible.

PROV.: Cartwright Bequest 1686; Inventory 117 *A man with a balld head in a gilt frame in 3 quarters Clouth don by grinhill.* £10.

EXH.: *Mr Cartwright's Pictures* 1987(35).

REF.: Lysons 1792, p.112; Collins Baker 1912, ii, p.157, as 'probably a copy of some Italian painting'; R.T. Jeffree in *Mr Cartwright's Pictures* 1987, pp.52–53; Waterhouse 1994, p.111, as 'could well be an actor's portrait in character'.

Dated mid-1660s by Jeffree who suggested the sitter may be foreign since both beard and costume are unusual for the Restoration period. The composition appears to be unresolved and the oval to have been imposed at a late stage (perhaps because of difficulties with the left arm). The drawing attributable to Greenhill in the Cartwright Album at Dulwich College shows the same head from a slightly different angle, apparently confirming this is a life study; it shows the ear drawn slightly better.

1 Brown Ledger, 2 November 1813, '*a Portrait of a Gentleman by Greenhill*'.

JOHN GREENHILL (1642–76)

DPG418 *Self Portrait*

Canvas 106.3 x 82.9 of three pieces joined horizontally through the elbow (73 from the top, as if originally a half length) and vertically from the elbow (52 from the left), lined; two large tears to the right of the figure, another to the left, and smaller ones in the jaw line and vertically through the near eye; a large stopping in the nose and a smaller one in the far cheek; a broad retouched craquelure disfigures the surface; Hell 1952–53; lined and cleaned 1988.

Blue eyes, brown hair; wearing a maroon jacket over a white shirt, with a brown cloak; holding a drawing of a profile head (see below).

PROV.: Cartwright Bequest 1686; Inventory 95 *grenhills pictur to ye knees in Read dun by himselfe. Grinhill.* £5.

EXH.: NPE 1866(1005); lent to Foreign and Commonwealth Office 1969–73; *Mr Cartwright's Pictures* 1987(18).

ENG.: A. Bannerman (Walpole *Anecdotes* 1763); G.T. Doo after W. Bone (Walpole *Anecdotes* 1862).

REF.: Lysons 1792, p.110 'a good picture'; Collins Baker 1912, ii, pp.8–9, 13, 157; R.T. Jeffree in *Mr Cartwright's Pictures* 1987, p.40.

A youthful and ambitious portrait in fancifully archaic dress, emulating Robert Walker's self portrait of c.1645 which shows the artist holding up a drawing before him in his right hand[1] (the drawing in Greenhill's hand possibly refers to his own portrait drawn by Lely c.1662).[2] The pose ultimately derives from Van Dyck's *Self Portrait with a Sunflower* of c.1635–36, engraved by Hollar in 1644.[3] The complicated construction of the canvas may indicate that DPG418 was first conceived as a half-length composition (to match the Van Dyck and Walker portraits) before the flowing drapery was added (conceivably to conceal difficulties experienced in drawing the right shoulder and upper arm) and the seated pose suggested. The head is rather stiffly drawn, and the left hand weak.

Copied in miniature by Bernard Lens II (from Ickworth; Sotheby's, 26 November 1992 lot 368), and in charcoal by C. Morcom 1901.

A youthful self portrait drawing is in the British Museum (1886-11-23-1).[4] Vertue mentioned a self portrait by Greenhill 'in a wig and that a capital picture' belonging to Mr Blow a relation,[5] and an etched self portrait;[6] with fine disregard for chronology he also mentioned 'Vandyke his head in Crayons of Greenhill' at Wroxton.[7]

1 Royal Collection; Millar 1963, i, no.207; ii, pl.94.
2 British Museum (1857-11-14-213); Croft-Murray & Hulton 1960, i, pp.417–18, ii, pl.213; formerly attributed to Van Dyck, cf. note 7 below.
3 Duke of Westminster collection; *Van Dyck* 2004, p.431(iv.4).
4 Croft-Murray & Hulton 1960, i, pp.339–40, ii, pl.141.
5 Vertue, iii, p.60; engraved by P. Gunst: Collins Baker 1912, ii, p.9.
6 Vertue, i, p.46.
7 Vertue, iv, p.192. See note 2 above.

JACOB HUYSMANS (c.1630–c.1696)

DPG362 *Portrait of a Lady*

Canvas 74.9 x 62.5; the head alone finished; much overpainted, with later dark retouchings on the hand, the curls on right shoulder and in the drape; Hell 1953–55.

Brown eyes, dark brown hair; wearing a white dress with a grey drape over her left shoulder; her left arm rests on a pink ledge.

PROV.: Cartwright Bequest 1686; Inventory 72 *a woman in a blue mantell, in a gilt frame on a 3 quarters Clouth don by housman. £5.*

EXH.: *Mr Cartwright's Pictures* 1987(37); Tredegar House 1991–.

REF.: Collins Baker 1912, ii, p.155; R.T. Jeffree in *Mr Cartwright's Pictures* 1987, pp.53–54.

This unfinished and much overpainted portrait study was dated in the early 1660s by Jeffree, who speculated that it may represent an actress from the King's Company, within the Cartwright circle. Collins Baker had proposed a slightly later date.

Unknown Artist

DPG354 *The Judde*[1] *Memorial*

Oak panel 80 x 102.2 of three horizontal members, from the top 32, 29 and 19 wide, with seven butterfly wedges on each join; supporting battens have been removed; described as 'much injured by time' in 1814 when it was cleaned by Brown;[2] described as 'cracked' in 1911; the panel remains in fragile condition; split through the hands on the skull; extensive losses through general blistering, and much over-painting; black dotted lines apparent beneath and on the corpse, indicating transfer from a cartoon (see below). Hell 1952–53; cleaned and consolidated 1990–92.

He has brown eyes and brown hair and wears a black hat and gown with 'kid' gloves; she has brown eyes and hair and wears a black hat, a black blouse with slashed sleeves, brown faced breast panels and a brown panelled skirt; the foreground corpse has brown hair. The husband's coat of arms, top left, show Judde quartered with Chiche with crescent for difference for a second son.[3] His wife's coat of arms has six quarterings, indicating her descent from Williams and other, principally Welsh, families.[4]The husband's age is inscribed above left: *AETATIS SVE 47* and his wife's above right: *AETATIS 28*.

Above the wooden sideboard between the two figures the inscription *THVS: CONSVMYTHE: OVR:TYME.* On the top ledge stand a burning candle, two vases of flowers with prominent irises, and two sacks of wool marked respectively *ano I* and *ano X*, each with a merchant's mark and the inscription: *Good. Lemster.p.daell.*, identifying wool from Leominster.[5]

Below on the sideboard are inscribed the sitters' initials: *WJ* and *JJ*, with between *BEHOWLDE. OWER.ENDE*, this inscription appearing above the sitters' hands which rest on a skull.

Beneath the skull, on the edge of the table, the inscription: *THE.WORDE.OF.GOD/ HATHE.KNIT.VS. TWAYNE/ AND. DEATH. SHALL.VS./DEVIDE. AGAYNE.* On either side the date *ANO 1560* is written above the Royal arms[6] and (perhaps) those of the Staple Merchants Company.[7]

Below, a corpse laid out on straw, symbolic of regeneration: *LYVE:TO.DYE: AND: DYE: TO LYVE: ETARNALLY.*

The contemporary inner frame is inscribed: *WHEN WE ARE DEADE AND IN OWR GRAVES, AND ALL OWRE BONES BE ROTTUN, BY THIS SHALL WE REMEMBERED BE, WHEN WE SHULDE BE FORGOTTYN.*

PROV.: Possibly Cartwright Bequest 1686;[8] in the College Audit Room 1814; by the Mausoleum before 1930.

EXH.: *Coronation Exhibition*, Manchester, 1953 (26); *Mr Cartwright's Pictures* 1987(33 attributed to Lucas de Heere); *The Story of Time*, National Maritime Museum, 1999(300).

REF.: Manning & Bray, iii, p.444; Young 1889, i, pp.480–81; L. Cust, *Wal. Soc.*, II, 1913, p.30 (as Hans Eworth); C.H. Collins Baker & W.G. Constable, *English Painting of the 16th & 17th centuries*, 1930, p.25 (as Hans Eworth); Collins Baker 1933, p.35 (as Hans Eworth); Strong 1969b, p.39 (as Unknown British Artist); N. Llewellyn, *The Art of Death*, 1991, pp.10–12.

The sitters have been identified by Lorne Campbell and Tarnya Cooper, from whose extensive notes most of the following entry is gratefully derived.

The initials WJ and JJ with the coats of arms in the top corners identify William Judde (c.1513–91)[9] and his wife Joan, *née* Williams (b. c.1532). William Judde, a merchant of the staple and member of the Skinners' Company of London,[10] was the second son of Thomas (d. c.1535), one-time member of the King's Household, and grandson of John Judde of Tonbridge (d. c.1493), and his wife Margaret *née* Chiche. William Judde's wife Joan was the daughter of Walter Williams (later Cromwell) and his wife Alice.[11]

It appears that the painting was made for remembrance rather than celebration. The texts emphasise transience and a hope for eternal life. The largest element within the composition is the ominous foreground corpse, the drawing of which was transferred from a pattern (see physical description above); it recalls images of *Christ in the Tomb* [as Holbein 1521 at Basle] and an identical corpse is seen in another less elaborate but equally rigorous painting which entered the collection of Claude Gouffier in 1557;[12] according to the inscription, it was found at Calais, the city of the Staplers until taken by the French in 1558; Judde's uncle, Andrew Judde, was Mayor of the Staple in Calais in 1552, 1555 and 1558.

In DPG354 neither husband nor wife looks at each other. Their hands (his right, her left) rest on a skull, but they do not touch. They are dressed as merchants; she carries a girdle book (a prayer book or psalter) and there are irises (which have been variously interpreted as symbolic of the Virgin Mary, the incarnation of Christ, or of trust)[13] in the vase, at her breast, and in his gloves. The date 1560 apparently indicates the date of the picture rather than their marriage. Four Judde children, Mary, ffrancis, Elizabeth and Grace, baptised at Allhallows, Lombard Street, between 12 January 1559 and 27 June 1563, were probably those of the William Judde who lived in Gracechurch Street in that parish at least from 1558 to 1560.[14] Grace and Ursula Judde were the administrators of the will of a 'Mr Wylliam Judde', buried at St Olave, Hart Street, on 7 June 1591.[15]

The execution does not seem to warrant an attribution to either Hans Eworth (see above) or Lucas de Heere (in Cook 1914 and 1926), but subject, style and inscriptions suggest an English artist. There is perhaps some similarity with the so-called Master of the Countess of Warwick, as seen in the *William, 10th Lord Cobham and his Family* at Longleat.[16]

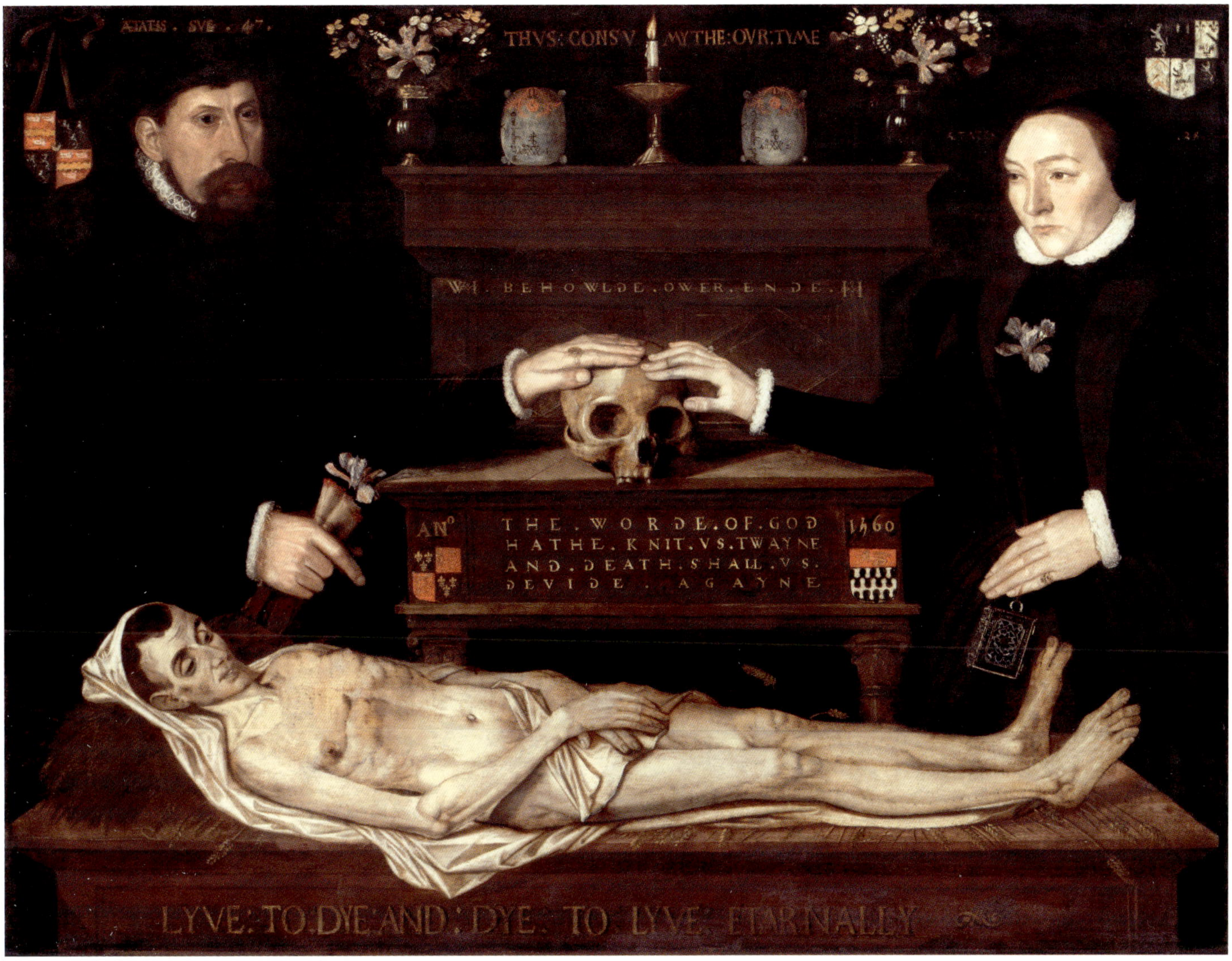

1 The name is generally spelled either 'Judd' or 'Judde'; H.S. Vere-Hodge, *Sir Andrew Judde*, n.d. [1953], p.3, remarks that 'in documents of the same time Sir Andrew's [William's uncle's] name appears in four different spellings, of which two are still rivals. I am calling him Judde, because the name is found more often in that form than in any other, and because that was how he signed his name in 1557 on an important document still preserved at Skinner's Hall'.

2 Manning & Bray, iii, p.444. Brown Ledger, 28 November 1814, '*a Picr on Panel husband & wife an ancient Pr*'.

3 *Gu. a fesse ragulée betw. three boars' heads heads couped ar.* for Judde, *quartering az. three lions ramp. ar. a border of the last* for Chiche.

4 1 and 6 *sa. a lion rampant arg.* for Williams; 2 *sa. two* [a third probably erased] *spears' heads arg.* for Pryce; 3 *arg. a chevron* [now incomplete] *betw. three fleurs de lys sa.* for Dixwell of Coton Hall, War. (or Aprice, according to Manning & Bray, at note 2); 4 *arg., three chevrons gu.* for Loughor of Tythegston, Glam.; 5 *arg. a lion rampant sa.* for Hughes of Gwerclas (Barons of Kymmer-yn-Ediernion), Lloyd of Dolglessyn in Edeimion (or Morgan, according to Manning & Bray, at note 2); 6 see 1.

5 Commonly called Lemster Ore (later celebrated in Drayton's *Polyolbion*, vii, 151–52: 'Where lives the man so dull, on Britain's further shore, To whom did never sound the name of Lemster Ore?').

6 *Quartered, or three fleur-de-lys and gu. three lions passant or.* Edward VI, who reigned until 1553 was the last English monarch to bear these arms; Queen Mary (reigned 1553–58) bore different arms and from 1558 Queen Elizabeth bore the same arms encircled by the Garter.

7 *Barry nebulée of two arg. and sa. on a chief gu. a lion passant gardant or.* The arms of the Staplers were in fact *Barry nebulée of six arg. and az. on a chief gu. a lion passant gardant or.*

8 Number *185* inscribed in ink, *verso*. Manning & Bray, iii, p.443, stated wrongly that 'The number is 185; unfortunately, there is a chasm of four numbers in the Catalogue [i.e. the Cartwright inventory] at this place'. But no.185 in the Inventory was *a great picture of fouls, & a Rabitt & a hare in a gilt frame a uery Long Large Pece* £12 (destroyed 1939–45; see Beresford 1998, p.306, Unknown DPG351). Edward Alleyn, on the other hand, may have particularly admired Sir Andrew Judde (William's uncle) as the founder of Tonbridge School, but that is pure speculation.

9 For whom, see Vere-Hodge (at note 1), pp.5–9, 125; J.J. Lambert, *Records of the Skinners Company of London*, 1933, pp.187, 370. These published references have been much expanded by the archival researches of Lorne Campbell, whose unpublished ms. notes of 1996 are on file.

10 A merchant of the staple exported materials for manufacture, principally wool, hides, leather, tin and lead (see Vere-Hodge, at note 1, pp.14–15, 25). Freemen of one Company could exercise the trade of another, and apprentices of one company could learn the trade of another. Thus Sir Andrew Judde (c.1495–1558), William's uncle – Mayor of the Staple in Calais (see above), Lord Mayor of London in 1550, Kt. 1551, and the founder of Tonbridge School in 1553, was apprenticed to a Skinner and was six times Master of the Skinners' Company.

11 For the Cromwell pedigree, see *Victoria County History of Huntingdon*, ii, 1932, pp.67, 69.

12 Louvre RF.1950-1 (on loan to the musée de Calais), see O. Meslay, *Les Trésors du Grand Ecuyer*, Château d'Ecouen, Val d'Oise, 1994, pp.89, 96, fig.44, as French School; the corpse lies beneath three skulls inscribed above: *RESPICE FINEM/SIC TRANSIT GLORIA MVNDI*; there is a later inscription below: *CE TABLEAU A ESTE APPORTE D LA PRISE DE CALAYS PAR LES MAINS DE … CLAVDE GOVFFIER.*

13 See M. Levi D'Ancona, *The Garden of the Renaissance*, 1977, p.186.

14 Sources quoted by Campbell: PROB 11/41 sig 58; C 142/123/95; Guildhall MS 17613. Judde was living at Harrowe Alley, St Peter, Cornhill, 1568-87 (R. Mark Benbow, 'Notes to the Index of London Citizens involved in City Governments 1558-1603', typescript, n.d., Institute of Historical Records, p.515).

15 Guildhall MS 9050/2, f.66; *Harleian Soc. Registers*, xlvi, 1916, p.123.

16 Exh. *Dynasties*, Tate Britain, 1995(51).

Unknown Artist

DPG375 *called Sir Martin Frobisher Kt*

Canvas 81.9 x 59.4 lined and cleaned by Brown 1813;[1] lightly cupped surface; discoloured retouchings and losses along the top edge, background and in the doublet; the head seems reinforced and details of the costume are very crudely executed.

Black hair, but fair beard and moustache, blue-grey eyes; wearing a black cape, white doublet and gold collar.

PROV.: Cartwright Bequest 1686; Inventory 174 *Sr Martin Furbishers pictur in a whit dublet & a great Ruff, with a gould Chaine in a black frame.* 10s.[2]

EXH.; NPE1866(351); *Mr Cartwright's Pictures* 1987(3).

REF.: Lysons 1792, p.108; R.T. Jeffree in *Mr Cartwright's Pictures* 1987, pp.29–30.

The Inventory suggests that Cartwright believed DPG375 represented the celebrated English navigator Sir Martin Frobisher (1535–?1594), who was given 'a fair chain of gold' by Elizabeth I for his Arctic exploration. But such chains were not uncommon amongst gentlemen of the later 16th century and the picture bears no resemblance to the swarthy, documented, portrait of 1577 in the Bodleian Library, Oxford.[3] DPG375 appears to be a copy of a late 16th-century portrait of a middle-aged man (in any case too young for Frobisher); Jeffree tentatively proposed the original might have been by Hieronimo Custodis. A copy in enamel by Henry Bone, from a drawing he made at Dulwich in 1818, was exh. BI 1835(12).[4]

1 Brown Ledger, 24 August 1813, '*a Portrait of Sr MartinFrobisher*'.
2 An old label *verso* reads *No 174 Sir Martin Frobisher.*
3 Strong 1969b, p.154, fig.100.
4 Bone's drawing is in the NPG, see R.J.B. Walker, *Wal. Soc.*, LXI, 1999, p.326, no.211.

Unknown Artist

DPG377 *Mrs Dirge*

Canvas 74.9 x 67.3 lined; very worn and considerably retouched; old tears, lower right, beneath the ring, in the ruff and on the left edge; a repaired hole above the hat; Hell 1949–55.

Inscribed bottom left: *Ao 1629*; blue-grey eyes, greying hair; wearing a broad-brimmed black hat, a black laced dress over a white blouse, and holding a white 'kerchief; a gold ring on the second finger of her right hand; painted oval.

PROV.: Cartwright Bequest 1686; Inventory 156 *mr dirges wife in a hat & ruff in a black fram 3 quarters Clouth.*

EXH.: *Mr Cartwright's Pictures* 1987(36); Tredegar House 1991–.

REF.: Collins Baker 1912, ii, p.193; R.T. Jeffree in *Mr Cartwright's Pictures* 1987, p.53.

Collins Baker in 1912 queried whether this portrait was not signed *W.D.F.* (and he listed another bust-length painted oval portrait of a man at Welbeck signed *D.F. 1633* [1]) – but no trace of a signature remains today.

1 Illus. Collins Baker 1912, i, f.p.110.

Unknown Artist

DPG430 *Michael Drayton*

Canvas 54.5 x 41.9 lined;[1] the original canvas wrapped round the stretcher, suggesting the painted oval was originally complete; the face distinctly worn with many retouchings; marked craquelure in background, the varnish discoloured; Hell 1949.

Inscribed bottom left: *ANO: 1628*; brownish eyes, greyish hair with green laurel leaves and a grey beard; wearing a dark costume, the details illegible.

PROV.: Cartwright Bequest 1686; Inventory 108 *mickill darayton ye poet in a black frame. 15s.*

EXH.: NPE 1866(338); *Le livre anglais*, Bibliothèque Nationale, Paris, 1951 (472); *Coronation Exhibition*, Manchester, 1953 (54); *Mr Cartwright's Pictures* 1987(4); *Edward Alleyn* 1994(25).

ENG.: R. Clamp after S. Harding 1794 (*Biographical Mirrour*, i, 1795), without the wreath and close buttons on the coat; I.H. Robinson after W. Green 1823.

REF.: Lysons 1792, p.108; Strong 1969a, i, p.72; G. Ashton in *Mr Cartwright's Pictures* 1987, pp. 30–31.

Michael Drayton (1563–1631), celebrated poet and playwright, author of the topographical narrative poem *Polyolbion* (1598–1622); it is said that between 1597 and 1604 he wrote some twenty unpublished plays for the Lord Admiral's Men (of whom Edward Alleyn was one) and he also collaborated with Dekker, Webster and Chettle for the stage; not lacking in ambition, he wished to be recognized as Britain's laureate bard, and each of his three authentic portraits shows him laureate.

DPG430, now very worn, was probably derived from the engraving by W. Hole 1613 used as the frontispiece for Drayton's *Poems* in 1619,[2] though he has much less hair and the laurel wreath is confined. The inscribed date of 1628 appears authentic. A copy in enamel by Henry Bone, from a drawing he made at Dulwich in 1818, was exh. BI 1835(18) and is now at Kingston Lacy.[3]

A laureate bust of Drayton attributed to Edward Marshall c.1631 is on his monument in Westminster Abbey.[4] A bust-length oval miniature attributed to Peter Oliver, wearing a laurel wreath and a falling lace collar, in a silver locket also containing a head of Christ, is in the collection of the Duke of Portland.[5]

1 Possibly '*a Portrait of a Gentleman with Lorels on his head*', lined and cleaned by Brown in 1813 (Brown Ledger, 24 August 1813), but see also DPG427, p.43.
2 Hind 1955, p.319, no.5, pl.196.
3 Bone's drawing is in the NPG, see R.J.B. Walker, *Wal. Soc.*, LXI, 1999, p.323, no.167.
4 Illus. Strong 1969a, ii, pl.133; Drayton's iconography is partly discussed in i, p.72.
5 R.W. Goulding, *Welbeck Abbey Miniatures*, 1916, pp.74–75, no.37, illus.; Vertue, v, p.78.

W. Hole, *Michael Drayton*, engraving, 1613
(National Portrait Gallery, London)

CORNELIS BOL (1589–c.1666)

DPG360 The Thames from Somerset House

Canvas 63.5 x 108.7 lined; substantial losses, principally in the trees in front of Somerset House; widespread retouching across the foreground area and in the sky above the Banqueting House; the boats had previously been embellished principally in the lower right area and the entire sky and dark foreground had been overpainted; revarnished 1987; cleaned and relined 2003.

Signed bottom right, on fencing: *CB*;[1] showing Somerset House[2] in the right foreground and Lambeth Palace in the left distance; in between, from left to right, the more prominent buildings are Westminster Hall, Westminster Abbey, the Banqueting House and Old Northumberland House (with the four turrets); the original canvas, as revealed during relining, inscribed *verso*: *Westminster/ nu 192*.

PROV.: Cartwright Bequest 1687; Inventory 192 (according to the inscription on the back of the canvas, see above; the number is from the missing part of the inventory).

EXH.: Aberystwyth 1947(3); *Image of London*, Barbican AG, 1987(32); *Mr Cartwright's Pictures* 1987(66); *Talking Peace 1604, The Somerset House Conference Paintings*, Somerset House, 2004(n.n.).

ENG.: J.P. Malcolm 1797, in two plates, *Somerset Palace 1650* (the right-hand section) and *Westminster 1650* (the left-hand section), showing slight variations in shipping and foliage (*Londinium Redivivum*, iv, 1807, f.pp.289, 303); H. & R. Wilkinson 1803 *'Somerset House in its original state ... from an antient painting in the possession of Dulwich College'*

REF.: M.H. Grant, *Old English Landscape Painters*, i, 1957, p.45, fig.13; Whinney & Millar 1957, p.263n1; Croft-Murray & Hulton 1960, i, pp.250–51; R.T. Jeffree in *Mr Cartwright's Pictures* 1987, pp.71–72.

The identity of the initials *CB* is inferred from Vertue. He listed in the possession of the Evelyn family c.1733 'three views of London from the River side Arundel House Somersett house Tower Lond. painted before the fire of Lond. by Cornelius Boll. A good free Taste'.[3] These pictures remain with family descendants. Two compare closely with views in the Guildhall Art Gallery (one of which, *The Thames from Bankside*, bears an indistinct *CB* or *CLB* monogram),[4] while the third, *View on the Thames with Old Somerset House*, much resembles DPG360 but is taken from a slightly higher angle.[5] These six paintings, virtually forming three pairs, may have emanated from the same studio, although the techniques vary in detail.[6]

DPG360 may be dated c.1650. The Diana fountain seen in the grounds of Somerset House, installed c.1637, was taken to Hampton Court in 1656 [7] and the two engravings of DPG360 by J.P. Malcolm (described above) were entitled *Somerset Palace 1650* and *Westminster 1650*. In 1662 a palladian gallery by John Webb considerably modified the appearance of the river frontage of Somerset House.

A signed replica was sold Sotheby's, 6 June 2007, lot 63.

1 The monogram appears in an undamaged area. M. Warner, *Image of London*, Barbican AG, 1987, no.32, added 'dated indecipherably'.
2 For a brief historical survey of Somerset House, see C. Knight, *British Art Journal*, ii, 2, 2000/2001, pp.6–13.
3 Vertue, iv, p.53.
4 *The Thames from Bankside* (160) and *The Thames from Dockhead* (159), each 61 x 91.5; illus. *Works of Art of the Corporation of London*, 1986, p.290.
5 Illus. *Burl. Mag.*, cxxvii, 1985, p.533; J. Harris, *The Artist and the Country House*, 1979, p.45; it includes the edge of Arundel House on the extreme right and more of the Somerset House façade is revealed as the trees are lower and there is a slightly different fenestration on the nearest tower (two vertical bars instead of one). All three Evelyn views (each approx. 66 x 102) were exhibited *Age of Charles II*, RA, 1960–61, nos.214, 224 and 230.
6 L. Goldsmith, *Topographical Painting in Seventeenth-century London*, Courtauld Institute, 1993 (final year diploma study; Department of Conservation), made a close technical examination of these paintings. She suggested that a drawing attributed to Alexander Keirincx in the British Museum (1855-7-14-60) was a source for both the *View of Shipping below the Tower* in the Evelyn collection (see note 5) and *The Thames from Dockhead* in the Guildhall AG (159).
7 See G. Fisher & J. Newman, *Burl. Mag.*, cxxvii, 1985, pp.531–33, and *The History of the King's Works*, ed. H.M. Colvin, iv, 1982, pp.269–70. The bronze figure of Diana, once thought to be by Fanelli but now known to be by Hubert Le Sueur, has stood in Bushy Park since 1713.

Lorenzo a Castro (fl.1672–1695)

DPG359 *A Galley of Malta*

Canvas 76.2 x 134.3 including two strips 89 and 45 long and 12.5 high across the top, lined; the canvas joins are crudely retouched; previous uneven cleaning reveals a red ground; Hell 1952–55.

Signed lower left: *L.A. CAS TRO*; a fighting galley of the Knights of Malta with, on the right, the flagship of the Dutch Mediterranean force and, in the left background, an English merchantman and the flagship of the English Streights Fleet (stationed in the Mediterranean).

PROV.: Cartwright Bequest 1686; Inventory 225 *A galley of malta ye Coulers Red with whit crosses full of passingers, a yard & a halfe Long & a yard deepe in a gilt frame. Castro £7...*

EXH.: *Mr Cartwright's Pictures* 1987(67); Tredegar House 1991–.

REF.: R.T. Jeffree in *Mr Cartwright's Pictures* 1987, p.72.

The Knights Hospitallers of St John ruled Malta from 1530–1798, defending it against Turkish attacks. Jeffree suggested a date of c.1680 according to the costumes of the foreground figures.

Lorenzo a Castro (fl.1672–1695)

DPG361 *Ships in Rough Water off a Mediterranean Port*

Canvas 95.3 x 178.7 lined; an old L-shaped tear in the sky near the centre ship; cleaned and consolidated 1991.

Signed bottom left: *L.a.Castro.fec.*; on the right the flagship of the English Streights fleet (stationed in the Mediterranean), beyond her the vice-admiral, and on the left the flagship of the Dutch Mediterranean force.

PROV.: Cartwright Bequest 1686; Inventory 224 *a Large Seascift of 2 yards Long, & a yard & somthing more depe, shipps a block hous a wharfe, & an Ale house, a Ruffe watter in a gilt frame Castro £10.*

EXH.: *Mr Cartwright's Pictures* 1987(72); Tredegar House 1991–.

REF.: R.T. Jeffree in *Mr Cartwright's Pictures* 1987, p.75.

Jeffree supposed that the foreground figures were dressed in the fashion of the later 1670s. Possibly the companion piece to no.223 in the Cartwright Inventory (untraced, see p.258).

Lorenzo a Castro (fl.1672–1695)

DPG428 *A Sea Fight with Barbary Corsairs*

Canvas 107 x 92.7 lined with new stretcher by Morrill; the surface is generally worn; vertical tears in the sky on the left between the ships, in the sea and in the wreck on the right; many small retouchings in the sky; Hell 1952–53.

Signed lower left, on side of ship: *Castro f*; in the left foreground an Algerine vessel; in the centre are grouped, from the left, a Dutch and Algerine frigate and an English galley frigate; in the right foreground a sinking Algerine ship.

PROV.: Cartwright Bequest 1686; Inventory 227 *A Large pece of a Sea fight in a gilt frame an elle deepe & a yard broud Castro* £4.

EXH.: *Mr Cartwright's Pictures* 1987(69); Travellers' Club 2001–.

REF.: R.T. Jeffree in *Mr Cartwright's Pictures* 1987, p.75; F.B. Cockett, *Early Sea Painters 1660–1730*, 1995, pp.101, 103.

Many actions were fought at this time in the Mediterranean between the British Streights Fleet and the Barbary Corsairs (mostly based at Algiers). Both Jeffree and Cockett have proposed that DPG428 may show the action of 22 May 1681 when the *Kingfisher* was attacked by seven Barbary ships and her captain Sir John Kempthorne was killed; the Algerine boats were then flying Dutch and English colours.[1]

1 The action is described by M.S. Robinson, *Van de Velde Drawings in the National Maritime Museum*, ii, 1974, pp.45, 75, and *The Paintings of Willem van de Velde the Elder and Younger*, 1990, i, pp.210–1; and by C. White, *The Dutch Pictures in the Collection of Her Majesty the Queen*, 1982, p.142. These references describe a painting by Van de Velde the elder in the Royal Collection (White 229) and a drawing in the National Maritime Museum (no.1215) by the Van de Veldes, both tentatively identified as showing the *Kingfisher* action.

LORENZO A CASTRO (fl.1672–1695)

DPG436 A Calm

Canvas 63.2 x 76.2 lined; generally worn with widespread retouchings, principally in the lower foreground and in the sky to the left; a repaired hole between the flags upper left; Hell 1952–53.

Signed bottom right: *L.CASTRO*; the principal ship is the commodore of the British Levant Company fleet off an eastern Mediterranean port; the figures on the wharf include turbanned eastern merchants.

PROV.: Cartwright Bequest 1686; Inventory 216 *a seascift of a calme with ships & a wharfe 3 quarters Clouth in a gilt frame castros.* £3.[1]

EXH.: *Mr Cartwright's Pictures* 1987(70); Travellers' Club 2001–.

REF.: R.T. Jeffree in *Mr Cartwright's Pictures* 1987, p.75.

1 An old ink inscription *verso* reading *No 176* is unrelated to any inventory/catalogue number.

LORENZO A CASTRO (fl.1672–1695)

DPG437 A Dutch East-Indiaman off Hoorn

Canvas 63.5 x 76.5 lined; widespread retouchings; discoloured varnish; Hell 1952–53.

Signed bottom right: *Castro*; the stork on her stern identifies the large boat as the *Ooeivaar* a Dutch East Indiaman, wearing the flag of a commodore of an East Indian fleet, anchored off Hoorn in northern Holland.

PROV.: Cartwright Bequest 1686; Inventory 218 *seascift sumthing calme with [five?] ships & wharfe in a gilt frame – Castros. Mr Hart has* 2.10s.[1]

EXH.: *Mr Cartwright's Pictures* 1987(73); Travellers' Club 2001–.

REF.: R.T. Jeffree in *Mr Cartwright's Pictures* 1987, p.75.

Perhaps the only known work by Castro in which a precise location is identifiable.

1 An old label *verso* reads *D.C.218*.

LORENZO A CASTRO (fl.1672–1695)

DPG517 *Dutch Levanters in a Rough Sea*

Canvas 47.3 x 63.8 lined; old tears and holes have been retouched; Hell 1952; cleaned and relined 2007-8.

Signed bottom left: *Castro*; in the centre and right are two Dutch levanters (merchant ships) seen off a Mediterranean port.

PROV.: Cartwright Bequest 1686; Inventory 219 *a Seascift ruffe watters with shipps & wharfe in a gilt frame* £2.10 *Castros.*

EXH.: Leeds 1952; *Mr Cartwright's Pictures* 1987(68).

REF.: R.T. Jeffree in *Mr Cartwright's Pictures* 1987, p.72.

LORENZO A CASTRO (fl.1672–1695)

DPG518 *A Storm at Sea*

Canvas 33 x 52 lined; uneven, much discoloured varnish; a patched tear in the stern flag of the left-hand vessel.

Dutch vessels with a British merchantman in the right-hand mid-distance.

PROV.: Cartwright Bequest 1686; Inventory 220 *an night Seascift castros* £2.10 (see below).

EXH.: *Mr Cartwright's Pictures* 1987(71 as attributed to Bonaventura Peeters the younger and as possibly Cartwright Inventory 213 *a small sea cift* or 214 *a small seascift don by peteres in a gilt frame a closit pece* 5s).

REF.: R.T. Jeffree in *Mr Cartwright's Pictures* 1987, p.75 as attributed to Peeters the younger.

An old incomplete label *verso* reading *No 220* may identify DPG518 in the Cartwright Inventory. But DPG518 has been described as Dutch by Jeffree and tentatively attributed by Archibald to the younger Peeters;[1] it was omitted from the list of works by Castro by Cockett.[2]

1 See *Mr Cartwright's Pictures* 1987, p.75.
2 F.B. Cockett, *Early Sea Painters 1660–1730*, 1995, pp.106–07.

ADAM COLONIA (1634–85)

DPG371 *Sheep Shearing*

Canvas 98.7 x 147 lined by Brown 1817;[1] battens are screwed to the sides and bottom edges of the stretcher; the paint surface is unstable, with general cupping; there is discoloured retouching and the thinner passages in the distance much abraded; discoloured varnish; surface cleaned 1986.

Signed bottom right, in yellow: *AG Colonia*, the *AG* in monogram.

PROV.: Cartwright Bequest 1686; Inventory 83 *A great Large pictur with a great hous, an ould man sheering a sheep, with Sheepe & gotes in it, & a woman milking a gote, with 2 oxon & a Cart of Corne.* £6.

EXH.: *Mr Cartwright's Pictures* 1987(64).

REF.: N. Kalinsky in *Mr Cartwright's Pictures* 1987, p.69.

The woman lifting two baskets is copied from *Autumn* and the sheep shearer from *Summer* by Jacopo and Francesco Bassano (originals in the Kunsthistorisches Museum, Vienna, but many replicas were produced by Francesco Bassano and his studio). According to Buckeridge, Colonia 'copied many pictures of beasts after Bassan',[2] but the copies of Bassano's *Seasons* in the Cartwright collection (DPG386, 398, 412 and 422; Inventory nos.69, 80, 70 and 79 – where three are described as after Bassano) are surely too crude to be by him.[3]

Kalinsky commented upon the uneasy relationship between the figures and landscape which, allowing for the poor condition, seems very weak; perhaps Colonia here collaborated with a landscape painter[4] – although his single signature does not necessarily corroborate this.

1 Brown Ledger, 15 July 1817, '*Harvest home with Sheep Shearing by Colonia*'.
2 B. Buckeridge, *An Essay towards an English School of Painting*, 1706, 1996 ed., pp.362–63.
3 Murray 1980, p.45, had suggested they might be by Colonia, but Kalinsky found the suggestion unconvincing. In the copies the animals in particular are poorly executed.
4 Waterhouse 1994, p.154, said Colonia sometimes placed his figures in landscapes by Adriaen van Diest, his son-in-law. Buckeridge, see note 2 above, said that Colonia's son 'often wrought upon the small figures in his brother Van Diest's landscapes'.

ADAM COLONIA (1634–85)

DPG431 *The Flight into Egypt*

Canvas 69.2 x 47.7 lined and cleaned by Brown 1817;[1] Hell 1953–55; cleaned 1980 when much old overpaint was removed from the sky area.

Signed bottom right in yellow: *AG Colonia*, the *AG* in monogram.

PROV.: Cartwright Bequest 1686; Inventory 82 *Josiph & mary & our Saviour, Josiph Leading an Asse & our Lady & our Saver on it in 3 quarters Clouth in a gilte frame.* £3.

EXH.: *Scholars of Nature*, Hull, 1981(4); *Mr Cartwright's Pictures* 1987(41).

REF.: N. Kalinsky in *Mr Cartwright's Pictures* 1987, pp.55–56.

The subject is taken from Matthew 2, 12–15; threatened by King Herod, the Holy family leave Bethlehem by night for Egypt.

The landscape is much superior to that in DPG371 above.

1 Brown Ledger, 15 July 1817, '*Upright pict.r of flight in to Egpet by Colonia*'.

after SIR ANTONY VAN DYCK (1599–1641)

DPG352 *The Infants Christ and St John*

Canvas 75.3 x 62.6 lined, cleaned and stippled by Brown 1813;[1] the surface is abraded and there are minor losses in the drapery above Christ and in the sky; discoloured varnish.

A red drape round Christ who has an aureole round his head; the lamb behind St John is now almost indistinguishable; the banner on his cross inscribed [EC]*CE AGN*[NUS DEI ECCE QUI TOLL]*IT P* [2][ECCATUM MUNDI]

PROV.: Cartwright Bequest 1686; Inventory 99 *our Saviour & John after van dik in an ould fasiond fram.* £4.

EXH.: *Mr Cartwright's Pictures* 1987(44).

REF.: O. Millar in *Van Dyck* 2004, p.429, under IV.1.

The subject is an elaboration of John 1, 29 (the text inscribed on the banner), the two children embracing on Christ's return journey from Egypt.[3]

The best of Cartwright's Van Dyck's copies. The original at Lamport (acquired by Sir Justinian Isham in 1655 when not in good condition) has been dated by Millar 'towards the end of Van Dyck's time in London', i.e. c.1638–40. Several other versions are recorded, including a picture in Lely's collection engraved in reverse by Arnolde de Jode in 1666, whose plate shows the lamb behind St John quite clearly.[4] A version in the Royal Collection, acquired c.1666–67, shows several minor differences from the Lamport (and Dulwich) pictures.[5]

1 Brown Ledger, 2 November 1813, '*a Picr of St John and Christ V. Dyck*'.
2 Although it appears to read *E*. De Jode's engraving (see note 4) clearly shows *P*.
3 For the Apocryphal texts describing this episode, see M.A. Lavin, *Art Bulletin*, xxxvii, 1955, pp.98–99, and J. Shearman, *Early Italian Pictures in the Collection of Her Majesty The Queen*, 1983, p.156, no.151.
4 New Hollstein, *Van Dyck*, vii, 2002, no.553. Compared with the Lamport/Dulwich pattern it appears to show only minor variations in Christ's drapery.
5 E.g. in John's right foot, the fold of his banner, the folds of the draperies and the height of the distant tree (and see O. Millar in *Van Dyck* 2004, p.429, IV.2)

after SIR PETER LELY (1618–80)

DPG408 *Susanna and the Elders*

Canvas 35.3 x 58.4 lined; a hole near the right edge on the right of the elder; much discoloured varnish; losses filled and pronounced craquelure consolidated 1987.

Susannah wears a white tunic with a blue drape; the central elder has a red turban, the right-hand elder wears a brown cloak.

PROV.: Cartwright Bequest 1686; Inventory 123 *Shusana & ye 2 elders, in a gilt frame a closit pece. £2 in ye Masters room.*

EXH.: *Mr Cartwright's Pictures* 1987(47).

REF.: R.T. Jeffree in *Mr Cartwright's Pictures* 1987, p.58.

The subject is taken from the History of Susanna in the Apocrypha; Susanna, wife of Joachim of Babylon, bathing in her own garden, repulsed the advances of two judges who afterwards by false charges condemned her to death; she was saved by the prophet Daniel who revealed their perjury.

A coarse, much-reduced, but near-contemporary copy of the Lely composition of c.1650 known by versions at the Tate Gallery (T00452), Birmingham City Art Gallery (P23'48) and at Burghley House. DPG408, which shows the nearer elder's right hand raised and Susannah's left breast covered, derives from the Birmingham version[1] (which belonged to the 1st Earl of Arlington in Lely's lifetime).

1 Illus. Beckett 1951, pl.26

Robert Streeter (1624?–79)

DPG376 Landscape

Canvas 102.2 x 129.1 lined with new stretcher by Morrill; small hole upper right at the edge of the foliage; a long tear across the bottom, parallel with the edge; the paint very thin within the trees; Hell 1953–61; cleaned 2002.

PROV.: Cartwright Bequest 1686; Inventory 228 *A Large Landscift don by Streeker in a black frame, fileted with gould.* £3.

EXH.: *Age of Charles II*, RA, 1960–61(303); *Mr Cartwright's Pictures* 1987(65); Travellers' Club 2000–03.

REF.: *Bur.l Mag.*, lxxxiv, 1944, p.7; M.H. Grant, *A Dictionary of British Landscape Painters*, 1952, p.188; H.V.S. Ogden & M.S. Ogden, *English Taste in Landscape in the 17th century*, 1955, p.115; Whinney & Millar 1957, p.265 (as attributed); R.T. Jeffree in *Mr Cartwright's Pictures* 1987, pp.69–71.

There is much improbability in the composition, and the figures are weak. Both Grant and the Ogdens suspected it was by Streeter's son (who is now only known for routine decorative painting).[1] Streeter *père* certainly showed more spatial certainty in, for example, his *Windsor Castle* (Knowsley) or *Boscobel House* of c.1670 (Royal Collection)[2] but the conventions of decorative and scenic painting, on which he was much employed, might sufficiently explain DPG379.[3]

1 Robert Streeter *fils* (fl.1679-d.1711), see Croft-Murray 1962, pp.227b, 228a. Since his earliest recorded works date from the 1680s DPG376 would have been a very prompt purchase by Cartwright.

2 Millar 1963, i, no.317; ii, pl.119.

3 Cf. his murals at Swakeleys (illus. *Burl. Mag.*, lxxxiv, 1944, p.9); Croft-Murray 1962, p.226, quotes records of Streeter executing 'all the ancient and fine scenes in the old playhouse' and 'very glorious scenes and perspectives' for Dryden's *Siege of Granada* at Whitehall in 1671.

Parry Walton (d.1702)

dpg429 *Still Life*

Canvas 63.9 x 55.2 lined; some background losses; a surface scratch through the upright glass; Hell 1953.

Prov.: Cartwright Bequest 1686; Inventory 122 *A pictur of a glass of Clarit a Lofe of bread an oring 2 apprecoks a Romer of Renish wine on a tabell couered with a green clouth in a gilt frame, 3 quarters Clouth by m walton.* £2.

Exh.: *Mr Cartwright's Pictures* 1987(76).

One of very few paintings known by Walton, dpg429 is wholly Dutch in character and much resembles the work of Simon Luttichuys (1610–61).[1]

1 Who was b. London but worked principally and d. in Amsterdam; I am grateful to Bernd Ebert for indicating this comparison.

THE BOURGEOIS BEQUEST 1811

The pictures in this section are catalogued in alphabetical order by artist

Desenfans' addiction to self advertisement and his eager promotion of Bourgeois have obscured their biographies. This brief account attempts to square salient facts.

Noel Desenfans

Noel Joseph Desenfans (1744–1807), linguist and art dealer, was born in France at Avesnes-sur-Helpe, near St Quentin. He studied at the university of Douai, where he may first have encountered Charles-Alexandre de Calonne (1734–1802, subsequently *comptroleur-général* of France, besides being a reputable collector of pictures, see studio of Reynolds DPG318) who was then a member of the local *parlement*. Desenfans moved on to the University of Paris, publishing in 1763 the first of a series of minor literary works, the Rousseauesque *Elève de la Nature*.[1] But it was as a language teacher that he came in 1769 to London. There he met the young Bourgeois whom he 'adopted' and who was to remain with him for the rest of his life, very much within his power.[2] In 1776 Desenfans embarked on a childless but convenient marriage with the middle-aged but affluent Margaret Morris (1731–1813, see p.218) who was said to have been the aunt of two of his pupils[3] and whose wealth enabled him to turn to picture dealing. This had started by accident, according to Farington: he had first lent money to a Dutchman 'who had brought over some pictures, and eventually he purchased them and sold them for £100 profit. This success induced him to go on'.[4] His eye was not perhaps the keenest, but he enjoyed some success, helped principally by his friend and business associate in Paris, the celebrated French dealer J-B-P. Lebrun. In 1784 Bourgeois and the Desenfans moved to a house in Charlotte Street, always crammed with old master paintings despite discreet sales of stock in 1785, 1786, 1795 and 1802. In 1790 they met in London Prince Michael Poniatowski, brother of King Stanislaus of Poland, through whom they agreed, it appears, to form a collection for the King. In 1791 Desenfans assumed the title of Consul-General of Poland and Bourgeois obtained a Polish knighthood (*Ordre du Mérite*) with the title of Painter to the King of Poland. But in 1795 Stanislaus was forced to abdicate and the scheme collapsed, leaving Desenfans, so he claimed, with a collection worth £9,000. It is not clear how many of the Dulwich pictures were ever intended for the Polish Royal collection, a term used, one suspects, quite freely by Desenfans to promote both his pictures and himself. Thereafter he devised a number of schemes for the ultimate disposal of his collection, including the creation of a National Gallery, but at his death he bequeathed it to his wife and to Bourgeois, who had meanwhile continued buying. Desenfans died on 8 July 1807 and lies in the gallery mausoleum, together with his wife and Bourgeois.

In her Will Mrs Desenfans left to Dulwich College 'three dozen of silver plates with the arms of Noel Joseph Desenfans Esquire engraved upon them' and directed that the servant of the Gallery's curator should wear 'the livery of my late dear husband'.[5] But, however much he craved them, no arms or pedigree are registered in the Herald's College to Desenfans (or Bourgeois),[6] and the plates bear the arms of his distinguished friend, Calonne.[7]

1 His obituary, *GM*, lxxvii, ii, 1807, p.690, also refers to his 'well-written novel, intituled, "Les Deux Hermites"' and the *Memoirs of the late Noel Desenfans* ...,1810, pp.4–5, mentioned *La Fête de Coulange* and see note 3 below.

2 Farington, vi, pp.2203, 2213 (25 December 1803, 8 January 1804).

3 They may first have met as Desenfans was preparing the pamphlet *Sulmiste et Sergit*, published in 1772, a study of educational methods, a subject in which Margaret was also interested.

4 Farington, ii, p.513 (21 March 1796).

5 The relevant extracts from her Will are printed as an Appendix to Sparkes 1876, Sparkes & Richter 1880, Sparkes & Richter 1892, and Cook 1914 and 1926.

6 Letter from Rouge Croix, 3 August 1874, to the Dulwich Committee (and see Young 1889, i, pp.483–84). An engraved portrait allegedly of Desenfans (see below under Northcote DPG28) bears the arms: *party per pale, dexter, az., a griffin rampant or. betw. three crescents arg., two and one; sinister, party per chevron az. two martlets arg.; below pean; crest, an ostrich*[?], *with; motto ATTACHED.*

7 See Cook 1914, p.311, and 1926, p.294. For the arms of Calonne, see d'Hozier, *Armorial général ou registre de la noblesse de France*, vii, 1868, p.383 [*D'argent au Lion léopardé de Gueules, mis en chef*].

Sir Francis Bourgeois

Peter Francis Bourgeois (1753–1811),[1] painter and collector, was born in London of a Swiss father, the watchmaker Isaac Bourgeois (1726–93), and an English mother, Elizabeth *née* Gardin. After his mother's death his father left England, leaving behind his two children, of whom Francis was 'adopted' by Desenfans (as described above). Having rejected a military career, he became an enthusiastic and ambitious painter of uneven talent, studying under De Loutherbourg c.1775–76 and travelling in France, Holland and Italy in 1776 (the first year of Desenfans' married life). He exhibited at the RA 1779–1810 and, after much canvassing by Desenfans, was elected ARA in 1787, RA in 1793 and Visitor in 1801. Apart from the Polish honours already described (George III allowed his *Ordre du Mérite* to count as an English Knighthood), Bourgeois was appointed Landscape Painter to the King in 1794 and to the Duke of Gloucester in 1807. Soane, Beechey and the young Turner were his friends, but Farington remained critical of his pretence; Leigh Hunt remembered that while he was a 'lively good-natured man, with a pleasing countenance, his oath and buckskins would never allow me to consider him a serious person'.[2] After Desenfans' death Bourgeois bequeathed their collection to Dulwich College, perhaps at the prompting of J.P. Kemble (the old friend of Desenfans) and through his friendship with the Rev Robert Corry, a Fellow of Dulwich. The Dulwich estate was then beautiful, secluded and remarkable for the cleanliness of the air, and the College, of course, already owned the pictures from the Alleyn and Cartwright Bequests.[3] Bourgeois died on 8 January 1811 and in his Will, apart from the collection, he gave the College a sum to be spent on the accommodation of his pictures. This was promptly increased by Mrs Desenfans (d. 1813) to enable Soane to build the Dulwich Picture Gallery with a mausoleum in which Bourgeois would lie with the Desenfans.

The Bourgeois Bequest comprises some 370 paintings, of which only 47 are British (see also DPG483, p.255), and of these 22 are by Bourgeois himself.[4] Desenfans, whose predilection was for seventeenth-century European masters, had not admired contemporary British art, with the exception of De Loutherbourg, Reynolds and Richard Wilson, and examples are otherwise principally confined to portraits of the Desenfans–Bourgeois circle.

1 His year of birth given me by Dr Paul Mathews. For Bourgeois see Waterfield 1989. An earlier account is given by D. Agassiz, 'Sir Francis Bourgeois, 1756–1811, Un paysagiste Suisse à la cour du roi George III d'Angleterre', *Revue Historique Vaudoise*, mai–juin, 1937 [offprint, pp.1–23, with a perfunctory list of the paintings by Bourgeois at Dulwich, pp.21–22].

2 Leigh Hunt, 'A Walk from Dulwich to Brockham' in *The Indicator and The Companion*, 1834, p.320.

3 See G.A. Waterfield in *Rembrandt to Gainsborough*, 1999, pp.25–26.

4 The Desenfans/Bourgeois sales of 1785, 1786, 1795 and 1802 reflect a similar ratio (with a particular liking for Bourgeois' teacher, De Loutherbourg).

Sir WILLIAM BEECHEY (1753–1839)

DPG111 *John Philip Kemble*

Canvas 76.8 x 64.1 lined;[1] broad craquelure in the impasted passages in the forehead and nose; discoloured varnish; revived and varnished in 1870; Hell 1949–1953.

Brown eyes, a small wig over his own powdered hair; wearing a deep blue-grey coat; the foreground table is covered with a green cloth.

PROV.: Commissioned by Desenfans 1798; Bourgeois Bequest 1811.

EXH.: RA 1799(174); *International Exhibition*, South Kensington, 1862(225); RA schools 1911, 1924; *Soane and After* 1988(4).

ENG.: P. Roberts 1802 (*Thespian Dictionary* 1802 and 1805); Mackenzie 1804; James Hopwood 1808; anon.

REF.: Britton 1813(92); Roberts 1907, pp.66–67, 268.

John Philip Kemble (1757–1823), Shakespearian actor and producer, brother of Sarah, Mrs Siddons (see DPG318, p.120) with whom he frequently played, and Charles Kemble (see DPG291, p.196); he studied at Douai University 1771–75 (as had Desenfans before him) and played in provincial theatre before making his London debut in 1783 at Drury Lane, where he became manager in1788; from 1802 he was manager of the Covent Garden theatre until his retirement in 1817; he died in Lausanne. He was said to resemble Napoleon on a larger scale and Lawrence told Farington 'there had been no other such countenance upon the stage',[2] which probably accounts for the fact that there are more original portraits of him 'than any other actor [*whose career was launched by 1800*], except David Garrick and Sarah Siddons'.[3] A friend of both Bourgeois and Desenfans,[4] according to J.T. Smith it was Kemble who first suggested to Bourgeois the gift of his collection to Dulwich.[5]

In an undated letter of 1798 from Charlotte Street, Desenfans fulsomely congratulated Beechey on his knighthood and added: 'I hope as soon as you are at leisure you will go on with [the] Kemble portrait, so that I may have to boast I possess *the first picture* of Sir William Beechey'.[6] There is a version in the Garrick Club.[7]

Bourgeois painted Kemble twice as Coriolanus, RA 1793(98) and RA 1797(344), but Kemble offended him by giving one of these away for his portrait by Lawrence.[8] For Kemble's extensive iconography, see Walker 1985, i, pp.292–94, and Highfill, viii, pp.373–83.

1 An old ink label *verso*: *No.2/ Portrait of John Philip Kemble Esqre/ painted by Sir W. Beechey/ for Noel De Senfans Esqre / 1798* [the last line now covered over].
2 See Farington, v, p.1883; x, p.3691 (29 September 1802, 16 July 1810).
3 Highfill, viii, p.373.
4 As revealed in his diaries in the British Library, Add.MS 31972, and in Farington's Diary. Both Desenfans and Bourgeois left him legacies (but Bourgeois's Codicil was not executed); Kemble attended the Dulwich College dinner with Beechey in 1817. Desenfans' Will had enjoined Kemble 'to continue his friendship to the Executor of this my Will' (as printed in Cook 1926, p.300, and in previous editions of the Dulwich catalogue).
5 *Nollekens and his Times*, 1920, ii, p.315.
6 Roberts 1907, p.66.
7 Ashton 1997, no.377, p.210; acquired in 1835 from the Mathews collection.
8 Farington, vi, p.2410 (13 September 1804); Kemble gave it to the writer James Boaden. The Lawrence portrait was very probably the half-length now in a private collection (Garlick 1989, no.451a). Lawrence painted at least eight portraits of Kemble, one a full length as Coriolanus in 1798 (Guildhall AG; Garlick 1989, no.451b); for Lawrence's stage portraits of Kemble, see S. West, *Art History*, 14, 1991, pp.225–49.

Sir William Beechey (1753–1839)

DPG169 Charles Small Pybus

Canvas 77.7 x 64.8 unlined, with plaster scraped on the *verso* behind the figure; some bitumen crazing in the face and curtain; pentimenti on the stock, curtain and, radically, above his left shoulder; some retouching in the eyes and shadow of nose; slightly discoloured varnish; Hell 1949–53.

Brown eyes; wearing a dark blue-grey coat and white stock; a deep red curtain behind.

PROV.: Bourgeois Bequest 1811.

REF.: Britton 1813(85); Roberts 1907, pp.82–83n.

Charles Small Pybus (1766–1810), MP Dover 1790–1802, Lord of the Admiralty 1791–97 and of the Treasury 1797–1803, was, according to Beechey, 'of an irritable temper & was always on ill terms with one person or other ... very vain of his knowledge of pictures, but in reality knew nothing abt. Them';[1] Brydges thought his 'vanity and pretension ... ridiculous and offensive'.[2] In 1799 Pybus approved Desenfans' scheme for establishing national picture galleries (*Plan, Preceded by a Short Review of the Fine Arts ...*), and in 1804 was described as having 'been in picture partnership with Desenfans for many years'.[3] DPG169 shows his left shoulder dropped and cramped, and the execution of the head is rather slipshod.

An engraving of Pybus by C. Wilkin after Henry Edridge published in 1798 (and used as the frontispiece for Pybus's pretentious poem *The Sovereign*, published in 1800),[4] shows a similar head, but the body is turned more to the right, there is no background drape and the coat and stock differ in detail.[5]

The infant Pybus stands in his mother's lap in a family portrait by Nathaniel Dance (NG Victoria; Felton Bequest 2003) of c.1769.[6] A portrait attributed to Bourgeois of an infant Martha Pybus was recently recorded in a private collection.[7]

1 Farington, xi, p.3882 (19 February 1811).
2 S.E. Brydges, *Autobiography*, 1834, i, pp.33–34. And see note 5 below concerning his armigerous status.
3 Farington, iv, p.1139; vi, p.2372 (19 January 1799, 6 July 1804).
4 Folio; 41pp. text, 13pp. notes and 2pp. postcript. *GM*, lxx, ii, 1800, pp.854–55: 'Mr Urban's reviewers are not a match for a Lord of the Treasury in putting together so small a number of lines, on fashionable paper [*folio*], in fashionable type, with his *own portrait*, not that of his *hero* – for so *small* a price as *one guinea*, or, with the portrait, £1.11s.6d'. The poem was addressed to the Tsar Paul, but it appeared just after Russia had withdrawn from the Napoleonic wars (see *House of Commons 1790–1820*, iv, 1986, p.906).
5 With arms: *paly of six arg, and az. with bend vair, a crescent for difference*, i.e. a second son; crest a lion rampant; motto *QUALIS AB INCEPTO*. This coat of arms is not recorded in Burke's *General Armoury* [1884], but the motto was shared by four familes, none of them Pybus. Burke records different arms and motto granted to Pybus of Greenhill Grove near Barnet, Herts., in 1768.
6 See E. Lauze, 'A Nabob's Return, the Pybus conversation piece by Nathaniel Dance', *ABV43* (*Annual Journal of the National Gallery of Victoria*), 2003, pp.33–41 (the picture had been offered to the NPG on loan in 1885).
7 Note on file c.2000; identified as Martha Pybus (1788–1875) who m . William Cooke (d.1863); both are buried in Leckhampton, Cheltenham.

SIR FRANCIS BOURGEOIS (1753–1811)

DPG6 *Tiger Hunt*

Canvas 114.3 x 142.2 unlined; revived and revarnished 1870; two repaired tears; Hell 1950–55; cleaned 1989, but subsequently damaged upper left.

The mounted hunter on the left wears a white turban and a red coat with a red sash.

PROV.: [Bourgeois sale, Christie's, 3 May 1794, lot 16, *A Tiger Hunting*, bt. Thompson; Desenfans sale, Skinner & Dyke, 2nd day, 26 February 1795, lot 85, *A Tyger Hunting*] Bourgeois Bequest 1811.

EXH.: possibly RA 1787(435 *Hunting of the royal Tiger*).

REF.: Britton 1813(43).

SIR FRANCIS BOURGEOIS (1753–1811)

DPG100 *Cupid*

Canvas 60.6 x 81.9 unlined; in poor condition: a vertical tear 26 long by Cupid's right arm and a small hole in the sky centre right; pronounced overall craquelure, bituminous in the shadows; much discoloured varnish.

PROV.: Bourgeois Bequest 1811.

REF.: Britton 1813(113).

Sir Francis Bourgeois (1753–1811)

DPG135 *Landscape with Cattle (A Young Shepherd with his Flock)*

Canvas 79.4 x 107.9 including vertical strips, 0.9 wide, added on sides of stretcher; lined; in poor condition; said to have 'suffered greatly' in 1842;[1] edges of lining partially secured in 1994 (there is now celluloid tape round all the edges); pronounced overall craquelure, bituminous in the shadows; discoloured varnish.

Inscribed lower left: *AC* [...*p*?] (previously recorded as *A. Cuyp*); the shepherd is taking his shoe off.

PROV.: Bourgeois Bequest 1811.

REF.: Britton 1813(66).

The inscription shows the remains of a false Cuyp signature (possibly added by Bourgeois) and DPG135 was exhibited in the early 19th-century as by Cuyp.[2] Bourgeois was also alleged to have added foreground cattle in the Cuyp DPG60[3] (removed in 1998).

1 Jameson 1842, p.452.
2 P.G. Patmore, *Beauties of Dulwich Picture Gallery*, 1824, p.19, no.38.
3 As stated in Denning 1858 and 1859, no.76.

Sir Francis Bourgeois (1753–1811)

DPG149 *Helena brought before the Altar to be Sacrificed*

Canvas 102.6 x 60.9 lined; some surface scratching on the left; pentimenti on the eagle's tail and left wing; bituminous in the shadows; discoloured varnish; surface cleaned and lining repaired 1992.

Helen is fair-haired and wears white; the priest in brown with a white tunicle; a black eagle; the heifer behind the tripod on the left.

PROV.: Bourgeois Bequest 1811.

EXH.: RA 1805(188) with a lengthy quotation from *Bell's New Pantheon* ('we are told that Helena once, ... which was therefore offered in her stead', see below).

REF.: Britton 1813(45 *Jephthah* [sic] *Rash Vow: Old Man, young Woman; an Ox-Altar-Eagle with sword.*).

The subject is taken from *Bell's New Pantheon*:[1] Helena, daughter of Helen of Troy by Paris, was to be sacrificed to save the city of Sparta ('Lacedemon') from a plague, but an eagle took the knife and placed it on a heifer which was slain in her stead; 'this circumstance, however, is assigned by some to *another* Helena'.

1 *Bell's New Pantheon; or, Historical Dictionary of the Gods, Demi-Gods, Heroes, and Fabulous Personages of Antiquity* ..., 1790, i, p.376.

Sir Francis Bourgeois (1753–1811)

DPG294 Landscape with Cattle (Cows by a Lake)

Canvas 91.7 x 145.1 surface cleaned 1874; lined by Holder 1911; losses along bottom edge, a small patched damage and a small tear in the sky; bitumen craquelure in the water and bottom right foreground; much discoloured varnish (demonstrated by the rebate); the foreground group of cows was painted over another illegible feature.

PROV.: Bourgeois Bequest 1811.

EXH.: Mausoleum 1873.

REF.: Britton 1813(204); Waterfield 1989, p.45.

Particularly dependent on Cuyp, a painter much admired and imitated by Bourgeois (see DPG135 above)

Sir Francis Bourgeois (1753–1811)

DPG301 Funeral Procession of a White Friar

Canvas 131.5 x 206 lined, surface cleaned and varnished 1875; bitumen in the darks, scattered retouchings and discoloured varnish.

Described in Desenfans 1802 (ii, pp.210–12): ... on the fore-ground ..., to the right, four children of the choir, are preceding the procession, according to custom, dressed in the habits of white friars – the head shaved, the feet naked, and surplices on for the funeral ceremony; the youngest walks first, and is carrying the incense; but having advanced too far before the others, he stops to wait their rejoining him; the two who are following, hold each a lighted torch before the crucifix, with which the fourth advances, holding it raised with both hands. A few steps behind them, walks the chorister of the convent, with a book open in his hand, and his eyes raised to heaven, singing psalms with the children. Immediately after him, are four friars carrying the body of their deceased brother, over whom they have thrown a white cloth, but his head and feet remain uncovered; he is followed by the rest of the community, who walk two and two, in prayers and meditation ....

PROV.: Painted for the King of Poland;[1] Desenfans sale, Christie's, 3 May 1794, lot 82, bt. in; listed in the Desenfans collection 1795;[2] Desenfans sale, Skinner & Dyke, 16–18 March 1802, lot 179 (Desenfans 1802, ii, p.210); Desenfans 1804(68 for £100); Bourgeois Bequest 1811.

EXH.: RA 1793(12); Mausoleum 1873.

REF.: Britton 1813(80); Waterfield 1989, pp.43–44.

1 According to Desenfans 1802, i, p.11.
2 *Freemasons' Mag.*, May 1795.

SIR FRANCIS BOURGEOIS (1753–1811)

DPG308 *Sea Shore with Horse and Cart*

Canvas 91.7 x 146.7 unlined; broad craquelure in the foreground darks; much discoloured varnish; abraded upper left; large pentimento of trees above the cliff on the right; strip lined 1994.

A man lies down to drink water in the foreground.

PROV.: Bourgeois Bequest 1811.

REF.: Britton 1813(209 *Sand men carts and horses on Brighton coast*).

SIR FRANCIS BOURGEOIS (1753–1811)

DPG310 *Friar in Prayer*

Mahogany panel 16.5 x 12 arched top; the surface rather abraded and the grain prominent; discoloured varnish.

Wearing a black habit.

PROV.: Bourgeois Bequest 1811.

EXH.: Osterley Park 2002–

REF.: Britton 1813(269).

Bourgeois exhibited *A Friar expiring before the cross* RA 1798(74), possibly indicating a date for DPG310.

SIR FRANCIS BOURGEOIS (1753–1811)

DPG311 *Soldiers*

Mahogany panel 16.5 x 12 arched top; old worm holes in sky and in the foreground soldier's nose; small imperfections in the panel surface and some minor losses; rather abraded and the grain prominent; discoloured varnish.

The foreground figure wearing a red beret and sash and buckskin trousers; behind him a soldier in black armour.

PROV.: Bourgeois Bequest 1811.

EXH.: Osterley Park 2002–

REF.: Britton 1813(264).

Sir Francis Bourgeois (1753–1811)

DPG325 Landscape with Cattle (Cows on a Hillock by a Stream)

Canvas 101 x 127.5 lined; pronounced overall craquelure, bituminous in the shadows; pentimento of a large tree behind the trees on the right and the cattle on the mound; varnish much discoloured.

Prov.: Bourgeois Bequest 1811.

Exh.: Mausoleum 1873.

Ref.: Britton 1813(194); Waterfield 1989, p.45.

Waterfield compared the treatment of the trees with those in the landscape from the Desenfans/Bourgeois collection, then thought to be by Jan Both (DPG12).

Sir Francis Bourgeois (1753–1811)

DPG335 *Sea Shore with Rearing Horse*

Canvas 101 x 126.3[1] surface cleaned 1874; lined by Reeve 1922; pentimenti within the waves; discoloured varnish; surface cleaned 1989.

Prov.: Bourgeois Bequest 1811.

Exh.: Mausoleum 1873; Travellers' Club 1994 –.

Ref.: Britton 1813(326).

The most accomplished of the Bourgeois paintings at Dulwich. He exhibited a *Sea coast with figures* and *A sea view with horses and figures*, RA 1792(52, 136), perhaps indicating a date for DPG335.

1 Incorrect measurements given in Murray 1980 and Beresford 1998.

Sir Francis Bourgeois (1753–1811)

DPG342 *A Man holding a Horse*

Canvas 21 x 15.8 (uneven) laid on oak panel; flaking top centre left and a pronounced craquelure down the left hand side; discoloured varnish.

Brown horse; the man wears a yellow turban with a black plume.

Prov.: Bourgeois Bequest 1811.

Ref.: Britton 1813(332 as panel).

Sir Francis Bourgeois (1753–1811)

DPG344 *Tobias and the Angel*

Bevelled oak panel 20.3 x 20.8 circular; surface cleaned and thinly varnished 1873; prominent grain, the varnish much discoloured.

The angel in white, Tobias in red.

Prov.: Bourgeois Bequest 1811.

Ref.: Britton 1813(319).

From the Apocrypha, Tobit, 6 and 11: Tobias, with the archangel Raphael, bears the fish whose gall would cure the blindness of Tobit, his father. According to the 1813 inventory DPG344 was painted as the companion to the *Hagar & the Angel* by Pietro Francesco Mola (DPG32, now considered to be by a follower of Mola).

Sir Francis Bourgeois (1753–1811)

DPG459 *Religion in the Desert*

Canvas 99 x 121.5 unlined;[1] surface cleaned and varnished c.1874; in very poor condition, damaged by bombs 1944.

A white-robed figure, apparently a Dominican nun, with a chalice and a crown of thorns by her side.

Prov.: Bourgeois Bequest 1811; Mausoleum 1873.

Exh.: Mausoleum 1873.

Ref.: Britton 1813(29).

1 Canvas stamp *verso*: *Poole/High Holborn/London.*

SIR FRANCIS BOURGEOIS (1753–1811)

DPG460 Landscape with Soldiers

Canvas 63.8 x 75.8 unlined; surface cleaned and varnished 1874; local losses top left and top right; marked overall craquelure; discoloured varnish.

PROV.: Bourgeois Bequest 1811; Mausoleum 1873.

EXH.: Mausoleum 1873.

REF.: Britton 1813 (270).

SIR FRANCIS BOURGEOIS (1753–1811)

DPG461 Figures in a Landscape

Canvas 43.2 x 76.2; unlined; surface cleaned and varnished 1875 by the attendant (T.F. Hodgkins); apparently unfinished; prominent craquelure lifting in places; marked impasto by the boy's head; discoloured varnish.

A brown-haired young man dressed in brown watching two girls in white who read, one fair, the other brunette; behind them a sheep; a dog in the foreground.

PROV.: Bourgeois Bequest 1811.

EXH.: Hatchlands 2000; Osterley Park 2002–.

REF.: Britton 1813(342).

SIR FRANCIS BOURGEOIS (1753–1811)

DPG462 *Landscape with Cattle (A Cow Resting)*

Canvas 42.9 x 53 unlined; surface cleaned and varnished 1875; bitumen in foreground; marked craquelure in blue sky; much discoloured varnish.

PROV.: Bourgeois Bequest 1811.

EXH.: Hatchlands 2000; Osterley Park 2002–.

REF.: Britton 1813(337).

Particularly reminiscent of Cuyp.

SIR FRANCIS BOURGEOIS (1753–1811)

DPG463 *Cavalry in a Landscape*

Canvas 40 x 67.9 lined; scattered retouchings and losses: two repaired holes (by the foreground horse's head and on bottom edge to right of the bridge); discoloured varnish.

PROV.: Bourgeois Bequest 1811.

EXH.: RA 1810(97, *Detachment of Horse in the Costume of Charles I*).

REF.: Britton 1813(195); Waterfield 1989, p.44.

At the RA in 1810 this was compared with 'Falstaff's ragged regiment mounted on stolen cattle, and equipped in stolen accoutrements'.[1]

1 Ackermann's *Repository of Arts*, iii, 1810, i, p.368

Sir Francis Bourgeois (1753–1811)

DPG465 Self Portrait, after Beechey

Canvas[1] 76.2 x 60.9 unlined; in very poor condition, damaged by bombs 1944.

Grey eyes, powdered white hair; wearing a grey coat with the ribbon and medal of the Polish *Ordre du Mérite* (see DPG17, p.194).

PROV.: Presumably Bourgeois Bequest 1811 (but not listed in Britton 1813).

For Bourgeois (1753–1811), see p.87.

Copied from the Beechey portrait DPG17 (see p.194), or a version of it.

Other portraits of Bourgeois[2] in the collection are: Bourgeois DPG466 (below) and DPG464 (p.195); Northcote DPG172 (p.115); the marble bust by Prosperi S1 (p.252); the drawings by William Daniell after George Dance D2 (p.246) and by Paul Sandby D9 (p.250), and the miniature by Charles Hayter after Beechey M1 (p.243). Further portraits of Bourgeois were by Timothy Collopy, listed in the Desenfans collection in 1791[3] and engraved by W. Ridley (1804), and a miniature by William Court exhibited RA 1797(951). Bourgeois' profile head appears among *The Royal Academicians* by Henry Singleton (Royal Academy), engraved by G. Bestland 1802, but a statuette by Westmacott, bequeathed to Dulwich by Mrs Margaret Desenfans in 1813, remains untraced (see p.252). The miniature M6 was unconvincingly identified as Bourgeois (see p.245).

1 Stamped, *verso*, partly behind stretcher bar: ... *524 0 173* ...
2 See also Walker 1985, i, pp.60–61; ii, pls.134–35. A doubtful portrait attributed to Beechey was offered to the NPG in 1860 (sketch by Scharf, 25 July 1860, Trustees' Sketch Book, 4, f.68; NPG archive), and an enigmatic unlettered mezzotint in the NPG archive (extra-illustrated *DNB*, vi, p.19). Bourgeois' name does not appear in CS.
3 Desenfans 1791–92.

Sir Francis Bourgeois (1753–1811)

DPG466 Self Portrait, after Beechey

Canvas1 76.5 x 64[1] unlined; considerable fold over on the left-hand vertical edge; retouching in cheek and waistcoat lapel.

Grey eyes, powdered white hair; wearing a grey coat with the ribbon and medal of the Polish *Ordre du Mérite* (see DPG17, p.194).

PROV.: Presumably Bourgeois Bequest 1811 (but not listed in Britton 1813).

A second copy after Beechey; see DPG465 above.

1 Stamped *verso*: *2 36.5 7.*

Sir Francis Bourgeois (1753–1811)

DPG467 William Tell

Canvas 76.8 x 110.2 lined; surface cleaned and varnished by the attendant (T.F. Hodgkins) 1875; heavily ironed surface; several old tears and blanched retouchings; pentimento on the rider's right arm; strip-lined and cleaned 1980.

Gessler dressed in a dull red costume; the composition reads as an elaborate sketch rather than a finished work.

Prov.: Bourgeois Bequest 1811.

Exh.: taken from the Mausoleum in 1875; returned from Alleyn's 1931; Dulwich College.

Ref.: Britton 1813(287).

The subject, doubtless of particular appeal to Bourgeois with his Swiss descent, illustrates the fourteenth-century legend of William Tell obeying governor Gessler's order to shoot an apple from his son's head, which he did, before killing the governor and liberating Switzerland from Austrian rule (Schiller's tragedy *Wilhelm Tell* appeared in 1804).

attributed to SIR FRANCIS BOURGEOIS (1753–1811)

DPG488 called Noel Desenfans on Horseback

Canvas 119.7 x 101 lined;[1] repaired, surface cleaned and varnished by the attendant (T.F. Hodgkins) 1875; the paint surface is generally very thin; old tears through horse's near back foot, to right of his tail, and in the saddle, and scattered small losses; pentimento of trees beneath the sky (from the clouds top left to within 15 of the right-hand edge); Hell 1952–55; cleaned 1994.

Faint traces of initials [*F.*]*B.* lower left; the rider has dark hair and brown eyes; he wears a black hat with gold piping, a red coat, white waistcoat, buckskin breeches and black boots; light blue saddlecloth with gold trim and a red border; the horse's head-piece includes a red rosette.

PROV.: [possibly Desenfans 1790–91 as *Portrait of an Officer – Bourgeois*] Bourgeois Bequest 1811.

EXH.: Mausoleum; Travellers' Club 1994 –

REF.: Britton 1813(273), see below.

For Desenfans (1744–1807), see pp.87, 114

A weak, reworked picture of uncertain status. Possibly an early painting by Bourgeios, c.1773–5(?), of his patron Desenfans 'disguised' as an army officer, listed in Desenfans' collection in 1790–91 as *Portrait of an Officer* by Bourgeois (see above), although it is odd that the sitter is not then identified. Possibly the picture described in Britton 1813, no.273: *Portrait of N Desenfans Esq on Horse* [by] *Bourgeois* [130 x 158 including frame] (but drawn as an upright picture). Comparison with portraits by Northcote DPG28 (p.114) and the anonymous DPG503 (p.127) does not altogether rule out the identification of Desenfans.

The faint initials recorded above emerged after cleaning in 1994; according to one obituary Bourgeois had been instructed 'while a child, in some rudiments of Painting by a Foreigner of inconsiderable merit as a Painter of Horses'.[2]

1 Stretcher stamped *W. Morrill/Liner.*
2 *GM*, lxxxi, ii, 1811, p.186.

SIR ANTHONY VAN DYCK (1599–1641)

DPG194 *Venetia, Lady Digby, on her Deathbed*

Canvas 73.5 x 81.8 lined; in 1859 the 'general tone was very cold & blue with high lights that have changed yellow';[1] revived and varnished 1871; the surface is generally worn with scattered retouchings and the necklace now appears incomplete; a large L-shaped tear in the sheet below the right breast; a horizontal grey band top centre cuts across the corner of the pillow; old vertical crease-marks pressed down during relining. Hell 1948–49; surface cleaned 1984 and cleaned 1997.

Auburn hair;[2] blue curtains round the bed, pale rose petals on the sheet in the foreground.

PROV.: [Sir Kenelm Digby; late in the 17th century Aubrey noted that in London 'at Mr Rose's, a jeweller in Henrietta-street in Covent Garden, is an excellent piece of hers, drawne after she was newly dead';[3] possibly Alexis Livernet sale, Christie's, 28 May 1806, lot 34, Van Dyck, *A Memento Mori* [4]] Bourgeois Bequest 1811.

EXH.: Leeds 1949–53; *Collection for a King*, Washington DC, Los Angeles, 1985–86(7); *Death, Passion and Politics* 1995(31); *Obras Maestras*, Madrid, Bilbao, 1999(24); *Van Dyck*, Antwerp, London, 1999 (69); *Rembrandt to Gainsborough*, Houston TX, Louisville KY, 1999–2000(77).

REF.: Britton 1813(343); Smith 1831, p.65, under no.222; E. Schaeffer, *Van Dyck*, Klassiker der Kunst, 1909, p.458; G.A. Waterfield in *Collection for a King*, 1985, pp.54, 56–57; N. Llewellyn, *The Art of Death*, 1991, pp.31–32; J. Egerton in *Van Dyck*, Antwerp, London, 1999, pp.251-52; O. Millar in *Van Dyck* 2004, p.506(IV.97).

Venetia, Lady Stanley (1600–33), daughter of Sir Edward Stanley (grandson of the 3rd Earl of Derby) and Lucy Percy (daughter of the 7th Earl of Northumberland), had had affairs with Sir Edmund Wyld and the 4th Earl of Dorset before marrying in 1625 the catholic Sir Kenelm Digby, Kt. (1603–65), who was much in love with her. They became prominent in cultured Court circles and she was said to have 'redeemed her honour by her strick't living' after her marriage; there were two surviving sons. On the night of 30 April–1 May 1633 she died quite unexpectedly in her bed. Digby, beside himself with grief, wrote copiously of his misfortune[5] and had casts taken of her hands, feet and face.[6]

Within two days Van Dyck was painting her as she lay. Digby received the picture in seven weeks, as he described to his brother in a letter of 19 June 1633:

> As I sate this morning meditating deeply on my blessed wife's death … her old servant brought in a picture and sett it downe before me … me thought I saw that Angell in her owne shape and substance lying in the same posture as I found her in, about the same hour this day is seven weekes … It was her picture so rarely made as not the eye but the touch onely could assure one whither it were a solide substance or no. …
>
> It is the Master peece of all the excellent ones that ever Sir Antony Vandike made, who drew her the second day after she was dead, & hath expressed with admirable art every little circumstance about her, as well for the exact manner of her lying, as for the likenesse of her face; & hath altered or added nothing about it, excepting onely a rose lying upon the hemme of the sheete, whose leaves being pulled from the stalke in the full beauty of it, & seeming to wither apace, even whiles you looke upon it, is a fitt Embleme to express the state her bodie then was in … When we came in, wee found her almost cold and stiffe; yet her blood was not so setteled but that our rubbing of her face brought a little seeming color into her pale cheekes, which continued there till she was folded up in her last sheete and Sir Anthony Van Dike hath expressed excellently well in his picture This is the onely constant companion I now have .. it standeth al day over aginst my chaire & table .. & att night when I goe into my chamber I sett it close by my beds side, & by the faint light of a candle, me thinkes I see her dead indeed; for that maketh painted colors looke more pale & ghastly than they doe by day light. …[7]

Aubrey hinted she might have been poisoned by her husband's viper wine which he had her drink to preserve her health and beauty,[8] and the King was said to have ordered an autopsy.[9] Perhaps the extravagance of Digby's mourning cannot altogether erase suspicion of blame, but there were no hints of mischief in the many elegies written on her death by poets of the Court circle (including Ben Jonson's *Eupheme*; 'What's left a Poet, now his Muse is gone?').[10]

In DPG194 the curtains, particularly on the right, are now quite lifeless (and may not have been painted by Van Dyck himself, as Millar has commented). Their original modelling and colour are better seen in a fine miniature copy by Peter Oliver (Sherborne Castle), inscribed *A.D.1633 AET.32.M.4.D.12*,[11] which shows the necklace with inset stones (would she have slept wearing a necklace?).[12] Copies of DPG194 are at Althorp,[13] differing in showing a double row of pearls, a simpler description of the pillow and sheets, a more emphatic rose with leaves, and different folds in the right-hand curtains; this was copied as an oval enamel by Henry Bone (Kingston Lacy).

Peter Oliver also made separate copies of the figures of Digby and his wife from Van Dyck's family piece in 1632 (see note 19). Two bronze busts of Lady Digby, one attributed to and one signed by George Larson, are in private collections,[14] probably unconnected with the monument Digby erected to his wife in Christ Church, Newgate, which was crowned by a copper gilt bust and destroyed in the Great Fire of 1666.[15] There is a much earlier miniature of Lady Digby by Oliver, her hair loose, at Burghley.[16]

Kenelm Digby, diplomat, naval commander and a learned, well-travelled man, was a discerning patron of Van Dyck 'with whom he had a mutual sympathy of mind and spirit'.[17] He acquired several of his pictures; besides other works now untraced,[18] he sat with his wife and two of their sons in 1632,[19] commissioned an allegorical whole-length portrait of Venetia as Prudence (completed posthumously),[20] and there are two portraits of Digby of c.1633 and c.1638 reflecting the philosopher and the soldier.[21]

1 G. Scharf, 8 November 1859 (Sketch Book, 57, f.23; NPG archive).
2 J. Aubrey, *Brief Lives and other selected writings*, ed. A. Powell, 1949, pp.46, 47–48, later described her as 'a most beautifull desirable creature' with 'a most lovely and sweet turn'd face [and] delicate darke browne hair.…Her face, a short ovall; darke-browne eiebrowe about which much sweeteness …The colour of her cheeks was just that of a damask rose, which is neither too hott not too pale. She was of a just stature, not very tall'.
3 Aubrey, *op. cit.* (at note 2), p.49.
4 First suggested by Egerton (see REF.), but the price then fetched, 12 shillings, was surprisingly low.
5 Forty-five of his letters with five 'meditations' were collected in a ms volume, 'In Praise of Venetia'; twenty-two were published by V. Gabrieli in the *National Library of Wales Journal*, ix, 1956, 2, pp.113–48; 4, pp.440–62; x, 1957, 1, pp.81–105; see also V. Gabrieli, *Sir Kenelm Digby, un inglese italianato*, Rome, 1957, pp.237–83. Further Digby lamentations appear in Digby's *Private Memoirs*, 1827, and *Loose Fantasies*, 1968.
6 Aubrey, *op cit.* (see note 2), p.48.
7 V. Gabrieli, *Sir Kenelm Digby*, 1957, pp.246–48 (from 'In Praise of Venetia').
8 Aubrey, *op cit.* (see note 2), pp.48–49. M. Foster (*ODNB*) states she died of a cerebral haemorrhage.
9 C. Gittings in *Death, Passion and Politics* 1995, p.60; *HMC Finch*, i, 1913, p.61.
10 A MS volume of such memorial verses is in the British Library (MS Add 30.259); see *Death, Passion and Politics* 1995, no.54 and pp.65–67. For the contemporary rivalry between painting and poetry, see, for example, C. Pace, 'Delineated Lives', *Word & Image*, 2, i, 1986, p.10, and G. Parry, 'Van Dyck and the Caroline Poets' in *Van Dyck 350*, Washington DC, 1994, pp.257–59.
11 Mounted in a black enamel frame with, engraved on the back, an armillary sphere; the inscription gives her age at her death, 32 years, 4 months, 12 days; see *Death, Passion and Politics* 1995(32), illus. p.76.
12 As Egerton (see REF.) queried.
13 K. Garlick, *Wal. Soc.*, XLV, 1976, p.24, no.167; listed in 1746 as 'after Van Dyck'. Jameson 1842, p.482, believed it was the original, as did Schaeffer (see REF. above) in 1909.
14 *Death, Passion and Politics* 1995(41, 42); no.42 was exhibited *British Portraits*, RA, 1956–57(169).

15 *Ibid.*, pp.110–12. In 1675–6 Aubrey saw a bust of Venetia on a stall at the Golden Crosse, a brasier's shop in Newgate Street, 'but the fire had gott-off the gilding' and, he said, it was melted down; Aubrey, *op. cit.* (at note 2) p.49.

16 *Death, Passion and Politics* 1995(27), illus. p.76, as c.1620.

17 G.P. Bellori 1672; translation as quoted in *Death, Passion and Politics* 1995, p.32, and *Van Dyck* 2004, p.504.

18 See O. Millar in *Death, Passion and Politics* 1995, p.35; *Van Dyck* 2004, p.268 (under III.29).

19 Private Collection; *Death, Passion and Politics* 1995(23); *Van Dyck* 2004, pp.503–04(IV.94).

20 Palazzo Reale, Milan, a version in the NPG (5727); *Van Dyck* 2004, pp.507–10(IV.98 & 99).

21 Private Collection and NPG (486); *Van Dyck* 2004, pp.505–06(IV.95 & 96).

Peter Oliver, *Venetia, Lady Digby, after Van Dyck*,
watercolour on vellum, 6.7 x 6.7 cms., 1633
By courtesy of John K. Wingfield Digby
Photograph: Photographic Survey, Courtauld Institute of Art

Sir Anthony Van Dyck (1599–1641)

DPG170 George Digby, 2nd Earl of Bristol

Canvas 103.2 x 83.2 lined; the vigorously-painted informal drapery appears to have lost a pink glaze (as suggested in the rebate area behind the frame); black underdrawing visible within the cloak; pentimenti in the collar, drapery and above his right arm; minor retouchings in his right cheek, eyes and hand; cleaned 1995.

Light brown hair, fair moustache, dark blue eyes; wearing a pink satin doublet with S-shaped slashings and a soft white collar beneath a deep red drape.

Prov.:[1] Richard Hulse, Blackheath (d.1805); his sale, Christie's, 22 March 1806, lot 79 as Philip, Earl of Pembroke ('painted with Dignity and fine execution') bt. Desenfans; Bourgeois Bequest 1811.

Exh.: RA schools 1836, 1840, 1847, 1852, 1854, 1863, 1866, 1877, 1878, 1881, 1892, 1896, 1901, 1913, 1919;[2] Aberystwyth 1945(41 as 5th Earl of Pembroke); National Gallery 1947(14 as Bedford); Leeds 1947–53(14); *Flemish Art*, RA, 1953–54(162 as ?2nd Earl of Bristol, probably c.1635); *Kolekcja dla Króla*, Warsaw, 1992(9); *Death, Passion and Politics* 1995(7); *Obras Maestras*, Madrid, Bilbao, 1999(25); *Rembrandt to Gainsborough*, Houston TX, Louisville KY, 1999–2000(78).

Ref.: Britton 1813(99, *Earl of Pembroke Kit cat Vandyck*); Smith 1831, p.146, no.521 (as Pembroke); G. Glück, *Van Dyck*, Klassiker der Kunst, 1931, p.479 (as Pembroke); O. Millar in *Van Dyck* 2004, p.503(IV.93).

The identity of the sitter had been much discussed (see note 1), but the resemblance to George Digby in Van Dyck's great double portrait of him with his brother-in-law, William Russell, 1st Duke of Bedford, c.1636 at Althorp (see note 7) leaves little room for doubt. In DPG170 Digby appears a little older, suggesting a date of c.1638. His pose was repeated in Van Dyck's *1st Duke of Bedford as William, Lord Russell* of c.1640 (Clifton Castle).[3]

George Digby, 2nd Earl of Bristol (1612–77), only son of John Digby (created Earl of Bristol in 1622), and a cousin of Sir Kenelm Digby (see DPG194 above), married in 1632 Anne Russell, daughter of the 4th Earl of Bedford; an active Royalist, he was MP for Dorset 1640, Secretary of State 1643–45, and fought at Edgehill; created Baron Digby in 1641 and in 1652 succeeded his father as 2nd Earl; KG 1653 (but not installed until 1661); he fought with the French 1651–56 and was re-appointed Secretary of State in 1657, an office he resigned on his conversion to Catholicism in 1659; his withdrawal from Court 1662–67 followed a disagreement with Clarendon who described him as 'a gracefull and beautifull person ... aequall to a very good parte in the greatest affayre, but the unfittest man alive to conducte it, having an ambition and vanity superiour to all his other parts ...'.[4] In DPG170 Van Dyck portrays the informal, sensitive Digby.

Many copies exist; at Coleshill, Woburn, formerly at Somerley, and in private collections in New York and Kansas; others were sold Christie's, 12 December 1958, lot 128, and 1 June 1962, lot 74; Christie's, New York, 23 May 2000, lot 283, and Sotheby's, 19 March 2003, lot 15.[5] There is a drawing by William Brocas (c.1794–1868) in a sketchbook in the National Library of Ireland (cf. DPG 201 below). A variant, in armour and wearing the Garter, sold Christie's, 23 April 1965, lot 23.

Other portraits of Digby include those attributed to Johann Priwitzer c.1627 (Sherborne),[6] and the Van Dyck whole length with his brother-in-law William, Lord Russell, at Althorp.[7] Two later three-quarter lengths in armour are by Lely c.1660[8] and attributed to Justus van Egmont c.1653 (Royal Armouries, London).[9]

1 Provenance established by Millar in *Van Dyck* 2004. Previously confused with a whole length Van Dyck of the *Earl of Pembroke* in the Reynolds sale, 14 March 1795, lot 43, and the Bryan sale, Coxe, 17 May 1798, 3rd day, lot 2, bt. Desenfans. And with the Van Dyck in the Desenfans sales at Christie's of 8 April ff. 1786, lot 208 (kit-cat of *Russell, Earl of Bedford*) and 2nd day, 14 July 1786, lot 44 (*Lord John Russell, 3rd son to the Duke of Bedford*). None of these sales is cited in *Van Dyck* 2004.

2 One of the copies then made was with G. Remus, Quebec, in 1995, with *verso* a label: *Miss Jacobs School of Art Royal Academy Burlington House.*

3 *Van Dyck* 2004, pp.442–43 (IV.20).

4 Clarendon (in D. Nichol Smith, *Characters*, 1918, p.120). Malcolm Rogers wrote how DPG170 not only showed an intensely reflective characterization of the head, but the hand seemed to stress 'the strength and privacy of his emotions' (*Kolekcja dla Króla*, Warsaw, 1992, no.9).

5 A version was offered to the NPG by Henry Eyre in 1877 as school of Van Dyck (sketch by G. Scharf, 16 February 1877; Trustees' Sketch Book, 23, f.9; NPG archive), Scharf then doubting the identity as the 5th Earl of Pembroke.

6 Illus. *Death, Passion and Politics* 1995, no.14.

7 O. Millar in *Van Dyck* 2004, pp.501–02(IV.92) also recording a drawing copied from the figure of Digby in the British Museum (1923 H.64).

8 A version from an American private collection illus. *Death, Passion and Politics* 1995, p.19.

9 *Death, Passion and Politics* 1995, no.17.

manner of SIR ANTHONY VAN DYCK (1599–1641)

DPG201 *Portrait of a Lady*

Canvas 118.2 x 93 lined on to a slightly larger canvas, the original edges cut; in poor condition; in 1831 the face and bosom were 'much injured by cleaning';[1] in 1842 it had 'suffered terribly';[2] in 1858 it was 'terribly injured by cleaning and scrubbing';[3] in 1867 Scharf observed that 'the hands dress & figure admirably painted in Van Dyck's richest & most mellow colours. The face & bosom poor flat & dirty. The hands modelled & shaded with his richest slaty grey & mulberry[?] browns'.[4] Revived and varnished 1870; many darkened retouchings; scattered losses, a large repaired tear in the left background and blistering down the left edge; discoloured varnish; partially cleaned by Hell 1955.

Dark hair, blue eyes; wearing a red dress with slashed sleeves and a white chemise, dull ochre scarf; a steel-blue curtain behind.

PROV.: Bourgeois Bequest 1811.

REF.: Britton 1813(90); Smith 1831, p.147, no.522 as Van Dyck, the Countess of Pembroke; J. Guiffrey, *Van Dyck*, 1882, p.274, no.753 as *la comtesse de Pembroke*; E. Schaeffer, *Van Dyck*, Klassiker der Kunst, 1909, p.460 as school of Van Dyck, *Lady Penelope Herbert.*

A much damaged portrait, identified between 1831 and 1926 as Penelope Naunton (1620–1647?) who married secondly in 1639 the 5th Earl of Pembroke. The identification was presumably made since the sitter was supposed to be the wife of the sitter in DPG170 (above), then identified as the Earl,[5] but her portrait by Van Dyck at Wilton[6] bears no resemblance to DPG201. The small pencil copy by William Brocas (c.1794–1868) in a sketchbook in the National Library of Ireland (cf. DPG170 above) was presumably made as of the Countess of Pembroke.

1 Smith 1831, p.147, no.522.
2 Jameson 1842, p.464.
3 Denning 1858, no.250.
4 G. Scharf, 1 March 1867 (Sketch Book, 78, f.61; NPG archive).
5 Denning 1858, no.250, was a little reluctant: 'by some it is supposed to represent the Countess of Pembroke ... [Vandyke] was apparently assisted by one of his pupils', but Sparkes & Richter 1880 recorded that 'Mr G. Scharf takes this to be the first wife of the above Earl Philip [of Pembroke].' After seeing a portrait of the Countess at Highclere (where described as Hanneman after Van Dyck) Scharf became more hesitant over the identity, calling her 'probably Penelope Naunton' (10 March 1878; Sketch Book, 96, f.78; NPG archive; see *Van Dyck* 2004, p.537, under IV.138)
6 *Van Dyck* 2004, pp.574–75 (IV.187).

THOMAS GAINSBOROUGH (1727–88)

DPG66 *Philippe-Jacques De Loutherbourg*

Canvas 76.5 x 63.2 double-lined, the surface heavily ironed and abraded; there are losses in the upper right quarter and a repaired tear runs in the lower left area, from the arm on the right to the left edge, perhaps the 'slight damage' repaired 'by the attendant' in 1870; pentimenti on the shoulders; surface cleaned 1980.

Brown eyes (showing a slight squint), grey wig; wearing a brown coat with a reddish waistcoat; his right elbow rests on his sketchbook; the mouth has been described as in two positions;[1] a green curtain behind.

PROV.: Desenfans 1790–91; Bourgeois Bequest 1811.

EXH.: RA 1778(408); RA schools 1926, 1933; Aberystywth 1946(19); NG 1947(21); Leeds 1947–53(21); *Gainsborough*, Tate, 1980 (122), and Paris 1981(50); *Collection for a King*, Washington DC, Los Angeles, 1985–86(8); *Nest of Nightingales* 1988(14.6); *Kolekcja dla Króla*, Warsaw, 1992(10); *The Young Gainsborough*, National Gallery, 1997(29); *Gainsborough*, Ferrara, 1998(20); *Obras Maestras*, Madrid, Bilbao, 1999(41); *Rembrandt to Gainsborough*, Houston TX, Louisville KY, 1999–2000(89); *Gainsborough*, London, Washington DC, Boston MA, 2002–03(53); *Sensation and Sensibility: Viewing Gainsborough's Cottage Door*, New Haven and San Marino, 2005–06 (n.n.).

REF.: Britton 1813(88); Waterhouse 1953, p.71; Waterhouse 1958, no.456; L. Stainton in *Collection for a King*, 1985, pp.58, 60; Ingamells 2004, pp.140–41.

Philippe-Jacques De Loutherbourg (1740–1812), the French landscape painter (see DPG 297 and DPG339 below) and scenic designer, settled in London in 1771 (with an introduction to Garrick). Bourgeois was his pupil c.1775–76 and several of De Loutherbourg's canvases appeared in the various Desenfans sales. De Loutherbourg also became a friend of Gainsborough (probably through Garrick) who came to admire his *eidu-phusikon* ('sequences of moving scenery on a model stage accompanied by dramatic sound effects and music by Dr Arne, an entertainment which took London by storm in 1781'), but was less fond of his lurid scene painting and bright stage lighting.[2]

DPG66, exhibited in 1778, is an intimate study of a friend, the urgency of the pose enhanced by the quick, sure touch of the execution.[3] In the nineteenth century it was duly criticized for lack of finish, Passavant finding it 'very insipid'[4] and Mrs Jameson 'very feebly coloured.'[5] A pencil and wash copy is in the National Library of Wales (13558176).[6] The rapid chalk sketch by De Loutherbourg of Gainsborough in the Yale Center for British Art (B1986.29.61) may have been made at the same time as DPG66.

For De Loutherbourg's iconography, see Ingamells 2004, pp.140–41.

1 '... the result of an ambiguity in the angle at which the face is depicted' (A. Asfour & P. Williamson, *Eighteenth-century Studies*, 31/4, 1998, p.420).
2 J. Hayes ed., *The Letters of Thomas Gainsborough*, 2001, p.106.
3 See Asfour & Williamson (at note 1), pp.419–20.
4 Passavant 1836, p.70.
5 Jameson 1842, p.460.
6 Illus. Manners and Williamson, *Zoffany*, 1920, p.12, as *Garrick* by Zoffany. Hugh Belsey has suggested an attribution to George Dance.

CORNELIUS JOHNSON (1593–1661)

DPG80 Portrait of a Lady in White

Canvas 73.3 x 54.6 lined; very faded, with many retouchings visible in flesh areas and dress; the figure cleaned but not the background; Hell 1953–55; the lower right-hand side of the lining relaminated 1990.

Blue-grey eyes, brown hair; wearing a double pearl earring, a pearl necklace, and a white dress with a purple sash.

PROV.: Bourgeois Bequest 1811.

EXH.: Tredegar House 1991–.

REF.: Britton 1813(345 as Van Dyck); Collins Baker 1912, ii, p.115; A. Finberg, *Wal. Soc.*, x, 1922, p.31, no.91 ('brown and opaque varnish which is cracked obscures the work').

Denning 1858 and Sparkes 1876 recorded an attribution to Van Dyck, suggesting DPG80 and DPG89 were among the three unidentified 'Van Dyck' portraits in Britton 1813 (as listed above). Collins Baker and Finberg proposed the attribution to Johnson with the date c.1639, later accepted by Malcolm Rogers.[1] It may be observed that in comparison with DPG89 below DPG80 is austere and the drawing weak, particularly of her left shoulder.[2]

1 Letter of 16 June 1997 on file.
2 Alastair Laing, for example, has raised some doubts concerning the attribution, suggesting van Leemput as a possible alternative (letter of 9 June 1991 on file).

CORNELIUS JOHNSON (1593–1661)

DPG89 Portrait of a Lady in Blue

Canvas 75.8 x 62.8; described in 1859 as 'in a terrible condition';[1] lined 1875; very faded in the face with numerous losses and some blistering in the background; hair retouched; Hell 1953–55; surface cleaned 1990.

Grey eyes, light brown hair; wearing a pearl necklace and a double pearl earring, a dark blue dress with gilt and pearl ornament, with yellow-brown sleeves and a golden-brown drape.

PROV.: Bourgeois Bequest 1811.

EXH.: Tredegar House 1991–.

REF.: Britton 1813(120 as anon., 3 x 2.9 [91.5 x 84]); Collins Baker 1912, ii, p.115; A. Finberg, *Wal. Soc.*, x, 1922, p.31, no.90 ('Traces of signature C.J. partly visible ... In bad condition through neglect').

Collins Baker and Finberg (who read traces of a signature invisible today) first suggested the attribution to Johnson with the date of c.1639, later accepted by Malcolm Rogers.[2]

1 Denning 1859, no.134.
2 Letter of 16 June 1997 on file.

Philippe-Jacques De Loutherbourg (1740–1812)

DPG297 *Landscape with Cattle*

Canvas 57 x 70.5 unlined; general fine craquelure revealing a light ground; retouching along the bottom edge; a small damage in the centre in the overhanging rock; discoloured varnish; Hell 1952–53.

Signed lower left: *P J de Loutherbourg 176*[7 or 5].

Prov.: Bourgeois Bequest 1811.

Exh.: *Obras Maestras*, Madrid, Bilbao, 1999(46).

Ref.: Britton 1813(272).

PHILIPPE-JACQUES DE LOUTHERBOURG (1740–1812)

DPG339 Landscape with Cattle and Figures

Canvas 70.8 x 97.2 lined and cleaned by Holder 1911; surface cleaned and thinly varnished 1873; strong craquelure in sky and trees; Hell 1953; cleaned 2002.

Signed lower left: *P.J. De Loutherb[ourg]*.

PROV.: Bourgeois Bequest 1811.

EXH.: [Paris Salon 1765(65), see below]; *France in the 18th century*, RA, 1968–69(457); *Kolekcja dla Króla*, Warsaw, 1992(16); *Obras Maestras*, Madrid, Bilbao, 1999(47).

REF.: Britton 1813(206).

Possibly the picture briefly described by Diderot in the 1765 Paris Salon, no.65.[1]

1 J. Seznec & J. Adhémar, *Diderot Salons*, ii, 1765, 1960, pp.39, fig.65, 171, proposed DPG339 may have been the exhibited picture *'où on voit des bestiaux qu'un pâtre mène abreuver au ruisseau qui coule sur le devant, et don't les eaux murmurent contre des cailloux jaunâtres'*

studio of PETER MONAMY (1681–1749)

DPG298 A Calm

Canvas 61.5 x 75.9 lined by Holder 1912; in 1859 described as much rubbed and much painted on;[1] an old Z-shaped tear in the sky centre right; the surface is much abraded, particularly the small boats in the centre; Hell 1953.

Galliot with man-of-war's pendant and a jackstaff at the end of the bowsprit like a man-of-war; a man on the galliot's gaff apparently disentangling the fly of the pendant which is foul of a part of the peak halyard with chafing gear on it.[2]

PROV.: Bourgeois Bequest 1811.

EXH.: Whitechapel Fine Art Exhibition, 1885;[3] Aberystwyth 1947(4 as Monamy); Osterley Park 2002–.

ENG.: R. Cockburn 1820.

REF.: Britton 1813(234 as Vandevelde); M.S. Robinson, *The Paintings of Willem van de Velde the Elder and Younger*, 1990. ii, pp.708–09, no.95 (4) as Monamy shop.

Described as Van de Velde until 1876, but already in 1859 Denning (see note 1) had remarked that 'if Willem van de Velde ever touched it, little of his handiwork remains'. Robinson considered it a Monamy shop production of c.1720 related to the picture by William van de Velde the younger of 1691 in the collection of the Baroness Bentinck (on loan to the Kunstmuseum, Düsseldorf, in 1977).[4]

A poorer version of DPG298 was in the collection of Erik Ekegren, Malmö, in 1984.

1 Denning 1859, no.92.
2 This nautical description taken from M.S. Robinson (see REF.).
3 Label *verso;* catalogue untraced.
4 M.S. Robinson, *The Paintings of Willem van de Velde the Elder and Younger*, 1990, ii, pp.707–08, no.95(1).

JAMES NORTHCOTE (1746–1831)

DPG28 Noel Desenfans

Canvas 73.3 x 60.9 oval, lined; Hell 1949–53; the painted surface is folded round the stretcher, suggesting it might once have been a square composition; in 1813 it was framed with an arched top, see below; darkened retouchings in the shadow of the nose, forehead and cheek.

Brown eyes, white hair; wearing a blue coat and red waistcoat.

PROV.: Bourgeois Bequest 1811.

ENG.: S. Freeman 1809, 1810 (as an oval: *Monthly Mirror* and *Memoirs of the late Noel Desenfans* 1810).

REF.: Britton 1813(346 *Portrait of Desenfans, at Mr Westmacotts, Northcote*, as an arch-topped composition); Gwynne 1898, no.305; J. Simon, 'The Account Book of James Northcote', *Wal. Soc.*, LVIII, 1996, p.66, no.320 ('pictures painted in the year 1796').

For Desenfans (1744–1807) see p.87.

In 1810 Desenfans was remembered as 'of the middle size, with a well proportioned form. His features were regular, and strongly expressive of benevolence and penetration. There was a spirit and vivacity in his eyes that strikingly resembled those of Mr Garrick. His manners were courteous, affable, and attractive, the natural effect of the urbanity of his disposition'.[1] When Passavant saw DPG28 in 1831 he thought it 'an excellent portrait'.[2] It was copied in miniature by Charles Hayter (see M2, p.243).

Other portraits of Desenfans were painted by Bourgeois (DPG488, p.103) and an unknown artist (DPG503, p.127), and drawn by Paul Sandby (D9, p.250); there is a bust by Prosperi (S2, p.252), but a statuette by Westmacott remains untraced (see p.252). A 'Head in crayons, with glass before it of Desenfans 2 x 1.8', although listed in Britton 1813 (291), remains untraced. An untitled engraving of c.1800 by W. Bond after W.P.J. Lodder, with a coat of arms and motto *Attached*, has been doubtfully identified as Desenfans.[3]

1 *Memoirs of the late Noel Desenfans* ..., 1810, p.20.
2 Passavant 1836, p.70.
3 NPG archive, with pencil inscription *Desenfans*. Desenfans was not armigerous (see p.87n6).

Pencil sketch of DPG172 by George Scharf, 1867 (National Portrait Gallery, London)

Photograph of DPG172 by Emery Walker, c.1910 (National Portrait Gallery, London)

JAMES NORTHCOTE (1746–1831)

DPG172 Sir Francis Bourgeois

Canvas 76.2 x 63.5 unlined;[1] the background much retouched (see below); smaller retouchings in the face and in his left upper arm; a small tear in the left tacking edge; pentimenti on his right shoulder and the collar; repainting above the head to the left (see below) and at the right on the arm; Hell 1949–1953.

Brown eyes, grey powdered hair; wearing a red coat with black fur trim; palette and brushes bottom left (the colours arranged yellow, red, blue and white) and a drawing in his right hand.

PROV.: Bourgeois Bequest 1811.

EXH.: RA 1794(65).

ENG.: S.W. Reynolds 12 July 1794; W. Leney 1795 (*Freemasons' Mag.*; oval, making the hair look more detailed, and fur collar more defined); a reduced version 1832 (*Library of Fine Arts*).

REF.: Britton 1813(91); Gwynn 1898, no.301 (as 1795).

For Bourgeois (1753–1811) see pp.87, 101.

Although the head was engraved in 1794 and 1795 as now seen, a sketch of 1867 and a photograph of c.1910 show the hair much restricted in width and his left ear visible,[2] so that the head somewhat resembled that by Beechey (DPG17, p.194). The disturbed area around the head betrays this alteration.

1 'Holder reported for lining 1911' but apparently not done.

2 Sketch by G. Scharf, 1 March 1867 (Sketch Book, 78, f.60r); Emery Walker photograph, neg.807/7 (both NPG archive). Scharf's sketch identified brown rocks in the right background.

JOHN OPIE (1761–1807)

DPG94 *Self portrait*

Canvas 60.3 x 50.8; lined by Holder 1911; much disfigured by broad shrinkage craquelure in the background, coat, hair and the shadows of the face; the face at one time partially cleaned and the craquelure filled; varnish much discoloured;[1] Hell 1953–55.

PROV.: Bourgeois Bequest 1811.

REF.: Britton 1813(103); A. Earland, *John Opie and his circle*, 1911, p.300; Walker 1985, i, p.378, undated.

DPG94 compares quite closely with an Opie self portrait of 1794, an enamel copy of which by Henry Bone was sold Bonham's, 19 March 1996, lot 87.

For Opie's iconography, see Walker 1985, pp.377-78.

1 No mention of this disfiguring craquelure was made by Passavant 1836, p.70 ('powerfully treated'), or Jameson 1842, p.443 ('powerful, rather coarse, but full of character and intellect').

SIR JOSHUA REYNOLDS (1723–92)

DPG102 *Recovery from Sickness*

Canvas 70.8 x 91 lined; Britton in 1813 noted 'paint chipp'd off'; pentimenti in the mother's hands and feet, in Death's left leg and the cloud on the left; very dark, with many repaired damages; the paint surface badly cracked and the glazes faded; loose paint fixed, revived and varnished 1870 'by the attendant'; cleaned by Reeve 1923; with Hell 1952–53; blisters treated 1972; strip lined, surface cleaned and consolidated 1991.

The mother has a blue veil over a golden-brown dress; a golden yellow drape above them; on the left an angel wards off the skeletal figure of Death.

PROV.: Reynolds sale, Greenwood's, 1st day, 14 April 1796, lot 16 'an emblematical subject of recovery from sickness', bt. Bourgeois, 8gn.; Desenfans 1804(96); Bourgeois Bequest 1811.

REF.: Britton 1813(150); GC 1901, iii, 1191 and iv, 1459–60; Waterhouse 1941, p.60 (as 1768-69); M. Postle in Mannings 2000, no.2143.

The composition appears a tame adaptation of Salvator Rosa's *L'umana fragilità* (Fitzwilliam Museum, Cambridge, PD.53-1958), using the same allegory of death and sickness,[1] while the mother and child group recall Reynolds' *Mrs Angerstein and her Daughter* of 1773 (private collection).[2]

1 Denning 1858, no.143, added *The Erl King* as a subtitle (a goblin that haunted the Black Forest carrying off children; the Goethe ballad of 1782, and Scott's translation of 1797, appeared after the picture was painted).

2 Mannings 2000, no.64. Both these comparisons indicated by R. Prochno, 'Sir Joshua Reynolds' use of Bolognese Art', in *Il luogo ed il ruolo della città di Bologna tra Europea continentale e mediterranea*, Fondazione Cesare Gnudi, 1990, pp.169–71.

Sir Joshua Reynolds (1723–92)

dpg223 *The Calling of Samuel*

Canvas 75.7 x 68 [sight 74.3 x 61.5] lined; revived and varnished 1866; prominent bituminous craquelure in the darks; heavily retouched, a large loss on his left shoulder; varnish much discoloured; loose paint fixed 1937; consolidated and surface cleaned 1993.

Brown eyes; wearing a white shirt and brown drape.

Prov.: Reynolds studio sale, Greenwood's, 3rd day, 16 April 1796, lot 12, 'sketch of Samuel', bt. Bourgeois, 17gn.;[1] Desenfans 1804(6); Bourgeois Bequest 1811.

Exh.: RA schools 1923; Aberystwyth 1946(16).

Ref.: Britton 1813(32); GC 1901, iii, p.1202 and iv, p.1461; Waterhouse 1941, p.102 as a school copy; M. Postle in Mannings 2000, no.2152 as Reynolds, possibly a studio copy.

The subject is taken from I Samuel, 3, 2–10: the Lord calls to the sleeping child; Samuel wakes and replies 'Speak, Lord; for thy Servant heareth'. The model was used on several occasions by Reynolds: an orphan beggar boy who sold cabbage nets, about fourteen years old, who 'though not handsome, had an expression in his eyes so very forcible, and indicating so much sense, that he was certainly a most excellent subject. …'[2]

Reynolds painted two Samuel pictures, *The Calling of Samuel* and *The Infant Samuel* – the latter showing a kneeling boy with his hands clasped together in prayer (cf. note 1). Early references confused the two,[3] so that it is now impossible to say which was the *Samuel* exhibited RA 1776(244) or which the *Samuel* bought by the Marquess of Granby in 1776 and burnt in 1816.[4] Two other versions of the *Calling of Samuel*, at Knole (bought by the Duke of Dorset in 1776) and formerly with Lord Darnley, differ from dpg223 in the shirt, wrap, bed and left arm.[5]

In dpg223 although the face shows quality, the overall appearance is not prepossessing and it has been described as possibly a studio production.[6] But circumstancial evidence suggests that it is by Reynolds himself: the composition is unique, the paint surface is characteristic of Reynolds and the picture came from the artist's posthumous sale.

1 In 1810 Desenfans wrote 'Being informed, a few years since, that a small picture, representing a Child at Prayers, by Sir Joshua Reynolds, was on sale at Paris, though I immediately sent Mr. Perregeaux, the banker, a commission of two hundred guineas, I could not obtain it, as the picture was deemed worth a great deal more' (*Memoirs of the late Noel Desenfans*, 1810, p.36). This was possibly Mannings 2000, no.2154.
2 W. Mason, quoted in W. Cotton, *Sir Joshua Reynolds's Notes and Observations on Pictures*, 1859, p.57.
3 E.g. Waagen 1854, p.348 called dpg223 *The Infant Samuel.*
4 Postle in Mannings 2000, nos.2149, 2150; his note under no.2150d encourages the idea that the Belvoir picture was a *Calling of Samuel.*
5 Cf. Mannings 2000, figs.1692–94.
6 Beresford 1998, p.199.

X-radiograph DPG333

SIR JOSHUA REYNOLDS (1723–92)

DPG333 An Officer on Horseback

Canvas 77.2 x 64.1 lined, with wooden strip extensions top and bottom hardly painted upon; revived and varnished 1871; a re-cycled canvas with two full-face portrait heads beneath – of a young lady in the upper half, and of a middle-aged man (reversed) in the lower; very sketchy, worn and faded, with old losses by the tower, above the horse's head, and in the bottom right foreground; Hell 1953; surface cleaned 1989.

PROV.: Reynolds studio sale, Greenwood's, 14 April 1796, lot 49 or 52, both sketches of generals on horseback, both bt. Bourgeois; Desenfans sale, Skinner & Dyke, 16–18 March 1802, lot 187;[1] Desenfans 1804(59 *Lord Ligonier on Horseback*); Bourgeois Bequest 1811.

REF.: Britton 1813(127); GC 1901, iii, p.1090 (as lot 52 in the Reynolds sale); M. Postle, *Apollo*, cxxxiv, 1991, p.374; Mannings 2000, no.1996 as 1760/65.

Ultimately derived from Bernini's equestrian statue of Louis XIV at Versailles; possibly a study for the equestrian portrait of Lord Ligonier of c.1760, in which he wears contemporary uniform,[2] or the equestrian Sir Jeffrey Amherst of c.1768 (which is reversed).[3]

The overpainted male portrait was first discerned by W.S. Spanton[4] and was later recognised by Postle as the head of a young man.

1 Desenfans 1802, ii, p.219, described as A General Officer – 'This portrait is asserted by some to be that of Lord Albermarle, by others of Lord Ligonier: we leave the decision to those who have known them.'
2 Of which there are two versions, Mannings 2000, nos.1127, 1128 (National Army Museum and Fort Ligonier, PA, 63.43.1).
3 Mannings 2000, no.56, as probably lot 49 in the Reynolds sale (Yale Center for British Art, B1981.25.522).
4 *A Discursive Handbook on Copying*, 1920, p.53.

Studio of Reynolds

DPG104 *Self Portrait*

Canvas 76.2 x 63.8 lined; revived and varnished 1870; faded, with pronounced bituminous craquelure; Hell 1949–51, 1952–53; surface cleaned 1986.

Brown eyes, white powdered wig; wearing a grey coat with the collar turned up on his left.

PROV.: Bourgeois Bequest 1811.[1]

EXH.: *Reynolds Bicentenary Commemoration*, RA, 1923 (n.n.); *Festival of Britain Exhibition*, Plymouth 1951(55).

REF.: Britton 1813(89); GC 1901, ii, p.806 (as Reynolds); Mannings 2000, no.26 as c.1788 (a replica).

A version of one of the last and best-known of Reynolds's self portraits now in the Royal Collection[2] which, according to Malone, showed the artist 'exactly as he appeared in his latter days, in domestick life'.[3] Reynolds wore spectacles to correct short sightedness; in 1782 he had suffered 'a violent inflammation of the eyes'; in 1790 one of his lenses was opaque and he was soon almost blind.[4] DPG104, one of several studio copies, shows minor differences from the Royal portrait, the right arm being slightly less raised and the collar less clearly lit.[5]

For Reynolds' iconography, see Mannings 2000, nos. 1-27, and Ingamells 2004, pp.393-96.

1 In a note on file Mannings very tentatively supposed it may have been given to Desenfans in 1790 when he negotiated the sale of the original *Mrs Siddons as the Tragic Muse* to Calonne (see DPG318 below).
2 On panel; Millar 1969, i, no.1008; ii, pl.105; Mannings 2000, no.22.
3 E. Malone in *The Works of Sir Joshua Reynolds*, 1798, i, p.lxxvii.
4 See Mannings 2000, no.22. The last *Self Portrait* of c.1788 (private collection; Mannings 2000, no.27) shows him without his glasses as he worked standing near a mirror.
5 Waagen 1854 (p.348) considered DPG104 'superior and more powerful in colouring' than the Royal Collection portrait, an opinion untenable today.

Studio of Reynolds

DPG 318 Mrs Siddons as the Tragic Muse

Canvas 239.7 x 147.6 lined 1882; extensive shrinkage craquelure has been retouched, principally in the brown areas; conserved 1998 when retouchings, notably in the face and arms, were corrected, and the thickest layers of discoloured varnish were thinned in the lighter areas; the soft and soluble painting medium (linseed oil, resin and a form of mastic) makes the picture otherwise almost uncleanable.[1]

Inscribed, on the hem of the drapery over her knees: *[JOSHVA] REYNOLDS PINXIT 1789*;[2] brown eyes, auburn hair; wearing a brown dress over a white shift, with a darker wrap across her lap; behind her the emblematic figures of *Pity* (left) and *Terror* (right).

PROV.: See below; Desenfans 1804(no.2); Bourgeois Bequest 1811.

EXH.: *International Exhibition*, South Kensington 1862(110); Lady Lever AG, Port Sunlight, 1949(171); *Georgian Playhouse*, AC, 1975(98); *Reynolds*, RA, 1986(151); *The Swagger Portrait*, Tate Gallery, 1993(37); *Reynolds*, Ferrara/Tate, 2005(69); *Citizens and Kings*, Grand Palais, Paris, 2006-07(107), RA, 2007(130).

ENG.: J. Bromley 1832. [Jos. Webb, S.W. Reynolds, H. Dawe 1826, A. Cardon 1812 and F. Haward 1787 engraved the prime Huntington version, see below].

REF.: Britton 1813(39); GC 1901, iii, pp.896–98, iv, p.1411; Waterhouse 1941, p.75 (as a replica); S. Bennett & M. Leonard in *A Passion for Performance*, 1999, pp.128–140 (as studio); Mannings 2000, no.1620 (as a replica); D. Mannings in *Clerics & Connoisseurs*, English Heritage, 2001, pp.305–06, no.96 (as perhaps a replica).

Sarah Kemble (1755–1831), the greatest tragédienne of her time, married William Siddons in 1773; her reputation was established in the 1782 London season and she came to dominate the English stage; in 1789 she was described as 'infinitely the most natural and affecting Actress on the English stage', while for Hazlitt 'she was tragedy personified, ... the stateliest ornament of the public mind'; she finally retired in 1812. Her three brothers John Philip, Charles (see DPG111 and DPG291, pp.88, 196) and Stephen also became actors of repute.

DPG318 is one of two full-size copies of the original portrait now in the Huntington Art Gallery, San Marino (21.2),[3] perhaps Reynolds's most successful attempt to reconcile his ambition as a history painter with the necessary business of portraiture. Exhibited at the RA in 1784, it shows the actress in an imagined classical costume, flanked by Pity and Terror, the traditional attributes of Melpomene, Muse of Tragedy. The source of her pose was variously explained,[4] but Reynolds appears to have recalled Domenichino's *St John the Evangelist* (Glyndebourne) and Michaelangelo's *Isaiah* from the Sistine Chapel ceiling; the background figure of *Pity* may derive from one of the companions of Michelangelo's *Jeremiah* or, with *Terror*, from the engravings in an English translation of Le Brun's *Traité de Passions* (1734).[5] The rich golden-brown impasted texture of the clothes owed much to a deep admiration of Rembrandt. The painting was extravagantly admired: Lawrence, for example, thought it 'indisputably the finest female portrait in the world',[6] and Farington 'a high refinement of Rembrandt'.[7] For some years Reynolds kept the picture priced prohibitively at one thousand guineas. On 4 June 1787 Francis Haward published his engraving of *Mrs Siddons in the Character of the Tragic Muse*, dedicated to the King. Then the earliest histories of the Huntington portrait, the Dulwich version and the second full-sized version now in the Cobbe collection become confused, so that it is necessary to look at each picture briefly in turn.

Huntington Art Gallery, the original picture, was bought from Reynolds by Desenfans for Calonne in 1790 for 700 gn.;[8] it subsequently appeared in Calonne's sale, 28 March 1795, lot 97, described as having being bought from Reynolds for 700gn.[9] The surface reflects how Reynolds had reworked certain areas (the bodice, the drapery round the knees, the chair arm finials; the removal of a kneeling putto, bottom left, and the remodelling of the figure of *Terror*).

Cobbe collection, Hatchlands,[10] a version acquired in 1789 by Robert Bateson Harvey of Langley Park, Stowe;[11] on 15 April 1789 *The Star* announced that 'Sir Joshua has agreed to copy his picture of Mrs Siddons – his payment a *Reubens* valued at 500£. The original Sir Joshua values at 1,000£.' In 1865 it was explained that Reynolds gave the copy to Harvey in exchange for 'a large Boar-hunt by Snyders, which Sir Joshua admired, and which used to hang in the place [at Langley Park] now filled by the Tragic Muse'.[12] The picture descended through generations of the Harvey family at Langley Park until sold at Christie's, 12 July 1990, lot 82. The surface is uniformly bland, the colour clear, and there is no trace of alteration (as in the Huntington picture). Particularly noticeable is the purple drapery over Mrs Siddons' lap, which Reynolds overpainted a warm brown in the course of completing the Huntington picture.[13] Of the three versions the Cobbe picture most closely resembles the Haward engraving[14] (and it might even be very tentatively attributed to William Score, who was alleged to have made a copy of the Mrs Siddons, but to have left Reynolds' studio in 1784).[15]

Dulwich Picture Gallery, DPG318 was insured by Desenfans in 1804 for £200, considerably less than the contemporary valuations of the previous two versions. Unlike them it is dated 1789 (when Reynolds's eyesight was rapidly fading, see DPG104 above) and appears to be entirely studio work. To judge by the surface it was copied from the Huntington rather than the Cobbe version, detailed differences being apparently due to an unskilled hand; the face is broader and coarser, the hair less articulated, the twisted strands of pearls are clumped together, her crown is more hesitantly executed, and the glowing texture of the original is lacking. Mrs Siddons herself, although an eccentric witness, pronounced it 'a poor imitation' of the original.[16]

Thus the Dulwich version was painted in 1789 just as the earlier Cobbe version left Reynolds' studio for Langley Park. *The Star* of 15 April 1789 was almost correct. But exactly how Desenfans acquired DPG318 sometime between 1789 and 1804 has not been established.

Another full size copy by Mary, Countess Temple (c.1759–1812), is at Somerley[17] and many reduced versions are recorded.[18]

1 The condition was thoroughly investigated at the Getty Center, see Bennett & Leonard, 1999, under REF. above. Hell had commented c.1945 that DPG318 'was in a horrid state. I'm compelled to admit that a thorough 'restoring' must not be attempted. An accumulation of dirty and discoloured varnish can advisedly be removed – but the whole picture is oozing bitumen, and nothing can be done about it. The large gaping cracks showing a white substructure can be tinted appropriately. The general appearance can be bettered. The treatment will take a long time, and I would rather see better pictures given priority' (typescript in Gallery archive of conversations between Sir Gerald Kelly and Dr Hell).

2 As recorded by Scharf, 8 November 1859 (Sketch Book, 57, f.18; NPG archive) and all sources thereafter.

3 R. Asleson & S. Bennett, *Catalogue of British Paintings at the Huntington*, 2001, no.79; Mannings 2000, no.1619. Signed on the drapery hem ... *REYNOLDS PINXIT 1784*. The Duveen catalogue 1921, no.4, advertising the picture for sale, described the signature as including *JOSHUA*. See also R. Wark, *Mrs Siddons as the Tragic Muse*, San Marino, 1965; R. Asleson, S. Bennet & M. Leonard, in *A Passion for Performance*, 1999, pp.69–72, 97–140. DPG318 was shown alongside the Huntington picture in *A Passion for Performance*, Getty Museum, Los Angeles, 1999 (n.n.).

4 Romantic explanations were provided by Samuel Rogers (see Mannings 2000, no.1619) and Mrs Siddons, although Peter Murray (1980, p.104) regarded her self-congratulatory accounts as 'probably no more untruthful than is usual in the memoirs of actresses'.

5 For the borrowing from Domenichino, see J.M. Merz, *Burl. Mag.*, cxxxvii, 1995, pp.516–17; from the Le Brun engravings, see R. Wark, *Ten British Pictures*, Huntington Library, 1971, p.50. In Denning 1858, no.340, it is recounted that Mr Eagles the sketcher used to say that Sir J. Reynolds took the idea of this from a picture by Domenichino. If so it is most likely 'La Force' London 69' – [no.69 in the National Gallery is now *St John the Baptist preaching in the Wilderness* by Mola; perhaps no.85, *The Vision of St Jerome* by Domenichino, was

intended]. The iconography has been much discussed, see also, for example, E. Wind, *Hume and the Heroic Portrait*, 1986, pp.44–46.

6 D. Williams, *Lawrence*, 1843, i, p.430.

7 Farington, ix, p.3309 (4 July 1808).

8 Reynolds accounts, February 1790: 'Mrs Siddons – sold to Mr Desenfans £735' (M. Cormack, *Wal. Soc.*, XLII, 1970, p.164). Leslie & Taylor 1865, ii, p.424n2, gave the date of the transaction wrongly as June 1789 (see Whitley 1928a, ii, p.12). This very high price (over three times Reynolds' charge for a whole length portrait at that time) was further inflated by the press: *The World*, 17 February 1790, reported 'Mrs Siddons by Sir Joshua. This picture, certainly sublime, perhaps beautiful, is sold for 1000 guineas, & to increase the wonder Desenfans is the buyer. It should have been M. de Calonne', and a week later the *Gazetteer*, 23 February 1790, announced that 'Mr Desenfans has, it appears, given a thousand guineas for the picture of Mrs Siddons'.

9 In the Calonne sale catalogue the *Mrs Siddons* was described as having been acquired from Reynolds for 800gn.; but a priced copy of this catalogue in the British Museum alters the 800 to 700gn. (Whitley 1928a, ii, p.12). Calonne, whom Desenfans is said to have known in Douai, had moved to England 'a short time after' the Assembly of Notables on 22 February 1787 and left for Coblenz shortly after the Revolution in July 1789 (*GM*, lxv, i, 1795, pp.287–88); he had returned to England by 1793 (Whitley 1928b, p.30).

10 See Mannings 2001 (see REF. above), pp.305–06, no.96; Mannings 2000, no.1621; Bennett & Leonard 1999 (see REF. above), pp.128, 140n84.

11 Whose daughter was sitting to Reynolds in May (Mannings 2000, no.857) and on 26 August 1789 Harvey was made an Irish Baronet.

12 Leslie & Taylor, 1865, ii, p.424n2. The Snyders may have been Reynolds's 'Rubens & Snyders, *Boar Hunting; the animals by Snyders*', exh. Ralph's, Haymarket, 1791, no.21 in the great room, or/and 'Rubens, *A Wild Boar Hunting*', lot 92 in the Reynolds sale, 4th day, March 1795 (see F.J.P. Broun, *Sir Joshua Reynolds' Collection of Paintings*, 1987, ii, pp.173–74, no.1).

13 See Bennett & Leonard 1999 (see REF. above), pp.126, 127, fig.30.

14 In such details as the three strands in the lowest pendant pearls on Mrs Siddons's bosom (there are four strands in the Huntington or Dulwich pictures); there is now some ambiguity as to whether the left-hand corner of the stool is covered by drapery, but it appears not to be, as in the engraving (but not in the Huntington or Dulwich pictures). Mannings has written that 'close comparison strongly suggests that it was the tidy Cobbe version, not the messy Huntington one, that was used by Francis Haward for his engraving' (Mannings 2001, see REF. above, p.306).

15 The idea of a copy by Score rests on confused proposals. Thus Hazlitt, *Essays on The Fine Arts*, 1873 ed., pp.441–42: 'While [*Mrs Siddons*] was in the possession of Mr Desenfans, a copy of it was taken by a pupil of Sir Joshua's, of the name of Score, which is now in the Dulwich Gallery ...', and Leslie & Taylor 1865, ii, p.215: 'another pupil [of Reynolds] about this time was Score, the painter, as Northcote used always to declare, of the copy of the 'Tragic Muse' now at Dulwich'. Whitley 1928a, ii, p.13, believed it was Hazlitt alone, and not Northcote, who had maintained this attribution: he said that Graves and Cronin had sought in vain for a Northcote reference to Score painting such a picture. There are two points to bear in mind; one, that Hazlitt talked much with Northcote, and two, that Northcote took a particular interest in Score who was in Reynolds's studio c.1778–84 (cf. Northcote, *Life of Reynolds*, 1819, ii, p.81, and Whitley 1930, p.226).

16 Bennett & Leonard 1999 (see REF. above), pp.130, 140n88, citing CUL, Add. 7621/481.

17 Mannings 2000, no.1621a. Described as being reputedly by a Reynolds pupil with his assistance by Bennett & Leonard 1999 (see REF. above), p.140n84.

18 E.g. by Rembrandt Peale and James Peale in American private collections, and by Moses Haughton, dated 1798, sold Sotheby's, 10 April 1991, lot 133. Holman Hunt made an untraced copy at Dulwich c.1845–46 (J. Bronkhurst, *Holman Hunt*, 2005, i, no.32).

RICHARD WILSON (1713/4–82)

DPG171 *View of Tivoli: the Cascatelle and the 'Villa of Maecenas'*

Canvas 73.3 x 97.2 lined by Holder 1911, heavily ironed; much retouched and the edges made up to the lining canvas; a small square damage bottom left beneath the artist and minor damages on the right side; pentimenti of a tree on horizon, and on the foreground rocks; Hell 1952–53; cleaned 1980.

The falls of Tivoli on the left and the so-called Villa of Maecenas (now identified as part of the foundations of the temple complex known as the Sanctuary of Hercules Victor[1]); a woman with a baby in her arms watches the painter at work.

PROV.: [possibly Dr Monro;[2] Norris of Manchester sale, Wright, Liverpool, 16 March 1804, lot 49, 'Wilson, Maecenas's Villa, Tivoli, with the Campana in the distance. This picture is allowed to be a chef d'oeuvre of the Master, and is from the collection of Dr Monro' (37 x 27in., i.e. 94 x 69), 105 gn.[3]] Hill, a dealer, from whom bt. Desenfans (d. 1807), 150gn (see below); Bourgeois Bequest 1811.

EXH.: BI 1817(92); RA schools 1820, 1823, 1864, 1913; Aberystwyth 1945(38); *Dulwich College – a School and its Art*, South London AG, 1981; *Collection for a King*, Washington DC, Los Angeles, 1985–86(36); *Obras Maestras*, Madrid, Bilbao, 1999(39); *Rembrandt to Gainsborough*, Houston TX, Louisville KY, 1999–2000(85).

ENG.: Normand fils.; R. Cockburn 1820; C. Turner (*Gems of Art* 1823).[4]

REF.: Britton 1813(201); W.G. Constable, *Richard Wilson*, 1953, p.225, pl.117a; G.A. Waterfield in *Collection for a King*, 1985, p.122.

Tivoli, a source of wonder for both classicist and painter, was believed to have been the home of Maecenas, the patron of Horace and Virgil.[5] In 1758 the young painter Jonathan Skelton wrote how he had been admiring the 'Thundering Cascades of Tivole bounding over lofty Rugged Rocks', adding that 'this antient city of Tivole I plainly see has been ye only school where our two most celebrated Landscape Painters Claude and Gasper studied.'[6]

There are several versions of this subject by, or attributed to Wilson. The prime version (now in the National Gallery of Ireland, 746), dated 1752, was painted for Joseph Henry of Straffan, co. Kildare; it is slightly smaller than the Dulwich picture and lacks the near foreground, most of the right-hand hill and the woman with her baby standing by the seated artist.[7] DPG171 appears to be a later reworking of the subject. It may probably be identified with the picture which Bourgeois showed Farington on 3 May 1809: 'a beautiful picture of Tivoli by Wilson, for which Desenfans gave Hill the picture dealer, 150 guineas. Wilson had 25 or 30 for it. In it He represented Himself with an Easel, painting'.[8] A studio version, the same size as DPG171, was in the Turner Bequest in 1856 (Tate Gallery, NO5538) and a copy was made by John Jackson in 1823 (see note 4).

In 1799 Farington recorded that 'Desenfans and Bourgeois acknowledged that some years ago they did not like [Wilson's pictures], from the execution being so slovenly compared with Loutherbourg & c, but now delight in them'.[9]

An untraced drawing by Wilson 'of Tivoli, as it deviates from the picture in the Dulwich Gallery, is curious, as exhibiting the changes made for the sake of composition', was exhibited at the Soho Square Academy in 1822.[10]

1 See D. Solkin, *Wilson*, exh. cat. Tate Gallery, 1982, p.182n1.

2 On 30 May 1796 Farington (ii, p.564) reported that Monro bt. two Wilsons from Mrs King for 70 gn. There was no Wilson in the Monro sale of 23 March 1804.

3 The late Frank Simpson (note on file) stated that in Winstanley's copy of T. Wright's *Life of Wilson*, 1824, there is a note saying this picture was in the Dulwich College Gallery.

4 Turner's plate was made from a full-size copy of DPG171 made by John Jackson RA while it was on loan to the Academy schools; the existence of a full-sized copy caused some concern with the Gallery Committee [Dulwich College Archive, Wodehouse Library, MS XVIIb, *Bourgeios Book of Regulations (Record of Art Gallery 1817–52)*, 31 July 1823]. The brief text accompanying the Normand engraving, identifying the original as that at Dulwich, stated that it had been 'repeatedly engraved'.

5 For example Denning 1858, no.215, was unable to refrain from quoting Horace, *Odes*, I, vii, 10–14 [*Me nec tam patiens Lacedaemon,… Mobilibus pomaria rivis*].

6 Skelton to William Herring, 23 April 1758; *Wal. Soc.*, XXXVI, 1960, p.42. See D. Solkin, *Wilson*, exh. cat. Tate Gallery, 1982, pp.181–82.

7 Inscribed in an unknown hand *verso*: *JOSEPH HENRY TIVOLI 2/ R: WILSON PINXT/ 1752/ NO.1*; 50 x 66; Constable 1953, p.225 as a version of his pl.117a; exh. *Wilson*, Tate, 1982, no.65.

8 Farington, ix, p.3446 (3 May 1809).

9 Farington, iv, p.1136 (17 January 1799).

10 Ackermann's *Repository of Arts*, 2nd series, xiii, 1822, p.174.

Samuel Woodburn (1780–1853)

DPG150 *Landscape in imitation of Jacob van Ruisdael*

Bevelled oak panel 49.5 x 39, chipped bottom left corner and small vertical split top left; varnish much discoloured.

Ruisdael scratched in the lower left corner, 'an imitation Ruisdael signature'.

Prov.: Bourgeois Bequest 1811.

Ref.: Britton 1813(344 Ruysdael);[1] Passavant 1836, p.62 (as Woodburn); S. Slive, *Burl Mag*, cxxxiii, 1991, p.606 (almost certainly by Samuel Woodburn); S. Slive, *Jacob van Ruisdael, a complete catalogue*, 2001, pp.660–62, dub139 (almost certainly by Samuel Woodburn).

When he visited Dulwich sometime in 1831–32 Passavant, who knew Samuel Woodburn, recognised that one of the Ruisdaels was entirely painted by Woodburn 'who made this very copy for his own pleasure, and which after passing through several hands[2] has at length here [*at Dulwich*] attained to the honour of originality'. In 1858 and 1859 Denning associated Passavant's comment specifically with DPG150. Successive Dulwich catalogues repeated this attribution but, variously and mistakenly, gave Woodburn's initials as W. or W.S. No original version of the composition has been traced and we are entirely dependant upon Passavant's words for the attribution.

1 '*Land[e] stump of tree &c Ruysdael 2.10 1.10* [68 x 56]'.
2 At the time of the Bourgeois Bequest Woodburn was 31; the picture must have been quickly passed around.

Unknown Artist

DPG151 Portrait of a Man

Oak panel 56.6 x 40.6 of two vertical members, the left 28.5 wide, the join covered *verso* with a canvas strip; old scattered losses in the lower area and in the hat; a scratch runs across the face, which is thinly painted; a slight pentimento on the rim of the hat across the forehead; in 1836 it was thought to be 'a fine picture, but nearly obliterated';[1] Hell 1953–68; cleaned 2005 when the top of the original panel was found to be arched (as opposed to rectangular); to restore this format old triangular additions on the top corners were replaced with oak additions retaining the overall rectangular format: the paint surface was then made up to an arch-top with small additions to the gessoed surface upper left and right.

Grey eyes, the right bigger than the left, the left eyebrow bushier than the right, white hair; wearing a sable-trimmed black gown over a black tunic, a stud on a cotton loop round his neck (to close the ruff collar), holding a leather-bound book with gilt fore-edge; traces of a thumb ring on his left hand.

PROV.: C-A. de Calonne sale, Skinner & Dyke, 4th day, 28 March 1795, lot 11 ('Holbein, A Man's Portrait a very expressive fine head, finished with great delicacy'); Desenfans sale, Skinner & Dyke, 16–18 March 1802, lot 73 (as Holbein); Bourgeois Bequest 1811.

EXH.: *Old Masters*, RA, 1880(199 as German School [with wrong size 83.8 x 39.4]); RA schools 1914, 1923, 1927.

REF.: Britton 1813(315 as Holbein).

A strongly characterized but unidentified portrait of some distinction. A traditional attribution to Holbein was first rejected in 1880 by Richter and most recent opinion favours an English origin.[2] The costume (as it now appears) may be compared, for example, with that worn by Sir Nicholas Bacon in portraits of the 1570s in the National Portrait Gallery (164) and at Gorhambury.[3] DPG151 was particularly admired by the young Holman Hunt[4] and the sitter's character was confidently read in 1841.[5]

1 Passavant 1836, p.68.
2 Susan Foister (letter of 19 December 1996 on file) felt 'fairly sure' it was English, as does Tarnya Cooper (orally 2004).
3 Strong 1969a, ii, pls.30, 31.
4 'A portrait of a man with a stubbly white beard by Holbein fascinated me with its delicate painting' (W. Holman Hunt, *Pre-Raphaelitism and the Pre-Raphaelite Brotherhood*, 1905, i, p.54; c.1840).
5 'We detect at a glance what sort of man he was; testy, opiniated, despotic in his household, but not without kindness – rough, hasty, irregular kindness – when he had his own way' (quoted by Cook 1914, 1926, as from *Bentley's Miscellany*, x, 1841, p.351, but an incorrect reference).

Unknown Artist

DPG200 *Portrait of a Lady*

Canvas 89.8 x 68.3 lined; in poor condition with widespread losses; varnish partially removed leaving large illegible matt areas (as her left forearm); partially cleaned by Hell 1955.

Fair hair, grey eyes; wearing a black hat, a damask-patterned black and grey bodice with a falling lace collar and grey sash; a green curtain behind.

PROV.: See below; Bourgeois Bequest 1811.

EXH.: RA schools 1915 (as After Johnson).

REF.: Britton 1813(123 *Portrait of a lady: rich laced collar Vandyck* 3.9 x 3.0 [114 x 91.5]).

DPG200 is by an unidentified English painter c.1630.[1] According to the size and the old attribution to Van Dyck, there is a slight possibility that DPG200 was the alleged portrait of Mrs Butler which appeared in three Desenfans sales between 1785 and 1786.[2] The attribution was first modified by Denning in 1858.

1 For costume cf., for example, Strong 1969b, p.276, no.262 (Gheeraerts, *Mrs Hoskins* 1629; private collection, exh. *Gheeraerts II*, Tate Britain, 2002, no.39), and p.303, no.313 (Gheeraerts, *Anne, Lady Fanshawe* c.1630; Valence House, Barking).

2 Desenfans sales at Christie's: 3rd day, 13 May 1785, lot 75 (Van Dyck, *Portrait of Mrs Butler who in her youth had been Maid of Honour of Queen Elizabeth*), bt. Jenkins; 8 April ff. 1786, lot 209 (*Mrs Butler* ..., 48 x 37 in.), and 2nd day, 14 July 1786, lot 80 (Van Dyck, *Mrs Butler*...), bt. Tessart. No such sitter is recorded in *Van Dyck* 2004.

Unknown Artist

DPG486 *Landscape with Horses*

Canvas 37.2 x 49.2 lined; diagonal scrape bottom right and another top left; varnish very discoloured; Hell 1953–55.

A bay and a grey with a peasant girl.

PROV.: Bourgeois Bequest 1811.

REF.: Britton 1813(116 as Zuccarelli).

An English picture probably of c.1760–70. Bourgeois bought a landscape by George Barret and Sawrey Gilpin (to whom DPG486 might conceivably have been attributed) at Christie's, 12 June 1784, lot 76 (it was presumably Desenfans sale, Christie's, 4th day, 14 May 1785, lot 65, Barret and Gilpin, *A landscape, cattle and figures*).

Mezzotint (*Gwin* [?] *delin.*, *JT* [sculp.?]), c.1780?
Dulwich Picture Gallery

Unknown Artist

DPG503 Noel Desenfans

Canvas 47.3 x 38 lined; cleaned by Holder 1912; losses down the edges and lower right.

Grey coat and breeches, yellow waistcoat, black shoes; an illegible inscription below the bust.

PROV.: Bourgeois Bequest 1811.[1]

ENG.: Anon. mezzotint (see below).

REF.: Britton 1813 (348 *Full length of N. Desenfans 2.1 x 1.9* [63.5 x 53.3]

For Desenfans (1744–1807), see pp.87, 114.

The subject is clarified by a similarly amateur mezzotint, bearing the name of *Gwin* as the designer and *J T* as the engraver,[2] in which the bust is identified as that of Fénélon, but the angel, lily, fountain and arbour are omitted.

In 1777 Desenfans published his *Lettre de Monsieur Desenfans à Madame Montague*, a vindication of the Abbé Fénélon, occasioned by the publication in 1774 of the *Letters* of the 4th Earl of Chesterfield. On 28 November 1752 Chesterfield had written to his son criticising the moral weakness of the Abbé in advising the King's *maîtresse en titre*, Mme de Maintenon: 'Love the King; be obedient to him, as Sarah was to Abraham … it is true, Madam, that your Station is a Riddle … You hold the place of a Queen, and yet have no more liberty nor Authority than the wife of a Tradesman'. Chesterfield commented 'no bawd could have written a more seducing letter to an innocent country girl'.[3] In 1777 Desenfans received the *Lettre de Monsieur Thomas de l'Académie Françoise à Monsieur Desenfans. Pour servir à la défense de Fénélon contre Milord Chesterfield.* Chesterfield's attack is here symbolised by the serpent, while Desenfans stands as the guardian of Fénélon's bust which is about to be crowned by a descending angel.

1 This was the only Bourgeois Bequest picture to be included in Sparkes & Carver 1890.

2 CS, iv, p.1725, no.52, as unattributed, but he supposed the plate may be in the 'style of Jehner'; the impression at Dulwich bears the scratched initials J.T. – possibly John Taylor (1739–1838), occasional engraver and painter, exhib. RA 1779 (CS, iii, p.1356; *Connoisseur*, lxvii, 1923, p.161; *ODNB*) and possibly the John Taylor author of 'Lines addressed to Noel Desenfans on his descriptive catalogue of pictures, purchased for the King of Poland' (*Memoirs of the late Noel Desenfans*, 1810, f.p.180). The mount of the Dulwich print bears a long hand-written inscription, suggesting that DPG503 'is probably a reproduction of a miniature made some years earlier when Monsieur Desenfans was about twenty or twenty-five years old'. But *de minibus* ….

3 *The Letters of Madam de Maintenon, translated from the French*, 1753, pp.192–93, letter clxxxv. See also *Memoirs of the late Noel Desenfans*, 1810, pp.121–58 (*Lettre de Monsieur Desenfans à Madame Montague* containing both Fénélon's letter, pp.132–34, and Chesterfield's, pp.134–40, with translations; the flattering letter from Monsieur Thomas, with translation, appears on pp.161–69, 171–80).

THE LINLEY BEQUEST 1835

The pictures in this section are catalogued in alphabetical order by artist

The nine Linley portraits include outstanding works by Gainsborough and Lawrence which, at the time of their arrival, considerably enhanced the quality of the British collection.

Thomas Linley (1733–95), the distinguished singing master and composer from Bath, had twelve children by his wife Mary Johnson (1729–1820) whom he married in 1752. Eight survived infancy and each was musically gifted. In order of age (and with references to their portraits at Dulwich) they were:

1 Elizabeth 1754–92 (Mrs Sheridan) [*Gainsborough DPG320*]
2 Thomas 1756–78 [*Gainsborough DPG331*]
3 Mary 1758–87 (Mrs Tickell) [*Gainsborough DPG320*]
4 Samuel 1760–78 [*Gainsborough DPG302*]
5 Maria 1763–84 [*Lawrence DPG475*]
6 Ozias 1765–1831 [?*Lawrence DPG474*; *A.J. Oliver DPG476*]
7 Jane 1768–1806 (Mrs Ward)
8 William 1771–1835 [*Lawrence DPG178*]

The Linley portraits finally came to Dulwich as the gifts of Ozias, a Fellow of Dulwich College from 1816 to his death, and of his brother William, the last surving sons of Thomas Linley. Gainsborough's *Linley Sisters* had been deposited by William in March 1822.[1] Following the death of Ozias on 6 March 1831 William, his sole heir, wrote to the College on 27 March announcing his intention of bequeathing 'his Family Pictures without exception':[2]

> Portrait of Himself by the late Sr Thos. Lawrence
> Do. of his Father, by Gainsborough
> Do. of Mrs Tickell when a little girl by Ozias Humphries
> Do. His Mother, by Oliver
> and also the Portraits in one Picture of Mrs. Sheridan and Mrs Tickell, by Gainsborough.

The same letter confirmed the Gift made by his brother the late Ozias T. Linley of:

> A Portrait of Mr Linley by Gainsborough
> Do. Mr Samuel Linley by Do.
> A crayon Portrait of Miss Maria Linley by Sr T. Lawrence

A second letter from William Linley, dated 1 April 1831[3] stated

> Mr Willm Linley presents as his Gift to the College his portrait when a Boy by Sir T Lawrence ... also the Picture painted by Gainsborough of his two sisters Mrs Sheridan & Mrs Tickell. He also bequeaths to the College the portrait of his Father & his two Brothers Thomas & Samuel painted by Gainsborough also a portrait of Mrs Tickell when a child by the late Ozias Humphries & moreover the two pictures of his Mother painted by Oliver & Lonsdale also the crayon Drawings of the late Miss Maria Linley & Mrs Ward by Sir T. Lawrence & also the portrait of the late Revd O.T. Linley, late Fellow of this College [*i.e. a portrait by an unnamed artist, presumably Oliver, see extract from his Will quoted below*].

After William's death in 1835 the College archives recorded[4]

> An Extract from the Will of the late William Linley Esq / 1832. January 17th
> William Linley Esqr of Furnival Inn ... by his Will of this date, gave and bequeathed (amongst other things) as follows,
> The Portraits by Gainsborough of my Father in the White Coat, and of my two Brothers Thomas, and Samuel, by the same Artist. Also the Portrait of my Brother Ozias painted by Oliver, and of my Sister Mrs Tickell painted when a Child by Humphreys.

There are slight discrepancies within these three lists, but they appear to describe a total of twelve portraits. Mrs Ward by Lawrence, Mrs Linley by Lonsdale, and Ozias Linley by Oliver appear only once. On 29 May 1835 the College Trustees agreed to return Humphry's pastel of the young Mary Linley (Mrs Tickell) to her daughter at her request.[5] The portraits of Ozias Linley by Lonsdale, two of Mrs Linley, and Mrs Ward by Lawrence were initially retained in the College but by 1905 the portrait of Mrs Ward[6] and one of the portraits of Mrs Linley had disappeared (i.e. they were omitted from the Dulwich Gallery catalogues). The other nine Linley portraits remain in the Gallery today.

1 Dulwich College Archives, Wodehouse Library, MS XVIIb, *Bourgeois Book of Regulations (Record of Art Gallery 1817–52)*: 'Ordered that a Picture by Gainsborough of Elizabeth Mrs Sheridan and Mary Tickle deceas'd, in the Possession of William Linley Esqr, should be allow'd at his request a place in the Picture Gallery, till it should be convenient to him to resume it'.
2 *Bourgeois Book of Regulations* (at note 1). *Nest of Nightingales* 1988, 10:12.
3 Dulwich College Archives, Wodehouse Library, box 321.
4 *Bourgeois Book of Regulations* (at note 1).
5 *Ibid.*, in compliance with a request made by Miss Tickell through her solicitor, Mr Henry C. Chilton. It may subsequently have been lot 151 in the Tickell sale, Christie's, 3 May 1884, 'Miss Linley by an unknown artist', or lot 158, 'Elizabeth Ann Tickell – in crayons – oval'.
6 William Linley left to his niece, Mary Esther Ward, 'a Crayon drawing of my sister Mrs Ward [Jane Linley] by the late Sir Thomas Lawrence' (January 1832; PRO Gloster 369) and in a Codicil of 8 May 1833 he left 'the Crayon drawing by the late Sir Thomas Lawrence of my late sister Jane Nash Ward' to the Rev Edward and Mrs Sophia Ward. A pastel of Jane attributed to Lawrence belonging to Ward descendants in 1911 is illus. *Nest of Nightingales* 1988, p.94.

Thomas Gainsborough (1727–88)

DPG140 Thomas Linley the elder

Canvas 76.5 x 63.5 lined by Holder 1911; revived and varnished 1870; small retouchings in the face, temple and cravat and minor scratches in the top spandrels; discoloured varnish; Hell c.1950–1953; surface cleaned 1995.

Light brown eyes, grey powdered hair; wearing a pale grey jacket, yellow waistcoat, white stock and collar; a vivid touch of vermilion by his ear; sheet of music inscribed *ELEGY* / *[f]or Three Voices*; Sloman tentatively suggested he might be playing some notes on a harpsichord with his right hand while directing a trio of singers.

PROV.: Bequeathed by the sitter to his wife 1795; bequeathed to Ozias Linley 1820; bequeathed to William Linley 1831; Linley Bequest 1835.

EXH.: Aberystwyth 1945(34); National Gallery 1947(17), Leeds 1947–53(17); *Gainsborough and his Musical Friends*, Kenwood, 1977(4); *Nest of Nightingales* 1988(1:1); *Gainsborough in Bath*, Bath, 1988(16); *Obras Maestras*, Madrid, Bilbao, 1999(42); *Pickpocketing the Rich*, Bath, 2002(29).

REF.: Waterhouse 1953, p.69, as c.1773–74; Waterhouse 1958, no.446, as probably later 1760s; S. Sloman, *Gainsborough in Bath*, 2002, pp.103, 105, and in *Pickpocketing the Rich*, 2002, pp.58, 59.

Thomas Linley the elder of Bath (1733–95), the son of a carpenter, became a composer, singing master ('almost unrivalled in England'),[1] and the father of a large musical family. He lived in Bath 1744–76 where in 1752 he married Mary Johnson; in 1771 he became director of music at the new Upper Assembly Rooms in Bath and in 1776 he moved to London as manager of the Drury Lane theatre; latterly his spirits were broken by the deaths of his son Tom in 1778 and daughter Maria in 1784. He was evidently a rather difficult man; Fanny Burney found him 'very sour, ill bred, severe & selfish'[2] and his pupil Mrs Crouch remembered him as a 'dark, stern, [and] gigantic'.[3]

Gainsborough settled in Bath in 1759, living close to Linley (they were at Abbey Street and Abbey Green respectively), and the two were close friends.[4] If Linley is shown here holding the manuscript of his *Elegies for Three Voices* (published in Bath on 25 January 1770) the portrait could date from the very late 1760s, but Sloman prefers a date in the early 1770s, associating it with Linley's appointment at the Upper Assembly Rooms in 1771. A copy by W. Rimer (1816–79), without the oval spandrels, is in an American private collection.

Another, earlier, Gainsborough portrait of Thomas Linley of c.1759–61, descended from the Tickell family, is in a private collection.[5]

1 W. Parke, *Musical Memoirs*, 1830, i, p.203.
2 *Early Journals and Letters of Fanny Burney*, ed. L.E. Trodie, i, 1988, pp.250–51 (1773).
3 M.J. Young, *Memoirs of Mrs Crouch*, 1806, i, p.83.
4 Sloman, *Pickpocketing the Rich*, p.59. Apart from the portraits now at Dulwich the Linleys also owned by Gainsborough another portrait of 'Miss Linley', the second portrait of Thomas Linley the elder (see above), two landscapes, and a pencil drawing of the Misses Linley; all were in the Tickell sale, Christie's, 3 May 1884, lots 150, 152, 153, 154 and 156 respectively.
5 See note 4. Exh. *Pickpocketing the Rich*, Bath, 2002, no.28.

Thomas Gainsborough (1727–88)

DPG302 *Samuel Linley*

Canvas 75.8 x 63.5 lined by Dyer; revived and varnished 1871; pentimenti round chin, his left shoulder, and in the hair; broadly brushed thin paint, the background stippled with a dry brush; minor retouchings (e.g. a small damage in the waistcoat); Hell c.1951–53; cleaned 2002.

Blue eyes, dark hair with pigtail and black ribbon; wearing a midshipman's uniform of black neckcloth, white shirt, black waistcoat, and a dark blue coat with a white tab and gold button on the collar.[1]

Prov.: Linley Bequest 1835.

Exh.: RA schools 1856; Aberystwyth 1945(32); National Gallery 1947(19), Leeds 1947–53(19); *Collection for a King*, Washington DC, Los Angeles, 1985–86 (9); *Nest of Nightingales* 1988 (6:1); *Kolekcja dla Króla*, Warsaw, 1992(11); *Obras Maestras*, Madrid, Bilbao, 1999(43).

Ref.: Waterhouse 1953, p.69; Waterhouse 1958, no.445, as 'traditionally 1777–8'; L. Stainton in *Collection for a King*, 1985, pp.60, 62.

Samuel Linley (1760–78), second son of Thomas Linley of Bath, performed as a singer and learned the oboe but, through his father's friend Captain Robert Walsingham, he sailed in 1778 as a midshipman on the third-rater *Thunderer*; fever broke out on board and the ship put into Portsmouth to land the sick, Linley among them; he was collected by his father and taken home, but died within weeks, three months after his brother Thomas (see DPG331 below).[2]

DPG302 is dated according to the uniform, Samuel being made midshipman in 1778. The wonderful verve makes credible Denning's recollection that it was 'commenced and finished in less than one hour, the authority for this [being] the testimony of his own brother'.[3] In his *Fourteenth Discourse* Reynolds wrote that he had often imagined that Gainsborough's 'unfinished manner contributed ... to that striking resemblance for which his portraits are so remarkable ....' (cf. *De Loutherbourg*, DPG66, p.108).

For Gainsborough and the Linleys, see DPG140 above.

A bust-length oval miniature of Samuel, attributed to Ozias Humphry, was sold Bonham's, 20 November 1997, lot 65A (possibly lot 157 in the Tickell sale, Christie's, 3 May 1884). A chalk drawing attributed to William Hoare, offered at Sotheby's, 19 May 1977, lot 185, was doubtfully identified as *Samuel Linley RN*.

1 R. Quarm (letter of 12 July 1988 on file) quoting Mrs Blackett Barber at the National Maritime Museum who thought it 'likely that Samuel Linley is indeed wearing midshipman's uniform. This seems to hinge on the white patch with a gilt button below his stock'.

2 See *Nest of Nightingales* 1988, p.87.

3 Denning 1858, no.361, and see G.W. Fulcher, *Gainsborough*, 1856, 1st ed., p.222 (2nd ed., p.226). Denning overlapped at Dulwich with Ozias Linley who doubtless told him the story (see also Lawrence DPG178, p.138).

THOMAS GAINSBOROUGH (1727–88)

DPG320 *Elizabeth and Mary Linley*

Canvas 199 x 153 lined; the composition was reworked after fourteen years (see below), resulting in a complex paint structure (discussed further below); underdrawing now visible by the left-hand figure's left hand; pentimenti show the hair of both piled higher and dressed with pearls and suggest the guitar may have been moved to the right; there was a drape around the right-hand figure's shoulders; cleaned and varnished 1914; Hell 1947; revarnished 1985; varnish thinned and a tear on the left-hand figure's arm repaired 1998.

Both sisters are brunette with pale brown eyes; Elizabeth on the left wears a pale blue underdress and a slightly darker blue overdress with white lace trim, flounced cuffs and a rose corsage; grey shoes; she leans on a five-stringed guitar with a blue strap; Mary on the right wears a golden brown under and overdress with narrow cuffs; blue shoes; an illegible libretto in her lap; there are primroses and a violet on the bank on the right and more primroses on the left.

PROV.: R.B. Sheridan; given to his brother-in-law William Linley by 1814 in part payment of a loan (see note 2); lent to Dulwich 1822 (see p.129); Linley Bequest 1835.

EXH.: RA 1772(95 *portrait of Two Young Ladies, whole length*);[1] BI 1814(97 *Portraits of the late Mrs Sheridan and Mrs Tickell, Gainsborough*), lent Rt. Hon. R.B. Sheridan;[2] *International Exhibition* 1862(74); Aberystwyth 1945(23); National Gallery 1947(20); Leeds 1947–53(20); *European Masters of the 18th century*, RA, 1954–55(64); *Masque of Beauty*, NPG, 1972(25); *Gainsborough and his Musical Friends*, 1977(6); *Nest of Nightingales* 1988(3:3); *Rembrandt to Gainsborough*, Houston TX, Louisville KY, 1999–2000(88); *Old Master Paintings*, Japan, 2000(50); *Gainsborough*, Tate, Washington DC, Boston MA, 2002–03(49); *Francesco Arcangeli*, Ravenna 2006(n.n.).

ENG.: [Mrs Noseda c.1878[3]] E. Gulland 1904.[4]

REF.: Waterhouse 1953, p.70; Waterhouse 1958, no.450; J. Hayes, *Gainsborough*, 1975, p.216n77; N. Kalinsky in *Nest of Nightingales* 1988, pp.63–65; D. Shawe-Taylor, *The Georgians*, 1990, pp.134–37; Ingamells 2004, pp.428–29.

Elizabeth Anne (1754–92), the eldest surviving child of Thomas Linley of Bath, began performing in public as a singer in 1767, her looks and voice at once attracting the highest praise. Following affairs with a Walter Long and a Captain Mathews in 1771 she eloped with Richard Brinsley Sheridan (1751–1816) on 18 March 1772 for France, when both were under age. Her father fetched them back, but on 13 April 1773 they married, thus depriving 'the family of the Linleys, in every sense, of its greatest treasure'.[5] Sheridan decreed that Elizabeth should sing no more in public and she promoted her husband's career, although both came to lead independent lives. She bore a son, Thomas Sheridan, in 1775, and a daughter Mary (who died in infancy) by Lord Edward Fitzgerald in March 1792, three months before her death by tuberculosis. Fanny Burney thought her

> really beautiful; her Complection , a clear, lovely, Animated Brown, with a blooming colour on her Cheeks; her Nose that most elegant of shapes, Grecian; fine, luxurious, easy setting Hair, a charming Forehead, pretty mouth, & most bewitching Eyes. With all this, her Carriage is modest & unassuming, and her Countenance indicates diffidence, & a strong desire of pleasing; a desire in which she can never be disappointed.[6]

Mary Linley (1758–87), Elizabeth's closest companion, sister and friend, made her public debut as an actress at the Theatre Royal, Covent Garden, in 1769–70 before joining her older sister in 1771 as a singer at oratorios, but she could not match her voice or looks. In 1780 she married Richard Tickell (1751–93),[7] a minor playwright, wit and close friend of Sheridan, whose waywardness he shared. She bore three children in four years and died of tuberculosis in 1787. Tickell remarried in 1789.[8]

Gainsborough could have received no further sittings from Elizabeth after mid-March 1772, when she eloped with Sheridan. The RA exhibition of 1772 opened on 24 April[9] and he was complaining on 31 March that he 'was just finishing her [Miss Linley's] Picture for the Exhibition'.[10] There is, perhaps, a reminiscence of Gainsborough's earlier portrait of c.1763–64 of two artistic sisters, his own daughters (Worcester Art Museum, Mass.), one engaging the viewer, the other distracted – although DPG320 is more deliberately staged. But Mary, it seems, had not been satisfied with the likenesses and in 1785, when she had become the mother of three and, according to Elizabeth, had 'compleately lost her beauty',[11] Gainsborough retouched the composition. On 2 November Mary wrote to Elizabeth, 'I found *our* picture come home from Gainsbro's very much improved and freshened up. My father and mother are quite in raptures with it; indeed, it is in *my* opinion, the *best* and *handsomest* of *you* that I have ever seen'.[12] Gainsborough had softened Mary's face, but other changes accommodated fashion:[13] their hair was now piled less high; Elizabeth's ear was covered by a lock of hair, her waist line raised by a dark blue velvet belt, and her flounced cuff shortened. The engraving of 1904 and a photograph of 1947 show Elizabeth still wearing her narrow cuff and 'dark blue velvet band and buckle round her waist';[14] one can only suppose that cleaning (by Hell in 1947?) removed them to expose the earlier paint layer.

A copy was sold Sotheby's, 30 October 1985, lot 251, and another, reduced, at Christie's, South Kensington, 15 November 2001, lot 223; other copies include a a pastel of 1899 by Ernest G. Beach, made for the Marquess of Dufferin and Ava, sold Christie's, 25 March 1999, lot 341,[15] and a pencil and watercolour study of the two heads alone, sold Christie's, South Kensington, 3 December 2003, lot 18. Two other drawings after DPG320 remain untraced.[16]

Gainsborough almost repeated Elizabeth's head in the bust-length of c.1775 now at the Philadelphia Museum of Art (E.24.4.13), possibly intended to form part of the series of half-length portraits of the Linley family, as Dorment has proposed.[17] Gainsborough painted two more remarkable portraits of her: a half length, begun in 1768, with her younger brother Tom (Sterling and Francine Clark Art Institute, Williamstown, MA, 1955.955; formerly at Knole)[18] and a whole-length of c.1785–86, seated beneath a tree (NG Washington, 1937.1.92). Gainsborough probably also painted Mary alone.[19] Fulcher recounted that Gainsborough also modelled a clay head of Miss Linley.[20]

1 There can be little doubt as to this identification, but Whitley 1928a, ii, p.378, simply said it likely that this was DPG320. At the RA 1772 it was described as 'executed in a fine natural style, the face of the young lady who is seated is uncommonly expressive and lovely, the draperies are well cast and the lights sweetly distributed' (*London Chronicle*, quoted by Whitley, *loc. cit.*), but the rich colouring was criticised as 'too glaring' (*Middlesex Journal*, 23–25 April 1772). See also H. Glanville in *Nest of Nightingales* 1988, p.20.

2 Sheridan was one of the sponsors of this exhibition; DPG320, although lent in Sheridan's name, had been described in a circular issued before the exhibition with a list of promised lenders as the property of William Linley (Whitley 1928b, p.230). Sheridan wrote an undated letter to an unidentified correspondent, presumably John Young, Keeper of the British Gallery, saying that he had just heard that of four pictures by Gainsborough he was lending, 'The late Mrs Sheridan and her sister the late Mrs Tickell' was to be described in the catalogue as Mr W. Linley's; '– This is an Errour – The Picture is *mine* – I beg the catalogue may be corrected – or the Picture not exhibited' (C. Price, ed. *The Letters of R.B. Sheridan*, 1966, p.200). Sheridan evidently believed that the picture was only temporarily with Linley as a security against a loan. Linley later recounted, in a letter of 17 November 1825, receiving DPG320 'in part payment (I considered it full payt), of the £100 loan, however, I have got *Gainsborough's charming picture* – it is now excellently placed in the Dulwich Gallery' (from an interleaved copy of T. Moore's *Memoirs of the Life of the Right Honourable Richard Brinsley Sheridan*, 1825; quoted in *NQ*, 11th series, x, 1914, p.62; Whitley 1928b, p.230; *Nest of Nightingales* 1988, p.102, 10:8).

3 At the Board Meeting of the Dulwich Governors, 11 December 1877, it was agreed that Mrs Noseda (Jane Noseda, 1813/14–after 1881?) should engrave the portrait of Mrs Tickell and Mrs Sheridan but on 14 January 1879 this permission was withdrawn since no start had been made.

4 Exh. RA 1905(1298), pub. Leggatt; illus. *Nest of Nightingales* 1988, p.66(3:4).

5 H. Angelo, *Reminiscences*, 1904, i, p.86.

6 *Early Journals and Letters of Fanny Burney*, ed. L.E. Trodie, i, 1988, pp.250–51 (1773).

7 For whose half-length portrait by Gainsborough, see *Nest of Nightingales* 1988, 13:1; it was last sold Sotheby's, 27 November 2003, lot 8.

8 Portraits of the second Mrs Tickell, Sarah Ley, are discussed by J. Bryant, *Kenwood, Paintings in the Iveagh Bequest*, 2003, pp.394–98.
9 I am grateful to Mark Pomeroy for this date.
10 J. Hayes ed., *Letters of Thomas Gainsborough*, 2001, p.96.
11 W. Lefanu ed., *Betsy Sheridan's Journal*, 1960, p.25.
12 W. F. Rae, *Sheridan*, 1896, ii, p.15.
13 As discussed by H. Glanville in *Nest of Nightingales* 1988, pp.17–18.
14 A colour plate showing this earlier state appears in M. Menpes & J. Greig, *Gainsborough*, 1909, f.p.152. See also *Nest of Nightingales* 1988, pp.64, 66. Sparkes 1876 had referred to a mass of 'much faded' violets at Elizabeth's feet, where now there are a few primroses, and Cook 1914 described a primrose plant in full blossom by Mrs Tickell on the right and a violet by Mrs Sheridan's feet on the left.
15 Letters of 3 September 1899 and 23 July 1900, from Beach to Lord Dufferin (a descendant of Elizabeth's granddaughter) concerning the pastel copy of a Gainsborough are in the PRO, Northern Ireland (xeroxes on file). A letter of 18 July 1900 mentions that the 'engraving of Gainsborough's picture at Messrs Dowdeswells … seems to me a good one & very interesting but to differ considerably in points from the photograph which I had' – perhaps DPG320.
16 See *A Nest of Nightingales* 1988(3:3a), presumably ex-Tickell sale, Christie's, 3 May 1884, lot 156, 'Gainsborough, The Sisters – in pencil'; another sold Anderson, New York, 9 April 1919, lot 172.
17 R. Dorment, *British Paintings in the Philadelphia Museum of Art*, 1986, p.124; also illus. *Nest of Nightingales* 1988, p.58.
18 Exh. *Great British Paintings from American Collections*, New Haven CT, 2001, no.16. For Elizabeth's iconography see *Nest of Nightingales* 1988, pp.58–66; Dorment (at note 17), pp.121–24, and Ingamells 2004, pp.428–29; an anonymous note on 'Early Portraits of Sir Thomas Lawrence', *Athenaeum*, 23 January 1830, p.46, stated that William Linley then owned a portrait of her in crayons by Lawrence 'about the same period' [i.e. 1789] – possibly that in the Tickell sale, Christie's 3 May 1884, lot 158 'Elizabeth Ann Tickell – in crayons – oval'. A bust-length oval miniature of Elizabeth attributed to Ozias Humphry was sold Bonham's, 20 November 1997, lot 65A.
19 For her iconography, see *A Nest of Nightingales* 1988, pp.79–81. A half-length by Gainsborough (illus. p.81) now at Kenwood, allegedly from the Tickell family in 1870, and lot 150 in the Tickell sale, Christie's, 3 May 1884 (as *Miss Linley*); see J. Bryant, *Kenwood, Paintings in the Iveagh Bequest*, 2003, pp.200–02, where identified as possibly Lady Eden.
20 G.W. Fulcher, *Gainsborough*, 1856, 1st ed., pp.88–89 (2nd ed. p.90): 'Mr Leslie had in his possession, some years ago, an exquisite plaster cast of a head of Miss Linley (from a clay model by Gainsborough).'

THOMAS GAINSBOROUGH (1727–88)

DPG331 *Thomas Linley the younger*

Canvas 75.9 x 63.5 lined by Dyer; revived and varnished 1870–71; the coat now lacking the original madder glazes; prominent craquelure and retouching in the right background, and minor retouchings in the face; pentimenti on the ear and behind the neck; discoloured varnish; Hell c.1951–53.

Pale grey eyes, powdered hair; wearing a red coat, yellow waistcoat, black hat trimmed with gold; trace of blue hair ribbon.

PROV.: Linley Bequest 1835.

EXH.: Aberystwyth 1946(17); National Gallery 1947(18); Leeds 1947–53(18); *Gainsborough in Bath*, Bath, 1988(17); *Nest of Nightingales* 1988(5:1); *Mozart, Prodigy of Nature*, Pierpont Morgan Library NY, BL London, 1991–92(n.n.); Gainsborough, Ferrara, 1998(17); *Rembrandt to Gainsborough*, Houston TX, Louisville KY, 1999–2000(87); *Old Master Paintings*, Japan, 2000(49); *Viva Mozart*, Salzburg, 2006-07(n.n.).

REF.: Waterhouse 1953, p.69; Waterhouse 1958, no.447.

Thomas Linley the younger (1756–78), violinist and composer,[1] eldest son of Thomas Linley the elder of Bath, studied under William Boyce in London and under Nardini in Leghorn from 1768; '*il Tommasino*' met Mozart in Florence before returning in 1771 to Bath, where he performed at his father's concerts; from 1774 he performed at Drury Lane, where he composed the opera *Selima and Azor* in 1776; he was accidentally drowned on 7 August 1778 at Grimsthorpe Castle, Lincs., while staying, with his sister Maria, with the Duke of Ancaster.

DPG331 appears to have been painted at Bath c.1772, after Linley's return from Italy and before both artist and sitter moved to London in 1774. A replica is recorded at Clandeboye in the collection of the Marquess of Dufferin and Ava.[2] Linley also appears in the double portrait with Elizabeth, in the Sterling and Francine Clark Art Institute, Williamstown, Mass. (1955.955; see DPG320 above, note 17).

1 For whom see also G. Beechey, *Musical Quarterly*, liv, 1968, pp.74–82.
2 Presumably by descent through Elizabeth Linley's granddaughter who m. the 4th Baron Dufferin (I am grateful to Hugh Belsey for this).

Sir Thomas Lawrence (1769–1830)

DPG178 William Linley

Canvas 76.2 x 63.5 lined; a small damage in the right background above shoulder; pentimenti down his right arm and behind the head; some bitumen in the coat and the overall craquelure has been retouched; Hell 1951; cleaned 1984.

Clear blue-grey eyes, rich brown hair; wearing a dark grey coat, white stock, 'the costume of the scholars of St. Paul's school in which he was then receiving his education'.[1]

Prov.: Linley Bequest 1835.

Exh.: RA 1789(171 *Mr Linley, brother of Mrs Sheridan*); BI 1833(32); RA schools 1831, 1866, 1891, 1898; *Deceased Masters of the British School*, RA, 1904(61); *First 100 years of the RA*, RA,1951–52(421); *Collection for a King*, Washington DC, Los Angeles, 1985–86(18); *Nest of Nightingales* 1988(10.1); *Obras Maestras*, Madrid, Bilbao, 1999(48); *Rembrandt to Gainsborough*, Houston TX, Louisville KY, 1999–2000(90).

Eng.: T. Lupton 1840; E. Gulland[?] 1904 (Leggatts).

Ref.: Garlick 1954, p.46; Garlick 1964, p.126; K. Garlick in *Collection for a King*, 1985, p.78; Garlick 1989, no.496; M. Levey, *Sir Thomas Lawrence*, 2005, p.77.

William Linley (1771–1835),[2] fourth surviving son of Thomas Linley of Bath; when his father moved to London in 1776 he was left in care in Bath with his brother Ozias and sister Jane; William went on to Harrow in 1780 and St Paul's school in 1785; although he had a good singing voice his lack of application to the study of technique led his father to decide he would be better employed in the public service; he worked for the East India Company at Madura and Dindigul from 1790 to 1795 when ill health brought him home; in London 1795–1800 he worked with his brother-in-law Sheridan at Drury Lane, composing operas with limited success; he returned to India in 1800 working in and around Madras until 1806 when again ill-health compelled him to return home; he then settled in London writing occasional songs, poems and novels and was remembered as having 'the sweetest and kindest temper, high and honourable principles … and a genius for poetry and music' (W.L. Bowles).

This most accomplished portrait was exhibited in 1789, when the sitter was eighteen and about to go to India, and Lawrence twenty (having spent two years in London). Denning recounted[3] that it was presented to George III as a specimen of the young artist's skill; after looking some time all the King said was 'Ah! Ah! Why doesn't the blockhead have his hair cut!' – an uncorroborated anecdote, but Denning doubtless knew William while his brother Ozias was a Fellow at Dulwich (see Gainsborough DPG302 and Oliver DPG476).

Several versions are recorded. One was in the Tickell sale, Christie's, 3 May 1884, lot 155 (perhaps that later with Peter Jones's brother which he recalled had, he thought, 'a label *verso*: '*Taken from the life, second time*'); another was in the collection of Gore Vidal in 2001.[4] Copies are in the Assembly Rooms, Bath; in the Royal College of Music, and formerly in the Groult collection, Bordeaux; others include those by M.P. Ward 1913 (with Marian Wilson, Norwich, 1997); sold Christie's, South Kensington, 14 December 1983, lot 80, and sold Sotheby's, Summers Place, 10 December 1996, lot 2201.

Other portraits of Linley were by William Lane, exhibited RA 1810(544 *Mr Linley, eminent musical performer*), and presumably a study for Lane's drawing of 'A group of portraits of eminent musical performers' in the Royal Collection.[5] A.J. Oliver exhibited a portrait of *W Linley Esq* at the RA 1810(179). His portrait in old age by William Lonsdale, exhibited BI 1831(214), is in the Gemäldegalerie, Berlin (1636).[6]

See also DPG474 below.

A miniature by John Barry in the Fitzwilliam Museum, Cambridge (3821),[7] dated c.1795, with long dark hair, is doubtfully identified as Linley (it had previously been called Thomas Linley); similarly a bust-length drawing by William Hamilton in the Huntington (63.52.92), probably c.1800, and a miniature attributed to George Engleheart, formerly belonging to Henry Yates Thompson.[8]

1 Anon., 'Early Portraits of Sir Thomas Lawrence', *Athenaeum*, 23 January 1830, p.46.
2 For whom, see G.A. Waterfield in *The Nest of Nightingales* 1988, pp.97–99.
3 Denning 1859, no.359.
4 Illus *Times Mag.*, 1 September 2001, p.43 (I am grateful to Alastair Laing for this reference).
5 A.P. Oppé, *English Drawings at Windsor Castle, Stuart and Georgian periods*, 1950, p.70, no.408, pl.67; Linley is possibly the left-hand figure.
6 Engraved W.R. Sherlock, exh. *Nest of Nightingales* 1988 (10.9). Linley left his portrait by Lonsdale to his niece, Elizabeth Ann Tickell.
7 R. Bayne-Powell, *Catalogue of Portrait Miniatures in the Fitzwilliam Museum, Cambridge*, 1985, p.4, and G. Reynolds, *British Portrait Miniatures*, Fitzwilliam Museum Handbook, 1998, p.118(b).
8 Illus. *Pictures in the Dulwich Gallery*, 1911, front.; sold Sotheby's, 2 July 1941, lot 127.

Sir Thomas Lawrence (1769–1830)

DPG475 *Maria Linley*

Pastel on paper laid on panel 31.5 x 26 oval; there may be brush marks in the blue sash and ribbon, suggesting watercolour; some mould round the head; a label *verso*: '*To be kept from the Sun and the Damp and to be hung with the front of the face towards the Light*'.

Brown hair, brown eyes; wearing a white dress with blue bow, neck ribbon and sash.

PROV.: Linley Bequest 1835.

EXH.: *Nest of Nightingales* 1988(7.2).

Lit:. Garlick 1964, p.263 (double entry); K. Garlick in *Nest of Nightingales* 1988, p.90.

DPG475 appears to be one of the pastel portraits the young Lawrence executed at Bath where he practised from before c.1779 to 1787. Garlick believes that the label on the *verso* was written by Lawrence, although it was unusual for it not to bear a date or signature. William Linley's original lists of the Linley Bequest made in 1831 (see p.129) include two pastels by Lawrence of Linley girls, Maria and Jane (Mrs Ward); but the latter, listed (as apart from described) in Dulwich catalogues 1876–92, was thereafter omitted altogether and remains untraced. It would appear, therefore, that the sitter in DPG475 was known to William Linley as Maria.[1]

Maria (1763–84),[2] the third daughter of Thomas Linley, showed the greatest promise as a singer; in 1775 Garrick proposed engaging both Mary and Maria at Drury Lane, where Maria sang regularly from 1776 until her sudden death in 1784. This portrait may have been taken when Maria was visiting her grandparents in Bath in September 1784, a visit which ended tragically when she was 'carried away' by 'brainfever'. One other portrait of Maria is known, a profile (wearing a man's surtout?) in watercolour in the Victoria Art Gallery, Bath, attributed to Ozias Humphry.[3]

1 In the Dulwich catalogues DPG475 was called simply Miss Linley 1876–80 and Mrs Tickell (Mary Linley) in 1892; this was corrected to Maria by C. Black, *The Linleys of Bath*, 1911, p.153.
2 For whom see *Nest of Nightingales* 1988, pp.88–90.
3 *Ibid.*, 7:1. .

attributed to SIR THOMAS LAWRENCE (1769–1830)

DPG474 *called the Rev Ozias Thurston Linley*

Pastel on paper on canvas 30.4 x 25.6 oval; some staining above the head; some fading in the lower area.

Brown eyes and hair; wearing a brown coat with silver buttons, white shirt and waistcoat.

PROV.: Linley Bequest 1835.

EXH.: *Science and Music in 18th century Bath*, Bath, 1977(74); *Nest of Nightingales* 1988(8.1).

REF.: Garlick 1964, p.263 (double entry); K. Garlick in *Nest of Nightingales* 1988, p.92.

For Ozias Linley (1765-1831) see A .J. Oliver DPG476 below.

Although listed in Dulwich catalogues from 1876 as a portrait of Ozias Linley by Lawrence, such a portrait was not identified by William Linley in his correspondence with the College in 1831 nor in his Will (see p.129). Both attribution and identity must remain tentative. Ozias was sent to Harrow in 1780, when the precocious Lawrence was beginning his pastel portraits.

Garlick has commented that the sitter appears to be under fourteen, when Lawrence was ten, and that the style does not seem to compare with Lawrence's at any stage of his career; he also considered DPG474 too unsophisticated for Ozias Humphry, but advocated retaining the traditional Lawrence attribution 'with reservation'.

JAMES LONSDALE (1777–1839)

DPG456 Mrs Thomas Linley

Canvas[1] 76.5 x 63.5 strip lined; Hell 1953; cleaned 1988; cleaned 2006-08.

Brown wig, blue-grey eyes; wearing a white muslin cap, a high-waisted brown day dress with a white fichu and a red wrap; she sits in a brown chair with a yellow cushion.

PROV.: Linley Bequest 1835.

EXH.: RA 1820(33); *Nest of Nightingales* 1988(2:3).

Mary Johnson (1729–1820) married Thomas Linley of Bath in 1752; herself musically gifted she was, as Ozias Humphry expressed it, compelled to relinquish her musical studies 'for the more useful and amiable offices of domestic concerns'; of her twelve children, all born in Bath, eight survived and were musically gifted; a shrewd, robust woman, she died on 18 January 1820, aged ninety-one, just before the opening of the RA exhibition in which this rather flattering portrait was shown.

The identity seems confirmed by the inscribed drawing by Lawrence of c.1795–1800 (Yale Center for British Art, B1977.14.5305).[2] Before 1980 DPG456 was catalogued as by Ozias Humphry (1742–1810),[3] who had drawn her youthful portrait while he was staying with the Linley family c.1762–64 (Victoria Art Gallery, Bath).[4] Her portrait by A.J. Oliver, exhibited RA 1807(109), and presumably that listed in the Linley Bequest, see p.129, remains untraced.

1 Canvas stamp *verso*: ... *99* ... *70/ BRO*
2 *Nest of Nightingales* 1988(2:2).
3 A label *verso* reads: *Portrait of Miss Linley/painted by Ozias Humphry.*
4 *Nest of Nightingales* 1988(2:1).

ARCHER JAMES OLIVER (1774–1842)

DPG476 The Rev Ozias Thurston Linley

Canvas 76.8 x 64.2 unlined; Hell 1953.

Brown eyes, dark brown hair; wearing a black coat.

PROV.: Linley Bequest 1835.

EXH.: *Nest of Nightingales* 1988 (8:2).

LIT.: G.A. Waterfield in *Nest of Nightingales* 1988, p.92.

Ozias Linley (1765–1831), the third son and least musical of Thomas Linley's eight surviving children, although he played the organ and composed some settings for the liturgy; his childhood was spent in Bath with Jane and William after their parents moved to London in 1776; he graduated at Corpus Christi College, Oxford, in 1789, became a minor canon at Norwich in 1790 and vicar of Stoke Holy Cross in 1807 and of Trowse and Lakenham in 1815; he was appointed a Junior Fellow and Organist at Dulwich College in 1816. An absent-minded and rather querulous bachelor, he was reputedly a good mathematician.[1]

Peter Murray first suggested DPG476 was the *Rev Ozias T. Linley by Oliver* which William Linley left to the College in his Will of January 1832 (but did not list as such in his correspondence with the College in 1831).[2] It had been discovered 'in or near the Mausoleum' in 1873 and from 1876 had been catalogued as showing Noel Desenfans (to whom the sitter bears no resemblance) by William Owen (a misreading of Oliver?).[3] Oliver painted a now unlocated portrait of Mrs Thomas Linley (see p.129) and exhibited a portrait of *W. Linley Esq* RA 1810(179). DPG476 may date from the same time.

A bust of *The late Rev. Ozias Linley* by C.A. Rivers was exhibited RA 1836(1109).

1 See G.A. Waterfield in *Nest of Nightingales* 1988, pp.90–91. For some lively first-hand reminiscences of Linley, see Young 1889, ii, pp.375–79. Ozias was a co-signatory of the Gallery accounts between 6 June 1817 and 9 August 1826.

2 Murray 1980, p.88. See p.129 above.

3 The features described as 'difficult to reconcile' with the more refined portrait by Northcote. DPG476 was illus. in J.E. Ross, *Radical Adventurer*, 1971, f.p.22, as Desenfans by David [*sic*] Owen.

THE FAIRFAX MURRAY GIFT 1911–17

The pictures in this section are catalogued in alphabetical order by artist

Charles Fairfax Murray

Charles Fairfax Murray (1849–1919), artist (see DPG612, p.214 and D6, p.248), collector and dealer,[1] was born in London. He worked with Edward Burne-Jones c.1866–67, was an assistant with William Morris & Co. and in 1869–70 became a general factotum in the Rossetti workshop. He first visited Italy in 1871 and by the 1880s was spending most of his time there, patronized by Ruskin 1872–83 as a 'heaven born' copyist of early Italian frescoes. In 1875 he married Angelica Colivicchi in Pisa and his Italian family eventually comprised six surviving children (born between 1877 and 1888); later, with Blanche Richmond, Murray raised an English family of six children (born between 1888 and 1905). By the 1880s his interests in the fine arts were turning increasingly to dealing in which he became eminently successful. His English clients included the National Gallery (of which he narrowly failed to become the director in 1894), the Victoria and Albert Museum, the Fitzwilliam Museum, Cambridge, and Birmingham Art Gallery. In 1900 he was working in partnership with both Agnews and Colnaghis.[2] He visited America twice in 1914 and sold over one thousand old master drawings to Pierpont Morgan. He died at Chiswick and was buried in Isleworth.

It was after completing a catalogue of the pictures at Welbeck Abbey in 1904 that he began to make a particular study of English art which was to culminate in his gift of forty-six English portraits to Dulwich.[3] He had been a frequent visitor to the Gallery in his youth and the donation was further encouraged by his friendship with the energetic Henry Yates Thompson (1838–1928), Chairman of the Dulwich Gallery 1908–19, who in 1910 funded new rooms (now galleries 10–12), mainly to accommodate a Fairfax Murray gift. The portraits were given in 1911, three additions being made in 1915 and 1917, and at his request the donor's name was withheld during his lifetime.[4] Murray told his friend William Spanton that 'it was not on acct. of the people represented that I gave those pictures to Dulwich, but as a series of pictures by artists, whether British or foreign, who have painted in England. … Most of the Dulwich pictures are signed, if not, mostly authentic like the 2 Dahls …'.[5] Fairfax Murray's gift transformed the British collection at Dulwich and led Collins Baker, then the most eminent historian of British art, to register his 'recognition of the great service Mr Murray has done to the study of English portraiture in collecting signed examples and presenting them in this way to public galleries'.[6]

1 For whom, see W.S. Spanton, *An Art Student and his Teachers*, 1927, ch.4; A.C. Benson, *Memories and Friends*, 1924, ch.12.; R. Barrington, *Apollo*, cxl, 1994, pp.15–21; D.B. Elliott, *Charles Fairfax Murray*, 2000; P. Tucker, *Journal of the History of Collections*, xiv, i, 2002, pp.115–37; J.F. Codell in *ODNB*.

2 Mr Richard Kingzett has kindly informed me that none of the Dulwich pictures is identifiable in the Agnew ledgers (9 March 2005); similarly the Colnaghi records (which are incomplete) have yielded nothing.

3 He gave a further nine pictures, not English: two Italian – after Giulio Romano (as Raphael DPG602), Master of the Annunciation to the Shepherds (as Ribera DPG558); one French – Bourdon (DPG557), and six Dutch – attributed to Cossiers (as a Dutch self portrait DPG605), Hanneman (DPG572), Honthorst (DPG571), Johnson the younger (DPG564), Nason (DPG556) and Sanders (DPG577).

4 Following Murray's death, Yates Thompson told his successor, E.T. Hall (letter of 15 March 1919; Gallery archive), that 'Dulwich were relieved of the pledge of anonymity which I gave him' and suggested that the portraits should be labelled 'Fairfax Murray Gift'.

5 Letter of 1 August 1913 (Gallery archive).

6 Collins Baker 1912, ii, p.68n. He later paid a second tribute to Fairfax Murray as 'a serious pioneer in the study of English portraiture' (*Burl. Mag.*, xxxv, 1919, p.150).

THOMAS BEACH (1738–1806)

DPG591 Portrait of a Man

Canvas 76.5 x 63.5 lined; pentimenti in the coat above the top button, and below the collar; two old tears, to the left of the fourth button down, and to the right of the face; unevenly cleaned; the eyelashes are retouched; there are drying cracks in the coat and the lower area is abraded with some overpainting; Hell 1952–55.

Signed in red, below left: *T Beach pt./1785.*; his right eye brown, and left eye grey; wearing a yellow coat with silver buttons and a white neckcloth; in a painted oval.

PROV.: Fairfax Murray Gift 1911.

EXH.: Possibly RA 1785(253 *Portrait of a gentleman; small oval*).

REF.: E.S. Beach, *Thomas Beach*, 1934, p.60, no.97.

Mary Beale (1633–99)

DPG574 *Portrait of a Youth*

Canvas 76.5 x 63.8 lined by Morrill; a filling in the top left corner and several large and darkened retouchings; uneven varnish; Hell 1953.

Signed in the bottom left spandrel: *Mary Beale*; blue-grey eyes, long brown hair; wearing a brown cloak; a painted oval.

PROV.: Col. E.A. Bulwer of Dereham sale, Christie's, 19 November 1910, lot 40 as of Cowley; bt. Agnew; Fairfax Murray 1910; his Gift 1911 as Cowley by Beale.

REF.: Collins Baker 1912, ii, p.40; R.T. Jeffree & E. Walsh, *The Excellent Mrs Mary Beale*, 1975, p.69, no.21.

DPG574 was dated c.1685 by Walsh and Jeffree (but it is perhaps earlier) and tentatively identified as a portrait of Bartholomew Beale (1656–1709), the artist's eldest surviving son. They listed three other portraits by Mary Beale which they considered might also show Bartholomew, dating between c.1670 and 1685.[1] Three portraits of him, from 1677 and 1681, are recorded in the Beale diaries,[2] but no certain portrait of him in his maturity survives.[3]

Previously identified as the poet Abraham Cowley (1618–67),[4] who had been a guest of the Beales in 1664, but the sitter in DPG574 is evidently much younger. For a second mistaken Cowley identity, see Lely DPG563, p.176.

1 Cf. *The Excellent Mrs Mary Beale*, 1975, nos.18–21 and pp.68–69: NPG 659, now called an unknown sitter (NPG, *Complete Illustrated Catalogue*, 2004, p.691); Rugby School (no.18 in the 1975 exhibition); Althorp, and DPG572. See also Lely DPG563n2, p.176.
2 On 5 March 1677 Charles Beale, Mary Beale's husband, sent 'my son Barth's picture done by [my wife] for Charles [Beale] to make an essay in water-colours', and in 1681 he listed two portraits by his wife of 'Son *Barth*; reading' and 'A 2nd picture of son *Barth's*' (Collins Baker 1912, ii, pp.164, 166).
3 See T. Barber, *Mary Beale*, Geffrye Museum, 1999, p.79. Mary Beale's *Self portrait* of c.1665 in the NPG (1687), may include portraits of her two sons as children, see Piper 1963, p.24. Like his younger brother Charles, Bartholomew had first assisted in his mother's studio, but in 1680 began his medical studies at Clare Hall, Cambridge, and subsequently maintained a medical practice in Coventry.
4 Collins Baker 1912, ii, p.40, rather enjoyed himself with this possibility: 'perfectly unleavened by any sentiment or emotion … [Mary Beale] might have been painting a young grocer instead of a poet of some grace and scholarship'.

MICHAEL DAHL (c.1659–1743)

DPG575 *Portrait of a Lady*

Canvas 125.7 x 101.6 lined; heavy retouched craquelure in the dress which has a yellowish overpaint and is irreversibly faded; Hell 1953.

Brownish hair, brown eyes; wearing a blue dress with green lining over a white shift; the spray of flowers on the ledge include honeysuckle.

PROV.: (with DPG576): Seymour Robert Delmé of Cams Hall, Hants.; his sale, Christie's 7 July 1894, lots 68(DPG575) and 70 (DPG576) unattributed, bt. Fairfax Murray; his Gift 1911.

Although they could be contemporary, probably 1700–10, and came from the same sale in 1894, DPG575 and DPG576 do not appear to be a pair.

Michael Dahl (c.1659–1743)

DPG576 Portrait of a Man

Canvas 125.7 x 101.6 lined; the deep blue of the sky irreversibly faded and the shadows in the face, eyes and hair abraded; there are repaired tears to the right of the head, along the bottom edge, either side of the hanging cravat and on the left side of the chest; scattered matt retouchings; Hell 1953.

Brown eyes, brown wig; wearing a white shirt and stock, with a brown coat with gold buttons and eyelets.

PROV.: see DPG575 above.

See DPG575.

Simon Dubois (1632–1708)

DPG584 *Sir William Jones Kt.*

Canvas 75.9 x 63.2 lined; repaired slit on forehead above his right eye; Hell 1952–53.

Signed bottom right: *S.du.Bois. fecit*; dated top left: *A.D.1682*. (in black) and inscribed top right: *Aet.77* (see below); a later inscription in yellow, bottom left: *Sr. Wm. Jones/Father to Ly./Pelham*; brown wig, grey eyes, slight grey moustache; wearing broad white bands, a black gown with black tasselled shoulders over a black waistcoat and vest; in a painted oval.

PROV.: [Probably by descent from the sitter's granddaughter who married the 2nd Viscount Townshend] 6th Marquess Townshend; Raynham Hall sale, Christie's, 7 March 1904, lot 172, bt. Agnew; Fairfax Murray 1904; his Gift 1911.

REF.: Collins Baker 1912, ii, 68; Duleep Singh, ii, p.206, no.52.

Sir William Jones (1630–82), lawyer and politician, Kt. 1671; solicitor-general 1673–75 and attorney-general 1675–79; MP 1680–82; he spoke for the Exclusion Bill and condemned the Popish Plot; Dryden characterized him as 'the Bull-faced Jonas' in *Absalom and Achitophel*; while his professional abilities were generally admired, Burnet, for example, found a 'roughness in his deportment that was very disagreeable.' He married in 1661 the widow Elizabeth *née* Alleyn (d. 1699) of Hatfield Peverel, see DPG585 below. Their daughter Elizabeth (c.1664–81) married in 1679 Thomas Pelham, 1st Baron Pelham of Laughton (and their daughter was the first wife of the 2nd Viscount Townshend, from whose descendants the portrait was purchased; see also Jervas DPG567, p.165).

Although the inscribed age *77* is mistaken, provenance and the lady's mourning dress support the identification of Sir William. He was 52 when he died on 2 May 1682 and the portrait of his wife in mourning, DPG585, would have been completed later. An effigy of Jones on his tomb in the Holy Cross church, Ramsbury, Wilts., is his only other recorded likeness.

These are the earliest dated English pictures by Simon Dubois who is said to have arrived in England in 1681.[1]

1 Waterhouse 1994, p.345n10.

SIMON DUBOIS (1632–1708)

DPG585 Elizabeth, Lady Jones

Canvas 75.9 x 63.2 lined; abrasions bottom centre and on the left-hand edge; scuff marks upper right and in her right shoulder; scattered retouchings; Hell 1952–53.

Signed bottom right in black: *S.du.Bois. fecit.1682*; a later inscription in yellow, bottom left: *Ly.Jones/Mother to Ly./Pelham.*; brown eyes, wearing a laced lawn collar, and a black mourning dress; a painted oval.

PROV.: See DPG584 above; Raynham Hall sale, Christie's, 7 March 1904, lot 173.

REF.: Collins Baker 1912, ii, 68; Duleep Singh, ii, p.206, no.53.

See DPG584 above. A comparable half-length painted oval portrait of a widow by Dubois dated 1689 was acquired by the Prado (3.158) in 1970.[1]

1 J.J. Luna, *Boletín del Museo del Prado*, vi, 16, 1985, pp.30–32.

attributed to ISAAC FULLER (c.1606–1672)

DPG569 Portrait of a Man

Canvas 62.8 x 49.5 lined; the edges were cut before lining, the canvas probably reduced from 76 x 63; small damages in the eye lids and through the upper lip; Hell 1949; cleaned 2007–08.

Blue eyes, chestnut hair; a slightly wandering right eye and a vestigial moustache and tuft on his lower lip; wearing a black jacket over a white shirt; his left hand rests on a classical stone bust.

PROV.: Colnaghi as an Unknown Portrait; Fairfax Murray by 1900 as '?J. Hanneman'; his Gift 1911 as Dobson? (and Picture Gallery Committee Minutes, 10 May 1915, as Artist unknown).

A forceful English portrait of 1645–50, evidently cut down, for which both sitter and attribution remain uncertain.[1] The slightly wandering eyes and the intensity of gaze encourage the idea of a self portrait and the features somewhat resemble those of Isaac Fuller as seen in his much later self-portrait of 1670.[2] A similar head appears in a kit-cat portrait by Fuller of c.1650 now in the Clarke Library, University of California at Los Angeles, which in the early 18th century was accepted as a self portrait,[3] and in a half-length of c.1645 in the Garrick Club attributed to Dobson.[4] Both these portraits show an unkempt figure in an open white shirt with long, untidy hair and a slightly wandering eye, the first set against a stormy sky, arms crossed at his breast, the second, a sketch, has one hand spread at his breast.[5]

The spirited execution of the sky and background wall in DPG569 further suggest the possibility of Fuller, but so little is known of his earlier portraiture that an attribution must be regarded as tentative. The (slightly later?) Los Angeles portrait shows a generally looser execution, as do the portraits of the *Unknown Man* (formerly called *John Cleveland*) inscribed 1644 but probably later (Tate Gallery, T00056),[6] and the *Sir William Petty* (National Portrait Gallery 2924)[7] of c.1650 (both these portraits show long-fingered hands as in DPG569); the *Sir Thomas Baines* of before 1653 (Christ's College, Cambridge)[8] provides the closest (but not conclusive) comparison.

The sitter in both the Dulwich and Garrick portraits was previously identified as the actor and playwright Nathaniel Lee (1645/52–92),[9] but both may date from before his birth. The inclusion of a classical stone bust recalls Vertue's mention of 'Latham (statuary) his head painted by *Fuller* leaning his hand on a bust',[10] but Latham's recorded activity began c.1670 and he died in 1693.

1 The stretcher is inscribed *verso*: *J. Mytens*. In a letter of August 1900 (Gallery archive) Murray told W.S. Spanton that the portrait by J. Hanneman? was being photographed by Braun and it was not of 'Lee the mad dramatist!'

2 Prime versions at Oxford in the Bodleian Library (Poole, i, p.57, no.142) and at Queen's College (Poole, ii, p.119, no.32), the head of the latter copied by Vertue (wash drawing at the Huntington, see R. Wark, *Early British Drawings in the Huntington Collection*, 1969, p.57, D, illus.).

3 'The Picture of Isaac Fuller' sold to Dorington at Covent Garden, 6 June 1717 (Vertue, i, p.43); Vertue drew a copy of the head inscribed *Mr Isaack Fuller se ipse pinxit. G.V. del. In posses. Dorington Esq* (British Museum; L. Binyon, *Catalogue of Drawings by British Artists in the British Museum*, iv, p.298, no.24 as 'Fuller the Painter in a Storm'); with Lady Walpole, Downing Street in 1736 (*Capital Collection* 2002, p.447; Vertue, v, p.126, and vi, p.177); by descent to Horace Walpole who renamed the sitter John Ogilby (1600–76); engraved W.C. Edwards 1820 as Ogilby by Fuller; Strawberry Hill sale, Robins, 20th day, 17 May 1842, lot 111; sold Christie's, 30 April 1954, lot 143; Clarke Library 1954. (The bust-length portrait of Ogilby in the Bodleian Library, Oxford, was considered 'Fulleresque' by Collins Baker 1912, i, p.159).

4 Ashton 1997, no.415, p.230; once belonged to Richard Cosway (*Cosway* 1995, no.192, and *Wal. Soc.*, LXVI, pp.188, 204n126, fig.89); engraved John Watts 1778 and B. Reading 1820 as Lee by Dobson; a crayon copy by William Faithorne (1616–91) in the Wellesley sale, Sotheby's, 28 June 1920, lot 313. At one stage Malcolm Rogers wondered whether it might not be by Fuller (note in NPG archive).

5 Malcolm Rogers first linked the three portraits (letters on file of 29 May and 11 July 1997). A. Laing, *Burl.Mag.*, cxli, 1999, p.549, emphasized the connection and wrote that 'the possibility that [DPG569] is an early *Self portrait* by Isaac Fuller ought to be given serious consideration'. DPG569 was illus. in D. Shawe-Taylor, *Dulwich Picture Gallery, a visitor's guide*, 2000, p.65, as British School (Isaac Fuller?), *Portrait of a Man (Self Portrait?)*.

6 Illus. Waterhouse 1994, p.89; see *Tate Gallery Report* 1955–56, pp.14–15; C. Macleod in *ODNB*.

7 Piper 1963, pp.275–76, pl.8g; NPG, *Complete Illustrated Catalogue*, 2004, p.490.

8 Illus. *Connoisseur*, cxxxix, 1957, p.70; J.W. Goodison, *Portraits in Christ's, Clare and Sydney Sussex Colleges*, 1985, no.2, pl.iv.

9 Who was confined in Bedlam 1684–88 (*ODNB* persists in listing DPG569 with the Clarke and Garrick portraits as an authentic image of Lee). See also note 1.

10 Vertue, ii, p.59. Vertue also mentioned (i, p.114) 'a square painting the head and picture of ... Pierce Sculptor a part of a Statue before him. Painted by ... Fuller', but his marginal sketch is sufficient to show this was not DPG569.

Isaac Fuller, *Self Portrait?*, c.1650
(William Andrews Clark Memorial Library, University of California, Los Angeles)

Thomas Gainsborough (1727–88)

DPG588 A Couple in a Landscape

Canvas 76.2 x 67 lined; painted over an inverted half-length figure (apparently a young woman with a rose corsage, her left hand by her head); damaged upper left where there was cleavage between canvas and paint film;[1] on the far right an old vertical tear in the sky, and a small damage through and below his right hand; there are scattered small losses in his coat, her skirt, and in the foreground landscape areas; in 1945 Hell said it was 'in very good condition but rather dirty – a light clean and revarnishing will be quite safe';[2] cleaned and relined 1972; cleaned and relined 2004–05.

He has brown hair and brown eyes and wears a blue coat over a red waistcoat with black breeches and white stockings; she has brown hair and brown eyes and wears a blue bonnet and an orange-yellow dress with a hooped skirt; in her right hand she holds a porte-crayon and in her left a crayon sketch on paper.

PROV.: John Carroll; John Doherty of Birmingham by 1858;[3] Carroll/Doherty sale, Foster's, 12 March 1879(90, 'Gainsborough, Pair of Portraits'), bt. in;[4] John Doherty of Foxlydiate House, Redditch 1880;[5] Adrian Lesser Lesser,[6] from whom bt. by Fairfax Murray in December 1888;[7] Fairfax Murray Gift 1911.

EXH.: [*Gainsborough, Constable and old Suffolk Artists*, Ipswich Fine Art Society, 1887(141 'Portraits by Gainsborough', lent L. Lesser)?]; lent to the Fitzwilliam Museum, Cambridge, 1910; RA schools 1931, 1936; Aberystwyth 1945(59); National Gallery 1947(16); Leeds 1947–53(16); *Gainsborough*, Victoria AG, Bath, 1951(1); *Collection for a King*, Washington DC, Los Angeles, 1985–86(10); *Manners and Morals*, Tate, 1987(189); *Young Gainsborough*, London, Norwich, Newcastle, 1997(29); *Rembrandt to Gainsborough*, Houston TX, Louisville KY, 1999–2000(86); *Old Master Paintings*, Japan, 2000(48); *The Art of Conversation*, York Art Gallery, 2006-07(n.n.).

REF.: Waterhouse 1953, p.117(as earlier 1750s); Waterhouse 1958, no.753 (as mid-1750s); D. Shawe-Taylor in *Rembrandt to Gainsborough*, 1999, p.232.

Dated 1753 by Belsey,[8] DPG588 is a particularly elegant example of the small-scale open-air portraits which Gainsborough painted in Suffolk; it may be compared with the rather earlier *Mr and Mrs Kirby* in the National Portrait Gallery (1421)[9] and the *Portrait of the Artist with his Wife and Daughter* in the National Gallery (6547)[10] The couple, presumably man and wife, are posed in a richly varied and carefully described landscape. The prominent decaying tree behind them may seem an inappropriate background for a young married couple, but it was a familiar presence in the young Gainsborough's landscapes and recalls his early admiration for Jacob van Ruisdael and Jacob Wijnants.[11]

DPG588 was once supposed to be a companion to the *Girl seated in a Park* in the Yale Center for British Art (B1977.14.55) which is the same size and shared the same 19th-century provenance.[12]

1 A photograph by Emery Walker of c.1910 (NPG archive), taken while DPG588 was in Fairfax Murray's collection, shows considerable disturbance in this area. On 5 November 1971 the Gallery Committee heard that DPG588 had a very elevated crackle and cleavage between the canvas and the paint film in the top left corner. Colour plates used in the exhibition catalogues of 1985, 1987 and 1999 and in Beresford 1998 all show this disturbance.

2 He went on: 'But I really believe it is difficult to clean any later pictures of his without removing some of the delicate finishing touches. The Dulwich ones are not very dirty, and look extremely nice. I hope they can be left alone, except for the removal of the yellowbrownish film.' These quotations from an undated and unsigned typescript in the Gallery archive, evidently by Sir Gerald Kelly from conversations with Hell.

3 The brushed mark *verso*: *866D* identifies a group of pictures sent to Christie's on 29 March 1858 by John Doherty of 15 Old Square, Birmingham; they were returned to him unsold (letter from W.A. Martin to E.K. Waterhouse, 25 April 1947; Fitzwilliam Museum, Cambridge, archives). I am most grateful to Hugh Belsey for help in disentangling this provenance (and see notes 4 and 5 below).

4 This sale was described as being 'the small but choice collection of Pictures … formed at the beginning of the present Century by John Carroll Esq and removed from Private Apartments at Hampton Court Palace'; Lugt 39053 described the sale as that of 'Carroll [Doherty]'; the names were presumably related and a stamp *verso*: *L27* may relate to this sale.

5 A second stamp *verso*: *544L* identifies 19 pictures consigned to Christie's on 10 March 1880 by John Doherty of Foxlydiate House, near Redditch, but delivered to Hampton Court Palace without appearing in a sale (letter from W.A. Martin to E.K. Waterhouse, 12 June 1947; Fitzwilliam Museum, Cambridge, archives).

6 His label, with his address at 123 New Bond Street, remains *verso*; he was listed at that address from 1880 until after 1888.

7 On 5 December 1888 Fairfax Murray wrote in his diary: 'Christie's met Lesser & arranged purchase of Gainsboro' for £[?50] – Lesser's after & concluded purchase of portrait of lady & gentleman (small whole lengths in a landscape) by Gainsborough an early work' (Fairfax Murray's Diary; Fondation Custodia, Paris). I am very grateful to both Paul Tucker and Paul Matthews for this reference. W.S. Spanton had alleged that Murray bought 'the small Lady and Gentleman' at Christie's, one of a number of portraits by Gainsborough he acquired there (*An Art Student and his Teachers*, 1927, p.106).

8 Orally 2005. M. Menpes and J. Greig, *Gainsborough*, 1909, p.178, list it as '1753' without supporting evidence.

9 Kerslake 1977, i, pp.162–63, ii, pl.449, as early 1750s. Comparing DPG588 with the Kirbys, C.H. Collins Baker found 'rounder modelling, greater freedom of pose (especially in the lady, who has an instantaneous, accidental kind of grace) and of more rhythmic play of line', and went on to suggest DPG588 was also 'rather later than the *Painter and his Family* (see note 10) which he dated c.1750 (*Huntington Library Quarterly*, x, i, 1946, p.107).

10 J. Egerton, National Gallery catalogues, *The British School*, 1998, pp.64–71, as ?1748.

11 Cf. the *Wood near The Hague* DPG210 or the *Landscape with a Hawking Party* by Wijnants (and Lingelbach) at Kenwood (J. Bryant, *Kenwood, Paintings in the Iveagh Bequest*, 2003, pp.100–03). Fairfax Murray also owned a drawing by Gainsborough of a comparable tree which he sold to Pierpont Morgan in 1910 (J. Hayes, *Drawings of Gainsborough*, 1970, no.150, pl.40).

12 It bears the same auctioneers' marks *verso*, as Waterhouse observed in 1953 (and see Waterhouse 1994, pp.249, 349n5). Listed in Waterhouse 1958, no.754, as on loan to the Fitzwilliam Museum, Cambridge, from the Francis Cook collection. It may be earlier than DPG588.

X-radiograph showing the head and shoulders portrait of a woman underneath DPG588

CHARLES GRIGNION the younger (1754–1804)

DPG595 *Thomas Haines*

Canvas 61.5 x 50.5 lined; losses along bottom edge; cleaned 2004.

Blue eyes, white powdered hair; wearing a light green waistcoat and mulberry coat.

PROV.: sold by the sitter's great-grandson, 'Interesting Relics of the famous Tom's Coffee-House in Russell Street, Covent Garden, 1714-1814', Sotheby, Wilkinson & Hodge, 3 July 1899, within lot 196, 'the original portrait in oils by *Charles Grignon*, of the son and successor of [Richard Haines], Thomas Haines, Proprietor 1764-1814, who from his polite manners and address, was called "Lord Chesterfield" amongst the members of the club';[1] Fairfax Murray Gift 1915 as 'The Younger Haines, Proprietor of Tom's Coffee House by Charles Grignon'.

Thomas Haines, proprietor of Tom's Coffee House in Russell Street, Covent Garden, from 1764 until its closure in 1814, had succeeded his father Richard (manager from 1723). Named after the founder, Captain Thomas West (d.1722), by the 1760s the Coffee House had become a well-known and fashionable resort.[2]

To judge by the costume DPG595 might be dated c.1775-80. Grignion had lived in Covent Garden, close by the Coffee House, before settling in Italy in 1781.

1 Also in this sale was an 'original sketch of Richard Haines, proprietor 1723-64, 'by Sir Nathaniel Dance, P.R.A. [*sic*] (then Mr Dance), one of the frequenters at "Tom's" ' – presumably the drawing listed with Spink in 1980 (NPG archives). The *Illustrated London News*, 10 June 1865, pp.545-46 described the relics as belonging to the sitter's eighty-four year-old daughter.

2 See A. Ellis, *The Penny Universities*, 1956, p.172; *Wal. Corr.*, xvii, p.296n16.

Joseph Highmore (1692–1780)

DPG566 Portrait of a Lady

Canvas 91.4 x 73.6 unlined; small loss bottom centre; slight retouchings; a small patch behind the right sleeve; Hell 1953.

Signed and dated, lower left: *J. Highmore / pinx:1734*; blue-green eyes, dark brown hair; wearing a blue velvet dress with white collar and cuffs, a white bow at her breast.

PROV.: Fairfax Murray Gift 1911.

EXH.: Eltham Palace 1991–92; Tredegar House 1992–.

REF.: E. Johnston, *Wal. Soc.*, XLII, 1970, p.68; Lewis 1979, ii, p.525, no.212.

Two years after visiting the Low Countries, Highmore went to Paris between June and August 1734, intent on seeing more works by Rubens.[1] In DPG566, dated 1734, the creamy flesh painting, costume and pose, strongly recall the master;[2] Collins Baker commented upon its 'fresh almost humorous vivacity'.[3]

While he was at Paris Highmore is known to have painted kit-cat portraits of Mrs Robert King and her friend Lady Ferrers[4] and it is tempting to associate DPG566 with one of these, but it was apparently acquired by Fairfax Murray as the unidentifiable Lady Ellenborough (although received at Dulwich in 1911 as *A Lady in Blue*).[5] An old photograph in the NPG archive is named *Mrs Arundel Windham*,[6] whom Highmore was to paint later, in 1748 and 1750.[7]

1 Johnston, 1970 (see REF. above), pp.61–104.
2 E.g. *Suzanna Fourment* (National Gallery, London, 852); *Isabella Brant* (Mauritshuis, The Hague, 250) and *Helen Fourment* (Munich, 349), portraits Highmore might have seen in the Low Countries in 1732. The pose relates to that adapted for a curtsy, according to eighteenth-century etiquette (F. Nivelon's *Rudiments of Genteel Behaviour*, 1737): the hands should be 'placed a-cross not high or low … the Inside of the Hands should be opposed to the Breast, the Fingers being easy and a little separated, the Wrists must bend inwards …' (see D. Mannings, *Connoisseur*, clxxix, 1979, pp.118–19). A signed miniature by Highmore of a half-length girl wearing a straw hat, uses the same Rubensian pose (Sotheby's, 5 February 1953, lot 76).
3 Collins Baker 1933, p.71.
4 Her husband was the exiled chief cashier of the South Sea Company; Mary Levinge m. the 2nd Earl Ferrers c.1704 and d. in Paris 1740 (Johnston, 1970, see REF. above, pp.64, 81, 87, 88, 90).
5 An old label, *verso*, is inscribed *Highmore/Portrait of Lady Ellenborough*; the 1st Baron Ellenborough was Edward Law (1750–1818), son of Edmund (1703–87), Bishop of Carlisle.
6 The negative presented to the NPG in 1929 by Collins Baker, who had apparently first noted the identification as Arundel Penruddock, 1717–80, who m. before 1736 Henry Wyndham (1708–88) of Salisbury (see Hon. H.A. Wyndham, *A Family History 1688–1837*, 1950, p.172).
7 Lewis 1979, ii, pp.518–19, nos.195, 197.

William Hogarth (1697–1764)

DPG562 A Fishing Party

Canvas 54.9 x 48.1 lined; a large damage above the 'mother's' head on the right and a prominent pentimento by the seated man's knee on the left; the painting of the lake and boating party is very thin; X-rayed 1950 (see below) when with Hell 1947–68; cleaned 2003. Murray 1980 alleged there was a signature lower left centre; for further discussion, see below.

The man on the left wears a blue coat, yellow waistcoat and black stockings; the seated lady wears a pink hat and white dress; the little girl is in white with a blue sash; the servant wears brown with a white bonnet.

PROV.: J.H. Manners Sutton, 3rd Viscount Canterbury (1814–77);[1] anon. sale, Robinson & Fisher, 29 May 1902, lot 87, 'The Fair Angler', bt. Agnew; Fairfax Murray 1902; his Gift 1911.

EXH.: *Old Masters*, RA, 1908(113 lent Murray); RA schools 1934; Aberystwyth 1945(53); *Hogarth*, Tate, 1971(34); *British Sporting Pictures*, AC, 1974(22); *Zwei Jahrhunderte Englische Malerei*, Munich, 1979(13); *Collection for a King*, Washington DC, Los Angeles, 1985–86(13); *The New Child: British Art and the Origins of Modern Childhood 1730–1830*, University Art Museum, Berkeley CA, 1995; *Rembrandt to Gainsborough*, Houston TX, Louisville KY, 1999–2000(81); *Old Master Paintings*, Japan, 2000(46); *The Art of Conversation*, York Art Gallery, 2006-07(n.n.).

REF.: A. Dobson & W. Armstrong, *Hogarth*, 1902, p.179 as with Fairfax Murray; R.B. Beckett, *Hogarth*, 1949, p.42; M. Webster, *Hogarth*, 1978, no.26; G.A. Waterfield in *Collection for a King*, 1985, p.68; R. Paulson, *Hogarth*, i, 1991, pp.212, 218.

The Fishing Party was apparently painted c.1730–31 (see below) as a family piece, possibly showing antecedents of the Manners-Suttons who owned the picture in the 19th century. Alterations to the composition, described below, involving a further six sitters, obscure the original intent. Elements of the composition recur in several Hogarth conversation pieces of 1730–31: the flanking figures, trees surrounding a central lake, and fishing rods in the *Popple and Ashley Families* dated 1730 (Royal Collection)[2] and the *Jeffreys Family* of c.1730 (Yale Center for British Art; B1981.20); in the *Vane Family* (private collection) and the *Conversation Piece with Sir Andrew Fountaine* (Philadelphia Museum of Art, M28-1-14), both of the early 1730s, Hogarth appears to have used a table similar to that originally in DPG562. But the composition of DPG562 only evolved with difficulty, as has been demonstrated by X-radiography and infra-red photography.[3]

The colourful group on the right now dominates a rather unbalanced composition, closed on the left by the much-reworked figure of the man with his back to the spectator. Hogarth modified the scene several times and some of his alterations, though not their exact sequence, may be identified as follows:

a) a conversation piece including a group of three male heads, centre right, with a fourth standing male figure in the centre; the canvas was subsequently cut along the bottom edge through the legs of this standing figure.[4] The group of three heads was exposed in the course of a previous cleaning and then covered up again; the fourth figure is now visible only through infra-red photography.

b) a second conversation piece included two men on the left, one seated in a Windsor chair as now seen but differing in detail, viz. he was pointing across to the right with his left hand and taking snuff (?) with his right; his head was turned up to the left towards a standing male companion whose profile head remains very faintly visible; the canvas was subsequently cut along the left-hand edge, through the chair and through the standing figure. The gestures of the seated man are now visible only through infra-red photography, but his altered legs remain as pentimenti.

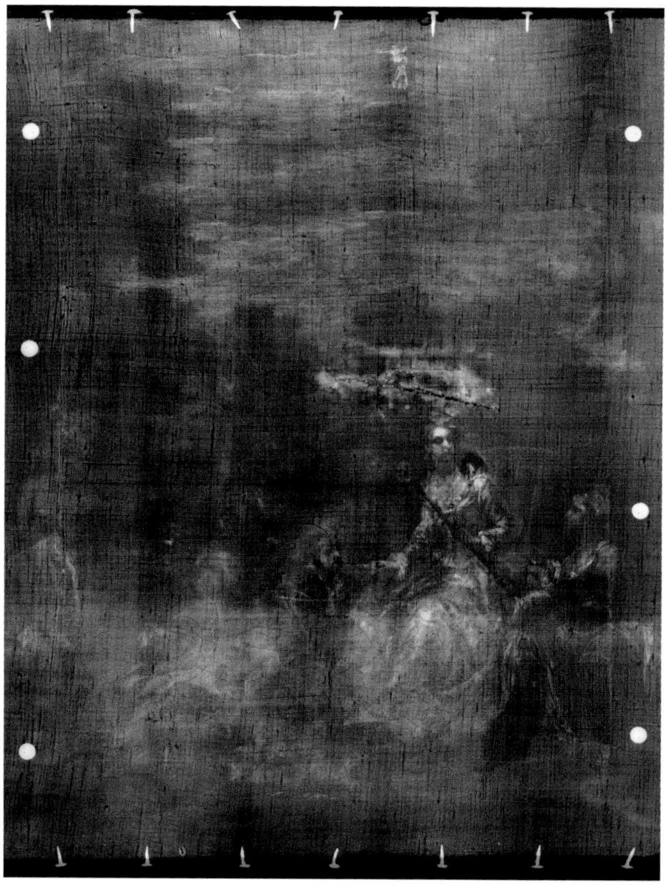

X-radiograph of DPG562

Infra-red photograph of DPG562

c) the woman on the right seated in a high-backed Windsor chair holding a fishing rod had the bait hook in her right hand resting on a wooden table (at some comparatively recent stage the top was strengthened by overpainting); her skirt (now an indeterminate grey) was blue; she was accompanied by the small child and his nurse, as now seen. This group may have coincided with stage b) described above.

d) much later, and probably not by Hogarth, the table was painted over, a bucket (for bait) was introduced by the seated woman's feet[5] and the colour of the woman's skirt was changed from blue to grey; the hook of the fishing line was transferred to the seated man on the left;[6] a *profil perdu* of his face was painted over his wig.

e) after 1934 the float of the fishing line was put back in the woman's right hand and the *profil perdu* painted out.

Some of the difficulties of conservation were reflected in a letter from A.P. Oppé to Sir Gerald Kelly (Chairman of the Gallery Board), printed in the Board Minutes, 15 December 1950:

> I saw the X-ray photos [of DPG562] with Rawlins [*scientific adviser to the National Gallery*] and have looked at the picture before and after. The X-rays show clearly that the lost figure [*the 'fourth standing male' described under a) above*] was never completed by the painter in the same way as the adjacent woman or was deliberately partially removed before being painted over. Hell is confident that all the present surface in this part of the picture is recent. The X-rays do not tell us anything about this; but as the figure could not have remained there after the other man's figure had been placed on the canvas I cannot see that anything would be gained by removing the new paint. Perhaps someone has tried to recover the obliterated figure before and having only found a mess, had to make good his own effacements. The same process would have to be repeated now.

Kelly then suggested that the cleaning should not be attempted, although the evidence uncovered by recent examination does not seem to confirm this.

1 Inscribed *verso*: *J H M S ... 70 Eaton Square*. Manners-Sutton *suc.* as Viscount Canterbury 1869; he is listed as living at 70 Eaton Square from 1855. He m. 1838 Georgiana, dau. of Charles Tompson of Witchingham Hall, Norfolk.
2 Millar 1963, i, no.561, ii, pl.210; exh. *Quest for Albion*, 1998, no.10.
3 I am most grateful to Elizabeth Einberg for help in deciphering the evolution of the composition. The Philadelphia composition also evolved through several stages, see R. Dorment, *British Painting in the Philadelphia Museum of Art*, 1986, pp.163–65.
4 The tacking edges are now cut.
5 As seen in Beresford 1998, p.128.
6 C. Beharrell, *CL*, 25 July 1985, pp.206–07, supposed the woman held a fish and that her daughter was looking eagerly at 'a male servant' on the left as he rebaited the hook; the idea that the woman should be holding the end of the fishing line showed (apparently) 'a total misunderstanding of the psychology of the picture'.

William Hogarth (1697–1764)

DPG580 Portrait of a Man

Canvas 76.2 x 63.8 lined; small losses upper left by the head and lower right on the cuffs; X-radiography reveals a flowered waistcoat, a painted oval format and a vase of flowers in the right background; there are pentimenti down the left sleeve, in the coat buttons, cravat and waistcoat; cleaned and relined 2003–04.

Signed bottom left centre: *W Hogarth Anglus pinxt 1741*; powdered bob wig, his hair combed back off forehead; pleated linen stock with shirt ruffle; red coat with shallow stand up collar (unusual at this period); some of the very large buttonholes may be sham, except for the top ones and a few at the waist, or they may even be half stitched up; cuff *à la marinère* – opened with a vertical slit slightly scalloped and edged with three or four buttons on the flap.

Prov.: In 1817 from 'the late Edward Coxe [c.1747–1814], of Hampstead Heath ... now in the possession of the widow of Mr Coxe [Mary, d.1833] ... with his name on it *Hogarth Anglus*';[1] Fairfax Murray by 1900;[2] his Gift 1911.

Exh.: *Old Masters*, RA, 1908(88); RA schools 1934; Aberystwyth 1945(33); National Gallery 1947(25); Leeds 1947–53(25); *Hogarth*, Tate, 1951(47); *Hogarth*, Tate, 1971(111); *Rembrandt to Gainsborough*, Houston TX, Louisville KY, 1999–2000(82); *Old Master Paintings*, Japan, 2000(47).

Ref.: A. Dobson & W. Armstrong, *Hogarth*, 1902, pp.130, 172; R.B. Beckett, *Hogarth*, 1949, p.49, 'probably the same as *A Gentleman in Red* signed *Hogarth Anglus* with Edward Coxe's widow in 1817', p.179; M. Webster, *Hogarth*, 1978, no.120; A. Ribeiro, *History of Costume*, 1983, p.51, no.45; R. Paulson, *Hogarth*, ii, 1992, p.154.

It has been supposed that the celebrated signature was a patriotic assertion in the face of the contemporary vogue for immigrant portrait painters[3] – in which case it is a little ironic that the pose relates so closely to Kneller's *Sir Richard Steele* of 1711.[4]

Without real evidence, the sitter has been supposed to be a member of the Coxe family, the earliest recorded owners.[5]

1 Nichols & Steevens, *The Genuine Works of William Hogarth*, III, iii, 1817, p.179.
2 A letter from Fairfax Murray to W.S. Spanton, dated August 1900 (Gallery archive), refers to his Hogarth man in a red coat being photographed by Braun. Listed in Fairfax Murray's possession by A. Dobson & W. Armstrong, *Hogarth*, 1902, p. 172.
3 It was in 1740 that the young Allan Ramsay declared he had 'put all your Vanlois and Soldis, and Ruscos, to flight' (letter to Dr Alexander Cunyngham, 10 April; SRO, GD331/5/20) – meaning the portrait painters J-B. Van Loo, Andrea Soldi and Carlo Rusca. Waterhouse 1994, p.174, hinted Hogarth's signature may have been specifically aimed at Van Loo.
4 NPG (3227), engraved in reverse 1713 and 1723, but it was probably the plate by Faber junior of 1733 which Hogarth had seen; see Stewart 1983, p.79, pls.77a, 77b.
5 Elizabeth Einberg has very tentatively supposed the sitter might be John Ranby (1703–73), Principal Sargeant Surgeon to George II; his portrait by Hogarth, according to Nichols writing in 1781, then belonged to Samuel Ireland; he had modelled the hero in *The Rake's Progress*, published in 1735 (J. Nichols, *Biographical Anecdotes of William Hogarth*, 1781, p.68) and comparison with the rake's head in pl.5 does not rule out the possibility.

Thomas Hudson (1701–79)

DPG578 Portrait of a Lady

Canvas 127.3 x 102 lined; the surface rubbed; the shadows in the grey dress reduced and retouched; a damage in the white skirt lower right; raised craquelure to left of the face; surface cleaned 1979.

Signed bottom right *T Hudson Pinxit.1750* (*TH* in monogram); brown hair, grey eyes; wearing a silver-blue underdress and white satin overdress; a deep red curtain behind.

PROV.: Robert Hollond (see DPG579); Christie's, 27 April 1889, lot 34, bt. Fairfax Murray; his Gift 1911.

EXH.: *Hudson*, Kenwood 1979(47); *Collection for a King*, Washington DC, Los Angeles, 1985–86(15).

REF.: E. Miles, *Thomas Hudson: Portraitist to the British Establishment*, University Microfilms, 1976, no.199; A. Ribeiro, *Art of Dress*, 1995, pp.8, 9, 237n25.

Pendant to DPG579. The dress, as Ribeiro has described, shows an imaginary mixture of the contemporary with references to Van Dyck and Kneller and may be compared with Kneller's *Countess of Ranelagh* at Hampton Court.[1] It recurs in a closely related drawing by Van Aken in the National Gallery of Scotland (D2190)[2] which probably indicates that the draperies in DPG578 were taken from his patterns.

1 Stewart 1983, pl.38b.

2 A. Smart, ed. J. Ingamells, *Ramsay*, 1999, fig.760. A copy by Richard Phelps in the British Museum (album 1918-6-8-39).

THOMAS HUDSON (1701–79)

DPG579 *Portrait of a Man*

Canvas 127.3 x 102 lined by Holder; surface cleaned 1979.

Signed bottom right: *T Hudson Pinxit.1750* (*TH* in monogram); clear blue eyes, white powdered wig; wearing a brown coat, silk waistcoat with gold trim; his black hat with gold trim under his left arm.

PROV.: Robert Hollond (1808–77);[1] Christie's, 27 April 1889, lot 33,[2] bt Fairfax Murray; his Gift 1911.

EXH.: *Hudson*, Kenwood 1979(46); *Collection for a King*, Washington DC, Los Angeles, 1985–86(14).

REF.: E. Miles, *Thomas Hudson: Portraitist to the British Establishment*, University Microfilms, 1976, no.200; A. Ribeiro, *Art of Dress*, 1995, pp.8, 9, 237n25.

Pendant to DPG578. The same pose, reversed, appears in the *Portrait of a Man* dated 1747 by Highmore in the Tate Gallery (N04107); it may be related to a passage in F. Nivelon's *Rudiments of Genteel Behaviour*, 1737.[3]

1 MP and philanthropist; he achieved particular fame by financing a two-day balloon voyage from London to Weilburg in 1836 (as described in the *Ingoldsby Legends*).

2 In a first edition of the sale catalogue lot 33 was described as by W. Hoare; this was subsequently corrected.

3 'The Head erect and turned … temper'd with becoming Modesty; the lips must be just join'd to keep the Features regular; … The arms must fall easy, not close to the Sides, and the Bend of the Elbow, at its due Distance, will permit the right Hand to place itself in the Waistcoat easy and genteel…'; see D. Mannings, *Connoisseur*, clxxix, 1975, pp.116–17.

circle of HANS HYSING (1678–1752)

DPG604 *John Dive*

Canvas 64.1 x 51.1 lined; minor retouchings in the face, stock and right background; larger losses lower left and in the middle near the bottom edge; Hell 1953.

Upper left the arms of Dive of Millwich charged with Aston;[1] inscribed in yellow upper right: *IOHN eldest son of IOHN DIVE / Esq^e^: married DOROTHY Daught^r^./ of. WALTER ASTON Esq^e^: of Millwich, com: Staffordshire*; grey-blue eyes, powdered tie wig; wearing a blue coat, white shirt and yellow waistcoat.

PROV.: Fairfax Murray Gift 1911 as 'apparently by a French artist about 1760'.

The sitter, as identified by the arms and inscription, was from Millwich, Staffs.; born in 1674, he married Dorothy Aston in 1704.[2] Portraits of his mother and father remain with the family at Wootton-under-Edge in frames similar to that round DPG604.

This fine portrait may date from the early 1730s, but this implies he would be some 55 years old in DPG604, indicating some flattery. The free execution and fluent drawing are suggestive of Hans Hysing, to whom it is very tentatively attributed.[3]

1 Dive (of Millwich, Staffs; and of Bromham, Beds.; and of Brompton, Harleston, Holwell, Quinton and Wyke, Northants.); *gu. a fess dancettée or betw. three escallops or* with crest (for Beds. and Northants only) *a wivern gu.*, with an inescutcheon (generally indicating marriage with an heir or co-heir) of Aston (Lord Aston of Forfar and Aston, or the uncle of Lord Aston of the House of Tixall, Staffs.) *ar. a fesse sa. in chief three lozenges of the last.*

2 A family tree was kindly supplied by Cynthia Walcot of Beaminster in 1993.

3 E.K. Waterhouse recalled (letter of 5 November 1977 on file) that Collins Baker had toyed with the idea of an attribution to Thomas Hill – whose activity ceased in 1725.

Charles Jervas (c.1675–1739)

DPG567 Dorothy, Viscountess Townshend

Canvas 127 x 103.8 including a strip 21.5 wide along the bottom edge, lined; the canvas join much retouched; X-radiography confirms her right hand was first held up by her shoulder[1] and the left reached across her waist (so that, for example, a string of pearls could have passed from right to left, or a lock of hair might have been held in her right hand); in the background a brown drape spread out behind the figure on both sides; her cloak was originally green; the spray in her turban is now half overpainted; Hell 1953.

X-radiograph of DPG567

Inscribed, upper right, below the coat of arms: *Dorothy, Sister of Sir Robert Walpole & / Second Wife of Charles Lord Viscount/ Townshend*; the arms show Townshend impaling Walpole within a Garter belt and a Viscount's coronet;[2] brown eyes, brownish hair, a black plume in her patterned silk headdress; wearing a blue cape (curdee) trimmed with ermine, red waistcoat (antery) and white skirt.

PROV.: Horace Walpole, listed at Strawberry Hill 1784 in the Great Parlour, 'Dorothy, sister of Sir Robert, and second wife of Charles lord Viscount Townshend, knight of the garter and secretary of state; in a Turkish habit: by Jarvis';[3] Strawberry Hill sale, Robins, 21st day, 18 May 1842, lot 37 (… 'in a Turkish habit, richly painted, by Jarvis'), bt. Lord Waldegrave; Waldegrave sale Christie's, 10 February 1900, lot 40, bt. Agnew from whom bt. 12 February 1900 Fairfax Murray; his Gift 1911.

EXH.: *Family and Friends*, Norwich, 1992(38); *Lady Mary Wortley Montagu*, Graves Art Gallery, Sheffield, 2007(n.n.).

ENG.: E. Harding 1802 (from a drawing by W.N. Gardiner);[4] W. Greatbatch 1858, 'From the original formerly at Strawberry Hill', slightly reduced all round (e.g. cut off just below her left hand, where there is now a join in the canvas) and emphasizing the spray in her head dress.

REF.: Kerslake 1977, i, p.189; A. Moore in *Family & Friends*, 1992, pp.106–07; *Capital Collection* 2002, p.315.

The arms and inscription, almost certainly added by Horace Walple, identify the 'lovely, careless and gay' Dorothy, Viscountess Townshend (1686–1726), sister of Sir Robert Walpole, the prime minister, and the great-aunt of Horace Walpole; she married in 1713 as his second wife Charles, 2nd Viscount Townshend of Raynham (1675–1738, see also Dubois DPG584 p.150), minister of state, KG 1724.[5] The Townshends lived next door to Jervas's London studio at Cleveland Court in St James's and, with Robert Walpole, were his consistent patrons.[6]

The Turkish costume finally adopted for DPG567 derived from an example set by Lady Townshend's particular friend, the writer, linguist and traveller Lady Mary Wortley Montagu, *née* Pierrepont (1689–1762), who has also been proposed as the sitter;[7] she married in 1712 Edward Montagu (1678–1761) whom she accompanied on a diplomatic mission to Constantinople 1716–18, where she adopted Turkish dress and encouraged the fashion in England on her return.[8]

There are undoubted portraits by Jervas of both Lady Townshend and Lady Mary. The earliest of Lady Townshend is the standing three-quarter length of c.1713 (perhaps to mark her marriage), which remains at Houghton[9] and a fine half-length oval version is at Holkham. Both show the same wide eyes and sensual mouth as DPG567.[10] Jervas painted Lady Mary three-quarter length, bare-headed, as a shepherdess c.1710 (Dumfries Castle)[11] and whole-length c.1718–20 (National Gallery of Ireland, 4341), wearing Turkish dress and with a view of Constantinople in the distance.[12] Compared with Lady Townshend, these portraits suggest narrower eyes and a less sensuous mouth.

Comparable whole-length 'Turkish' portraits of English ladies who hadn't been to the Orient, standing before a prospect of Constantinople, include those of Jemima, Countess of Ashburnham (Wrest Park), Mary, Duchess of Montagu (Boughton),[13] and Lady Fanny Shirley (private collection) and her sister Lady Selina (by Jervas dated 1724).[14] Thus the Turkish tents in the background of DPG567, suggesting, as Isobel Grundy has it, the daring explorer rather than exotic sophisticate,[15] may also be interpreted as fashionable embellishment rather than documentation.

Two versions are recorded of DPG567 which, according to the costume, must date from after Lady Mary's return from Turkey in 1718: a copy, without the coat of arms and inscription, sold Christie's, 21 November 1975, lot 60 as *Lady Wortley Montagu* by Kneller, and a version in the National Portrait Gallery (2506), differing in details of costume and landscape, acquired as Lady Mary Montagu but now called Dorothy, Viscountess Townshend.[16] A miniature bust-length copy attributed to C.F. Zincke, set in a box, is in the National Museum, Stockholm (NMB.1058).[17]

1 The raised right arm, a familiar device in portraiture at this time, recurs, for example, in Jervas's portraits of *Catherine, Lady Walpole* (Lady Townshend's sister-in-law), of c.1710 (Houghton; *Capital Collection* 2002, no.216) and *Martha and Teresa Blount* 1716 (Mapledurham; exh. *Manners & Morals*, Tate, 1987, no.19).

2 Walpole: *or, on a fesse betw. two chev. sa. three crosses crosslet of the first*; Townshend: *az. a chev. erm. betw. three escallops or.*

3 H. Walpole, *A Description of Strawberry Hill*, 1784, p.5.

4 Illus. E. Sherson, *The Lively Lady Townshend*, 1926, f.p.170.

5 Legend has it that her ghost haunts Raynham and a photograph of this presence appeared in *CL*, lxxx, 1936, p.673.

6 A. Moore, *Family and Friends*, Norwich, 1992, pp.34–35, and *Houghton Hall*, 1996, pp.52, 130; E. Bottoms, *Apollo*, cxlv, February 1997, pp.44–48; I. Grundy, *Lady Mary Wortley Montagu*, 1999, p.91. Lady Townshend commissioned Jervas to paint a whole-length of her husband immediately after his installation as KG (version at Blickling; illus. *Family and Friends*, Norwich, 1992, p.225); and a Townshend family piece by Jervas (including five small children), was sold Christie's, 24 April 1987, lot 77 (illus. *Apollo*, cxlv, February 1997, p.47).

7 Most recently by Isobel Grundy (at note 6), p.202.

8 Cf. A. Ribeiro, *Connoisseur*, cci, June 1979, pp.17–23. She also pioneered vaccination (and it was after innoculating her family that Lady Townshend died of smallpox).

9 Houghton Hall; *Capital Collection* 2002, pp.314 (no.217), 371, 446(109), 464.

10 A standing whole-length at Audley End (formerly at Brome) is also attributed to Jervas.

11 A miniature copy was engraved by Caroline Watson 1803 as dated 1710.

12 N. Figgis & B. Rooney, *Irish Paintings in the National Gallery of Ireland*, i, 2001, pp.305–08. Versions are in the Mappin AG, Sheffield, and sold Sotheby's, 15 July 1987, lot 52; the type was engraved by Caroline Watson as a portrait by Jonathan Richardson of 1719.

13 *Boughton*, ed. T. Murdoch, 1992, p.182 as attributed to E. Seeman. Versions recorded with the Chichester Estates 1954 and with Lord Montagu of Beaulieu 1962.

14 See the Ferrers family catalogues of Lough Fea, 1869, p.5, and Lower Ettington, 1880, p.31, no.5, where another version of the Lady Selina is listed at Clarendon Park.

15 Grundy (at note 6), p.202.

16 Kerslake 1977, i, pp.189, 281, ii, pl.552; she wears a blue waistcoat, a bracelet, has a jewel on the headdress, a brooch fastening the blouse, and an embroidered cloth in her left hand; her gown has no ermine, and the distant landscape is seen only below the outstretched arm.

17 Identified by Mary Poole-Wilson of Dulwich in 2000.

Tilly Kettle (1734–86)

DPG582 *Eliza and Mary Davidson*

Canvas 127 x 101.9 lined; scattered losses mostly in the lower foreground area and in the two skirts; cleaned 1947; consolidated 1994; cleaned 1997.

PROV.: Anon. Sale, Christie's, 16 June 1900, lot 103, bt. Fairfax Murray; his Gift 1911.

Mary Davidson on the left has brown eyes and dark brown hair dressed with pearls and a white muslin Indian scarf with gold threads; she wears a purple dress with a light brown drape; Eliza Davidson on the right has brown eyes and dark hair with a white band; she wears a white dress with a pearl corsage; an ochre drape and purple slippers.

EXH.: *Art chiefly from Pakistan and India*, RA, 1947(1327).

REF.: Milner 1927, pp.72–73, 94–95; M. Archer, *India and British Portraiture 1770–1825*, 1979, pp.94, 96 as c.1784.

Painted in India c.1784. The sitters were the daughters of Elizabeth, *née* Pigou (d.1791), and Alexander Davidson (d.1791), provisional Governor of Madras 1785–86.[1] Eliza (c.1769–1837) married Alexander Falconar of Falcon Hall, Edinburgh; Mary (1775–1839) married Colonel Younge of Little Durnford, Wilts., and died in a fire.[2] There was a third sister, Margaret (1770–1784) who died in England in October 1784 and a son Alexander Hector (b. c.1780?).[3] The children had been brought back to England in 1784.

1 He was painted by Kettle in Madras 1770 (Milner 1927, p.94), a half length with Spink in 1968, illus. M. Archer, *India and British Portraiture 1770–1825*, 1979, p.68.

2 A 19th-century label, *verso*, reads: *Portraits of Eliza and Mary Davidson daughters of Alexander Davidson then Governor of Madras. Eliza married Alexdre Falconar of Falcon hall, Edinburgh – died 1837. Mary married Colonel Younge of Little Durnford, Wilts & was accidentally burnt to death in 1839.* See also Archer (at note 1), p.441n52.

3 A portrait of Mrs Davidson with her small son Alexander Hector, previously attributed to Kettle (Milner 1927, p.98), was sold Sotheby's, New York, 17 July 1991, lot 181 as by Hugh Barron.

Tilly Kettle (1734–86)

DPG583 *Portrait of a Lady*

Canvas 68.5 diameter, lined by Holder; originally circular, it had been converted to a standard 76 x 63 rectangle with added spandrels (four separate pieces of canvas) sometime before Murray bought it before 1911;[1] an old vertical tear in to the right of the head, and two smaller ones in the face; two damages in left-hand background; fine craquelure in the flesh; pentimento of hair over her ear; lightly varnished 1989; restored to original circular format 1991 when the previous lining was stripped off and the circular canvas relined; narrow strips at the centre of the left and right edges were made up to complete the circle.

Signed lower left: *T. Kettle./ Pinx.*; grey eyes, very dark hair with a white lace head-dress and a pearl ear-ring; wearing a blue-grey dress with black lace fichu and white lace cuffs.

Prov.; Fairfax Murray Gift 1911.

Ref.: Milner 1927, pp.52, 80–81.

Milner suggested a date of 1760, very tentatively equating DPG583 with *A half length portrait of A Lady* exhibited by Kettle FS 1761(88).

1 See Milner 1927, pl.xiva.

George Knapton (1698–1778)

DPG606 *Lucy Ebberton*

Canvas 76.5 x 64.1 lined; restored 1984.

Dark brown eyes, black hair; wearing a yellow hat with purple lining and ribbon; wearing a necklace of paste pearls,[1] a Spitalfields silk dress, the floral pattern echoed by the flowers in her basket, which include a plumed pink (traditional symbol of betrothal); a light purple bow at her waist.

Prov.: Thomas McLean, dealer, bt. Agnew 1905; Fairfax Murray 1907; his Gift 1917.

Exh.: *Old Masters*, RA, 1908(107) lent Murray; *Cent Portraits de Femmes*, Paris, 1909(21); *Collection for a King*, Washington DC, Los Angeles, 1985–86(17); *Obras Maestras*, Madrid, Bilbao, 1999(37); *Rembrandt to Gainsborough*, Houston TX, Louisville KY, 1999–2000(83); *Flower Power*, Sheffield, Norwich, 2003(n.n.)

Eng.: J. McArdell (CS, ii, p.857, no.58) as by Knapton (the second state has an entirely altered face with smaller cap and hat, the strings and necklace removed).

Ref.: A. Staring, *Nederlands Kunsthistorisch Jaarboek*, xix, 1968, pp.200–02 (proposing an attribution to Frans van der Mijn); G.A. Waterfield in *Collection for a King*, 1985, p.76; A. Moore in *Flower Power*, 2003, p.56.

The attribution to Knapton is confirmed by the (undated) McArdell engraving, and a date of c.1745–50 is suggested by the particular floral designs on her silk dress.[2] The sitter's identity rests solely upon annotations made by Horace Walpole on his impression of McArdell's print: '*Lucy Ebberton – afterwards the wife of Captain Greeg of the Marines by whom she had three or four children. She resided sometime at Blandford and afterwards removed to Exeter. Barton, who kept the London Tavern in Poole, was her uncle*.'[3] No mention of Ebbertons or Greggs survives in the parish registers of Blandford or Exeter, but a Captain Thomas Gregg is recorded in the Royal Marines between 1757 and 1782 and a 'Mr Barton' resided in a modest property in Poole High Street between 1761 and 1769.[4]

An interesting comparison is provided by Hudson's portrait of 1752 (private collection) showing the young Esther Hamner in a comparable floral-patterned dress with a basket of flowers before her.[5]

1 D. Scarisbrick (letter 21 September 1984) identified the necklace as almost certainly artificial pearls and paste. This description agrees with that given by Moore in the *Flower Power* exhibition catalogue, 2003.
2 See N. Rothstein, *Silk Design of the Eighteenth Century in the collection of the Victoria and Albert Museum*, 1990, pp.48–49, and cf. pls.236–37, designs of 1745; see note from Dr A. Ribeiro, cited in *Collection for a King*, 1985, p.76,
3 Cited by CS, *loc. cit.*, and see G. Goodwin, *J. McArdell*, 1903, no.130.
4 As recounted by G.A. Waterfield, *Collection for a King*, 1985, p.76, and a letter from the Royal Marines Museum, Southsea, 14 January 1971, on file.
5 Illus. Rothstein (at note 2), p.185, pl.182.

attributed to George Knapton (1698–1778)

DPG596 *Portrait of a Man*

Canvas 75.7 x 63.5 lined; scattered retouchings; pentimento on front of the collar; Hell 1953.

Brown eyes, powdered wig; wearing a red-brown coat with gold facings and buttons; gold waistcoat; his black hat with gold trim under his left arm.

PROV.: Fairfax Murray Gift 1911 as a 'Gentleman by Ramsay'.

A version was sold Sotheby's, 9 July 1980, lot 39 as the 4th Duke of Leeds (Thomas Osborne, 1713–89, who *suc.* as 4th Duke of Leeds 1731; KG 1749, PC 1757) by Knapton. If the sitter were the Duke of Leeds the portrait is likely to date from before 1749 since it does not show the Garter ribbon or badge, but a half-length circular portrait of the 4th Duke by Hudson, sold Phillips, 10 July 1972, lot 45, showing the Garter badge, is not easily reconciled with DPG596.[1]

DPG596 appears to date from the earlier 1740s. Fairfax Murray's attribution to Ramsay, maintained in Murray 1980, is now untenable, and current opinion is divided between Knapton and Hudson. In 1992 Jacob Simon suggested (orally) Knapton rather than Hudson, to whom an attribution has been proposed by Ellen Miles,[2] as cited in Beresford 1998.

1 An enamel copy by C.F.Zincke, from the collection of the Dukes of Leeds, sold Christie's, 14 October 1998, lot 9.

2 Letter on file of 23 July 1997.

Sir Godfrey Kneller (1646–1723)

DPG570 *called The Howard Children*

Canvas 127.3 x 102.9 unlined;[1] a large pentimento at the bottom of the boy's red drape; Hell 1953; cleaned and given a loose canvas lining 1993.

Signed lower left: *G. Kneller.f. / 1694*, the last digit altered from a 5; the seated girl is fair haired, wearing blue over a white shift, a spaniel in her lap; the standing boy is fair haired wearing a white tunic with a gold trim and a red drape fastened by a gold clasp.

Prov.: [Hon. Mary Howard];[2] Fairfax Murray Gift 1911 as Lord Carlisle and his Sister by Kneller.

Ref.: Stewart 1983, no.133 as ?Lord Carlisle (1686–95) and Lady Mary Howard (d.1694), see note 4 below.

Traditionally known as *Lord Carlisle and his Sister*, but this identification cannot be confirmed. Fairfax Murray recalled that when the 9th Earl of Carlisle (d. 1911) saw the picture he thought it represented 'the [3rd] building earl & his sister but was doubtful about it after. Anyway there is (or was) a printed label on the back, the girls name I think was Katherine but am not sure. I have never taken the trouble to catalogue my own pictures.'[3] The children appear to be a girl under five and a boy under three years old, but no recorded children of the Howards of Castle Howard fit these approximate ages and the date of the portrait.[4]

Two preparatory drawings by Kneller are in the British Museum.[5]

A slightly earlier family group of c.1680–85 by Kneller called *Children of the Howard Family* (Bradford City Art Gallery) came from the collection of the Earls of Suffolk and Berkshire.[6]

1 There is an illegible wax seal on the canvas *verso* (which appears to show a standing fisherman with helmet?, rod and line with a fish biting).
2 A label *verso* reads: *Honble Mary Howa[rd]* who cannot be identified with certainty. There was an Hon. Mary Howard (d.1892), 6th dau. of the 6th Earl of Carlisle, who m.1852 Lord Taunton. (There was also an Hon. Mary Howard of Elford Hall, Elford, Northumb., 1785–1877, and an Hon Mary Howard, b.1865, of the Norfolk Howards).
3 Letter of 11 October 1913, lent to the Gallery by Mrs Yates Thompson in 1936 and transcribed. The label to which Fairfax Murray refers is no longer there and a 'Katherine Howard' defies identification.
4 The nearest identifiable seem to be Edward Howard (1686–before 1692), 5th son of the 2nd Earl of Carlisle (d.1692), and his sister, Lady Mary (d. unm.1694). A Philip Howard (b. 1687/8) and his sister Mary (who m. in 1698), were children of Lord Thomas Howard of Worksop (d.1689).
5 Stewart 1983, nos.25 (1897-8-13-9, 95) and 26 (1897-8-13-9, 94)), pls.91a & b.
6 Stewart 1983, no.365. Probably showing the three sons of Henry Howard, 5th Earl of Suffolk (Henry (c.1670–1718), Edward (1675–1731) and Charles (1675–1733).

Sir Peter Lely (1618–80)

DPG555 *Nymphs by a Fountain*

Canvas 128.9 x 144.8 lined; with Holder 1911; generally abraded; the outlines of the sleeping foreground figures retouched; old tears by the left-foreground nymph's left arm and in the white drapery by her left hip; old damages top and bottom left and in the fountain's base; Hell before 1949; in 1978 Millar commented that the picture had been 'rather harshly treated in a recent restoration'; conserved 2006.

A signature and date, *P L fe 1670* [*sic*] was [doubtfully] recorded in Cook 1914 and 1926;[1] Beckett saw only the signature in 1951, but neither was visible in 1980; the left-hand figure, loosely swathed with a blue drapery, lies on a pink and white drape; the left leg of the distant reclining figure on the left is covered with a light brown drape; to the right an elaborate fountain with three putti and a long-tailed dolphin.

PROV.: 'Bought in Paris' by Fairfax Murray; his Gift 1911 as 'painted in Holland'.[2]

EXH.: Leeds 1949–53; *Age of Charles II*, RA, 1960–61 (17); *Lely*, NPG, 1978(25); *Collection for a King*, Washington DC, Los Angeles, 1985–86(20); *The Artist's Model*, Nottingham & Kenwood, 1991(12); borrowed by Christie's 1993; *Obras Maestras*, Madrid, Bilbao, 1999(36); *Rembrandt to Gainsborough*, Houston TX, Louisville KY, 1999–2000(79); *Rembrandt & Co.*, Dulwich and Rembrandthuis, Amsterdam, 2006(n.n.).

REF.: Collins Baker 1912, i, 139n; Becket 1951, no.594; O. Millar in *Lely*, NPG, 1978, p.9; M. Rogers in *Collection for a King*, 1985, pp.83–84.

When Lely first arrived in England sometime before 1647 he 'pursu'd the natural Bent of his Genius in Landscapes, with small Figures, and Historical Compositions', before realizing that portraiture was 'generally more encourag'd.'[3] His friend Richard Lovelace (see DPG363, p.56) wrote that an 'un-understanding Land' had treated such works with 'transalpine barbarous Neglect'.[4] DPG555, an elaborate example of a landscape with small figures, was presumably painted in the early 1650s as Millar and Rogers proposed.

There is an element of contrivance within the composition and the five nymphs seem awkwardly combined. It seems unlikely that the covering of half of the frontal head by another's drapery (at the base of the fountain) was of Lely's doing, but the insertion of that head is curious. Two of the other poses suggest a particular knowledge of Van Dyck and Titian; the sleeping left-hand figure (whose blue drapery has now suffered so badly) recalls the figure of Psyche in Van Dyck's *Cupid and Psyche* of c.1638–39 (Royal Collection) which was owned by Lely during the Commonwealth,[5] and the (stiff) sleeping background nymph echoes the bottom-right-hand figure in Titian's *Andrians* (Prado, Madrid; engraved in reverse by G.A. Podestá c.1636).[6]

A drawing attributed to Lely and latterly to Subleyras (Sotheby's, Amsterdam, 18 April 1977, lot 40)[7] has been related to the right-hand foreground nymph, but it is more directly connected with Lely's *Cimon and Iphigenia* (Doddington Hall, Lincs.).

1 Collins Baker 1912 (but writing when DPG555 was still in Fairfax Murray's collection) wrote it was 'said to be signed by Lely and dated earlier than his arrival in England', which he then supposed was in April 1641 (i, pp.139–40).
2 At Dulwich, Spanton found the picture 'in the lumber room, where the copies are kept and where nobody is admitted, for fear it should injure the morals of the boys at the College!' (W.S. Spanton, *An Art Student and his Teachers*, 1927, p.114).
3 Graham, p.384.
4 From '*Peinture. A Panegyric to the best Picture of Friendship Mr.* Pet. Lilly' in *Lucasta, posthume Poems*, 1660 (*The Poems of Richard Lovelace*, ed. C.H. Wilkinson, 1930, pp.180–81); see Millar 1978, p.11; Rogers 1985, p.83. Lovelace was said first to have met Lely in 1647.
5 Royal Collection; *Van Dyck* 2004, p.430(IV.3).
6 See H.E. Wethey, *Titian*, iii, 1975, p.152.
7 Millar 1978, pp.10–11, illus. (and exhibited *hors* catalogue); *Collection for a King* 1985, pp.83–84, illus.; *Subleyras*, Paris, Rome, 1987, pp.232–33, illus., as Subleyras c.1739.

Sir Peter Lely (1618–80)

DPG559 *Portrait of a Lady with a Blue Drape*

Canvas 126.7 x 102.5 relined with a new stretcher 1934; damages on the edges; very thinly painted landscape 'almost unfinished'; many retouchings and uneven varnish.

Signed bottom right *PL* in monogram.; brown eyes, dark brown hair dressed with pearls; wearing a green-gold dress with a rich blue drape.

PROV.: 6th Marquess Townshend; Raynham Hall sale, Christie's, 5 March 1904, lot 81 as Lely, bt. Murray; Fairfax Murray Gift 1911 as A. Mytens [*sic*][1] formerly attributed to Lely.

REF.: Collins Baker 1915, p.107 as c.1660; Duleep Singh, ii. p.221, no.149.

Both DPG559 and DPG560 were bought at the Townshend sale in 1904 and may show sisters from that family.[2] Unaccountably, and despite the signature on DPG559, both were attributed to Daniel Mytens by Fairfax Murray (as maintained in the 1914 and 1926 catalogues), although they were correctly given to Lely c.1660 by Collins Baker in 1915.

1 DPG560 bears a label *verso*: *A Mytens 1590–1642* (the dates of Daniel Mytens).
2 Sir Roger Townshend, 1st Bt., had five daughters, of whom Mary (d.1668) m.1650 the 2nd Lord Crewe of Stene, and Anna (d.1667) m. William Cartwright of Aynho; Jane m. John Windham, and Edith d. unm. Whole-length portraits by Lely of their brother Horatio, 1st Viscount Townshend, and of Mary, his Viscountess , were formerly at Raynham (lots 71, 72 in the Raynham sale; Beckett 1951, nos.537, 538); and see DPG573 n2, p.182.

Sir Peter Lely (1618–80)

DPG560 Portrait of a Lady in Blue holding a Flower

Canvas 126.7 x 102.5 relined 1934; pentimento in dress on the right; unevenly cleaned; slight discoloration; Hell 1953.

Brown eyes, brown hair; wearing a blue dress with a pearl necklace and holding a spray of white jasmine in her left hand.

Prov.: 6th Marquess Townshend; Raynham Hall sale, Christie's, 5 March 1904, lot 80 as Lely, bt. Murray; Fairfax Murray Gift 1911 as A. Mytens [*sic*], formerly attributed to Lely.

Ref.: Collins Baker 1915, p.107 as c.1660; Duleep Singh, ii, p.221, no.148.

See DPG559 above.

Sir Peter Lely (1618–80)

DPG563 A Boy as a Shepherd

Canvas 91.4 x 75.6 lined; the little finger on the recorder retouched; dirt in impasto noticeable in upper lip, chest and sky; retouchings by his left forefinger and in right sleeve; retouched 1974; conserved 2008.

Signed lower right below arm *PL* in monogram; golden hair, blue eyes; wearing a golden-brown wrap and white shirt; he holds a shepherd's crook and a recorder.

PROV.: Edward Lovibond (1724–75), Hampton, by c.1770, when seen by Walpole and identified as Abraham Cowley; Lovibond sale, Skinner, 27–28 May 1776, bt. Walpole;[1] Strawberry Hill sale, Robins, 11th day, 6 May 1842, lot 21 as Cowley ('in a splendidly carved frame'), bt. Seguier; Sir Robert Peel;[2] Peel Heirlooms sale, Robinson & Fisher, 10 May 1900, lot 203 as Cowley, bt. Agnew; Fairfax Murray by 1908; his Gift 1911.

EXH.: *Old Masters*, RA, 1908(157 as Cowley by Lely, lent Murray); Aberystwyth 1945(45 as Cowley); National Gallery 1947(27); Leeds, 1947–53(27); *Lely*, NPG, 1978(28); *Collection for a King*, Washington DC, Los Angeles, 1985–86(21); *Kolekcja dla Króla*, Warsaw, 1992(15); *Rembrandt to Gainsborough*, Houston TX, Louisville KY, 1999-2000(80); *Old Master Paintings*, Japan, 2000(45).

ENG.: W.P. Sherlock 1800 after S. Harding (*Biographical Mirrour*, iii, c.1810); Simon (both as Cowley).

REF.: Collins Baker 1912, ii, p.122 as Cowley 1642; Beckett 1951, no.129 c.1657, rejecting Cowley identification; O. Millar in *Lely*, NPG, 1978, pp.51–52; M. Rogers in *Collection for a King*, 1985, p.86.

Dated c.1658–60 by Millar and related to the Arcadian portraits painted by Lely for the Sidney family at that time.[3] Horace Walpole, considering its 'impassioned glow of sentiment' and 'eyes swimming with youth and tenderness', believed DPG563 to be a portrait of the poet Abraham Cowley (1618–67).[4] This identification was finally dismissed in 1951 when Beckett pointed out that Cowley would have been roughly forty years old (and rotund) when the picture was painted. The young sitter meanwhile remains unidentified. Edward Lovibond, who once owned DPG563, also owned several pictures which had belonged to Mary Beale[5] – which led Rogers to question whether the sitter might not have been Bartholomew Beale (see DPG574, p.147) and to propose a date of c.1665 (which may be a little late). It is nonetheless of interest (and perhaps relevance) that a small copy in oils and a drawing by Charles Beale of the head of DPG563 were in Lovibond's collection.[6] Another drawing by Charles Beale (the same?) is in the British Museum.[7]

A miniature bust-length oval copy by Zincke dated 1716, also from Strawberry Hill, is now in the Fitzwilliam Museum, Cambridge (PD.1–1949).[8] Cook 1914 and 1926 mentioned a duplicate or copy 'in which the colour of the mantle is changed to blue' and a copy (the same?) was in the Dutton sale, Rumsey & Rumsey, Bournemouth, 20 February 1930, lot 151.

1 In his *Works*, ii, p.424, Walpole records buying the picture at Lovibond's sale in 1776; Lovibond's sale is noted in *Wal. Corr.*, xxxii, p.294n13 (but is not listed in Lugt).
2 *Wal. Corr.*, xxxii, p.294n11, stated in error that it was bt. Seguier for Queen Victoria 'from whom it went to Dulwich College'.
3 Millar, *Lely*, NPG, 1978, no.19, p.45. See also Lely's *Jocelyn Percy* (Petworth).
4 Walpole, *Anecdotes of Painting*, ed. R.N. Wornum, 1888, iii, p.29. It is curious how Collins Baker 1912 managed to date DPG563 1643 to accommodate this identity. DPG574, p.147, was also once believed to show Cowley.
5 Walpole *Visits*, p.69; *Wal. Corr.*, xxxii, pp.294–95nn10–13.
6 Walpole *Visits*, p.69.
7 Croft-Murray & Hulton 1960, i, p.183 (G.g.4. W.5-65).
8 Strawberry Hill sale, Robins, 18th day, 14 May 1842, lot 51; R. Bayne Powell, *Catalogue of Portrait Miniatures in the Fitzwilliam Museum, Cambridge*, 1985, p.212–13; G. Reynolds, *British Portrait Miniatures*, Fitzwilliam Museum Handbook, 1998, p.76.

Robert Muller (1773–c.1800)

DPG587 *Mrs George Morland*

Canvas 76.3 x 63.5 lined; sparse retouchings in the dress, hair and in the dog's muzzle which has been slightly altered; the dog was painted over her extended left arm; discoloured varnish; Hell 1953.

Powdered grey hair; blue-grey eyes, yellow hair band; wearing a white dress.

PROV.: Joseph Flack of Hemmings Row, Charing Cross;[1] Robinson & Fisher, 29 May 1902, lot 110, bt. Agnew; Fairfax Murray 1902; his Gift 1911.

Anne Nancy Ward (c.1768–1804) married in 1786 the painter George Morland (1763–1804); one of her brothers, the engraver William Ward (1766–1826), married Morland's sister Maria the same year, and her second brother was the painter and engraver James Ward (1769–1859). She died within two days of her husband, her health 'most seriously impaired from his cruel treatment.'[2] The identity of DPG587 seems consistent with other incidental likenesses of Mrs Morland: a pencil sketch as *Louisa* by James Ward (Sotheby's, 28 November 2002, lot 218),[3] a head painted and engraved by William Ward,[4] a drawing by George Morland (Christie's, 17 June 1969, lot 26) and a painting by him showing her seated on a sofa.[5]

Ribeiro has dated the dress in DPG587 c.1792–95.[6] The vigorously painted pug dog was said in Cook 1914 and 1926 (plausibly but without documentation) to be by H.B. Chalon (1770–1849) who had been Morland's contemporary at the RA schools.

The probable companion piece of her husband by Muller is at Port Sunlight (LL3559)[7] but the two portraits seem soon to have been separated.[8] Muller was said to be 'intimately acquainted' with Morland.[9]

1 W. S. Spanton, *An Art Student & His Teachers*, 1927, p.33.
2 J. T. Smith, *Nollekens and his Times*, 1920, ii, pp.339–40.
3 A version of this in the collection of Mrs E.M. Ward, illus. C.R. Grundy, *James Ward*, 1909, pl.28. Both were studies for Ward's painting, *The Clean Face rewarded*.
4 Illus. *ibid.*, f.p.viii.
5 Engraved by W. Ward 1787. Another alleged portrait of her by him illus. *Connoisseur*, xxxvi, 1913, f.p.145. Additional portraits of Mrs Morland are cited in the *Connoisseur*, *loc.cit.*, p.188, as the mother in *The Mother's Bribe* by James Ward, and as the mother in George Morland's *The Disconsolate and her Parrot*. G. Dawe, *Life of George Morland*, c.1910, listed an unattributed half-length oval engraving showing 'Mrs Morland' in a wide-brimmed hat (illus. p.118).
6 Verbally to A. Kidson, 26 February 1998; see note 7 below.
7 A. Kidson, *Earlier British Paintings in the Lady Lever Art Gallery*, 1999, pp.109–10, illus. Kidson found no evidence that it was exh. RA 1796 as suggested in Murray 1980.
8 The Liverpool portrait was sold alone in the Charles Chatfield sale, Coxe 8 May 1807, lot 45.
9 See Kidson 1999 (at note 7), p.111n8, quoting catalogues of the European Museum where Muller's portrait of George Morland was exhibited 1808–14.

John Riley (1646–91)

DPG565 *John Somers, Baron Somers*

Canvas 70.5 x 63.5 lined; a large wrap round along the lower edge shows that the painted oval on the recto was originally complete; Hell 1953; conserved 1997.

Inscribed on the lining canvas *verso*: *Sr. John Sommers Knig[ht] / by Mr. Riley Given to Sr. Philip Yorke by the Righ / Honble. Sr Robert Walpole Knight. Of / The most noble order of ye Garter*; grey-blue eyes, brown hair; wearing a grey-blue gown; in a painted oval.

PROV.: Given by Sir Robert Walpole (1676–1745; KG 1726) to Sir Philip Yorke (1690–1764; cr. Lord Hardwicke 1733) of Wimpole Hall, sometime between 1726 and 1733;[1] by descent to the 5th Earl of Hardwicke (1836–97);[2] probably Christie's, 30 June 1888, lot 44 (Sir John Sommers by Kneller 1692 in an oval), bt. Burn 54gn; [possibly Lord Bateman of Kelmarsh Hall, Northants., sale Christie's, 11 April 1896, lot 82, Kneller Portrait of a Gentleman, oval, bt. Upton, £9]; Fairfax Murray; his Gift 1911 (as from the 'Bateman Heirlooms').[3]

REF.: Piper 1963, p.320.

John Somers (1651–1716), lawyer and whig politician, was called to the Bar in 1676; MP 1689–93; Kt. 1689; Keeper of the Great Seal and Privy Counsellor 1693; Lord Chancellor 1697–1700; created Baron Somers 1697; President of the Royal Society 1698–1703, he was a member of the Kit-Cat Club, a bibliophile and collector of prints and drawings; unmarried, he was 'of a grave deportment, easy and free in conversation; something of a libertine, of middle stature brown complexion' (Macky).

The inscription on the *verso* of DPG565 might suggest it was painted between 1689, when Somers was knighted, and 1691 when Riley died, when the sitter was between 38 and 40 years of age. But the inscription was surely added, for his apparent age and his costume suggest a date nearer 1680. He certainly appears to be younger than in the unattributed miniature in the National Portrait Gallery (3658) dated c.1690–1700.[4] A portrait of Somers in later life, c.1715–16, forms part of Kneller's Kit-Cat series (National Portrait Gallery 3223).

1 As stated in the inscription. Somers, Walpole and Yorke were eminent whig statesmen. Lord Hardwicke was Somers's nephew, and his son, Charles Yorke, owned Lord Somers's papers (destroyed by a fire in his chambers in 1754).
2 An indistinct Christie's stencil *394L* on the stretcher might identify a group of pictures brought in from 17 Cork Street and returned to Lord Hardwicke at Wimpole Hall in June 1882. I am most grateful to Margie Christian for this information.
3 Picture Gallery Committee minutes 20 January 1911.
4 NPG, *Complete Illustrated Catalogue*, 2004, p.574.

John Riley (1646–91)

DPG568 William Chiffinch

Canvas 76.1 x 64.4 lined; pentimento behind his left shoulder; an old large tear runs across the hair and chin down to the collar; there are losses by his right cheek, left shoulder and in the lower left background, and abrasion across chest; Hell 1953–55; relined 1994, when a double lining was removed.

Inscribed top left: *W.m CHIFFINCH* in yellow; dark blue eyes, white hair; wearing a white shirt, blue-grey cloak; a wart on his left cheek.

PROV.: Col. E.A. Bulwer of Dereham sale, Christie's, 19 November 1910, lot 115 as by Soest, bt Agnew; Fairfax Murray; his Gift 1911 as Soest.

EXH.: RA schools 1912.

REF.: Graham, p.396; Vertue, ii, p.131; Collins Baker 1912, ii, pp.23, 159 as Riley; Collins Baker 1915, p.106; Piper 1963, pp.70–71.

William Chiffinch (c.1602–88), born in Salisbury, succeeded his brother Thomas as page of His Majesty's Bedchamber and Keeper of his private closet in 1666; MP 1685–87; his influence at Court was incalculable as he humoured the private wishes of Charles II;[1] he was characterized as a 'time-server and libertine, wasteful, unscrupulous, open to bribery and flattery' (*DNB*). His daughter married Edmund Villiers, 1st Earl of Jersey.

In 1716 Graham recorded that, on Lely's death in 1680, Riley's friends 'being desirous that he [Riley] should succeed that excellent *Master* in the Favour of King *Charles* II. engag'd Mr *Chiffinch* to sit to him for his *Picture*; which he perform'd so well that the *King*, upon the sight of it, sent for him, and having employ'd him in Drawing the Duke of *Grafton's Portrait*, & soon after his *own*, took him into his Service ...' .[2]

DPG568 was presented by Fairfax Murray as a work by Soest and was

catalogued as such until 1926, but by then it had already been convincingly given to Riley by Collins Baker. Several versions exist, including those in the Town Hall, Salisbury;[3] at Cirencester Park (Lord Bathurst);[4] in Lord Jersey's collection; from the Pearson collection at Augill Castle, Cumbria (Christie's, 11 May 1987, lot 343, and Sotheby's, 18 November 1987, lot 23),[5] from the Earl of Dartmouth's collection (Sotheby's, 17 December 1980, lot 149) and from the Bob Jones University, Greenville OH (Christie's, New York, 15 June 1977, lot 217); a reduced oval copy from Strawberry Hill is in the National Portrait Gallery (1091).

1 In 1674 Mary Beale borrowed some drawings 'of William Chiffinch, esq, cleaner of His Maties Italian drawings.' (Collins Baker 1912, ii, p.163). Was this the same man?
2 Repeated, verbatim, by Vertue, ii, p.131.
3 C. Haskins, *Salisbury Corporation Pictures*, 1910, pp.1–8, front.; exh.NPE 1866(835).
4 *Bathurst Catalogue*, 1908, no.66, illus.
5 Illus. Stewart & Cutten, *Dictionary of Portrait Painters in Britain*, 1997, pl.61.

George Romney (1734–1802)

DPG590 *William Hayley*

Canvas 76.2 x 63.3 lined; white cracks in background and chest; the coat appears discoloured; treated by Reeve 1923 and Hell 1953.

Brown eyes, grey wig; wearing a grey coat (now discoloured) over a ruddy brown waistcoat; his right arm rests on an upright drawings folder.

PROV.: Colnaghi; Fairfax Murray by 1904;[1] his Gift 1911.

EXH.: Aberystwyth 1946(21); *Obras Maestras*, Madrid, Bilbao, 1999(45).

ENG.: J. Jacobi 1779; T. Holloway 1796 (*European Mag.*); W. Ridley 1798 (*Monthly Mirror*).

REF.: Ward & Roberts 1904, ii, p.74 no.1 (as the prime version, with Murray); A.B. Chamberlain, *George Romney*, 1910, pp.331–32 (as the prime version); J. Watson, *George Romney in Canada*, Kitchener-Waterloo AG, Ontario, 1985, p.56 (as replica); Walker 1985, i, p.241 (as 1779); B. Maclean-Eltham, *Romney Transactions*, 1996, p.36 (as c.1778); R.N. Blass, *Romney Transactions*, v, 2000, p.11.

William Hayley (1745–1820), poet, patron, biographer and amateur artist, met Romney in 1776; thereafter Romney worked for some time each autumn at Eartham, Hayley's country home in Sussex; Hayley published *Epistles on Painting addressed to George Romney* in 1778 and a life of Romney in 1809. In 1794 Romney told him that 'if you should go before me, I should lose every thing that is dear to me, and the best friend I ever had',[2] yet Hayley subsequently came to be regarded as a malign influence and, in his father's biography, John Romney rancorously observed that his friendship had been 'grounded on selfishness, and the means by which he maintained it was flattery'.[3] In 1814 Hayley was described as 'most charming and very distinguished … tall and portly, with a commanding air and a carriage more suited to a military man than a hermit'.[4]

DPG590 is probably an autograph replica of the picture sold Sotheby's, 8 November 1995, lot 59, from a private collection in Canada,[5] which shows slightly more of the spine of the upright folder. A third version was sold Sotheby's, New York, 16 May 1996, lot 193. The type was engraved in 1779 and these portraits presumably relate therefore to the sittings Romney received from Hayley between September and November 1777 and in June 1779. Jacobi's mezzotint of that year does not exactly agree with any of these, e.g. in the background shadows, and in the curves of the left lapel, the folds of the sleeve, and the hair line (which agrees more with DPG590); both the Canadian and Dulwich versions appear to have lost something of their original surface.

Further sittings by Hayley are listed in May 1788 and February 1797 and other Romney portraits of him include:

c.1779 Half-length holding rolled papers in his left hand, the head relating to that in DPG590, sold Christie's, New York, 24 January 2003, lot 8.

c.1781 Half-length oval, painted for Anna Seward according to an inscription *verso*, ex-collection Sir Robert Witt (private collection).

c.1795 *Flaxman modelling the bust of William Hayley*, whole-length figure, Yale Center for British Art (B1981.25.538), exh. *George Romney*, NPG, 2002(145). A half-length portrait of Hayley derived from this composition is at Newnham Hall (Chandos-Pole coll.).

1796 *The Four Friends* Abbot Hall AG, Kendal (AH674/68); Hayley with his son Thomas, William Meyer and Romney; engraved by C. Watson 1823 with the head of Romney omitted.

For Hayley's iconography, see Walker 1985, i, pp.241-42.

1 Fairfax Murray also owned at one time some Hayley correspondence, containing letters between Romney and Gibbon (letter to W.S. Spanton, 26 July 1890; Gallery archive).
2 Letter of 20 August 1794 (W. Hayley, *Romney*, 1809, p.220).
3 J. Romney, *Life of George Romney*, 1830, p.139.
4 Mrs John Opie; quoted in M. Bishop, *Blake's Hayley*, 1951, p.335.
5 Exh. NPE 1868 (859) lent by William Hayley Mason, librarian to the Duke of Richmond at Goodwood (the frame still bears the NPE label), and *George Romney in Canada*, Kitchener-Waterloo AG, Ontario, 1985(19).

Gerard Soest (1602–81)

DPG573 called Aubrey de Vere, 20th Earl of Oxford

Canvas 73.7 x 63.2 lined; the surface is rubbed and the varnish unevenly blanched[1] except in the darker background area, lending a flat and inconsistent appearance to the figure; retouchings on the nose, mouth and in his right eye; pentimento on the chin; Hell 1952–53; surface cleaned c.1978.

Crudely inscribed in black, above right: *AET:A.T./ SU../ 30: 1662.*; fair hair, half greyed, blue eyes; wearing a red sash.

PROV.: 6th Marquess Townshend;[2] Raynham Hall sale, Christie's, 5 March 1904, lot 5 unattributed, bt. Fairfax Murray; his Gift 1911 as attributed to Samuel Cooper.

EXH.: *Old Masters*, RA, 1908(161 as by Samuel Cooper); *Marvell*, Hull 1978 (42).

REF.: C.H. Collins Baker, *Burl. Mag.*, xxxv, 1919, pp.150, 155 as Soest; Duleep Singh, ii, p.215, no.114 unattributed; Collins Baker 1933, pp.55–56. Whinney & Millar 1957, p.183.

Aubrey de Vere, the impoverished 20th Earl of Oxford (1627–1703, the last of the old creation); his father was killed with the Dutch army in 1632 and he was brought up in Holland, fighting with the Dutch 1644–46; he upheld the Royalist cause during the English Commonwealth, being twice imprisoned in the Tower in 1654 and 1659, and acted as an envoy to recall Charles II in 1660; KG and Lord Lieutenant of Essex 1660; subsequently he opposed James II and supported William III; in 1665 Pepys was surprised to discover 'so rude and dirty a family' and Macaulay, for whom Oxford was an (unlikely) whig hero, declared he was 'of loose morals, but of inoffensive temper'.

The traditional identity is supported by the provenance, but the absence of the garter ribbon, which the 20th Earl was awarded in 1660 and received in April 1661, is not consistent with the inscription.[3] Costume indicates an earlier date and Millar has suggested c.1656–57.[4] A later whole length by Kneller of c.1685–90[5] shows the same ovoid face.

While the attribution to Soest is now above suspicion, Fairfax Murray (who had bought DPG573 as an anonymous portrait) had attributed it to Samuel Cooper (c.1608–72). He told William Spanton:

> The Cooper is my attribution on acct. of its likeness to his miniatures. I am told Bell (Oxford) [the connoisseur C.F. Bell 1871–1966] made merry over it – but I have not heard that he could suggest any other name equally likely. It is certainly of a very high class I gave some 400g. for it at the sale of the Townshend heirlooms.[6]

In 1919 Collins Baker gave Murray credit for this 'happy inspiration', reflecting that 'our minds must have been as blank as regards an attribution as a handless clock-face'.

1 A 1935 photograph seems to show no blanching.
2 Many portraits passed from the Vere family to Raynham through Lady Mary Vere (1581–1671), widow of Horace Vere, Baron Vere of Tilbury (1565–1635, 3rd s. of the 15th Earl of Oxford), see A. Moore, *Family & Friends*, Norwich, 1992, p.34. Their dau. Mary (c.1611–69) m. 1627 Sir Roger Townshend, 1st Bt. , and their s. Horatio (1630–87) was cr. 1st Viscount Townshend (see DPG559n2, p.174).
3 A. Laing, *Burl. Mag.*, 1999, p.549, was unhappy concerning the identity of the 20th Earl of Oxford for this reason.
4 Letters of 30 September 1974 and December 1993 on file; a date slightly later than 1651 was proposed in Whinney & Millar 1957, p.183. In 1919 Collins Baker had suggested c.1648.
5 NPG (4941). A half-length attributed to Kneller is at Antony House (National Trust).
6 Letter of 1 August 1913 in Gallery archive. Murray gave 380 gns for the portrait, a remarkably high price for an unattributed picture. O. Millar in Whinney & Millar 1957, p.95, indicated some similarities between Soest and Cooper's style in the last twelve years of his life: 'Soest's best portraits provide the closest parallel in English painting before the eighteenth century to the power and sympathy of such male portraits [by Cooper] as James, Duke of York at Upton and Ecton.'

Gerard Soest (1602–81)

DPG592 *Sir Henry Vane the younger Kt.*

Canvas 77.5 x 63.8 lined; damages centre and upper right (with rectangular insertion); worn areas round his right shoulder and along lower strip; some cupping and discoloured retouchings; his brown hair appears to have been greyed over, and the outline of his chin is now grey; Hell 1953.

Grey hair, blue eyes; wearing a black cloak.

PROV.: Fairfax Murray Gift 1911 as 'Sir Harry Vane by Dobson'.

REF.: Collins Baker 1915, p.106 as Soest; C.H. Collins Baker, *Burl. Mag.*, xxxv, 1919, p.155 as Soest c.1655–60.

Sir Henry Vane the younger (1613–62) emigrated to Boston MA 1635–37 'to enjoy the ordinances of Christ in their purity', becoming Governor in 1636;[1] dissension led to his return to England, where he became joint-treasurer of the navy in 1636 and treasurer 1639–41 and 1642–50; MP 1640–53; Kt. 1640; a leading figure of the Commonwealth, he retired from government 1653; of his many politico-religious pamphlets, *A Healing Question* 1656, critical of the government, led to imprisonment, but he returned as MP 1659–60; at the restoration his non-conformity led to his arrest and execution, and he died 'as much a martyr and saint as ever man did' (Pepys).

The key portrait of Vane is a half length by Lely of c.1650 at Raby Castle,[2] and comparison with DPG592 would seem to confirm the identity (although it is a soemwhat later portrait). DPG592 was catalogued as by Dobson in Cook 1914 and 1926,[3] but an attribution to Soest c.1655–60 proposed by Collins Baker in 1915 has since found general acceptance.

1 A statue of Vane by MacMonnies was given to the Public Library, Boston MA, in 1895 (illus. J. Willcock, *Sir Henry Vane*, 1913, f.p.64).

2 Exh. *Age of Charles II*, RA, 1960–61(11), illus. pl.10; engraved Faithorne (reversed) for G. Sikes's *Life* 1662, Vertue 1713 and Houbraken 1742. A version is in the Museum of Fine Arts, Boston MA (43.1319). Piper 1963, pp.360–61, discussed Vane's tangled iconography without mentioning DPG592.

3 An ink label *verso* reads: *Wm Dobson/Sir Harry Vane.* There is a generic similarity between the ovoid heads of DPG592 and the so-called Dobson DPG363 (see p.56).

Andrea Soldi (c.1703–71)

DPG603 *Louis-François Roubiliac*

Canvas 97.5 x 83.2, lined and heavily ironed in the late nineteenth century.[1]

Signed and dated, centre left: *Aw Soldi/Pin Ao 1751*;[2] brown eyes, mousey hair; wearing working dress of a purple fur-lined cap, pink fur-lined coat and a white cambric shirt, the left cuff link undone; he holds a spatula in his right hand and on the adjustable stand lie dividers and two spatulas with the clay model of a partly-draped lady with turban pointing upwards with her left hand accompanied by a small boy (see below).

PROV.: [possibly Sir Henry Gott sale, Christie's, 24 February 1810, lot 26: 'A capital Portrait of Roubilliac', bt. Lane, with 'The Companion, the Portrait of Rysbrack', bt Blakesey][3] DPG603 and a portrait of Rysbrack by Soldi were with W. White, London, c.1848, when bt. by J. Mathews of Edgbaston House, Birmingham;[4] both were seen in his collection in November 1858,[5] and were with Fairfax Murray by 1913;[6] his Gift 1917.

EXH.: *Italian Art and Britain*, RA, 1960(155); *Art and Design in Hogarth's England*, VAM, 1984(S17); *Obras Maestras*, Madrid, Bilbao, 1999(38); *Rembrandt to Gainsborough*, Houston TX, Louisville KY, 1999–2000(84); *Creative Quarters*, London Museum, 2001(n.n.); *Wettstreit der Künste*, Munich, Cologne, 2002 (157).

REF.: K. Esdaile, *Roubliliac*, 1928, pp.67, 190–91; J. Ingamells, *Connoisseur*, clvi, 1974, p.181; Kerslake 1977, i, p.238; J. Ingamells, *Wal. Soc.*, XLVII, 1980, p.14, no.50.

Louis-François Roubiliac (1702–62), sculptor, born in Lyons, came in 1730 to London where he became the leading sculptor of his generation, his many works include the celebrated seated statue of Handel (Victoria and Albert Museum, A.3-1965) made for the Vauxhall Gardens in 1738; he died in London.

This vivid portrait was much admired by Vertue, who wrote:

> lately Mr Rubilliac, the Statuary, his picture painted by Mr Soldi – portrait painter – Nov. 1751. his portraits are freely & well drawn and his Colouring true and very natural, he is certainly a painter of superior merrit in the portrait way. very light and ary.[7]

The sculptural group seen in DPG603 somewhat resembles, in reverse, the figure of Charity which Roubiliac incorporated in his monument to the 2nd Duke of Montagu (d. 1749) in Warkton Church, Northants, completed in 1752 and installed in 1753. Soldi's accurate portrayals of such sculptural detail in his portraits of Rysbrack and in the later Roubiliac (see below and note 6), suggest that an actual model is here depicted. Bindman and Baker, while admitting the group may have related to an

entirely different project, also stress that, if it was a study for the Montagu project, DPG603 provides a unique record of the sculptor using a separate model for a single figure in the design of a monument.[8]

Soldi painted Roubiliac again in 1757/8, a slightly larger portrait showing the sculptor working on his bust of Garrick (Garrick Club);[9] another half-length portrait was sold Foster's, 25 July 1835, lot 9.[10] For Roubiliac's iconography, see Kerslake 1977, pp.236-38.

1 The stretcher is stamped *F. Leedham Liner*. The previous stretcher had diagonal corner pieces, whose impression remains discernible on the picture surface.
2 An example of Soldi's anglicized signature, i.e. *Andrew* for *Andrea*.
3 Henry Thomas Gott (d.1809) Kt. 1784, changed name from Greening in 1796; both he and his father, John Greening, a Royal Gardener, sat to Soldi (see Ingamells, *Wal. Soc.*, XLVII, 1980, pp.10–11, nos.32 and 35).
4 Letter from Mathews of 11 August 1859 (NPG archive) explained he had bought them 'some 12 or 14 years ago from White'; the label of '... White Picture Frame Maker, Brownlow Street, Holborn' remains on the stretcher of DPG603. There is also a 19th-century cutting from an unidentified sale catalogue: 'Companion picture, 38in. x 33in. The Sculptor RulIallac [*sic*]'; this is not the 1810 Gott sale.
5 G. Scharf at 'Mr Matthews's, Hagley Road, Birmingham, 24 November 1858' (Sketch Book, 54, f.105; NPG archive).
6 The slightly larger Rysbrack dated 1753, 112 x 91, retains a Fairfax Murray label on the stretcher. On 1 August 1913 Murray told William Spanton that he had '2 Soldi's portraits of Rysbrack and Roubilliac signed and dated both the Rysbrack is here [*in Florence*] but I have left the Roubilliac still in London' (letter in Gallery archive). The Rysbrack later belonged to his son Edward Murray in Florence in 1929; sold Sotheby's, 24 June 1970, lot 109; with Martin & Sewell, London; private collection, Switzerland; sold Christie's, 24 May 1991, lot 68 (when the provenance was first established, demonstrating that Ingamells, *Wal. Soc.*, XLVII, 1980, pp.14–15, nos.54 and 55, are the same picture). A second *Rysbrack*, 115 x 91, dated 1753, sold Christie's, 10 April 1970, lot 94, was bought from Cyril Humphris in August by Paul Mellon and is now in the Yale Center for British Art (B1976.7.75).
7 Vertue, iii, p.159.
8 D. Bindman & M. Baker, *Roubiliac and the eighteenth-century Monument*, 1995, p.304, cat. 5 (L.mod.8). The Montagu monument is examined in detail pp.298–304.
9 Ashton 1997, no.727, p.381 (104 x 89; ex-Christie's, 3 March 1883, lot 84).
10 J. Taylor sale, 'Soldi A Portrait of Roubiliac the Sculptor Canvass 2 foot 5 ? high by 2 feet 1 wide' [74 x 63].

JOHN VANDERBANK (1694–1739)

DPG581 Portrait of a Lady

Canvas 127 x 101.9 lined; paint powdering at the top; the sky has many crude retouchings; an old tear in the bodice; varnish somewhat discoloured, the flowers and right hand quite dark; Hell 1953.

Signed and dated, bottom left: *1738/ Jno Vanderbank Fecit.*; brown eyes, brown hair dressed with pearls; wearing a white satin dress, the bodice decorated with jewelled clasps, and a pink shawl.

PROV.: [Very probably Delmé sale, Christie's, 7 July 1894, lot 77, 'Vanderbank, A lady in a white dress and crimson scarf, signed, and dated 1738', bt. Colnaghi] Wallis & Sons sale, Christie's, 31 May 1902, lot 106, bt. Fairfax Murray;[1] his Gift 1911.

REF.: A. Ribeiro, *A History of Costume*, 1983, p.48, no.39 (described as 1736).

In 1738, the year DPG581 was painted, Vertue noted that 'Mr John Vanderbank has of late for some years had a great run of Busines – painting persons of Quality and distinction …' .[2] The costume may be compared with that worn in Vanderbank's *Georgiana Cartaret*, dated 1737, at Althorp.[3]

1 Label *verso*: *Mr Fairfax Murray June 2 1902*.
2 Vertue, iii, p.82.
3 K. Garlick, *Wal. Soc.*, XLV, 1976, p.84, no.650, pl.16.

attributed to HENRY WALTON (1745/6–1813)

DPG589 *Portrait of a Man*

Canvas 76.2 x 63.5 lined; pentimento above his right arm and coat collar which may first have been drawn beneath the wig; cleaned 1994.

Grey eyes, powdered wig; wearing a black coat, clerical grey waistcoat, white stock.

PROV.: Fairfax Murray Gift 1911 as 'Hoppner, Portrait of a Divine'.

REF.: E. Bell, 'The Life and Work of Henry Walton', *Gainsborough's House Review*, 1998/99, p.73, no.169 as Walton, A Gentleman, possibly a Cleric.

Given by Murray as a portrait of a divine by Hoppner, DPG589 was first attributed to Walton by Hugh Belsey. Evelyne Bell suggested a comparison with his portrait of William Crowfoot of c.1805, although dating DPG589 c.1785.[1] Nothing in the sober dress confirms the sitter is a cleric.

1 Letter 8 September 1998 on file: 'I have the strong feeling that it could very well be a Walton'.

Benjamin West (1738–1820)

DPG586 Mrs Benjamin West II with her son Benjamin West III

Canvas 91.4 x 71.1 lined; Hell 1953; cleaned 1989.

Signed in black on the chair arm: *B. West. 1805*; the mother has light brown hair, brown eyes, a black blouse and green skirt with a floral pattern; the baby, holding a red and black rattle, wears a white smock and purple drape; a red-upholstered chair with a red curtain behind.

PROV.: By descent to Mrs Albert F. West;[1] her sale, Christie's, 19 March 1898 ('part of the collection of Benjamin West PRA … in the possession of the family since the Artist's death', the sitters unidentified), lot 146, bt. Fairfax Murray; his Gift 1911.

REF.: H. von Erffa & A. Staley, *The Paintings of Benjamin West*, 1986, no.544.

The sitters seem first to have been identified in Cook 1914 as the artist's daughter-in-law and grandson. Benjamin West III was born late in 1804/early 1805, the son of the artist's younger son, Benjamin II (1772–1848), who married c.1803 a daughter of Edward Dickinson of Perthall;[2] Benjamin III was their only surviving child.[3]

1 Wife of the artist's great-grandson.
2 See Farington, vi, p.2162 (12 November 1803), when West reported his son's marriage to a beautiful young lady, and vi, p.2275 (24 March 1804), when West spoke of his son Benjamin bringing 'His Wife to town, & that she was a very fine young Woman, – and in a state likely to add to the family'.
3 Farington, xiii, p.4667 (11 July 1815). The family descent is documented by Erffa & Staley, see REF. above.

BENJAMIN WILSON (1721–88)

DPG593 *Portrait of a Lady with Mask and Cherries*

Canvas 91.7 x 70.7 lined by Holder and heavily ironed; Hell 1953–55; cleaned 2006 when considerable repaint in the hat was removed and prominent retouchings in face, neck and lower left area were repaired.

Signed bottom left: *AE20 / B. Wilson.pinxit./1753*; brown hair, grey eyes; wearing a small bergère hat, a gauze shawl with a white and gold floral pattern over a pink and turquoise dress; a brown mask hangs from her left arm, and in her left hand a basket from which she takes grapes; a round window to the right.

PROV.: C.J. James, Bristol, sold Christie's, 22 January 1898, lot 88 (B. Wilson 1753, 'supposed to be Anne, daughter of Horatio Orford'), bt. Phillpot; Christie's, 18 April 1903, lot 21 (B.W. Wilson 1753, 'A Lady in Fancy Costume, holding a basket of cherries'), bt. in; Fairfax Murray Gift 1911.

An adaptation of Rembrandt's *Saskia as Flora* (1634; St Petersburg), though that does not preclude the idea of a portrait (cf. Knapton DPG606, p.168). Whether it is of Lady Anne Walpole (1733–97), as diffidently alleged in the 1898 sale catalogue, might be doubted, although the inscribed age and date would be correct for her. She was one of the three rather plain daughters of Horatio, 1st Baron Walpole of Wolterton (1678–1757)[1] and no portraits of her in her maturity are recorded. The face somewhat resembles that of her cousin Lady Mary Walpole (c.1725–1801, who married in 1745 the poet Charles Churchill) as seen in J.G. Eccardt's portrait in the Lewis Farmington Library,[2] or in Benjamin Wilson's so-called *Peg Woffington* in the Garrick Club (848).[3]

Fairfax Murray told William Spanton 'Benjamin Wilson is very little known rather smooth The specimen I had'.[4]

1 Lord Walpole's three daughters were described in their maturity as 'not handsome women, and as [their father] finds by various trials are not likely to be married' (*Wal. Corr.*, xxxvi, p.298).
2 Illus. W.S. Lewis, *Horace Walpole*, 1961, p.31.
3 Ashton 1997, no.848, p.446. There are many versions.
4 Letter of 1 August 1913 in Gallery archive.

Unknown Artist

DPG561 *Portrait of a Baron*

Canvas 127 x 102.2 lined by Holder; retouchings lower left and losses along the bottom edge; pentimenti on the coronet; discoloured varnish; Hell 1953; surface cleaned 1980.

Blue eyes, powdered wig; wearing a Baron's robes and the collar of the Bath; a Baron's coronet on a table to the right; a green curtain behind.

PROV.: Sir Hugh Lane;[1] Christie's, 25 November 1911, lot 121 as the Earl of Egremont by Richard Wilson, bt. Agnew; Fairfax Murray Gift 1911.

EXH.: *Richard Wilson*, Tate 1925(32 as by Richard Wilson).

REF.: W.G. Constable, *Richard Wilson*, 1953, pp.46n2, 232, pl.133b.

The traditional identity as the 2nd Earl of Egremont (1710–63) may be discounted since the sitter is shown as a Baron and a Knight of the Bath. The date of the portrait would appear to be c.1735–40 and the age of the sitter perhaps forty. This reduces the number of possible sitters to five:

1 John West (1693–1766), 16th Baron de la Warr 1723, KB 1725; cr. Earl de la Warr 1761.

2 John Monson (1693–1748), KB 1725; cr. Baron Monson 1728.

3 Robert Walpole (1701–51), cr. Baron Walpole 1723; KB 1725; suc. as 2nd Earl of Orford 1745.

4 John Hobart (1694–1756), KB 1725; cr. Baron Hobart 1728; cr. Earl of Buckinghamshire 1746.

5 Thomas Coke (1699–1759), KB 1725; cr. Baron Lovel 1728; cr. Earl of Leicester 1744.

Of these, there are no extant portraits of 1 and 2; none of the portraits of 3 (an unattributed whole-length in robes in a private collection), 4 (a whole length in robes by Hudson engraved by Faber) or 5 (by Casali, Hudson and Richardson, all at Holkham), agrees closely enough with DPG593 to confirm an identity.

The attribution also remains uncertain. It is clearly not by Richard Wilson under whose name it was sold in 1911 (perhaps Benjamin Wilson was meant, as proposed in Murray 1980). In 1998 an attribution to William Hoare (who had painted the 2nd Lord Egremont more than once) was published in Beresford 1998, but the proposed date and loose execution might indicate a painter nearer Vanderbank.

1 Information kindly supplied by L.M. Sampson of the Getty Art History Information Program 1985.

ACQUISITIONS 1831–1961

The pictures in this section are catalogued in alphabetical order by artist with unattributed works at the end

Besides the major gifts and bequests already described, there had been a steady trickle of individual gifts from 1831. The quality varied greatly.

The fine Gainsborough of *Mrs Moody* arrived unexpectedly in 1831; Beechey bequeathed his portrait of *Sir Francis Bourgeois* in 1836 and there were further individual gifts of portraits painted by Briggs and Lane in 1854 and by Bourgeois in 1866; three paintings by John Wood arrived in 1883 and 1897. Works by two of the Dulwich Gallery Curators had also been accepted; Denning's charming *Princess Victoria* was purchased in 1891 and three of Hodgkins' much less charming copies were received in 1892 and 1894 (the Gallery Committee must have been in a tight corner when he offered them). Henry Yates Thompson (1838–1928), the first knowledgeable and active Chairman of the Gallery Committee (1908–19), effectively presented the splendid Canaletto of *Old Walton Bridge* (DPG600), one of four important gifts he made between 1898 and 1917 (he also funded a Gallery extension and provided interior furnishings).

Closely related to Dulwich history were Sir James Leigh Wood's gift in 1920 of W.C. Horsley's *Old-time Tuition at Dulwich College*, and the commissioned copy of *Mrs Margaret Desenfans* by Reynolds in 1930. In 1934 Margaret Spanton, whose father had been one of Fairfax Murray's closest friends, bequeathed three last Fairfax Murray paintings, but there ensued a protracted period of very minor (and undocumented) donations during the tolerant Chairmanship of Sir Gerald Kelly. His reign was, of course, otherwise a triumph; it was primarily due to his resolve and influence that, after the Gallery had been hit by a flying bomb in 1944, it was repaired and re-opened in 1953.

Moussa Ayoub (fl.1903–38)

See DPG627, after Sir Joshua Reynolds, p.218.

attributed to Mary Beale (1633–99)

DPG611 *Portrait of a Physician*

Canvas 75.9 x 63.5 lined; a mended tear in the drawing and another in the lower left corner (see note 2 below); scattered small retouchings, principally round the hand and in the hair; pentimenti to left and right of the gown.

Blue-grey eyes, greying hair; wearing a brown cloak and holding a sanguine anatomical drawing (in which the arm is shown separately from the standing figure).

Prov.: Anon. sale, Christie's, 14 July 1877, lot 87 as Boerhaave by Kneller,[1] bt. Hughes; Fairfax Murray who gave it to W.S. Spanton;[2] bequeathed by his daughter, H. Margaret Spanton 1934.

Exh.: Aberystwyth 1947(7 as Dr Boerhaave by Kneller).

Purchased and presented as a portrait of Dr Herman Boerhaave (1668–1738) by Kneller, but neither name is defensible.[3] The sitter was later tentatively identified as Sir Richard Blackmore (1654–1729), physician and writer,[4] but his surviving portraits do not furnish a convincing comparison;[5] there is perhaps some resemblance to the physician Sir Edmund King (1629–1709).[6]

The pose matches that of Kneller's 1690 portrait of the shipbuilder *Sir Anthony Deane* holding a drawing of a ship (National Portrait Gallery, 2124). An attribution to Mary Beale seems more probable and has been independently suggested;[7] the weak 'tubular' hand is characteristic of her work, but not the strongly characterised head. An attribution within the Riley-John Closterman orbit was offered as a possibility by both Millar and Rogers.[8]

1 A cutting from the catalogue remains on the *verso*; I am most grateful to Mrs Marijke Booth of Christie's for the identification.
2 W.S. Spanton's niece, Miss Tarrant, confirmed the gift to her uncle when she visited the Gallery on 29 November 1935 (note on file); she also recorded that the frame on DPG611 had been much admired by Fairfax Murray and her father. An undated letter from Fairfax Murray to W.S. Spanton (Gallery archive) refers to a damaged Kneller which Spanton had from him.
3 G.A. Lindeboom, author of the *Iconographia Boerhavii*, Leiden, 1963, rejected outright the identification of Boerhaave.
4 By both Murray 1980 and Beresford 1998.
5 His engraved portrait by John Closterman c.1697 illus. *Closterman*, NPG, 1981, no.13. Another by Vanderbank engraved G. White relates to his portrait with the Royal College of Physicians (illus. *Cat. of Portraits in the Royal College of Physicians*, 1964, p.65 attributed to Closterman).
6 Cf. the portrait engraved by R. Williams after Lely.
7 Orally in 1997 by B. Allen, T. Barber and K. Hearn; rejected by M. Rogers, letter of 16 June 1997 (on file).
8 Letter from O. Millar, 17 July 1975, and a note from M. Rogers, 25 November 1982 (on file).

Sir William Beechey (1753–1839)

DPG17 Sir Francis Bourgeois

Mahogany[?] panel 74.9 x 62.2; painted on the *verso* of a painting by Reynolds (see DPG17A, p.215);[1] revived and revarnished 1872; much bitumen in coat and background; discoloured varnish; Hell 1953.

Grey eyes; black coat, white hair, red curtain; wearing the ribbon of the Polish *Ordre du Mérite* (red with green edges and a silver stripe down the centre) with the gold medal bearing the head of King Stanislaus Augustus;[2] a fluted column to left.

PROV.: Given by the artist 1836 (see DPG17A, p.215).[3]

EXH., ENG., see below.

REF.: Roberts 1907, pp.125–26; Walker 1985, i, pp.60–61.

For Bourgeois (1753–1811) see pp.87, 101.

Two copies from this Beechey type by Bourgeois (DPG465 and DPG466, p.101) indicate a date before January 1811 when Bourgeois died. The first engraving of Beechey's portrait was published on 7 May following.[4] The portrait was not exhibited at the RA until 1813 (221 *The late Sir F. Bourgeois RA*) and then again at Suffolk Street (RSBA) in 1830(101).[5] It is no longer clear which of three surviving autograph versions was Beechey's original, DPG17, National Portrait Gallery 231[6] or Soane Museum 114;[7] DPG17, being painted on the back of another picture, seems an unlikely candidate; the earliest history of the National Portrait Gallery version is unclear, leaving the Soane portrait, which remained in Beechey's possession until 1836, the likeliest contender.[8]

Beechey's portrait was copied by Charles Hayter in miniature (M1, p.243).

1 According to Cook 1914 and later Dulwich catalogues, Beechey used to say he did this 'in order that it might be sure of preservation' (his, not Reynolds's, picture?).
2 Medal and ribbon are preserved in the Gallery archive. The medal shows on the obverse a bust, the hair in a band, lettered: *STANISLAUS AUGUSTUS D. G. REX POLONIAE M.D. LITUA*, and on the reverse: *MERENTIBUS* with oak and laurel wreaths. Bourgeois was awarded the Order in 1790 and a British Royal licence was issued 12 April 1791 accepting the Polish knighthood.
3 A frame provided by Biggs for £7 was paid for on 5 April 1837.
4 By J. Vendramini from a drawing by W. Evans (such a drawing was sold Bonham & Brooks, 11 September 2001, lot 166, paired with one of Lord Barham), published on 7 May 1811 and included in Cadell's *Contemporary Portraits*, i, 1822. A reduced vignette engraved by E. Scriven appeared in the *Library of the Fine Arts*, 1832.
5 On both occasions lent by the artist.
6 See Walker, *loc. cit.*, and, ii, pl.134. Having been offered for sale to Dulwich in 1866 by Mrs Mary E Dixcee, an artist's widow of Red Hill, near Edgware, it was bought from her by the NPG the following year.
7 Also presented by the artist in 1836; cleaned in 1988. Roberts did not know of this version.
8 Although Roberts, who called DPG17 a posthumous work and did not know of the Soane picture, wrote that of the two versions he knew 'that at the Dulwich Gallery is probably the RA portrait of 1813' and 'the second portrait … acquired by the National Portrait Gallery in 1867 … may have been the picture exhibited at Suffolk Street in 1830' (Roberts 1907, pp.125–26).

Sir Francis Bourgeois (1753–1811)

DPG464 Self Portrait

Canvas 61 x 50.8 including an addition of 4 at the top, lined 1873;[1] unfinished and in poor condition; flattened surface; marked overall craquelure, particularly prominent in the head, and much discoloured varnish; the top of the jacket is painted red, the lower part modelled in browns.

Light brown hair, grey eyes; in a painted oval.

PROV.: Given by the Executors of Sir Felix Agar Kt.[2] 1866.

For Bourgeois (1753–1811) see pp.87, 101.

Bourgeois here appears appreciably younger than in the Beechey portrait DPG17 (p.194) and there is no evidence of the Polish *Ordre du Mérite*, suggesting a date of c.1790.

1 The stretcher is stamped *W Morrill/Liner.*
2 c.1781–1866, MP Sudbury 1807–12; his father had invested £25,000 in collecting pictures (*House of Commons 1790–1820*, iii, 1986, pp.51–52).

Henry Perronet Briggs (1791–1844)

DPG291 *Charles Kemble*

Canvas 76.5 x 63.8 unlined; a scratch and ruck at the bottom of the right edge; pentimenti on the collar; surface cleaned and tacking edges strip lined 1996.

Brown hair, blue-grey eyes; wearing a black cravat and a black cloak with brass clasp over a red jacket.

PROV.: [probably Briggs sale, Christie's, 27 April 1844, lot 565 ('Briggs, a head of Charles Kemble')[1] but see below] gift of the actor George Bartley 1854 (on the death of the sitter);[2] College Board Room 1880.

EXH.: Whitechapel Fine Art Exhibition, 1885.[3]

Charles Kemble (1775–1854), comic actor, the brother of John (see DPG111, p.88) and Sarah (Mrs Siddons, see DPG318, p.120); he became manager of Covent Garden in 1822; pre-eminently 'a gentleman', he was described as being in private life 'the very noblest of men'.[4]

Briggs painted three portraits of Charles Kemble. Ashton believed the kit-cat in the Garrick Club showing Kemble holding the masks of tragedy and comedy may have been that exhibited RA 1832(477)[5] and another kit cat formerly belonging to O.Wister at Bryn Mawr PA, was that shown RA 1835(346);[6] he suggested that DPG291, the least ambitious composition, preceded both.[7] A version, formerly with Lady Butler, is in the Garrick Club.[8]

For the extensive iconography of Kemble, see Highfill, viii, pp.317–21.

1 The Christie's copy of the catalogue has the buyer's name '*Bell*' deleted.
2 See p.212, DPG500 note 2.
3 Label *verso*; catalogue untraced.
4 See Highfill, viii, p.317 (Kemble's biography is given pp.302–17).
5 Ashton 1997, no.366, p.204. A half-length version acquired by the NPG in 1983 (5687) was exh. NPE 1868(87) lent Mrs Noseda.
6 Ashton 1997, p.204. Photograph in NPG archive.
7 *Ibid.*, pp.204–05.
8 *Ibid.*, no.367, p.205.

Kate S. Brodie (fl. 1891–1900)

DPG632 *Landscape (Four Figures in a Wood)*

Canvas 91.4 x 60.9, revarnished 1988 [not seen].

Signed bottom left: *S. Brodie.*

Prov.: Anonymous Gift 1956.[1]

1 The donor possibly lived in Grove Hill Road, Camberwell, SE5.

Giovanni Antonio Canal called Canaletto (1697–1768)

DPG600 *A View of Walton Bridge*

Canvas 49 x 76.5 lined in 1850 (see below), when the surface was ironed quite heavily; pentimenti in the bridge, in the trees on the horizon, by the cow and in the figure of the seated artist; cleaned 1996. The remains of a mid nineteenth-century label *verso* [the missing passages given in square brackets]:[1]

> *Behind this picture on the original canvas is the following inscription by Canaletto:*
>
> *Fatto nel anno 1754 in Londra per la pri*[ma] *ed ultima* [volta con ogni maggior attenzione] *ad instanza* [del Signor Cavaliere Hollis] *padrone mio* [stimatissimo/ Antonio Canal detto il Canaletto].
>
> *It was nece*[ssary to new line the picture in 1850] *so the inscript*[ion is hid. John Disney, 1850].

Walton-on-Thames, Surrey, twenty-five miles south west of central London; the bridge depicted is seen from the north, looking upstream, against an approaching rain cloud; a boat approaches with lowered mast; to the left a seated artist in a fur cap turns towards the spectator (his identity as Canaletto is of course possible but academic); Thomas Hollis and Thomas Brand stand in the centre (see below); across the Thames, in the trees on the left, the 'large plain edifice' of Mount Felix, home of Samuel Dicker (see below).

Prov.:[2] Painted for Thomas Hollis (1720–74); bequeathed by him to Thomas Brand (later Brand-Hollis; 1719–1804); bequeathed by him to the Rev John Disney (d.1816); his son John Disney (d.1857); his son Edgar Disney; Mrs E. Disney sale, Christie's, 3 May 1884, lot 130, bt. C. Becket Denison; his sale, Christie's, 13 June 1885, lot 858, bt. H. Yates Thompson for George Murray Smith (1859-1919);[3] lent to Dulwich by Mrs George Murray in February 1914 and presented by Miss E. Murray Smith in 1917.

Exh.: BI 1864(158) lent Edgar Disney; Aberystwyth 1945(29); National Gallery 1947(2), Leeds 1947–53(2); *European Masters of the 18th century*, RA, 1954–55(24); *London and the Thames*, Somerset House, 1977(15); *Canaletto*, Venice, 1982(108); *Manners and Morals*, Tate Gallery, 1987(178); *Collection for a King*, Washington DC, Los Angeles, 1985–86(3); *Canaletto*, New York, 1989(73); *Canaletto & England*, Birmingham, 1993(35); *Rembrandt to Gainsborough*, Houston TX, Louisville KY, 1999–2000(12); *Old Master Paintings*, Japan, 2000(10); *Canaletto in England*, Dulwich, 2007 (37); *Canaletto e Bellotto*, Palazzo Bricherasio, Turin, 2008.

Ref.: *A Catalogue of some Marbles, Bronzes, Pictures, and Gems, at the Hyde, near Ingatestone, Essex, the greater part successively the property of Thomas Hollis, Esq. F.R.S. and S.A. and Thomas Brand Hollis Esq. F.R.S. and S.A. and now of John Disney, D.D. F.S.A. with an appendix*, 1809, p.12; H. Finberg, *Wal. Soc.*, IX, 1921, pp.42, 66; W.G. Constable & J.G. Links, *Canaletto*, 1976, no.441; J.G. Links in *Collection for a King*, 1985, pp.44, 46; C. Beddington in *Canaletto in England*, 2006, p.130.

Walton Bridge, designed by William Etheridge, was completed in August 1750 and the structure painted in the summer of 1751; it was built of wood, at the expense of Samuel Dicker,[4] and had stone additions at each end, with a long raised causeway on the south side. The central arch was much admired, as an account of 1750 makes clear:[5]

> The prodigious compass of this great arch, to a person below, occasions a very uncommon sensation of awe and surprise, ... and his wonder and attention are raised, when he proceeds to take notice, that all the timbers are in a falling inclination, (there not being discoverable one upright piece) and considers also the very small dimensions of the piers that support the whole. It is, without doubt, a noble work, and very well worth the trouble of going many miles to take a view of it, and will be so more especially in the summer, when it will be painted over.

Dicker later wrote that the outer arches should have been wider, to lessen the gradient of the bridge, but he was confident it would last two hundred years.[6] He was mistaken; the bridge decayed and was demolished in 1780 (twenty years after his death), to be rebuilt in stone and brick.[7] The 1809 Hollis catalogue stated that 'in this picture, the portraits of T.H. his friend T.B. his servant Francisco [*Giovanni*], and his dog Malta, are introduced'. Hollis, the traveller and radical (T.H.), was a large man 'over six feet tall, Herculean in size and strength',[8] and may be identified as the tall figure in the yellow coat, with Brand (T.B.) on his left pointing with his stick.

Hollis had been in Venice from late 1750 to February 1751[9] when he probably met Canaletto and when he befriended the British consul, Joseph Smith, the artist's agent and extensive patron. (Canaletto had first been in England from 1746; he returned to Venice for some months from late 1750 before returning to England where he stayed from mid-1751 to 1755).[10] It is clear from contemporary descriptions and engraved elevations of 1750[11] that in 1754, when Canaletto dated DPG600, the bridge did not appear as he painted it; he omitted the stone additions at each end (which he was to include in his 1755 view, see below) and hinted that the bridge was wider in the centre, giving it a curved appearance (such inaccuracy was not unprecedented in his English work[12]). It is now generally accepted that the subject was chosen by Hollis from a drawing made when the bridge was first opened. Hollis commissioned a total of six Canalettos, each inscribed and dated 1754 or 1755, three others apparently based on an earlier drawing or engraving.[13]

Canaletto painted a second view of Walton Bridge for Samuel Dicker in 1755 from a slightly different angle, including the stone approaches and the long raised causeway to the south; this painting bears an inscription which follows exactly the formula of DPG600 but with Samuel Dicker's name and the date 1755; it is now in the Yale Center for British Art (B1981.25.86),[14] together with a directly related drawing (B1981.25.2409) also dated 1755.[15]

1 The missing passages taken from the similar labels on the other Hollis Canalettos, see note 14 below.
2 The provenance is further attested by two Christie's stamps, and additional labels: *Mrs Murray Smith* and [Becket D]*enison; No.16 Disney* is scratched into the stretcher.
3 William Whitley recorded (Whitley Papers, iii, 216) lunching 'at Portman Square with Yates Thompson, July 9, 1916. Miss Murray Smith also there. Yates Thompson bought picture for George Smith in 1885 at Christie's, Smith thinking the bridge had association with his courtship (wrong bridge)'. Yates Thompson's brother-in-law George Smith, 1859-1919, m. Ellen Strutt 1885; she was perhaps the lender (the Committe minutes of 10 May 1915 recorded the loan of DPG600 'in the last few years'); the donor, and Whitley's fellow-guest at Portman Square, was perhaps their only daughter.
4 Samuel Dicker (d.1760), for whom see *History of Parliament 1754–90*, ii, 1964, p.320; West India merchant and MP for Plymouth 1754–60; his enthusiasm for bridge building earned him the title *Pontifex Maximus*.
5 *GM*, xx, 1750, pp.588–90. Manning & Bray, ii, p.769 described the central arch as 26 feet and the side arches as 18 feet high above water at high flood, and as 144 and 44 feet wide, with five smaller arches of brickwork on each side of the causeway. See also Brayley 1850, ii, pp.339–41.
6 *GM*, xxiv, 1754, pp.116–17.
7 Brayley 1850, ii, p.341. The new bridge by James Paine was completed in 1783 (H. Colvin, *Dictionary of Architects*, 3rd ed., 1995, p.723).
8 From the Latin of Cipriani, see J. Ingamells, *Dictionary of British and Irish Travellers in Italy 1701–1800*, 1997, p.512. The servant identified in Hollis's diary (information from W.S. Anthony, letter of 18 April 1989 on file). A bust of Hollis by Joseph Wilton is on loan to the NPG from a private collection (2004); it is fully discussed, along with the sitter, by D. Wilson, *British Art Journal*, v, 3, 2005, pp.4–26.
9 J. Ingamells, *Dictionary of British and Irish Travellers in Italy 1701–1800*, 1997, p.512.
10 C. Beddington, *Canaletto in England*, 2006, p.10. Constable & Links, 1989, i, pp.21, 40 had previously said that Hollis could not have met Canaletto in Venice (and that Brand was with him in Venice).
11 *GM*, xx, 1750, f.p.589, and see illustration below.
12 A painting of Walton Bridge from a similar view-point by Francis Towne dated 1785, five years after the bridge was demolished, shows a steeper central span (Yale Center for British Art, B1976.7.155; illus. *Canaletto to Constable*, New Haven CT, 1998, no.30). And cf. Canaletto's *View of Eton College* in the National Gallery (942), also of the 1750s (Constable & Links, 1976, no.450: 'details of the chapel and of the College building are far from the facts').
13 Listed in the 1809 *Catalogue*, pp.12–13. Apart from DPG600, they were: *A View of Whitehall* (Constable & Links, 1976, no.472, inscribed 1754), *A View of Westminster Bridge* (no.437b, inscribed 1754), *A View of St Paul's Cathedral* (no.422, inscribed 1754; now Yale Center for British Art, B1976.7.95), *A View of the inside of Ranelagh* (no.420, inscribed 1754; now National Gallery, London, 1429) and *The Capitol at Rome* (no.396, inscribed 1755 and said, in the 1809 *Catalogue*, to include *the portraits of T.H.*[ollis] *T.B.*[and] *Francisco and his dog*). Four were exhibited at the BI 1841, all six were exhibited at the BI 1864 and all six were sold Christie's, 3 May 1884, lots 128–133. (A further three pictures attributed to Canaletto were in the 1884 sale, lots 134–36, two Capriccios and *The Municipal Palace, Piazza dei Mercanti, Milan* (Constable & Links, 1976, nos.496j, 497k, with lot 136 unlisted).
14 Constable & Links, 1976, no.442.
15 Constable & Links, 1976, no.755, inscribed: *Disegnato da me Antonio Canal detto il Canaleto appresso il mio Quadro Dippinto in Londra 1755/ Per il Signore Cavaliere dickers*. An engraving by A. Walker dedicated to Dicker, probably derived from this drawing, identifies Dicker's house.

A. Walker, *A View of the New Bridge over the Thames at Walton in Surrey*, after Canaletto, hand-coloured engraving, 1750 (Yale Center for British Art, Paul Mellon Collection)

Canaletto, *Old Walton Bridge*, 1755
(Yale Center for British Art, Paul Mellon Collection)

attributed to Marmaduke Cradock (c.1660?–1716)

DPG519 *Mallards on a Pond*

Canvas 45.4 x 55.3 lined, possibly by Brown 1815;[1] scratched surface and scuffed vertical edges; losses in the right wing of flying duck, in the left-hand tree, in the pond and by the tail of the left-hand duck; discoloured varnish.

A crested albino mallard disturbs other mallards.[2]

Prov.: Dulwich College by 1890 (see below).

The attribution was first suggested by F. Meijer.[3] A comparable view by Cradock shows frightened ducks with a diving bird, with reeds in the background.[4]

Cradock's approximate date of birth makes it unlikely that this was a Cartwright picture, although it appears to agree with his taste; it was probably restored for the College in 1815 (see note 1) and was otherwise first described as being in the College in Sparkes & Carver 1890 (as were the other Cartwright pictures).

1 Possibly the *Pic^r. of Ducks &c.* lined and cleaned by Brown, 13 October 1815 (Brown Ledger).
2 I am grateful to Dr Jim Brock of the Horniman Museum for the identification of these birds.
3 See Beresford 1998, p.78.
4 Illus. M.H. Grant, *Old Landscape Painters*, i, 1957, fig.38 (as 'Gradock').

attributed to John de Critz the elder (c.1551/2–1642)

DPG548 *James VI and I*

Canvas 200.5 x 129.5 lined; a vertical join runs up the right-hand side; retouchings in the nose, stockings, fur, doublet and tablecloth; the face worn; raised craquelure; discoloured varnish; cleaned 1953 by Hell; revarnished 1994.

Brown hair, grey eyes, the great Feather jewel[1] in his black hat; wearing a silver costume with the ribbon and Badge of the Garter beneath a brown fur cape.

Prov.: [The Countess of Warwick of Holland House, who m. 1716] Joseph Addison of Bilton Hall, Warwicks.; Miss Addison (d.1797), bequeathed to the Hon. John Simpson, by descent to the Rev. Bridgeman-Simpson at Bilton Hall; Bilton sale Christie's, 28 June 1898, lot 12, bt. Henry Yates Thompson and given by him 1898.[2]

Exh.: *Kings & Queens*, RA, 1953 (113, attributed to Gheeraerts); *Christian IV and Europe*, Copenhagen, 1988(110); *Edward Alleyn* 1994(44); *Death, Passion and Politics* 1995(12); *Talking Peace 1604, The Somerset House Conference Paintings*, 2004 (n.n.).

Ref.: L. Cust, *Wal. Soc.*, III, 1914, p.26 (as by Gheeraerts the younger).

James (1566–1625), son of Mary, Queen of Scots, and Lord Darnley; crowned as James VI of Scotland 1567 and James I of England 1603. He was a reluctant sitter and in his few portraits Henry Peacham found artists committed two principal errors, 'the one in the complexion and haire, the other is in the mouth, which commonly they draw with a full and great netherlip very apparent, wherein they commit the chiefest error.'[3]

A good example of a standard type of portrait of James I now generally associated with John de Critz the elder and dated c.1606.[4] Cook 1914 and 1926 attributed DPG548 to Marc Gheeraerts and stated it was signed,[5] but there is now no trace of a signature or inscription; the RA 1953 catalogue said it was 'wrongly stated to be signed'. A survey of the many versions of

this pattern was made by Strong;[6] they include whole lengths at Loseley Park,[7] in the Prado (1954), from the Ellesmere collection,[8] and in the Old Schools at Cambridge.[9] Three-quarter length versions of 1610 are in the National Maritime Museum (BHC2796) and from Hemingstone Hall, and a half-length at the Middle Temple appears to bear the inscription *1604 Aetatis suae 38*.[10] See also DPG384, p.31.

1 'One fayre jewell like a feather of gold containing a fayre table diamond in the middest and five and twentie diamonds', see D. Scarisbrick, *Tudor and Jacobean Jewellery*, 1995, p.19.
2 The date of 1898 printed by Cust 1914 (see REF.); the Committee minutes 10 May 1915 record that DPG548 had been presented by the Chairman 'in the last few years'. For the descent of the Bilton pictures see G. Scharf MS, Portraits in Private Collections, iv, ff.11–12 (NPG archive).
3 H. Peacham, *The Gentleman's Exercise*, 1612, p.25.
4 K. Hearn in *Dynasties*, Tate, 1995, p.184.
5 In 1931 Hake alleged he read *Mark Garr* bottom left and thought there was an inscription in the extreme right-hand corner (notes on file).
6 Strong 1969a, i, p.179; a general survey of James I's iconography pp.176–80.
7 Exh. *Elizabethan Image*, Tate, 1969–70, no.174.
8 Exh. *Dynasties*, Tate, 1995, no.125.
9 J.W. Goodison, *Cambridge Portraits*, 1955, i, *The University Collection*, pp.15–16, no.16, pl.iv.
10 *Catalogue of Paintings and Engravings in the Middle Temple*, 1931, p.26.

STEPHEN POYNTZ DENNING (1795–1864)

DPG304 Princess Victoria aged Four

Mahogany panel[1] 27.9 x 22.7; a scratch lower right and minor losses by the left arm and above the head; pentimenti round the hat.

Fair hair, blue eyes; wearing a black pelisse, with a fox fur tippet (shoulder cape), a large black hat decorated with feathers, black shoes, white stockings and grey gloves; roses lie on the ground before her.[2]

PROV.: Purchased 1891, having been declined in 1880.[3]

EXH.: *Jubilee Exhibition*, Royal Room, Earls Court, 1897(651); Aberystwyth 1945(47); London Museum, *Dearest Children*, 1978; *Dulwich College – a School and its Art*, South London AG, 1981; *In Royal Fashion*, Museum of London, 1997; *Obras Maestras*, Madrid, Bilbao, 1999(49); *Our Highland Home*, Scottish NPG, Edinburgh, 2005.

ENG.: Chromolithograph 1895 (*Golden Penny*); mezzotint by J.W. Chapman 1901.

REF.: Ormond 1973, i, p.479 (as a water-colour of 1823).

Victoria (1819–1901), daughter of Edward, Duke of Kent (1767–1820), and Victoria of Saxe-Coburg-Saalfeld, Duchess of Kent (1786–1861), acceded as Queen 1837; she married in 1840 her cousin Albert (1819–61), son of Ernest, Duke of Saxe-Coburg-Gotha. Her isolated childhood was spent principally at Kensington Palace, attended by a nurse until she was five (and thereafter by a governess); she was often in the Palace gardens, where Leigh Hunt first saw her (with another girl and attended by a footman);[4] it was observed how her remarkably transparent complexion, with 'a tinge of the sweet blush rose upon her cheeks' lent 'a peculiar brilliancy to her clear blue eyes. Whenever she met any strangers in her usual paths she always seemed by the quickness of her glance to enquire who and what they were'.[5] In 1823, at the age of four, she was not inevitably destined to be Queen[6] and was frequently pitied as a fatherless child.

Such sympathy may be expressed in DPG304, doubtless painted from memory as a result of a chance encounter. It has always been described as Princess Victoria aged four, but where this (entirely plausible) assertion of her age was first made is not known.[7] She is rather overdressed (although the sky is blue and the trees and plants in leaf she wears several layers of fur, rather than a white muslin dress), and her black clothes with the fallen rose appear deliberately melancholy. The picture remained in the artist's collection until his death and was engraved in 1901 by J.W. Chapman, with the approval of the Royal Chamberlain's Office, as a portrait of the young Queen Victoria.

Denning came to enjoy some minor Royal patronage. In 1835 his copy of Lawrence's portrait of Sir Jeffrey Wyatville at Windsor was presented to the sitter by William IV for engraving[8] and before 1845 he had made a watercolour copy of Sully's portrait of the Queen for the 2nd Duke of Buckingham.[9] In 1847 the Queen commissioned from him a copy of Winterhalter's *Royal Family*[10] and at some stage he painted Prince Albert in miniature; an example is at Gotha, perhaps the 'Portrait of His Royal Highness the late Prince Consort, *from the life in water-colours*'[11] which, like DPG304, remained in Denning's collection until after his death.

Such Royal patronage in the 1840s might suggest that DPG304 also dates from that period and shows Princess Victoria, Queen Victoria's eldest child.[12] But it seems impossible to determine whether the costume dates from 1823 or 1844[13] but, to judge by other contemporary portraits, while the Queen's hair was still fair at the age of four, her daughter's had turned darker at that age.[14] It is further slightly disconcerting to find that Denning's style evolved very little; a comparative portrait of a young girl standing in a landscape being dated 1859.[15]

A slightly larger copy of DPG304 by W.B. Morris, with simplified trees, is in the Walker AG, Liverpool (347), presented by Henry Yates

Thompson in 1904.[16] Thompson had previously commissioned from Morris copies of portraits of Edward Alleyn and Francis Bacon for Alleyn's school (see DPG551 and DPG549, p.235).

1 Stamped *Brown/163/High Holborn* (Thomas Brown, artist's colourman, was at this address from 1805).
2 F. Weiss (*Marco*, September 1967, p.57) suggested the pelisse must be of seal skin. In 1956 C.G. Heise observed that 'the great English Queen barely changed the style of her dress in 80 years' ('Mäzen hinter Glaswand', *Die Zeit*, 5 July 1956; transcript on file).
3 Minutes of the Board Meeting, 21 April 1891.
4 L. Hunt, 'The Old Court Suburb', ii, [1851], see The Marquis of Lorne, *V.R.I., Her Life and Empire*, 1901, p.25. Her earliest years were very closely supervised (see, for example, M. Charlot, *Victoria*, 1991, p.52).
5 Quoted by the The Marquis of Lorne (see note 4), p.27, as from a letter from Jane Porter.
6 She was third in line of succession, after the Duke of Clarence (later William IV) and his possible legitimate offspring.
7 An ink label *verso* reads: *The Princess Victoria by S.P. Denning, Curator of Dulwich Gallery.* and in pencil *By Denning/* B[?t,@ his Sale] – but it was not in Denning's sale, Christie's, 17 August 1864.
8 According to an inscription now on the *verso* of the drawing which is in a private collection (Gallery archive).
9 *Wallace Collection Catalogue of Pictures*, i, 1985, pp.77, 179–81.
10 Millar 1992, p.294 under no.823, as possibly the watercolour in the Royal Library (13334); D. Millar 1995, no.5920.
11 Denning sale, Christie's, 17 August 1864, lot 92.
12 Victoria (1840–1901), Princess Royal, Crown Princess of Prussia and German Empress; m. 1858 Frederick William (1831–88), Crown Prince of Prussia, Frederick III, German Emperor.
13 I am grateful to Aileen Ribeiro (letter of 5 January 2004), Edwina Ehrman (letter of 8 February 2005) and Christine Rose (letter of 25 February 2005) for their considered opinions on the child's dress.
14 Cf. the young Queen as painted by Beechey in 1821 (Millar 1969, i, no.671; ii, pl.170) or by William Fowler in 1825, holding a hat decorated with a large ostrich feather (Millar 1992, i, no.236; ii, pl.184) and seated holding a rose (Millar 1992, p.67, fig.11), with her daughter as painted by Lucas in 1844 (Millar 1992, i, no.472; ii, pl.398).
15 Oil on panel, the same size as DPG304, sold Christie's, South Kensington, 27 September 1990, lot 20.
16 Canvas 32.9 x 25.5 (*Concise Illustrated Catalogue of British Paintings at the Walker Art Gallery and at Sudley*, 1995, p.189).

Stephen Poyntz Denning (1795–1864)

DPG655 *A Woodman*

Canvas 76.5 x 64 lined; discoloured retouchings top left corner; disfigured by craquelure and much discoloured varnish.

Brown hair, brown eyes, holding a curved knife in his right hand; wearing a red hat, white shirt and red waistcoat, a black scarf over left shoulder; very loosely painted.

PROV.: [Denning's sale, Christie's, 17 August 1864, lot 88, 'Head of a woodman']; transferred to the Gallery from the College 1988.

EXH.: [?BI 1844, no.170 *A Woodman* 3.1 x 2.7 (i.e. 94 x 79, framed)].

after Sir Anthony Van Dyck (1599–1641)

DPG405 *Portrait of a Man*

Canvas 68.6 x 57.1 lined; damage in the upper right corner; reinforced black background; much discoloured varnish.

Dark eyes, chestnut hair; wearing a dark coat.

PROV.: Dulwich College by 1890.

DPG405 appears to derive from Van Dyck's whole-length portrait of an unknown man c.1638 at Hagley.[1] Other versions include a half-length formerly at Littlecote (sold Sotheby's, 21 November 1985, lot 813) and a bust-length miniature sold Sotheby's, 13 July 1982, lot 100.

It is possible that this was a Cartwright picture; it appears to agree with his taste and was first catalogued as being in the College in Sparkes & Carver 1890, as were the other Cartwright pictures.

1 *Van Dyck* 2004, p.619(IV.245); formerly identified as James Hay, 2nd Earl of Carlisle.

Thomas Gainsborough (1727–88)

DPG316 *Mrs Elizabeth Moody with her sons Samuel and Thomas*

Canvas 234 x 154.2 lined; cleaned and varnished 1914; the composition was altered by Gainsborough some six years after completion with the addition of the two children (see below); Mrs Moody's right hand was originally raised, fingering a string of pearls at her breast, her blue cape swirled round her (beneath the standing child), and her feet were placed to the left of the foot now seen;[1] Hell c.1951–1953; cleaned 1993 when minor losses behind and above the left-hand child, behind and above Mrs Moody's head and a pronounced craquelure in the children, were retouched.

Mrs Moody has brown eyes and brown hair dressed with pearls; she wears a white gown with a pale green sash beneath a light-blue overdress and a pale lavender gauze scarf; both children wear white tunics and red shoes; Thomas, the left-hand child, has red hair, Samuel, is fair;[2] there are foxgloves bottom left.

PROV.: Bequeathed by the sitter's widower 1808 to their younger son, Thomas,[3] and presented by him, Captain Thomas Moody, September 1831.

EXH.: Aberystwyth 1946(18); National Gallery 1947(22); Leeds 1947–53(22); *European Masters of the 18th century*, RA, 1954–55(63); *Conserving Old Masters* 1995(12); *Obras Maestras*, Madrid, Bilbao, 1999(44).

REF.: Waterhouse 1953, p.77 as mid-1770s; Waterhouse 1958, no.498 as later 1770s; A. Sumner in *Conserving Old Masters* 1995, pp.58–60.

Elizabeth Johnson (1756–82) of St. Ives, Hunts., married in 1779 Samuel Moody (1733–1808; see DPG601, p.219); her two sons, Samuel and Thomas, were born respectively on 24 April 1781 and 10 May 1782; she died, while taking a cure for tuberculosis, at Bristol Hot Wells, on 26 December 1782, aged 26 (as stated on her tablet in Bristol Cathedral). Both sons followed military careers: Samuel served as Captain in Bengal and died unmarried in 1826; Thomas, a Captain in the 41st Foot in India, married in 1826 Lucy Wood of Reigate, and was still living in 1841. On 23 February 1786 their father remarried Mary Paterson (c.1767–1820).[4] Thomas's diary is said to reveal an aversion to his step-mother[5] and by giving this Gainsborough to a public gallery he would have prevented it from passing to her four children (see note 3).

The portrait was probably originally painted on the occasion of Moody's first marriage in 1779.[6] Ann Sumner indicated that the 'quasi-Turkish' ensemble of hairstyle and costume was of the late 1770s and the original elegant pose compares closely with Gainsborough's *Mrs Henry Beaufoy* shown at the RA 1780(84). Later the widower returned DPG316 to Gainsborough to have their two sons added. When their mother died the sons were 20 and 7 months old; when their father remarried they were nearly 5 and 4 years old. To judge by their apparent ages in DPG316 the portrait was modified sometime before Moody's second marriage, implying a date of 1784/5. While Gainsborough painted each child with evident affection (Samuel recurs in an anonymous and undated lithograph after Gainsborough, *Boy with a Birdcage*)[7] the changes did not enhance the picture. The original graceful figure became a somewhat dysfunctional mother, without her pearls, inconvenienced by her two sons, and looking askance.

A so-called oil sketch from the H.J. Pfungst sale, Christie's, 15 June 1917, lot 80, is a crude copy, and a miniature copy of 1831 by James Warren Childe (1788–1862) is noted on file.

1 A composite X-radiograph demonstrating these changes illus. *Conserving Old Masters* 1995, p.60.
2 The identities of the children confirmed in a note from the diary of Miss Sylvester, great grand-daughter of the second Mrs Moody, which was with Knoedler sometime before 1921 (letter from Knoedler, 31 March 1921, on file): '[Samuel Moody's] first wife was painted by T. Gainsborough and is now in the Dulwich Gallery, having been presented to the Gallery by her son, Captain Murray (the child seated on her arm in the picture)'. See also note 3.
3 Samuel Moody's Will dated 19 April 1808, proved 20 October 1808 (xerox on file), named his son Thomas as the recipient of his mother's picture – and named Thomas and Samuel as his sons by his first wife.
4 *GM*, lvi, 1786, i, p.180. His second wife bore four children: James Andrew (*d.s.p.* 1814), John Baker, Mary (Mrs Mackintosh) and Elizabeth (Mrs Sylvester) – as named in Samuel Moody's Will. She sat to Romney between April and December 1786 for a three-quarter length (Ward & Roberts 1904, ii, p.108; last sold Christie's 22 November 1985, lot 130), and to John Russell for a pastel (with Leggatt 1915 and Knoedler before 1921) cf. DPG601, p.219.
5 'An extant diary of Thomas Moody is full of complaints about her, and it is possible that a desire that his mother's portrait should not fall into the hands of the second family may have led to his presenting the fine Gainsborough to the Gallery' (Cook 1914, 1926).
6 As Moody's second wife was to be painted by Romney the year of their marriage, see note 4.
7 Illus. A. Asfour & P. Williamson, *Gainsborough's Vision*, 1999, p.249.

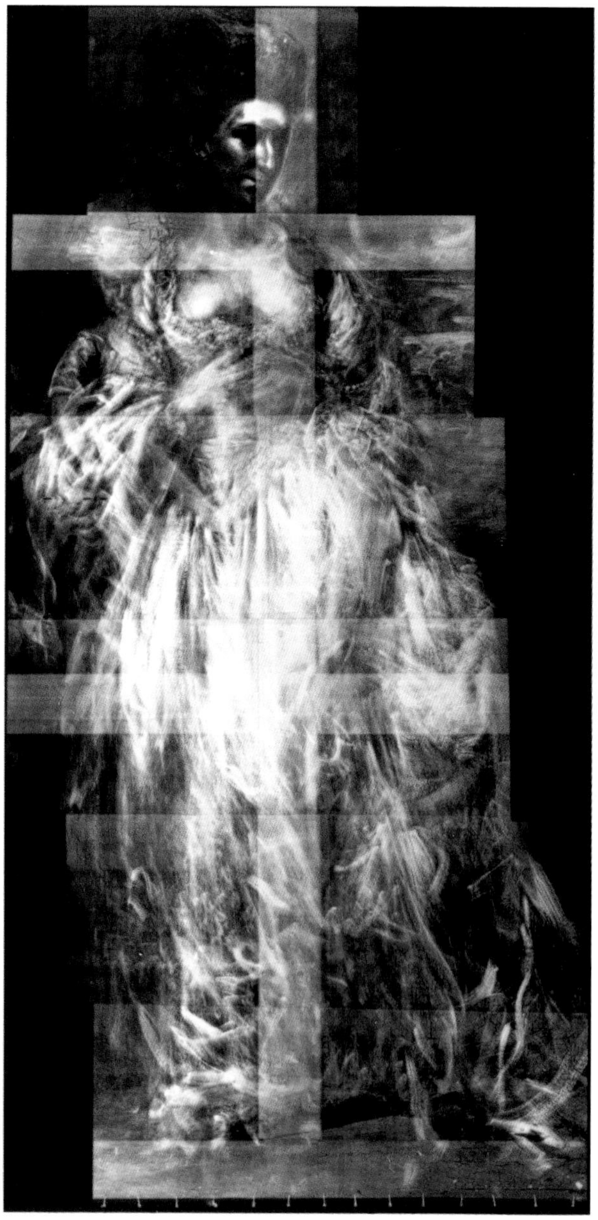

X-radiograph DPG 316

Thomas Francis Hodgkins (fl.1835–d.1903)
DPG446 The Tribute Money

Canvas 64.5 x 86.7 lined; in poor condition with prominent craquelure and discoloured varnish.

Prov.: Presented by the artist 1894.[1]

The subject is taken from Mark, 12, 14–17 and Luke, 20, 22–26.

A crude copy of the Rembrandt in the collection of Lord Allendale.[2]

1 A canvas strip is nailed to the stretcher with the printed inscription: *Miss Woodburn March 13* [1886?], signed [T F H?].

2 Bredius Gerson, *Rembrandt*, 4th ed., 1971, no.586.

Thomas Francis Hodgkins (fl.1835–d.1903)
DPG492 Samson and the Lion

Poplar panel 31.7 x 101 of two horizontal members (12 and 19.7 wide), supported by three vertical battens; the join opening and there are two additional splits on the right hand side; slight warping; some gouged damages; the surface scratched and spotted all over; much discoloured varnish.

Prov.: Presented by the artist 1892.

The subject is taken from Judges, 14, 5–6.

Both DPG 492 and DPG493 are poor copies from pictures originally from the Palazzo Grimani, near Genoa, purchased by George Lucy in 1839 as by Titian; they remain at Charlecote Park (National Trust) as Venetian early 16th century.[1]

1 *Charlecote Park*, Warwickshire, NT guide, 1996, pp.24–25.

Madeline Green (1884–1947)
DPG618 Self Portrait (The Chenille Net)

Linen 39.5 x 25 unevenly stretched over a coarser linen.[1]

Signed centre right, in red: *M.G.*; brown eyes, dark hair; wearing a grey dress.

Prov.: Bequeathed by the artist's sister 1951.

Exh.: RA 1938(625); Glasgow Institute 1938(116); Paris Salon 1947(2149).

The acquisition of this picture was minuted (20 July 1948) as 'a Self-portrait from Miss Green painted by her deceased sister which she wished to bequeath'.

1 The stretcher inscribed *verso*: *"The Chenille Net" By Madeline Green who died Feb 17th 1947/ awarded Médaille D'Or/ Société des Artistes Français No2149 Salon 1947…*

Thomas Francis Hodgkins (fl.1835–d.1903)
DPG493 Samson and the Philistines

Poplar panel 31.7 x 101 of two horizontal members 15.8 and 15.9 wide, supported by three vertical battens; splits right and left and warping on the right; the surface scratched all over; much discoloured varnish.

Prov.: Presented by the artist 1892.

The subject is taken from Judges, 15, 14–16.

See DPG492.

WALTER CHARLES HORSLEY (1855–1934)

DPG607 *Old-time Tuition at Dulwich College*

Canvas 84.1 x 107.3; a small loss on the lower right-hand edge.

Signed bottom left: *Walter. C. Horsley*;[1] the boys in black gowns, the central figure with red hair; the master wears a green dressing gown with an elaborate pattern; red curtains above; on the wall to the right a framed engraving of Dulwich College (by J. Rogers 1829 after N. Whittock).[2]

PROV.: Presented in 1920 by Sir James Leigh Wood on behalf of the relatives of the late Mr Alexander Horsburgh Turnbull, a scholar of Dulwich College from 1881 to 1884; Headmaster's study, Dulwich College.

EXH.; RA 1906(578); Aberystwyth 1947(5); *350th Anniversary*, Dulwich, 1969 (664); *Nest of Nightingales* 1988(8.3 as by J.C. Horsley).

Towards the end of his life the painter's father, the artist John Callcott Horsley (1817–1903), recalled how the Rev. John Lindsay (d.1875), usher of Dulwich College 1814–34, invited him to stay at Dulwich 'when he was about 11 years old' (i.e. c.1828). Lindsay he described as the tutor of the twelve boys but

> not being an early riser arranged that his class should come up to his bedroom for their lessons at eight o'clock every morning. I remember well seeing him sitting up in his old four-poster, propped up by pillows and swathed in a flannel dressing-gown of a quaint design, a tasselled nightcap of the period on his head, and a long clay pipe in his mouth, while grouped round the bed were the twelve scholars repeating their lessons. It made a never-to-be forgotten picture.[3]

It is not clear how seriously DPG607 should be taken as portraiture, if at all; perhaps Horsley enjoyed the parallel with *Isaac blessing Jacob*.

1 Inscribed *verso*: *W C Horsley II/ 1 High Rw. Kensington, W.*

2 From T. Allen, *History of the Counties of Surrey & Sussex*, 1829, i, f.p.433 (I am grateful to Dr Jan Piggott for this identification).

3 J.C. Horsley, *Recollections of a Royal Academician*, 1903, pp.294–95; the editor, Mrs Edmund Helps, believed DPG607 was painted by J.C. Horsley. While Lindsay was the College usher, John Vane (1792–1870) was the master (a post he held 1818–34); S. Hodges, *God's Gift*, 1981, p.23, wrote that 'the gentleman in the bed must be the formidable John Vane' – but, right or wrong, the painting illustrated J.C. Horsley's text. W.S. Spanton, *An Art Student and his Teachers*, 1927, p.114, wrily commented that it was 'a pretty example to set the boys!' (in contrast to the Lely *Nymphs by a Fountain*, see DPG555, pp.172-73, which was then not displayed for fear of corrupting the pupils' morality).

SAMUEL LANE (1780–1859)

DPG449 *George Bartley*

Canvas 76.2 x 63.5 unlined; extensive craquelure and discoloured varnish.

Dark brown hair, blue-grey eyes; wearing a dark coat with a red drape, seated in a red chair.

PROV.: Presented by the sitter 1854.

EXH.: possibly RA 1822(391, *Mr Bartley*).

George Bartley (c.1782–1858), comic actor, made his debut at Drury Lane in 1802; he played in the provinces 1809–14 before returning to Drury Lane and becoming stage manager at Covent Garden in 1829; he retired in 1852; he was twice married, secondly in 1814 to Sarah Smith whose reputation rather overshadowed his own (see DPG500 below). Samuel Lane also exhibited a portrait of the *Infant Son of Mr & Mrs Bartley of the Theatre Royal, Drury Lane*, RA 1826(49).[1]

A number of engraved portraits show Bartley in character.[2]

1 Thomas Williams Bartley matriculated at Exeter College, Oxford, in 1841 aged 18, and d. 1843.

2 See *Catalogue of Engraved Dramatic Portraits in the Theatre Collection of the Harvard College Library*, i, 1930, p.74. A portrait of Bartley as Hamlet by Isaac Pocock is in the Garrick Club (Ashton 1997, no.51, p.32). Macready's *Diaries*, 15 November 1836, recorded 'Lane called with drawings of Miss E. Tree and myself, C. Kemble, Mr and Mrs Bartley and Mr Farren' – but this was probably R.J. Lane.

Samuel Lane (1780–1859)

DPG500 *Mrs Sarah Bartley*

Canvas 136.5 x 102.2 unlined;[1] discoloured varnish and bad flaking; edges reinforced with cotton tape and staples; faced with tissue and a wax-resin adhesive 1994–.

Black hair, brown eyes; wearing a deep red dress, seated in a red chair.

Prov.: Presented by the sitter's husband 1854.[2]

Mrs Sarah Bartley, formerly Smith (1783–1850),[3] tragédienne, played in Edinburgh, York, Birmingham and Bath (where she was hailed as the 'Siddons of Bath') before making her London debut at Covent Garden 1805; after Mrs Siddons's retirement in 1812 her fortunes rose and in 1818 an American tour with her husband (see DPG449 above), proved very successful.

The pose in DPG500 may subtly refer to *Mrs Siddons as the Tragic Muse* (see DPG318, p.120). A number of engraved portraits show Mrs Bartley in character.[4]

1 Stamped twice *verso*: *0 45 55 12*.
2 On 2 May 1853 the National Gallery had rejected the offer by George Bartley of 'a portrait of the late Mrs Bartley, painted by Mr Samuel Lane, and, as an inducement to them to accept it, stating the fact, that he has some four other pictures which he would very gladly present to the Trustees, namely, a head of Molière, a portrait of Charles Kemble by Briggs, and a very fine picture by Mr Unwins'. The Molière is now DPG188 (attributed to Claude Lefèbvre) and for the Kemble, see DPG291, p.196; the Unwins remains unidentified.
3 Her parentage is not established; her original maiden name is variously said to have been Williamson or O'Shaughnessy, but she adopted the name of Smith in 1793 (J. Knight & J. Gilliland in *ODNB*).
4 See *Catalogue of Engraved Dramatic Portraits in the Theatre Collection of the Harvard College Library*, iv, 1934, pp.80–82. A water-colour showing her reciting, by Samuel De Wilde, is in the Garrick Club (Ashton 1997, no.767, p.403).

Samuel Lane (1780–1859)

DPG648 Frederick Lane

Canvas 76.2 x 63.5 lined by C. Robinson;[1] a strip 0.3 wide made up on stretcher on the left-hand side; scattered losses; there is a series of old fold marks: horizontal lines above the head at 6.5 and 10 from the top edge, and 10 above the bottom edge; a vertical mark runs 24 from the left-hand edge; scuffs and losses round the edges; heavy craquelure in hair and face with prominent retouchings; discoloured varnish.

Dark brown hair, brown eyes; wearing a dark coat with brass buttons; a red curtain to left.

Prov.: Presented by Mrs E.U. Hutton, date unknown.[2]

The identity of the sitter is given in a recent chalk inscription *verso*. Frederick Lane (1788–1846), the artist's brother, was Town Clerk of King's Lynn from 1832; he married Miss Everard of King's Lynn in 1815.[3]

Another portrait of Frederick Lane by Samuel Lane (panel 30.5 x 25.4), was exhibited *Samuel Lane*, King's Lynn, 1959. Samuel Lane exhibited a portrait of *Mr F Lane*, RA 1806(141), when his brother was sixteen, but he appears older in DPG648.

1 Label *verso* of *C. Robinson & Co, 51 Long Acre, London, backliners.*
2 A handwritten and largely illegible label, *verso*, reads *Mrs Hutton* [Hulton], *of 33 Malam* [Malvern] *Court, London, S W 7*; London Directories take us no further (there was a Miss Hutton at 40/1 Elvaston Pl. SW7 in 1953).
3 Farington, xiii, p.4687 (8 August 1815). I am grateful to Clare Agate for her help with Frederick Lane.

Charles Fairfax Murray (1849–1919)

DPG612 *The King's Daughters*

Mahogany panel 25.8 x 36.5; a fine craquelure in the dresses of the central and right-hand figures; conserved 1980.

Signed lower left *C.F.M.*; the three princesses, from the left, wear gold, red and blue.

PROV.: Given by the artist to W. S. Spanton 1882;[1] bequeathed by his daughter, H. Margaret Spanton, 1934.

EXH.: *The Last Romantics, Burne Jones to Stanley Spencer,* Barbican AG, 1989(42); *Nel segno di Ingres*, Palazzo Squarcialupi, Siena, 2007-08(99).

REF.: J. Christian in *The Last Romantics, Burne Jones to Stanley Spencer*, 1989, p.91.

Fairfax Murray was working in the Rosetti workshop in 1869–70. The subject of DPG612 was taken from Rossetti's 'My Father's Close' (*Poems* 1870, from the Old French), where 'three King's daughters fair' sat below apple blossoms. Spanton remembered it was painted in Murray's studio in Holland Park Road, and that Murray later gave him many books of which 'the most precious to me is the 1870 volume of Rossetti's 1870 Poems'.[2] A 'preparatory' *Study for the King's Daughters* is in the Philadelphia Museum of Art (1994-165-001).[3] Burne-Jones had made two pen and ink drawings entitled *The King's Daughters* in 1858[4] (twelve years before Rossetti's poem was published).

The date c.1875 proposed by John Christian implies DPG612 stayed seven years in Murray's studio before he gave it to Spanton.

1 Inscribed *verso* in yellow paint: *"King's Daughters"/ painted by Charles Fairfax Murray,/ and given by him to W S S// May 1882.*

2 W. S. Spanton, *An Art Student and his Teachers in the Sixties*, 1927, pp.84, 101.

3 It does nor relate closely to DPG612, showing only two figures with distant Italianate thatched houses instead of the enclosed garden and fountain.

4 Exh. *Burne-Jones*, AC, 1975–76, no.14, and see *The Little Holland House Album*, Dalrymple Press, 1981, pp.19, 36.

attributed to ABRAHAM PETHER (1756–1812)

DPG624 *Coast Scene by Moonlight*

Canvas 69.2 x 92.3; in very poor condition, a tear in sky, a hole upper right centre; brittle canvas and very discoloured varnish.

Figures unloading a boat to the left; a castle on a distant hill.

PROV.: Given by Miss Gibbs 1951.

Condition prevents a close evaluation, but DPG624 appears close to Pether.

SIR JOSHUA REYNOLDS (1723–92)

DPG17A *Girl with a Baby*

Mahogany[?] panel 74.9 x 62.2; in very poor condition, the paint surface over-worked, abraded and with prominent bituminous craquelure; Hell 1953.

PROV.: Probably Reynolds sale, Greenwood's, 2nd day, 15 April 1796, lot 49, bt. Cooper;[1] gift of William Beechey 1836.

REF.: Mannings (Postle) 2000, no.2079.

The composition is barely legible. Denning 1858 (f.356) included a pencil sketch of the picture, the tree on the left quite clear and on the right a 'very young lady & an infant child', with a note below reading 'It was a Lady … from Scotland – Much more like a girl with her little sister'.

Reynolds perhaps used the same model, with her distinctive pointed chin, for the *Lesbia* he sold in 1786 and the *Girl warming her hands*.[2]

See Beechey DPG17, p.194.

1 Beechey bought two of Reynolds' own pictures on the second day, 'dear' commented Farington (ii, p.524, 15 April 1796), but his purchases are not recorded, cf. GC 1901, iv, p.1637. On the second day, within lot 49, there was an unfinished *Mother and Child*, bt. Cooper, 2½ gn.

2 Respectively Mannings (Postle) 2000, nos.2101 and 2078.

Pencil sketch of *Girl with a Baby* by S.P. Denning, 1858

Sir Joshua Reynolds (1723–92)

DPG598 Robert Dodsley

Canvas 75.8 x 63.5 lined; bituminous craquelure to right of the face and in the coat; pentimenti in stock, hands, cuffs and table; the flesh tones faded; discoloured varnish; Hell 1953; surface cleaned 1979.

Inscribed on envelope: *To Mr Dodsley in Bruton* [St] *London*; brown eyes, white powdered wig; wearing a dark coat and grey waistcoat.

PROV.: Given by the sitter to William Shenstone, on whose death in 1763 it returned to the Dodsley family; by descent to James Dodsley Tawney; Miss Ann Cuff; Miss Charles, Bristol; bequeathed to Miss Margaret Wigmore; Christie's, 2 April 1887, lot 112; George Ware sale, Christie's, 10 December 1898, lot 62, bt. Adrian Lesser Lesser; by 1901 with Henry Yates Thompson who had given it to Dulwich by 1915[1] in memory of his father-in-law, George Murray Smith (founder of the *DNB*).

EXH.: *Obras Maestras*, Madrid, Bilbao, 1999(40).

REF.: GC 1901, i, pp.255–56, and iv, p.1299 as with Thompson; Waterhouse 1941, p.48; Mannings 2000, no.512.

Robert Dodsley (1703–64), bookseller, poet and playwright; he suggested the compilation of a Dictionary to Samuel Johnson and published works by Johnson, Pope, Akenside and Goldsmith, a *Select Collection of Old Plays* in 1744, and founded *The Annual Register* in 1758; a close friend of the poet William Shenstone (whose executor he became).

The evolution of this portrait is described in the Dodsley–Shenstone correspondence. On 1[–4] December 1759 Dodsley wrote 'as to my Face, it is a Subject not worth considering; however I will make you an imprudent Proposal: if you will exchange Faces with me when you come up to Town, we will both sit to the same Painter'.[2] But Shenstone was already sitting to Edward Alcock.[3] Sometime between 18 February and 21 April 1760 Dodsley asked him 'And will you really consent to an Exchange of Pictures? Upon my Word, you make but a sorry Bargain for yourself: however, to give you as little Reason as may be to regret your Compliance, I will sit to one of our best Artists; and to supply the Want of Merit in the Original, will endeavour to give as much as I can to the Copy. If you have any Thing to suggest on this Subject, (as you seem to hint) you will be so good as to let me have a Line, because, as soon as I am able to get abroad, which I hope I will be in a few Days [he was suffering from gout], I intend to consult with Reynolds about it'.[4] Dodsley had appointments with Reynolds in 1760 on 21 April; 23, 28 May; 3, 9, 11, 16, 20, 26 June, and 3 July. On 17 June Dodsley conceded that 'Shenstone by Alcock, will certainly be more valuable than a Dodsley even by Reynolds ... [who] desires his Compliments, and would be glad, if you came to Town, that you sate to him'.[5] On 24 June Dodsley wrote 'My Face is quite finished, and I believe very like.... If the picture should be turned yellowish, by being packed up, Mr. Reynolds advises, that it be set in the Sun for two Hours, which will quite recover it'.[6] On 7 July 1760 Shenstone told the Rev. Richard Graves that Dodsley was 'to *give* me his picture done by Reynolds'[7] and on 11 August he told Thomas Percy that Dodsley 'has given me a Portrait of his head by Reynolds, ye Price of which I am asham'd to mention';[8] on 20 July he had told James Prattinton, a Merchant of Bewdley, that he had received Dodsley's portrait 'yesterday' and that it 'cost him at least 10 Guineas'.[9] Dodsley paid Reynolds 20 guineas sometime in 1760.

A later copy was in a British private collection in 1994.

Shenstone's portrait by the provincial painter Edward Alcock is now in the National Portrait Gallery (1436)[10] together with a small oval he painted of Dodsley (1436), the composition of which somewhat resembles DPG598.[11]

1 The Committee Minutes of 10 May 1915 record the gift of this picture 'in the course of the last few years'.
2 *The Correspondence of Robert Dodsley 1733–64* ed. James E. Tierney, 1988, p.432.
3 *Ibid.*, p.530; letter of 13 November 1759.
4 *Ibid.*, pp.437–38.
5 *Ibid.*, p.439.
6 *Ibid.*, p.441.
7 M. Williams, *The Letters of William Shenstone*, 1939, p.556.
8 *Ibid.*, p.559.
9 *Ibid.*, p.655.
10 Kerslake 1977, i, p.247, ii, pl.727.
11 *Ibid.*, i, p.72, ii, pl.191.

after SIR JOSHUA REYNOLDS (1723–92)

DPG627 *Mrs Margaret Desenfans*

Canvas 75.9 x 63.5; fine overall crazing; discoloured varnish.

Inscribed *verso*: *Copy by Ayoub*; brown eyes, dark brown hair with blue ribbon; wearing a grey cap, a golden brown drape round her blue dress, and holding a bunch of narcissi with a pink rose.

PROV.: Commissioned by Sir Evan Spicer (Chairman of the Dulwich Gallery) 1930, when the original was with Agnew (see below).

REF.: Mannings 2000, no.1300a.

Margaret Morris (1731–1813), second daughter of Robert Morris, the Swansea industrialist, married Noel Desenfans (see p.87) in 1776, bringing him a considerable fortune; following her husband's death in 1807 she assumed a life interest in his collection, giving additional sums and furnishings for the completion of Soane's Gallery; she is buried in the Gallery Mausoleum, alongside her husband and Bourgeois.

Reynolds's original portrait, which has been on loan to the Gallery since 2002, was painted in 1757,[1] twenty years before the sitter's marriage to Desenfans. It was listed in the Desenfans collection in 1790,[2] but after the sitter's death reverted to the Morris family, descending to Sir Robert Armine Morris, 4th Bt., of Sketty Park, Swansea.[3] Following his death in 1927 the portrait was sold at Sketty Park on 1 May 1930, lot 168, and bought by Agnew.[4] The College Governors commissioned DPG627 from Moussa Ayoub in 1930, while the original remained with Agnew, and her copy was received in September that year.

Margaret Morris's sisters Bridget (b. 1729, Mrs Lockwood) and Mary (b.1736) were also painted by Reynolds c.1757,[5] and her sister-in-law Henrietta Musgrave, Lady John Morris, by Reynolds c.1775–76[6] and by Romney 1777[7] (sold Sotheby's, New York, 11 April 2005, lot 119).

1 Mannings 2000, no.1300; Waterhouse 1941, p.42; at one stage framed as an oval; engraved in 1757 as Margaret Morris.
2 Desenfans 1790–91.
3 The route was somewhat tortuous; as it had also appeared in a Morris sale, Christie's, 1 March 1873, lot 39, bt. Agnew, and in the Gaunt House sale, Christie's, 17 March 1877, lot 59, bt. Colnaghi.
4 I am grateful to Dr Paul Matthews for the date of the Swansea sale. Agnew subsequently sold it to J. Connell & Sons and it was later sold at Christie's, 29 April 1938, lot 45.
5 Mannings 2000, nos.1298, 1301. Both were listed in Desenfans 1790–91 ('Portrait of Mrs Lockwood her [Mrs Desenfans's] sister – Reynolds' and 'Portrait of Miss Morris – Reynolds'). There was a third sister Jane.
6 Mannings 2000, no.1296.
7 Ward & Roberts 1904, ii, p.109.

JOHN RUSSELL (1745–1806)

DPG601 Samuel Moody the elder

Pastel on paper 60.3 x 44.8 oval; the edges torn and the surface much rubbed, particularly in the face.

Blue eyes, powdered hair with a black hair ribbon; wearing a russet coat turning to maroon below with gold buttons and a blue waistcoat.

PROV.: By descent to Miss Sylvester, one of the sitter's great grand-daughters, on whose death in 1915 acquired by Leggatt; bt. Henry Yates Thompson and presented by him 1917.

REF.: A. Sumner in *Conserving Old Masters* 1995, pp.58–59.

For Samuel Moody (1733–1808), see Gainsborough DPG316, p.206. The companion pastel of Moody's second wife, Mary Paterson (1767–1820) whom he married in 1786, was with Leggatt in 1915, when offered to Dulwich, and later with Knoedler.[1] DPG601 appears to date from c.1790, or perhaps on the occasion of his second marriage.

1 A letter from whom, dated 31 March 1921 (on file), states that the firm owned it 'a few years ago' (see DPG316 n2, p.206).

John Smart I of Ipswich (1755–after 1830)

DPG635 *Self Portrait*

Canvas 76.5 x 62.6 cut from stretcher; discoloured varnish and scattered losses.

Brown eyes, powdered wig; wearing a green coat, his right arm stretched across the front of the picture; in a painted oval.

PROV.: Given by Douglas Ion Smart[1] 1956.

Probably painted c.1785–90. Evidently the same sitter as in DPG639 below. A twentieth-century label *verso* reads: *Portrait of John Smart of Ipswich by himself for Douglas J M Smart great grandson of the above.*

A closely-related miniature self portrait was with H.L. Smart, another direct descendant, in 1963.

1 Douglas Ion Smart (1879–1970) watercolourist and engraver, exh. RA 1906–61, claimed direct descent from John Smart of Ipswich (letters in NPG archive) and lived several years in East Dulwich. Presumably the Douglas J.M. Smart mentioned in the label.

John Smart I of Ipswich (1755–after 1830)

DPG636 *Mrs John Smart I*

Canvas 76.2 x 62.8 cut from stretcher; a long diagonal damage runs from centre left to lower centre, the losses filled with white paint with white tape applied *verso*; marked craquelure within the figure; discoloured varnish.

Brown eyes, powdered hair; wearing a grey hat with pale blue ribbon, a white dress with pale blue sash; she holds an open book in her lap inscribed *sentimen.. journal* [intended for Sterne's *Sentimental Journey*?].

PROV.: Given by Douglas Ion Smart 1956 (see DPG635 note 1).

Probably painted c.1785–90. A twentieth-century label *verso* reads: *For Ouida V Smart/ Portrait of Mrs John Smart/ Wife of the Artist/ John Smart sen.*; presumably the wife of John Smart I.

JOHN SMART I of Ipswich (1755–after 1830)

DPG637 *Miss Planner*

Canvas 76.2 x 61.6 cut from stretcher; losses round edges; discoloured varnish; marked craquelure in arm, neck and sky; damaged along bottom edge.

White head dress, brownish hair and eyes; wearing a dark grey dress with white collar, holding an opened (illegible) letter; a red curtain behind.

PROV.: Given by Douglas Ion Smart 1956 (see DPG635 note 1).

Painted probably c.1820. A twentieth-century label *verso* reads: *Portrait of Miss Planner By John Smart Senr. for Douglas Smart.* A portrait of a Miss Planner was in the collection of Horace Barker (d. 1869), Bury St Edmunds.[1]

1 E. Farrer, *Portraits in Suffolk Houses (West)*, 1908, p.69, with the note 'This is not supposed to be anyone connected with Suffolk'.

JOHN SMART I of Ipswich (1755–after 1830)

DPG639 *Self Portrait*

Canvas[1] 60.3 x 50.5 cut from stretcher; damage below right ear; marked craquelure in face; general flaking with discoloured retouchings; discoloured varnish.

Brown eyes, powdered hair; wearing a green jacket, yellow waistcoat and white stock.

PROV.: Given by Douglas Ion Smart 1956 (see DPG635 note 1).

Painted c.1810. A twentieth-century label *verso* reads: *Portrait of John Smart senr. by Himself.*

1 Stamped *verso*: *106 JT 17 … 31 St Martins Lane* and *British Linen.*

JOHN SMART II of Ipswich (fl.1822–50)

DPG634 called George and Charles Smart, sons of John Smart II

Canvas 91 x 71 cut from stretcher; losses in skirt of seated boy, in sky upper left and in the bottom right-hand corner; discoloured varnish.

Both fair haired and brown eyed, holding bows; the standing figure wears a black hat with a gold tassel, a red plaid shawl, a black dress and black shoes; the seated child wears a tartan blouse with a light brown skirt and black shoes; in the foreground a large straw hat and a green quiver with red ribbon; a brown and white dog on the right.

PROV.: Given by Douglas I. Smart 1956 (see DPG635 note 1).

Probably painted c.1840. A twentieth-century label *verso* reads: *Portraits of George and Charles Smart sons of John Smart.* Formerly (and optimistically) called Pickersgill, according to a contemporary and separate label.

JOHN SMART II of Ipswich (fl.1822–50)

DPG638 Mrs John Smart II

Canvas[1] 76.2 x 62.8 cut from stretcher; in very poor condition; extensive flaking, four slits; losses along left and right vertical edges and bottom edge; holes by the head upper left and right; pentimento by her right shoulder.

Brownish hair with an ornamental clasp, blue eyes; wearing an ornate white dress with gold-buckled belt and a pearl necklace.

PROV.: Given by Douglas I. Smart 1956 (see DPG635 note 1).

Probably painted c.1830–40. A twentieth-century label *verso* (now missing) identified the sitter as Mrs J Smart wife of the artist.[2]

1 Stamped *verso*: *9[85] J7 70.*
2 A more recent Dulwich label read: *Queen Charlotte by Haslone or oylas* [Hayter?].

John Smart II of Ipswich (fl.1822–50)

DPG640 *Portrait of a Lady*

Pine? panel 21.9 x 17.7; a vertical scratch in the hair, scratches and scuffs round edges of the hair; wide craquelure in shoulders and by her right arm; general retouchings and discoloured varnish.

Brown eyes, black hair; wearing a white dress with a blue fichu and brown shawl; a blue background; incised *verso*: *By Lawrence.*

PROV.: Given by Douglas I. Smart 1956 (see DPG635 note 1).

Probably painted c.1830. Possibly the same sitter as in DPG638, and presumably by Smart II.

H. Margaret Spanton (1874–1934)

DPG641 *Female Nude*

Canvas[1] 35.5 x 30.5; uneven streaked varnish.

Signed bottom left, in white: *H.M. Spanton*; the figure has red hair.

PROV.: Given by Miss Gliddon 1960.

1 Stamped *Winsor & Newton … Rathbone Place ….*

H. MARGARET SPANTON (1874–1934)

DPG642 *Portrait of a Lady*

Canvas[1] 117 x 66; there are small losses along a horizontal seam 16 above the bottom edge.

Grey eyes, brown hair; wearing a dark grey dress; a reflection of the artist appears in the mirror.

PROV.: Given by Miss Gliddon 1960.

A Whistlerian exercise, painted possibly c.1900–10. Identified by a 1960 ink label *verso*: *Miss Gliddon/ Gift (artist H.M. Spanton).*

1 Stamped *verso*: *Percy Young/ Gower Street London/ WC.*

JOHN WOOD (1801–70)

DPG346 *Thomas Stothard*

Canvas 127.2 x 101.9 lined; cleaned, repaired and varnished by Reeve 1923; pentimenti show the curtain was laid over the end of the bookshelves and the scroll on the table added over the cloth; lined and cleaned 2000.

Signed lower right: *John WOOD / 1833*; white hair, brown eyes; wearing a black coat, sitting in a red chair; the books and the print on the table (which can just be identified as James Heath's 1817 plate from Stothard's *Canterbury Pilgrims*)[1] are not inscribed; a red curtain behind.

PROV.: Given by Miss Elizabeth Wood, the artist's sister, 1883.

EXH.: RA 1833(246 *T. Stothard, Esq., R.A., Librarian*).

Thomas Stothard (1755–1834), painter and celebrated illustrator, studied at the RA schools 1778; ARA 1791 and RA 1794. 'As he grew old', Leslie remembered, 'his appearance became very venerable; his head, or rather the expression of his face, resembling the antique in the British Museum called Homer'[2] and another moving account of the aged Stothard was written by Redgrave:

> The venerable artist has left an additional picture in our minds, when in his last years, deaf and feeble, he was occupied in his evening duties as librarian of the Royal Academy. There bending over some books of prints, with many unconscious sighs and moans, his unsteady hand was unable to pour out the cup of tea in which he found solace, yet even then, retiring into the recess of the window, he would, from time to time, occupy his pencil for a few moments, in the realization of some thought, in a slight but still elegant and graceful sketch.[3]

For Stothard's iconography, see Walker 1985, i, pp.483–84.

1 This celebrated image also appears in the background of Stothard's portrait by G.H. Harlow of 1817–18 (Petworth; illus. Walker 1985, ii, pl.1185).
2 C.R. Leslie, *Recollections*, 1860, i, p.133.
3 R. Redgrave, *A Century of Painters of the English School*, 1866, i, p.453.

John Wood (1801–70)

DPG453 *Endymion*

Canvas 127 x 101.5 lined; gouging left and right of the horn in the centre foreground; tenting and marked craquelure in the figure of Diana; surface damages and discoloured varnish.

Signed bottom right: JOHN WOOD. / *1832.*; Diana, the moon goddess, descends robed in white and with a blue drape; Endymion wears a pelt, with beside him two dogs (spotted brown and black), a horn and crook; a ram to the left.

PROV.: Given by Thomas Gray 1897; Dulwich College.

EXH.: BI 1833(483, 'Methought I lay watching the zenith,/ And lo! from opening clouds I saw emerge/ The lovely moon'); [Midland Counties Art Museum, Nottingham, 1885?].[1]

ENG.: see note 2.

The subject is taken from Keats' *Endymion*, 1818, the quotation supplied in the 1833 BI catalogue seems garbled from book one, lines 578–92;[3] the beautiful shepherd Endymion, beloved by the Moon (Diana/Selene) who visits him on Mount Latmos as he sleeps enchanted under her spell.

With DPG454, DPG453 was cited in Wood's obituary as a work which particularly contributed to his contemporary reputation.[4]

1 According to an incomplete label *verso* which seems to bear the pencilled date 1885 (see DPG454 note 1)
2 An incomplete label verso reads *The dream of Endymion engraved by …/Royal Academy*
3 Cf. 'Methought I lay watching the zenith, where the milky way/ Among the stars in virgin splendour pours;' (578–80) … 'And lo! From opening clouds, I saw emerge/ The loveliest moon, that ever silver'd o'er / A shell for Neptune's goblet:' (591–93).
4 *Art Journal*, ns ix, 1870, p.204.

John Wood (1801–70)

DPG454 The Orphans

Canvas 143.2 x 105.4 lined; scratches top right; a slash by the larger child's head and pentimento on her right arm and shoulder; abrasion across the smaller child's red dress at the hips; scattered retouchings and discoloured varnish.

Signed bottom left: *John Wood./ 1830.*; the taller girl has a very dark skirt and dark hair, a tear falls from her red eyes; the smaller girl wears a red skirt; both wear white shifts.

PROV.: Given by Miss S. Wyatt Gray 1897.[1]

EXH.: RA 1830 (197, 'Silently eloquent/ By the way-side those gentle orphans stood,/ Not asking aid, save by those looks and tears/ That tell their tale – poor desolate ones! –/ The blight of winter hath come o'er their spring./ Oh! For some blessed beam to cherish them' – S.C. Hall [1800–89]); BI 1831(112 without quotation); [Midland Counties Art Museum, Nottingham, 1885?].[2]

ENG.: C. Rolls 1831 (*The Amulet*).

See DPG 453 above. The left-hand figure recalls Lawrence's *Lady Georgiana Fane* of 1806 (Tate Gallery, N00922), engraved in 1826.[3]

1 A label *verso* reads: *Aighburton House, Heathfield Gardens, Turnham Green, London W.*
2 A faded label *verso* reads *Midland Counties Art Museum/Nottingham Castle* ... cf. DPG453 above.
3 Garlick 1989, no.290a, pl.42.

John Wood (1801–70)

DPG650 *Susan Jay and her Dog*

Canvas 68.5 x 56.5; in poor condition; blistering, a hole and tear lower left centre; marked shrinkage craquelure upper left; discoloured varnish.

Signed bottom right: *John Wood* ....; fair hair, blue eyes; wearing a white dress with blue sash; a black and white dog.

PROV.: Bequeathed by Mrs Harriette Estill Mason 1942.[1]

The identification is given by a label formerly *verso* (now on file): *John Wood/1821/ a portrait of/ Susan Jay/ and her dog.* The donor provided an undated note concerning Susan Jay, saying she became a Catholic convert and entered a convent at Croydon, upon which her father condemned her portrait to the attic; it descended through her younger brother, John Jay, at the death of whose widow the portrait was received by Mrs Mason who presented it to Dulwich.

1 The anticipated bequest approved in 1938 on the grounds that DPG650 was better than the pictures by Wood already in the Collection.

Unknown Artist

DPG445 *Francis Bacon, Viscount St Alban*

Canvas 61 x 47 lined; retouching under his right eye and along the lower edge; small losses to the right of his hat; discoloured varnish.

Brown hair, brown-grey eyes; wearing a black hat and the chancellor's gold-braided black robe.

PROV.: Given to the College by Miss Love 1873 in fulfilment of the wishes of her brother Admiral Henry Omanney Love.[1]

EXH: *Edward Alleyn* 1994(73).

REF.: Young 1889, i, p.490.

Francis Bacon (1561–1626), lawyer, politician, eminent essayist and philosopher, was lord chancellor in 1618 when he was made Baron Verulam; in 1621 he was created Viscount St Alban; he published *Essays* (1597 and 1625), the *Novum Organum* (1620) and the *Advancement of Learning* (1605). His seal was attached to the Charter of Foundation of Alleyn's College of God's Gift in 1619.

Despite the alleged provenance (see note 1) DPG445 is a pedestrian derivation from the whole-length portrait at Gorhambury of c.1618 – but the hat is now uncomfortably square and a knotted white cord hangs at his breast. An 18th-century copy of the Gorhambury portrait was acquired by the National Portrait Gallery in November 1900 (1288)[2] and this, in turn, appears to have been the portrait copied by W.B. Morris in 1901 for the picture now in Alleyn's School (DPG549, p.235).

A closely comparable three-quarter length portrait belonging to the Royal Society, which has been attributed to Abraham van Blyenberch,[3] shows a different ruff collar, the lord chancellor's sack more prominently displayed to the right and a paper hanging from his left hand inscribed *To the/Honrobll Francis/Lord verulam/ Lor Chanceller/ of England.*

1 As described in a discursive MS label *verso*: *Sir Francis Bacon ... after he had regained his full liberty* [following a brief confinement in the Tower in 1622], *presented them* [the Andrews family of Wandsworth] *with this Portrait of himself, as a compliment for their kindness. The last of the said Andrews was a female, who married Mr John Acworth, who were Grandfather & Grandmother to the late Mrs Sedgwick, who being the surviving eldest descendant, became poss-ess'd of both Pedigree ... By the title of Marian Sedgwick eldest daughter of the above Ann Blagrave Sedgwick This Portrait with the Pedigree came into the possession of her first cousin, Rear Admiral Love of Yarmouth Isle of Wight – Marian Sedgwick died on the 16th January 1860 aged 80 years.*

2 Illus. Strong 1969a, ii, fig.24.

3 Strong 1969a, i, pp.11–12, ii, fig.21. Bacon's iconography is discussed by Strong 1969a, pp.10–14.

Unknown Artist

DPG494 John Churchill, 1st Duke of Marlborough

Canvas 75.5 x 63.1 lined; discoloured retouchings; a tear top left was repaired and the edges strengthened 1991.

Wearing ermine, with the George collar over black armour; in a painted oval.

PROV.: Dulwich College by 1890.

John Churchill, 1st Duke of Marlborough (1650–1722), defeated the French at Blenheim 1704, Ramillies 1706, Oudenarde 1708 and Malplaquet 1709.

An exceedingly crude derivation from a portrait by Kneller, it was rightly described in Sparkes and Carver 1890 as a 'wretched painting, intended for a representation of the Duke of Marlborough, [it] deserves notice only from its association with a great name. It could otherwise have no title to a place in any collection of works of art'.

Unknown Artist

DPG613 Portrait of a Lady

Canvas 127 x 101.6 lined; very rubbed with an uneven surface; consolidated 1990.

Grey eyes, brown hair; wearing a brown dress over a white shift with a (very faded) blue wrap; behind her a deep blue gold-fringed curtain with a vase and foliage to the left.

PROV.: W.S. Spanton (see below); bequeathed by his daughter, H. Margaret Spanton, 1934 as by Highmore.

EXH.: Tredegar House 1991–.

REF.: Lewis 1979, ii, p.638, no.87 as probably not by Highmore.

In 1935 Spanton's niece, Miss Tarrant, said she believed that DPG613 had been purchased by her uncle, time and place unknown, and that the attributions may have been reversed between two of Spanton's pictures, the 'Kneller' (DPG611, p.192) and the 'Highmore' (DPG613).[1] But DPG613 has nothing to do with Highmore (or Kneller) and is the work of an anonymous late-17th/early-18th century hand.

1 29 November 1935; note on file.

Unknown Artist

DPG646 Landscape

Canvas[1] 43.5 x 33, painted area 41.5 x 31; in poor condition; a hole lower right, tape-repaired tear lower centre; flaking along top and bottom edges; much discoloured and uneven varnish.

Four figures, two men and two women, in a landscape.

PROV.: Given by Miss Davies of Herne Hill 1961.

A late 19th-century work. Listed as by 'Montanini' in Murray 1980.

1 Stamped *verso*: *Artists Canvas /prepared/ Hone La … / London.*

Unknown Artist

DPG647 The South Downs, with the Belle Tout Lighthouse

Canvas[1] 30.2 x 40.4; scattered losses and retouchings; discoloured vanish.

A standing lady and seated man looking at the Belle Tout lighthouse and the Seven Sisters cliffs in Sussex.

PROV.: Given by Miss Davies of Herne Hill 1961.

Probably painted c.1900. Listed as by 'Shayer' in Murray 1980.

1 Stamped *verso*: *Winsor & Newton*; and printed *276704*.

ACQUISITION 2006

Although acquired after the completion of this catalogue, a Constable oil sketch, a copy of the Dulwich Ruysdael DPG168, merits inclusion.

John Constable (1776–1837)

DPG657 *Landscape with Windmills, after Jacob van Ruisdael*

Bevelled oak panel 31.6 x 34 x 1(maximum); pentimenti on windmill sails, on the distant church and on the horizon; minor fillings in the foreground bottom left and centre right; cleaned 1967; faint traces, bottom right, suggest a copy of the Ruisdael's monogram (as seen on DPG168); inscription *verso*, not in Constable's hand (recorded in 1967, now illegible): 'copied by John Constable R.A. feb 1831 from the original picture by J. Ruysdael in the Dulwich Gallery'.

The distant church was once identified as the Groote Kerk, Haarlem.[1]

PROV.: Constable posthumous sale, Foster's, 15 May 1838, lot 47 ('The Windmill, from the original picture, by Jacob Ruysdael, in the Dulwich Gallery'), bt. White; R.K. Haselden, whose father had owned it for many years; Miss Forn by 1947/48; her sister Mrs Jack; Christie's, 5 May 1967, lot 173, bt. Barclay 1966-67;[2] T.A. Gore Browne before 1970; his son James Gore Browne,[3] from whom bt. through Johnny Van Haeften and anonymously given to the Gallery in memory of Bill and Anita Greenoff, 2006.

EXH.: *Shock of Recognition*, Tate Gallery, 1970-71, no.2, lent T.A. Gore Browne; *Constable, a Master Draughtsman*, Dulwich, 1994, n.n., lent T.A. Gore Browne.

REF.: G. Reynolds, *The Later Paintings and Drawings of John Constable 1817-1837*, 1984, i, p.242, no.32.44, ii, pl.855 with the assigned date of 1831, and *The Early Paintings and Drawings of John Constable,* 1996, p.252, no.32.44, confirming date of 1831; I. Dejardin, *In View*, Dulwich, Autumn, 2006, pp.8-9; S. Slive, *Jacob van Ruisdael, a complete catalogue*, 2001, app.2, p.698.

Constable had always greatly admired Ruisdael (whom he called Ruysdael in the manner of the time); together with Richard Wilson and Claude, he considered him one of the greatest of landscape painters. He made frequent copies ('memoranda') of his works throughout his life,[4] four appearing in his posthumous sale.[5]

DPG657 is a copy of the Dulwich Ruisdael, DPG168,[6] made after the latter, apparently on Constable's advice, had been lent to the RA schools for copying by the students in 1830.[7] It differs in showing a boy walking besides a man with a red coat on horseback in the right foreground. These figures were first recorded in the Ruisdael in 1835[8] and it is a reasonable assumption that they were there when Constable made his copy in 1831; but in 1997 boy, horse and rider were discovered to be additions and were removed. Bourgeois was not above 'improving' landscapes he had acquired.[9]

DPG657 is a vigorous 'memorandum', capturing all the drama of Ruisdael's windy sky and fitful light, but without close attention to his crisp detail; the distant church in particular is muddled, the fence by the cottage simplified, the foreground bridge perfunctory. The muddier tonality doubtless reflects embrowned varnish then on the Ruisdael.

1 Seymour Slive considered it bore 'some resemblance to St Bavo at Haarlem but the setting is unrelated to topographical views of the city' (Slive 2001, no.131).
2 Largely based on information kindly supplied by the former owner David Barclay.
3 The picture was stored at Christie's from October 1986 to February 1989 (the stencil FV787 refers).
4 The earliest being from 1799, before he entered the RA schools (Constable, *Corr.*, ii, 1964, pp.22, 24).
5 Apart from DPG657, these were *Winter*, lot 45 (Reynolds 1984, no.32.43, subsequently sold Christie's, 21 March 2001, lot 69); a *Small upright landscape, after Ruysdael*, lot 50, and *The Cornfield, after Jacob Ruysdael*, lot 52.
6 Bourgeois Bequest 1811; Beresford 1998, p.217; Slive 2001, no.131.
7 Constable visited the gallery on 30 July 1830 with five Academicians to choose six paintings for copying in the RA schools (*Bourgeois Book of Regulations*, Dulwich College; Constable, *Corr.*, iv, 1966, p.330). Dejardin 2006 believed that it was Constable who had particularly argued for the Ruisdael. Before it was properly examined DPG657 was thought to date from 1799 (see note 4 above).
8 J. Smith, *Catalogue raisonné of the Works of the Most Eminent Dutch Painters* ..., vi, 1835, p.99.
9 See ante, DPG135, p.93. Constable would sometimes make additions to his copies to avoid confusion with the originals (see Reynolds 1984, nos.23.7 and 32.43) but not, apparently, in this case.

DPG168, Jacob van Ruisdael, *Landscape with Windmills*, before cleaning

DPG168, Jacob van Ruisdael, *Landscape with Windmills*, after cleaning

DULWICH COLLEGE PORTRAITS

The portraits in this section are catalogued in alphabetical order by sitter with unidentified sitters at the end

Between 1619 and 1814 the Alleyn and Cartwright pictures, together with any other gifts or commissions from that period, were displayed in the College (see p.19). They remained there after the Dulwich Picture Gallery was opened in 1814 and in April 1883 there were 129 pictures in the Master's house alone. In 1890 Sparkes and Carver published the *Catalogue of the Cartwright Collection and other Pictures and Portraits at Dulwich College*, and these were incorporated into the picture gallery catalogues from 1892. Since then the Alleyn and Cartwright pictures have been displayed in the Picture Gallery and the College has acquired several more pictures in its own name, principally portraits, which have never been catalogued.

In 1994 the administration of the Gallery passed from the Governors of the College to an independent Board of Trustees.

The following seventeen portraits are described since they have appeared in previous Gallery catalogues.

JOHN ELLYS (c.1701–57)

DPG441 *James Allen*

Canvas 239.7 x 147.3 lined; the surface is generally rubbed revealing grey-green underpainting in the head; surface scrapes across the lower part of the figure, minor losses on the forehead and a damage in the back of his left hand; the bottom edge much worn; varnished 1939; relined 1988 when large tears across the centre of the figure were repaired.

Signed lower right edge: *J. Ellys p.* and dated lower centre right: *JALLEN* [monogram]/ *42/ 1724*, the scroll inscribed: *Sussex &/ Wigorn /*[1] *Rotulus Jacobi Allen*; blue eyes, powdered wig; wearing a black gown trimmed with black fur over a grey coat, black stockings and black shoes with silver buckles, white gloves.

PROV.: A payment to Ellys of £26.5.0 appears in the College accounts for the week ending 27 November 1724,[2] but an old label *verso*: '*This for the Right Honourable my Lady Pitsligo*',[3] confirms that Allen bequeathed it to his sister, Elizabeth, Lady Pitsligo (d. 1759), a benefactress of the College;[4] College Board Room 1892; James Allen's Girls School.

James Allen (1682/3–1746), Warden of Dulwich College 1712, Master 1721, founder of the Dulwich Reading School in 1741 (later known as the Free School, which became James Allen's Girls School in 1857), '*Was Six feet High, Skilful as a Skaiter, a Jumper, Athletic, and Humane*'.[5]

See also DPG 495 and DPG 496 below.

1 I.e. Cursitor for the counties of Sussex and Worcestershire, an administrative appointment within the High Court of Chancery. Allen had begun work at the Cursitors' Hall in 1701 as clerk to his half-brother Thomas Barnes (then Cursitor for Leicestershire and Cornwall) and was promoted Cursitor in 1727 as his second half-brother Stephen was appointed assistant to the Principal, see M.A. Wren & P. Hackett, *James Allen*, 1968, pp.34, 54, 68.
2 Dulwich College, 2nd series xxii, *Weekly Account Book 1722/3-1733*.
3 James Allen's Will directed that all his pictures 'except that drawn by Mr Ellis which I leave to my sister Pitsligo' were left to the College (Wren & Hackett, at note 1, p.76).
4 She m. 1731 the Jacobite philosopher Alexander Forbes, 4th Lord Forbes of Pitsligo (1678–1762). In January 1739 the College borrowed £200 from one Elizabeth Wakeham, spinster, from moneys held in trust for Lady Pitsligo (Young 1889, i, p.273).
5 Quoted from a tablet on the frame of DPG495.

attributed to JOHN ELLYS (c.1701–57)

DPG495 *James Allen*

Canvas 125.7 x 102.2 lined; varnished by C. New 1931; the surface is rubbed; restored old horizontal tears in the necktie and a small loss across the mouth; discoloured varnish.

Blue eyes, white powdered wig; wearing a dark grey velvet coat and waistcoat, white gloves.

PROV.: Acquired before 1814 when in the Master's Room; College Board Room 1890; James Allen's Girls' School 1892–.

For Allen (1682/3–1746), see Ellys DPG441 above and Stoppelaer DPG496 below.

The similarity of the head to that in DPG441 suggests the attribution to Ellys. Presumably the 'kit-cat picture of Mr James Allen, who was master in 1717' listed in the Master's room in 1814.[1]

1 Manning & Bray, iii, p.443.

CHARLES STOPPELAER (fl.1703–57)

DPG496 *James Allen*

Canvas 236.1 x 147.2 lined after 1926 (see below); scattered discoloured retouchings and minor abrasions lower left.

Inscribed on the scroll bottom left: *JAL* (monogram) *Born ye 4th/ of May: 1683/ 1737/ AE:54*, lower left, and *Sussex &/ Worcester/ s. The Roll/ of James Allen/ of the Vacation after/ Trinity Term and of/ Michaelmas Term/ following. Anno/ 1737*;[1] blue eyes, white powdered wig; wearing a plum-coloured suit and stockings, a black gown trimmed with black fur, an ornate gold waistcoat and a white shirt, with black silver-buckled shoes; a silver-blue cloth on the table to the right; a green drape round the two columns, upper left; Cook 1914 and 1926 recorded an inscription on the *verso*, before the relining, as *J. Allen AE 54, 1757* [1737?], *G.G.C.*[?].

PROV.: Bequeathed to the College by the sitter; College Board Room.

For Allen (1682/3–1746), see DPG441 above.

In 1745 it was observed that 'the present master's picture is also painted at full length, by Mr Charles Stoppelaer, lately a player; but it is not exposed in the gallery'.[2] In 1746 James Allen directed in his Will that 'my own picture at Length drawn by Mr Stopilear' should be given to the College,[3] and in 1791 'a late master's picture painted by Mr Charles Stoppelaer, formerly of Covent Garden Theatre' was listed there.[4]

1 For this inscription, see DPG441 note 1.
2 *Biographia Britannica*, i, 1747, p.119. I am most grateful to Dr Jan Piggott for this reference.
3 M.A. Wren & P. Hackett, *James Allen*, 1968, p.76.
4 *European Mag.*, xx, 1791, ii, p.88; Young 1889, i, p.465.

George Romney (1734–1802)

DPG440 Joseph Allen MD

Canvas 128.3 x 102.2 lined; pentimento on his right shoulder; minor damages round the extreme edges; Hell 1953; recently cleaned.

Blue-grey eyes, white powdered wig; wearing a black gown trimmed with black fur over a light faun suit with striped white stockings; his chair encased in a red cloth; to the right a green covered table with (unlettered) books and a statue of Aesculapius.

Prov.: Commissioned by the College 1775;[1] College Board Room.

Exh.: RA schools 1925; *Dulwich College – a School and its Art*, South London AG, 1981.

Eng.: C. Townley c.1786–92.[2]

Ref.: Ward & Roberts 1904, i, p.87; ii, p.3; B. Maclean-Eltham, *Romney Transactions*, 1996, p.14 (as 1775–78).

Joseph Allen (1713–96), surgeon (the figure of Aesculapius behind him referring to his profession), travelled round the world with Anson; at Dulwich he was Warden 1745–46 and Master 1746–75, resigning in order to marry Elizabeth Plaw, a widow from Dulwich (she d. 1781); he left an ample fortune on his death.[3]

Allen sat to Romney on 13, 17, 23, 30 October and 6, 13 November 1778.

1 Joseph Allen wrote to the Master on 10 September 1775 concerning, *inter alia*, the 'additional Honour also in your Request to sit for my Picture to remain in the Said College for ever' (Dulwich College, *Register of Accounts* 1755–88, n.f.; Young 1889, i, p.303).
2 For this dating see CS, iv, p.1382.
3 *GM*, lxvi, i, 1796, p.85; Young 1889, i, pp.300–01.

William Bright Morris (1844–1915)

DPG551 Edward Alleyn

Canvas 139.6 x 96.5; small scratch by right elbow; slight vertical marks and some spotting caused by water damage; several losses along bottom edge; discoloured varnish; surface cleaned 1993.

Brown eyes, brown hair; wearing a black gown with sable fur edging and black fur across the sleeves, with small blue bows.

PROV.: Given by Henry Yates Thompson to Alleyn's School 1901.[1]

A copy made c.1900 from the whole-length DPG443, see p.20. See also the drawing by Sylvester Harding, D4, p.247.

1 Thompson also commisssioned copies from Morris of the Denning DPG304, see p.202, and of Francis Bacon, see DPG549 below.

William Bright Morris (1844–1915)

DPG549 Francis Bacon, Viscount St Alban

Canvas 139.6 x 96.5; vertical damage down the right-hand side of the cloak; small loss in the red tablecloth and a small area of shrinkage craquelure below the paper; faint traces of a long vertical mark down the centre and some spotting caused by water damage; discoloured varnish; surface cleaned 1993.

Brown eyes, brown hair; wearing the lord chancellor's black hat and black robe with gold trim, with his seal bag on a table to the right; a yellow paper in his left hand and a stick in his right; a red tablecloth to the right and a red curtain behind.

PROV.: Given by Henry Yates Thompson to Alleyn's School 1901.

For the sitter see DPG445, p.228.

DPG549 was apparently copied from the whole-length portrait acquired by the National Portrait Gallery (1288) in November 1900,[1] as described under DPG445, p.228.

1 See Strong 1969a, i, pp.11–12; ii, pl.24.

Samuel Melton Fisher (1860–1939)

DPG497 *The Rev Alfred James Carver*

Canvas 151.4 x 93.9; damaged by his left shoulder; broad craquelure by his left wrist; slight surface scratching lower left.

Signed and dated, bottom left: *S. Melton Fisher.1882*; blue eyes, greying hair; wearing clerical dress with a doctor's red-hooded gown; the Dulwich arms upper left (*ar. a chevron gu. with three cinquefoils gu., two and one, with crest, a mailed fist holding a heart, proper*) above a scroll: *A.D.1882 DULWICH* .

Prov.: Given by Francis Peek 1883; College Board Room.

Exh.: RA 1882(504).

The Rev A.J. Carver (1826–1909), a 'man of educational vision and dogged independence',[1] was the Master of Alleyn's College of God's Gift 1858–83; under his mastership the school was divided in 1882 into Dulwich College (New College; designed and built by Charles Barry 1866–70) and Alleyn's School, and the date on the inscription beneath the College arms in DPG497 appears to commemorate this distinction. Carver was the co-author with Sparkes of the 1890 Dulwich picture catalogue.

Carver was also painted by Hastain, see DPG553 below, and the College has other portraits of him by E.U. Eddis, exhibited RA 1867(283), with his preliminary drawing, and an unattributed bronze bust. A portrait by Trevor Hadden c.1905 is in Alleyn's School. Edith Gorham exhibited a portrait of a Rev Canon Carver DD, at the RA 1907(1178), her only RA exhibit.

1 J.R. Piggott, *Dulwich College*, 1990, p.34.

Eugène Hastain (b.1884)

DPG553 *The Rev Alfred James Carver*

Canvas1 81.3 x 66; his left hand repainted (an open crack reveals underlying flesh tones); losses below right arm; surface cleaned 1988.

Signed and dated bottom left, in red: *Eugène Hastain 1907*; blue eyes, white hair; wearing a doctor's red-hooded gown.

Prov.: Given by W. Miller to Alleyn's School 1908; Dulwich Picture Gallery 2004.

For Carver (1826–1909), see DPG497 above.

1 Stamped *verso*: *Winsor & Newton*.

Unknown Artist

DPG438 Thomas Clark

Canvas 75.3 x 63.8 oval, lined and repaired by Brown 1815;[1] relined and cleaned 2004.

Grey powdered wig, dark eyes; wearing a red gown over a green waistcoat with white stock.

Prov.: Dulwich College by 1815.

Thomas Clark, fourth Fellow of Dulwich College and College organist 1714–15.[2]

1 Brown Ledger, 13 October 1815, '*a Portrait of T. Clark*'.
2 Young 1889, i, pp.226, 431.

Unknown Artist

DPG439 Miss Clark

Canvas 74 x 61.6 oval, lined, probably by Brown 1815;[1] late 19th-century stretcher;[2] large losses lower right in the area of the drape, possibly due to damp, and old tears to the right of the nose and to the right of her chin; small scattered losses throughout; cleaned and restored 2005.

Blue eyes, brown hair; wearing a brown dress over a white smock.

Prov.: Dulwich College by 1815 (see note 1).

Traditionally identified as the sister of Thomas Clark, see DPG438 above. The two portraits were doubtless conceived as a pair.

1 Probably Brown Ledger, 13 October 1815, '*Portrait of a Lady Half-Length Sise*', which he lined, cleaned and stippled at the same time as DPG438.
2 Bearing the stamp of *W. Morrill Liner.*

Henry Perronet Briggs (1791–1844)

DPG499 *Charles Druce*

Canvas[1] 238.4 x 146.7 lined with poor adhesion; in poor condition with punctured surface; bituminous in the darks and in the table cloth, with bad drying cracks elsewhere; numerous losses corresponding to old fold lines; pentimento on chair back (which was originally rounded); discoloured varnish.

Blue eyes, white hair; wearing a dark grey suit; a green curtain to the right, a red chair and yellow tablecloth; one of the books inscribed *dulwch/port*[?].

Prov.: Given by the sitter's family 1846.[2]

Charles Druce (1762–1845), Steward of the Manor at Dulwich and solicitor to Dulwich College for sixty years, in which office he was succeeded by his son, also Charles Druce.

1 Stamped *verso*: *GEO:ROWNEY MANUFACTURER/ 51* [Rathbone] *PLACE LONDON.*
2 Young 1889, i, p.394.

Unknown Artist

DPG498 *called Sarah, Lady Falkland*

Canvas 127.3 x 102.9 lined; diagonal scratch, bottom right; scuffed bottom edge; numerous heavy retouchings; much discoloured varnish.

Fair hair, dark eyes; wearing a white bonnet, a red dress with a gold striped revers worn over a white chemise; a black scarf is draped over her left arm, and a string of pearls hangs from her left hand.

Prov.: College Board Room 1890, as *Lady Falkland, Dowager Countess of Suffolk, benefactress of the College*; Dulwich Picture Gallery 2004.

Traditionally but doubtfully identified as showing Sarah Inwen (1714–76) who married firstly Henry, 10th Earl of Suffolk (d. 1745), and secondly Lucius Cary, 7th Viscount Falkland (d. 1785); she bequeathed £300 to be invested and shared between the twelve Dulwich College pensioners. This would imply a date of c.1745–50 for DPG498, but this seems far too late.

Unknown Artist

DPG448 *John Reading*

Canvas 76.1 x 63.5 lined and repaired by Brown in 1815;[1] fine overall craquelure; an old tear in nose and upper lip; many retouchings and an uneven discoloured varnish.

Grey eyes, white powdered wig; wearing a brown suit; in a painted oval.

PROV.: Acquired by 1815 (see note 1); College Board Room 1880; College Music Department 2005.

The identity of Reading is traditional.[2] John Reading (d.1764) organist and composer, studied at the Chapel Royal under John Blow until 1699; he was acting organist at Dulwich College 1700–02; junior vicar and Master of Choristers at Lincoln Cathedral until 1707, and organist at St John's, Hackney, 1708–27, until dismissed for playing 'Airy and Jyggy Tunes'; thereafter he was at St. Mary Woolnoth and St. Mary Woolchurch Haw with St Dunstan's-in-the-West; a founder member of the Royal Society of Musicians 1738; he donated 12 volumes of musical scores to Dulwich.[3]

DPG448 may be dated c.1720–30.

1 Brown Ledger, 13 October 1815, '*a Portrait of John Reading*'.
2 A label *verso* reads: *John Reading, organist at Dulwich College 1700*.
3 *The New Grove*, xx, 2001, p.896; Young 1889, i, pp.212–13.

Sir Arthur Stockdale Cope (1857–1940)

DPG442 *The Rev William Rogers*

Canvas 125.7 x 92.7 lined; pentimenti round the books on the right with pronounced drying cracks in that area; cleaned and repaired 1998 after vandalisation (holes and tears concentrated in the head area and in the knees).

Signed lower left: *A.S. Cope/1894*; the books and papers, lower left inscribed: *Dulwich/ College; Bishopsgate/ Foundation/Institute …/ EDUCATION … ENGLAND AND WALES* and markers in another volume read: *CRIPPLEGATE SCHEME / ALDGATE SCHEME* ; the standing books on the right include *Jowett's Poetics* (Jowett was his life-long friend); very thin grey hair, blue-grey eyes; wearing a clerical grey suit and black waistcoat.

PROV.: Presented to the sitter on his 75th birthday by his Friends 1894; given to the College by Lorance H. Carter, the sitter's nephew, 1896.

EXH.: RA 1895(368).

The Rev. William Rogers (1819–96), an energetic educational reformer, was Governor of Dulwich College from 1857 and Chairman 1862–95; his advocacy of secular education led to his being called 'Hang theology Rogers' and led to friction with Carver (see DPG497, p.236). DPG442 was presented to the sitter on his 75th birthday, 24 November 1894, which coincided with the opening of the Bishopsgate Institute, one of many educational establishments he sponsored; from the mid-1880s he was badly lame.

On 21 July 1896 the Board allowed Charles Holroyd to take a copy for Balliol College, Oxford, albeit without consulting Cope.[1]

1 Poole, ii, p.38, no.69; the portrait presented to Balliol by Lord Rosebery.

Sydney W. White (fl.1892–1917)

DPG552 *The Rev Joseph Henry Smith*

Canvas 111.7 x 83.8; horizontal scratches across left arm and through the centre, with scattered minor losses upper right and a small abrasion in the forehead; the canvas sagging and the varnish discoloured.

Signed lower right: *Sydney W. White/1902*; blue-grey eyes, greying brown hair; wearing a clerical grey suit, holding his academic cap with a gold tassel in his right hand, his left resting on a closed book on the table beside him by his spectacles; dark red background.

PROV.: Given by subscribers to Alleyn's School 1902.

Joseph Henry Smith (1836–1918), headmaster of the Lower School at Dulwich 1875–1902 (and thus the first headmaster of Alleyn's School in 1887) and senior Curate of St Botolph's, Bishopsgate; he died in Worthing.[1]

1 A brief, bland obituary appeared in the *Edward Alleyn Mag.*, July 1918, pp.24–26, 28–29 (I am grateful to both Dr Jan Piggott and Peter Rodway for this reference).

Unknown Artist

DPG415 *Portrait of a Man*

Canvas 71.7 x 61 lined; repaired damages above his right shoulder; the edges abraded; Hell 1949–55.

Brown eyes, dark brown wig, his complexion very pale; wearing a golden-brown gown, white stock, with a blackstone hanging round his neck; in a painted oval.

PROV.: Dulwich College by 1890.

EXH.: Tredegar House 1991–.

Probably painted c.1690.

Unknown Artist

DPG504 *Portrait of a Man*

Canvas 75.9 x 62.9; large L-shaped tear across the forehead, a large repaired damage above his right eyebrow and another to left of the face; much wide craquelure; large area of overpainting in lower half of left background and down centre of the coat; discoloured varnish; cleaned and repaired 2006-07.

Blue eyes; wearing a maroon coat; in a painted oval.

PROV.: Dulwich College by 1890.

Probably painted c.1740–50.

Britton 1813(284) has *Head of Mr King* [and] *Mrs Ds father*[1] *3.6 x 5.4* [two in one frame]; it is perhaps conceivable that DPG504 was one of these, although that does not explain why it was first recorded in the College in 1890 (i.e. not a Bourgeois picture).

1 But the father of Mrs Desenfans was Morris, see DPG627, p.218.

APPENDICES

APPENDIX I

MINIATURES AND SELECTED DRAWINGS

These works have not previously been catalogued. They are given M (miniature) or D (drawing) numbers; any previous archive numbers are given in brackets following the title.

Arranged alphabetically by artist, with unattributed works at the end.

CHARLES HAYTER (1761–1835)

M1 Sir Francis Bourgeois, after Beechey (DPG 654)

Oil on card 9.5 x 7.2

Inscribed *verso*: *Sir Francis Bourgeois/ copied (from a Picture by/ Sir William Beechey)– / by Chas Hayter/ Sept 1811/ No.60 Wells Street.*

PROV.: Probably Bourgeois Bequest 1811.

EXH.: *Kolekcja dla Króla* 1992, II.6.

For Bourgeois (1753–1811) see pp.87, 101. Copied, shortly after the sitter's death, from the Beechey portrait of c.1810 of which DPG17 (p.194) is a version.

CHARLES HAYTER (1761–1835)

M2 Noel Desenfans, after Northcote (DPG 653)

Oil on card 9.5 x 7

Inscribed *verso*: *Noel Desenfans Esqr/copied from a Portrait by John Northcote Esqr RA/ by Charles Hayter/ November 1811/ No.60 Well Street/ Oxfd St/ London.*

PROV.: Probably Bourgeois Bequest 1811.

EXH.: *Kolekcja dla Króla* 1992, II.5.

For Desenfans (1744–1807) see pp.87, 114. Copied from the Northcote portrait DPG28, see p.114.

JOHN HOSKINS (c.1595–1665)

M3 *Portrait of a Man* (*DPG 658*)

6.9 x 5.7 watercolour on vellum; faded.

Signed centre right: *1652/IH*; brown eyes and hair; wearing armour over a white shirt; a tree half in leaf on the left.

PROV.: Anonymous Gift 2000.[1]

It is possible that M3 is by John Hoskins the younger (c.1617–after 1693) who used his father's monogram; there is much uncertainty in distinguishing between the works of father and son after 1640.

1 Delivered to the Gallery anonymously in October 2000 with M4 and M5 from an unknown donor with a letter explaining that 'I am dying and have asked a dear friend to deliver the enclosed three miniatures to the trustees of the Dulwich Art Gallery as an anonymous gift, because I have lived in obscurity into old age and wish to remain so in death'.

C.P. (fl. c.1640–50)

M4 *Portrait of a Youth* (*DPG 659*)

Gouache 4.9 x 4 oval; faded with several small losses in the face.

Signed lower left: *CP*; blue eyes, grey powdered hair; orange-red sash, white stock

PROV.: Anonymous Gift 2000 (see M3).

attributed to GERVASE SPENCER (fl. 1740–63)

M5 *Portrait of a Lady* (*DPG 660*)

3 x 2.5 oval

Blue eyes, brown hair; wearing a silk dress with floral pattern and a blue trim; pearl necklace and ear-ring; a black bracelet on her left arm.

PROV.: Anonymous Gift 2000 (see M3 above).

Probably painted c.1750.

UNKNOWN ARTIST

M6 *Portrait of a Young Man* (*DPG 554*)

Gouache on ivory 15.2 x 11; large pentiment around head, perhaps indicating a large hat; conserved 1989.

Wearing a blue coat; seated in a red chair, his left arm resting on three books on a table; with a nineteenth-century hand-written label below: *Sir Peter Francis Bourgeois Knt R.A./ Founder of the Dulwich Gallery –/ Born – 1756 Died 1811/ By W. Beechey./ on Ivory.*

PROV.: Given by Canon A.J. Carver (1826–1909).

The head appears well finished, the remainder very slipshod; the attribution to Beechey is impossible, while the sitter, who appears to be under twenty years old, cannot be Bourgeois. Probably painted c.1820.

GEORGE CRUIKSHANK (1792–1878)

D1 *The Duke of Sussex in his Library* (G9)

Pencil on paper 15.3 x 12.2, the sheet 18.5 x 15; conserved 1989.

Looking down the length of the long library at Kensington Palace, the perspective lines faintly ruled; the seated, dark-haired figure of the Duke in the mid distance attended by his Librarian, while a third figure in the distance examines the shelves; inscribed in ink bottom left: *G Cruikshank* and titled, in a different hand, in the bottom margin *Library of the Duke of Sussex Kensington Palace* (ink over pencil); inscribed in pencil in the top right margin: *right*.

PROV.: Given by Henry Yates Thompson by 1918 (see below).

ENG.: *Pictorial Times*, 8 May 1843.[1]

REF.: D. Hudson, *Kensington Palace*, 1968, f.p.62, dated 1826.

Augustus Frederick, Duke of Sussex, (1773–1843) kept his remarkable library of 50,000 books in the Long Gallery on the first floor of Kensington Palace, with its collection of Biblical manuscripts and 5,000 Bibles in a special Divinity Room. Between 1818/20–30 the Duke's Librarian was T.J. Pettigrew (1791–1865), a surgeon and antiquarian who was also Cruikshank's family doctor. Cruikshank provided five engraved plates for volume I of Pettigrew's *Bibliotheca Sussexiana* (1827)[2] and D1 was most probably drawn when Cruikshank was working in the Library making those plates.[3]

The ink 'signature' on D1 appears to have been added. Some elementary pencil sketches for this interior appear on a small card (70 x 143 mm) in the Cruikshank collection in the Victoria and Albert Museum (6496T); they bear a title and signature (which does not absolutely agree with that seen on D1). Both drawings relate directly to the unsigned woodblock (slightly smaller than D1) printed in the first number of the *Pictorial Times*, 8 May 1843 (following the death of the Duke on 25 April).

The Alleynian (July 1918, pp.139–40) recorded Queen Mary's (inevitable?) admiration for this drawing on a visit to the Dulwich Gallery.

1 Illus. M. Gillen, *Royal Duke*, 1976, f.p.193 (but said to be from the *Illustrated London News*, 1843).
2 Four more were engraved by Robert Cruikshank, the brother of George.
3 R.L. Patten, *George Cruikshank*, 1992, i, pp.302, 463n38; Hudson 1968 (see REF.). The Duke's dark hair and long sideboards, just visible in D1, would further confirm such a date.

WILLIAM DANIELL (1769–1837)

D2 *Sir Francis Bourgeois, after G. Dance* (G4)

Pencil with black and red chalk on paper 23 x 18; inscribed in pencil below: *Sir Francis Bourgeious* [*sic*].

PROV.: Given by William Drummond 1982 in memory of his father, John Neil Drummond JP, one time Governor of the Dulwich Estates.

EXH.: Sabin, *Sublime and the Beautiful* 1973(4); *Soane and After* 1988(3).

REF.: Walker 1985, i, p.61 (as an overworked copy by Dance); *Rembrandt to Gainsborough*, 1999, p.14.

For Bourgeois (1753–1811), see pp.87, 101.

Inscribed on the backing by the donor 'at what stage this portrait comes is not altogether clear', but it is a copy by the engraver William Daniell from George Dance's original drawing in the RA which is dated 16 March 1793. Daniell's subsequent plate is undated.

Richard Doyle (1824–83)

D3 *Lord John Russell 'at home'* (G18)

Pen, ink and pencil 17 x 21

Prov.: Richard Doyle, Grosvenor Gallery, 1885(359?),[1] bt. Henry Yates Thompson, by whom given 1919.

Preparatory drawing for a cartoon which appeared as the title page in *Punch*, 1 May 1847, when the small banners carried by the surrounding figures were inscribed with the Prime Minister's problems, e.g. Ireland, the railways, state education, law reform, army reform and emigration. On the *verso* are mounted the relevant *Punch* cover and a copy of the print; on the backboard there is a typed description of how, and how rapidly, the drawing would have been transferred to a wood block for printing and publication.

1 Doyle's drawings were then shown together with works by Gainsborough; his works were frequently numbered in groups: the present drawing may have been among no.221 *Design for the Title Page of Punch, Pen and ink, and Political Caricatures, pencil*; 359 *Two Designs for Cartoons in Punch*; 360 *Six Designs for Punch – Marshal Pelissier and others*, 369 & 370 *Designs for Punch Cartoons* and 384 contained a sketch portrait of Lord John Russell – each lent by Miss Doyle; drawings 'catalogued as belonging to the family of the late R. Doyle' were then for sale. A sale of Doyle's works, Christie's, 7 June 1886, included sketches and cartoons for *Punch*.

Sylvester Harding (1745–1809)

D4 *Edward Alleyn* (G5)

Pencil and watercolour on paper 37 x 25.9; much discoloured.

A label, *verso*: *Drawing (for engraving) of the Founder/of Dulwich College Edward Alleyn/ by Sylvester Harding* A.D. 1.7.9.0./ *Executed before the original/ painting had been restored/* A.D. *1790 letters mounted on board// Purchasd by* [Dr Carver?] *A.D.1870.*

Prov.: Given by Henry Yates Thompson.

Exh.: *Kolekcja dla Króla* 1992(II.13).

Eng.: T. Nugent 1792 (*Biographical Mirrour*).

For Alleyn see pp.19, 20. Copied from DPG443, see p.20 n.5.

T.F. Hodgkins (fl.1835–1903)

D5 *London from Flamsteed Hill, after Jan Looten* (G14)

Pencil and watercolour on card 7 x 11

An old label, separately conserved, reads: *View of London/from Flamstead Hill, Greenwich Park/ with the ruins of Duke Humphrey's Tower./ After J. Loten, time of Charles II/ Drawn by T.F. Hodgkins/ Keeper of the Dulwich Gallery/ and presented by him to the Governors/ of the same/ 1899.*

Prov.: Presented by the artist 1899.

A copy of an untraced picture by the Dutch painter Jan Looten (1618–c.1681).

Charles Fairfax Murray (1849–1919)

D6 *called Andrea del Sarto and his Wife* (G11)

Pencil and wash on paper 18.5 x 24

Signed top left: *C.F.M.*

Prov.: Given to Robert Browning on his 71st birthday, 7 May 1883; Browning sale, Sotheby's, 1st day, 1 May 1913, lot 9, bt. Maggs; given by Henry Yates Thompson c.1917 (see below).

Eng.: (an example mounted on the *verso* of D6) lettered: *Andrea del Sarto pleading with his Wife, from the Picture by himself in the Pitti Palace, Florence, which suggested Browning's "Andrea del Sarto", drawn by C. Fairfax Murray & reproduced by Dawson's fotograving process for the Browning Society 1882–3.*[1]

The original painting in the Pitti (118) is now considered not to be by Andrea del Sarto and not to show del Sarto and his wife Lucrezia.[2] Browning's poem *Andrea del Sarto*, inspired by this painting, had been written c.1853.[3]

This was perhaps the drawing over which there was subsequently a mild dispute: Murray wrote to Yates Thompson on 8 May 1918 'I am told by a friend of mine who has been to Dulwich within the last few days that my picture of Andrea del Sarto is labelled as presented in 1917. I never gave you this picture. If you look at your notes of our meeting you will not find any mention of the picture. I cannot understand how this mistake was made'.[4]

1 The Browning Society, founded in 1881, held its last public meeting in London in 1891–92 (but many Browning Societies exist today).
2 S.J., Freedberg, *Andrea del Sarto, catalogue raisonné*, 1963, p.223.
3 See *Robert Browning, The Poems*, ed. J. Pettigrew, i, 1981, pp.643–50, 1129.
4 D. Elliott, *Fairfax Murray*, 2002, p.199; Elliott says he then offered a Gainsborough sketch to make it all up (not identifiable today).

John Nixon (c.1750–1818)

D7 'Dulwich – Berry' (G6)

Ink and wash on paper 8.4 x 9

Half-length figure of an elderly man with an open book on a ledge before him; inscribed below: *Dulwich – Berry*; numbered top left: *99*.

Prov.: Haines bequest 1923? [W.D. Haines bequeathed a Nixon drawing to the British Museum in 1923] to the French Hospital of La Providence, Rochester; sale Christie's,[1] bt. William Drummond, by whom presented 1987.

The identity of Mr Berry remains unknown; he may have been Fleetwood Bury, who was negotiating for property from the Dulwich estates in 1788 and leasing property in 1808.[2]

1 Neither of the Dulwich Nixon drawings is specifically identified in the fourteen sales of his drawings from the French Hospital between 1974–85: Christie's: 5 November 1974, 9 November 1976, 14 June 1977, 22 November 1977, 14 March 1978, 21 November 1978, 18 November 1980, 24 March 1981, 29 March 1983, 20 March 1984, 10 July 1984, 20 November 1984, 19 March 1985 and 19 November 1985.

2 Young 1889, i, pp.310, 329.

John Nixon (c.1750–1818)

D8 Allen and Allen (G7)

Ink and wash on paper 12.3 x 11.5

Inscribed bottom right: *Allen Master/Allen Warden/ Dulwich College 1786*; numbered top right: *116*.

Prov.: as D7.

Exh.: *Kolekcja dla Króla* 1992(II.14).

The inscription (though not the drawing) identifies Thomas Allen, Master 1775–1805, and William Allen, Warden 1775 and Master 1805–11.

PAUL SANDBY (1730–1809)

D9 *Noel Desenfans and Sir Francis Bourgeois* (DPG645)

Watercolour on card 14.3 x 15.3; conserved 1989.

Inscribed below in pencil: *Sr F Bourgeois* [left] *Mr Desenfans* [right]; Bourgeois in blue coat dozing, Desenfans in white cap and jacket apparently engaged in lively conversation.

PROV.: With W.A. Sandby 1888;[1] said to have been given by Henry Yates Thompson before 1926 (see below);[2] Christie's, 24 March 1959, lot 129 (one of three drawings); presented by M. P. Bernard of Dulwich, in memory of his brother Arthur Basil Bernard, 1959.

EXH.: *350th Anniversary*, Dulwich, 1969(173); *Soane and After* 1988(2); *Kolekcja dla Króla* 1992(II.8).

REF.: C. Monkhouse, *The Portfolio*, 1888, pp.11, 14; Cook 1926, as given by H. Yates Thompson; Walker 1985, i, p.61 as c.1795.

For Desenfans (1744–1807) and for Bourgeois (1753–1811) see pp.87, 101, 114. The scene has been described as showing the pair as crossing the channel[3] or in their home at Charlotte Street (which seems far more likely).[4] It may date from c.1805.

1 *The Portfolio*, 1888, pp.11, 14.
2 Not in the Yates Thompson sale, Sotheby's, 22 July ff. 1941; he d. 8 July 1928. It remains unexplained how the drawing left Dulwich to be re-acquired in 1959.
3 Monkhouse 1888 (see REF.); *Soane and After* 1987(2).
4 *Rembrandt to Gainsborough*, 1999, p.10.

SIR JAMES THORNHILL (1675–1734)

D10 *A Group of Connoisseurs* (G3)

Bodycolour, wash and chalk on grey paper 18.5 x 19 laid down; conserved 1989.

PROV.: 'Ulverston Bequest' after 1926.[1]

D10 relates directly to a drawing by Thornhill in the Art Institute of Chicago (1922.1283)[2] and is evidently by the same hand. Each is set before a curving arcade with a prominent foreground drape, and the five figures are modelled with emphatic light and shade. Otherwise the compositions differ. D10 reads from the left, the Chicago drawing from the right. As the Chicago drawing has a scale beneath it, indicating a proposed canvas of some 230 x 300 cm., it was perhaps the later version. No related painting is known.

A more rudimentary Thornhill sketch in the British Museum (1865-6-10-1334), showing five figures looking to the front with an architectural background, may show the first stage of the composition.

The intended identities of the figures are inscribed in a contemporary hand on the Chicago drawing as *1 Mr Dahl – Prior in Sketch/ 2 Mr Thornhill – Models St Pauls &c / 3 Mr Wootton – Horses & Dogs/ 4 Mr Gibbs – new Church Strand/ 5 Mr Wanley – Looking over Medals &c.* – and we may assume these are also the figures in D10. Thus Michael Dahl (1656–1743) sits at his easel painting the poet Matthew Prior;[3] the antiquarian Humfrey Wanley (1672–1726) sits on the right; behind Dahl stand James Gibbs (1682–1754) with the T-square, Thornhill with the portfolio and John Wootton (c.1686–1756). These were the 'Harley Virtuosi', members of that intellectual Tory circle gathered round Edward Harley, 2nd Earl of Oxford, for whom Thornhill painted the Chapel at Wimpole in 1721–24.[4]

1 On 4 March 1986 Giles Waterfield (copy letter on file) wrote: 'all the information I have on provenance is that the drawing was left in the "Ulverston Bequest" earlier this century': since it was not listed in Cook 1926 it presumably arrived after that date. An old, perhaps 18th century, label *verso*: *Hogarth painting Sir James Thornhill standing behind him/ Hogarth*; the old backing is inscribed in pencil *Lot 73; Miss Potter/Chester* and bears a printed Colnaghi label.
2 Illus. *Apollo*, cxxii, 1985, p.204; T. Friedman, *James Gibbs*, 1984, p.22; A. Meyer, *Wootton*, exh. cat. Kenwood, 1984, no.45.
3 While the portrait on the easel in the Chicago drawing can be related to the Dahl portrait of Prior now at Knole, the corresponding portrait in D10 agrees with no known Prior portrait. The poet died at Wimpole on 18 September 1721. The identity of the figures to the key in the Chicago drawing was made by A. Meyer, 'Wootton at Wimpole', *Apollo*, cxxii, 1985, p.212, who pointed out that Gibbs was there holding the ground plan of St Mary-Le-Strand, and Thornhill a cartoon for one of his paintings for St Paul's.
4 See B. Allen, *Apollo*, cxxii, 1985, pp.204–11; Friedman and Meyer at note 2; Croft-Murray 1962, p.273b. A visit to Wimpole by Thornhill, Gibbs, Wootton and the landscape gardener Charles Bridgman was celebrated in Thornhill's *A Hue and Cry after Four of the King's Liege Subjects*, 1721.

Samuel Woodforde (1765–1817)
D11 Copies from Murillo (G22)

Three drawings in black and white crayon with white heightening:

a) the standing boy's head on brown paper 18.4 x 13.2

b) whole picture on grey paper 24.7 x 17.7; the sheet uneven and divided vertically in two (division at 14.7/13.7)

c) seated boy's head on brown paper 18.4 x 13.2

Prov.: Given by William Drummond 1989.

Copies from the Murillo DPG224; possibly made on 15 March 1785 when the young artist 'went with Mr Wyatt to see Mr Desenfans collection of Pictures'.[1]

1 *Woodforde Papers and Diaries*, ed. D.H. Woodforde, 1932, p.92.

Unknown Artist
D12 Portrait of a Young Man (G8)

Watercolour, pencil and chalk on paper 20 x 16; the sheet has been folded across the centre.

Half length to right; light brown eyes, dark hair with large sideburns, light brown coat, white waistcoat and stock .

Prov.: Discovered c.1980 in a copy of the *Memoir of Noel Desenfans* (1810) in the Dulwich Gallery Library.

Probably drawn c.1810.

APPENDIX II

SCULPTURE

Christopher (Cristoforo) Prosperi (fl.1800–16)

S1 *Sir Francis Bourgeois*

Marble bust 49 high, on a socle 11.5 high; inscribed down the right shoulder: *Mr. Crus. Prosperi Fecit.*

PROV.: Bequeathed by Mrs Margaret Desenfans 1814.

REF.: *Collection for a King* 1985, p.17 as by Westmacott.

For Bourgeois (1756–1811) see pp.87, 101. The bust may derive from the portrait by Beechey (DPG17 (p.194) or from one of the copies from it made by Bourgeois (DPG465, DPG466, p.101).

In her Will dated 19 April 1813[1] Mrs Desenfans bequeathed to the Master, Warden and Fellows of Dulwich College, to be 'placed and preserved in the Mausoleum attached to the same College, viz: two Marble Busts one of my said dear Husband Noel Joseph Desenfans and the other of the said Sir Peter Francis Bourgeois'.

The bodies of Bourgeois and Desenfans were placed in the Mausoleum in March 1815.

Mrs Desenfans also bequeathed 'Two Statues one of Noel Joseph Desenfans Esquire and one of Sir Peter Francis Bourgeois by Westmacott' to be 'preserved with the Collection of Pictures in the Gallery'; they remain untraced and are otherwise unrecorded.[2]

1 PRO Prob 11 1559(9 Bridport) f.461, p.283; extracts are printed as an Appendix in Dulwich catalogues 1876–1926.

2 See REF. above. Britton 1813 included '9 bronzes' at the end of his inventory of pictures.

Christopher (Cristoforo) Prosperi (fl.1800–16)

S2 *Noel Desenfans*

Marble bust 48 high, on a socle 11.5 high; the tip of the nose repaired; inscribed down the right shoulder: *Mr. Cr. Prosperi Fecit.*

PROV.: Bequeathed by Mrs Margaret Desenfans 1813.

Lit: *Collection for a King* 1985, p.16 as by Westmacott.

For Desenfans (1744–1807) see pp.87, 114. The bust appears to derive from his portrait by Northcote DPG28 (p.114).

See S1 above.

APPENDIX III

LOST or DESTROYED PICTURES

as described in previous Dulwich catalogues.

after HEINRICH VON ANGELI (1840–1925)

DPG550 *Queen Victoria*

Canvas 121.9 x 99

PROV.: Acquired by subscription of friends, boys and masters, 1901, following the death of the Queen on 22 January; listed in the Hall of Alleyn's School in 1926; untraced.

For Queen Victoria (1818–1901), see DPG304, p.202.

Described as 'half length standing to front, after the full-length portrait at Windsor' – presumably the standing three-quarter length now at Buckingham Palace painted in 1875,[1] Angeli's first portrait of the Queen and first displayed at Windsor. It was much copied.[2]

1 Millar 1992, no.5.
2 See Ormond 1973, p.476, pl.961.

SIR FRANCIS BOURGEOIS (1753–1811)

DPG491 *Children at their Mother's Grave*

Canvas 142.2 x 114.3.

PROV.: Purchased in 1889 'a Picture for the Gallery, by Sir F. Bourgeois'; destroyed by bombing 1944.

EXH.: RA 1794(204).

ENG.: John Ogbourne 1797 (the tombstone dated October 22 1774, the plate dedicated to Desenfans). Reproduced below.

REF.: Waterfield 1989, p.44.

after Sir Edwin Landseer (1802–73)

DPG447 Dr John Allen

Canvas 45.7 x 60.9; an undated photograph shows a hole in the chair back and losses along the lower edge.

Allen's whiggism and his *Inquiry into the Rise and Growth of the Royal Prerogative in England*, 1830, are suggested by the bronze bust of Cromwell by Edward Pierce on his desk.[1]

Prov.: Presented by Col. C.R. Fox 1843, the year of Allen's death;[2] listed in the Board Room of Dulwich College in 1926; untraced.

John Allen (1771–1843), medical doctor, and whig historian; MD Edinburgh 1791; Warden 1811–20 and Master 1820–43 of Dulwich College; his life was divided between the school and Holland House, where he lived from 1802; General Fox (see note 2), who owned two portraits of Dr Allen (DPG447 and NPG384, the latter inherited from his mother in 1845), remembered his 'dear old friend' as 'a stout strong man, with a very large head, broad face, enormous round silver spectacles on his nose, and with the thickest legs I can remember. His accent Scotch, his manner eager but extremely good-natured'.[3]

DPG447 is a copy from the Landseer portrait commissioned by the 1st Lord Holland as a birthday present for his wife in 1836 and presented by their son's widow to the National Portrait Gallery in 1873.[4] Mrs Norton thought it 'the best little picture of dear old Mr Allen that could be done if they tried for a century.[5] Four copies of this original are known:

a) DPG447.

b) University Library, Oklahoma State University, given by Mr and Mrs Burton D. Salmon 1984, inherited from the estates of their parents, Walter J. and Elizabeth Davy Salmon. A 19th-century label *verso* reads: '*Portrait of Dr John Allen MD Master of Dulwich College. Author of An Enquiry into the Rise and Growth of the Royal Prerogative. By Sir Edwin Landseer RA (1802–1873) from the Collection of Lord Brougham and Vaux*'.[6]

c) formerly at Holland House; given by the Hon Mrs Drewitt in 1935 to replace the original given to the National Portrait Gallery; Melbury sale, Rawlence & Squarey, 20 July 1967, lot 18.

d) Sotheby's, 16 May 1990, lot 58, a reduced copy, from the collection of the Marquess of Londonderry.

A crayon portrait of Dr Allen by William Lane 1810 was also listed at Holland House in 1904.[7]

1 The 'Newstead Bust', identified by C.F. Bell (his annotations to *Chronicles of Holland House*, 1937, p.164, NPG copy).
2 Charles Richard Fox (1797–1873), illegitimate son of the 1st Lord Holland, b. 6 November 1796; his mother, Lady Webster, becoming Lady Holland on 6 July 1797. The presentation of the portrait on 11 September 1843 is recorded in Young 1889, i, p.392.
3 Ilchester, *The Home of the Hollands*, 1937, p.179. For Allen, see also Young 1889, ii, pp.380–419.
4 Walker 1985, i, p.5, no.384; ii, pl.12; exh. *Art Treasures*, Manchester, 1857(MM491) lent Gen. C.R. Fox; *International Exhibition*, 1862(396) lent Maj.-Gen. C.R. Fox; RA, *Old Masters*, 1874(195).
5 Ilchester, *Chronicles of Holland House*, 1937, p.164.
6 Henry Brougham, 1st Baron Brougham and Vaux (1795–1868) had been very friendly with Allen whom he described at his death as 'the oldest friend I now had in the world ... Fifty years friendship without a shade or cloud is a thing not often granted to any one' (Ilchester, *The Home of the Hollands*, 1937, pp.178, 308–09). The principal Brougham residence, Brougham Hall, near Penrith, was demolished in 1934. I am very grateful to Emma Lauze of the Paul Mellon Centre, London, and to Dr Jennifer F. Paustenbaugh of Oklahama State University Library for additional information on this picture.
7 *Holland House Catalogue*, 1904, pp.62–63, no.88.

SIR JOSHUA REYNOLDS (1723–92)

DPG483 *Death of Cardinal Beaufort*

Canvas 134 x 163.2

PROV.: ?Reynolds sale, Greenwood's, 16 April 1796, lot 69, bt. T. Holcroft; Christie's, 28 March 1800, lot 10, bt in; Holcroft sale, Christie's, 29 April 1803, lot 64, bt. Nixon; Farebrother, 2 February 1804, lot 45; Bourgeois Bequest 1811; destroyed by bombing 1944.

REF.: Britton 1813(280); GC, iii, p.1146; iv, p.1453; Waterhouse 1941, p.81 as a partial study for the Petworth picture; M. Postle, *Reynolds, the Subject Pictures*, 1995, pp.258–59; Mannings (Postle) 2000, no.2064.

The subject was taken from Shakespeare's *Henry VI part 2*, 3, iii, where the King, Salisbury and Warwick witness the Cardinal's death. A reduced version of the picture now at Petworth (218 x 157)[1] and exhibited in Boydell's Shakespeare Gallery in 1789, DPG483, lacking the fiend and much reduced in height, was apparently executed some years earlier, as Postle has shown. By 1787 Reynolds had 'some scenes from Shakespeare, which he has sketched at the desire of a nobleman a few years since',[2] and in 1788 it was announced that 'Sir Joshua's transcendental work of Cardinal Beaufort was one of his earliest designs. It was resumed entirely at his own impulse. Mr Boydell has bought it and to fit it for his undertaking, the Canvas is enlarged'.[3]

In 1836 Passavant found it a 'slightly painted picture, and now almost colourless: upon the whole a most painful composition';[4] nearly twenty years later Waagen wrote 'the expression of the Cardinal here is extravagantly frightful; and to the feeble drawing, so usual with Reynolds, is added a pale and cold colouring'.[5]

1 Mannings, Postle 2000, no.2063.
2 *Morning Herald*, January 1787.
3 *The World*, 27 December 1788
4 Passavant 1836, p.69.
5 Waagen 1854, p.348. Master Clive Newcome found 'it frightens me so, I daren't look at it' (W.M. Thackeray, *The Newcomes*, xii).

JAMES WARD (1769–1859)

DPG631 A Bay Hunter

Panel 69.8 x 93.7

Signed bottom left: *JWARD* (monogram) *R.A. 1817.*

PROV.: Anonymous gift 1956; stolen c.1987–88.

UNKNOWN ARTIST

DPG502 Portrait of a Clergyman

Canvas 221 x 127

PROV.: Dulwich College by 1890; last recorded in 1926.

Described from 1890 onwards as an early 18th century portrait, somewhat resembling Henry Sacheverell (1674–1724).

INDICES

BIOGRAPHICAL INDEX OF ARTISTS

ANGELI, HEINRICH VON (1840-1925)
Portrait painter; b. Sopron, Hungary; studied in Dusseldorf and Vienna, entering the Academy in 1854; a history painter at Munich 1859-62; returned to Vienna, taking up portraiture; he quickly became a distinguished painter of Royalty in the courts of Germany, Austria, Russia and England - where he worked on nine occasions between 1875 and 1899; d. Vienna.

550 *Queen Victoria*, after p.257

AYOUB, MOUSSA (fl.1903-38)
Portrait and genre painter; exhibited RA 1906-34 from London addresses.

627 *Mrs Margaret Desenfans*, after Reynolds p.218

BEACH, THOMAS (1738-1806)
Portrait painter; b. Abbey Milton, Dorset; studied at the St Martin's Lane Academy and under Joshua Reynolds 1760-62; by 1770 he had settled in Bath where he established a comfortable portrait practice, but exhibiting from London addresses SA 1772-83 and RA 1785-90 and 1797; retired to Dorchester c.1798.

591 *Portrait of a Man* p.146

BEALE, MARY (1633-99)
Portrait painter, née Cradock at Barrow, Suffolk; in 1652 married Charles Beale (1631-1705) who administered the studio of his 'Dearest Heart'; apart from a spell in Albrook, Hants., during the plague years 1664-70, she worked in London receiving in her puritan house distinguished sitters from church, state and the world of learning; from c.1672 she was discreetly encouraged by Lely whose portraits she sometimes copied.

574 *Portrait of a Youth* p.147
611 *Portrait of a Physician*, attributed p.192

BEECHEY, SIR WILLIAM (1753-1839)
Portrait painter; b. Burford, Oxfordshire; studied at the RA schools 1774; exhibited RA 1776-1839; ARA 1793, RA 1798; Kt. 1798; in Norwich 1782-87; Portrait Painter to Queen Charlotte 1793 and later described as Principal Portrait Painter to William IV; Painter to the Duke of Gloucester 1813(?); some subject pictures by him exhibited BI 1806-36; a friend of Sir Francis Bourgeois; d. London.

111 *John Philip Kemble* p.88
169 *Charles Small Pybus* p.90
17 *Sir Francis Bourgeois* p.194

BOL, CORNELIS (1589-1666)
Topographical artist; b. Antwerp; master at Antwerp 1615; worked in Paris before coming to London 1635; member of the Dutch Church in London 1636; etched the Spanish Fleet off the Kent coast 1639 and etched and painted several prospects of London before the Great Fire of 1665; buried in Haarlem 1666.

360 *The Thames from Somerset House* p.76

BOURGEOIS, SIR FRANCIS (1753-1811)
See p.87. In the 1780s Bourgeois exhibited mostly landscapes with some banditti and battle scenes, and in the early 1790s hunts and sea storms; he endeavoured to 'attain Mr Loutherbourg in execution, Mr Gainsborough in colouring, & Mr Wilson in forms & grandeur' (*The World*, 7 May 1790), but Denning thought it impossible to give Bourgeois high rank as an artist: 'heavy, leaden, and unpleasing, his works are placed in the Gallery merely in honour of the munificence which induced him to found it. Regard for his fame would have removed them' (1859, f.183). Only two paintings by Bourgeois appeared in the Desenfans insurance list of 1804: no.68 *A Funeral Procession* (now DPG301) and no.65 *Smugglers Defeated* (not in the Bourgeois Bequest).

6 *Tiger Hunt* p.92
100 *Cupid* p.92
135 *Landscape with Cattle (A young Shepherd with his Flock)* p.93
149 *Helena brought before the Altar to be Sacrificed* p.93
294 *Landscape with Cattle (Cows by a Lake)* p.94
301 *Funeral Procession of a White Friar* p.94
308 *Sea Shore with Horse and Cart* p.95
310 *Friar in Prayer* p.95
311 *Soldiers* p.95
325 *Landscape with Cattle (Cows on a Hillock by a Stream)* p.96
335 *Sea Shore with rearing Horse* p.97
342 *A Man holding a Horse* p.98
344 *Tobias and the Angel* p.98
459 *Religion in the Desert* p.98
460 *Landscape with Soldiers* p.99
461 *Figures in a Landscape* p.99
462 *Landscape with Cattle (A Cow Resting)* p.100
463 *Cavalry in a Landscape* p.100
465 *Self Portrait, after Beechey* p.101
466 *Self Portrait, after Beechey* p.101
467 *William Tell* p.102
464 *Self Portrait* p.195
491 *Children at their Mother's Grave* p.257
488 *called Noel Desenfans on Horseback*, attributed p.103

The following paintings by Bourgeois, listed in Britton 1813, remain untraced:

68 *Landscape Cattle barge Bourgeois panel 1.5 x 1.9*
194 *Landscape with Bridge & Figures 1.10 x 2.6*
310 *Sketch of Sir F Bourgeois' Greadr*[sic] *& children very slight 2.6 x 2.2*
359 *Two small heads studies 7 x 11 & 6 x 12* (apparently circular within rectangular frames)

BRIGGS, HENRY PERRONET (1791-1844)
Portrait and history painter; b. London; studied at the RA schools 1811; ARA 1825, RA 1832; exhibited RA 1814-44, BI 1819-35; until 1832 specialised in Shakespearean and historical scenes, thereafter concentrated on portraiture; a friend of Margaret Gainsborough who left him some of her father's works; d. London.

291 *Charles Kemble* p.196
499 *Charles Druce* p.242

BRODIE, MRS KATE S. (fl. 1891-1900)
Landscape and genre artist; exhibited Royal Scottish Academy 1891-1900, from Edinburgh 1891-94 and from Glasgow 1895-1900, and at the Royal Glasgow Institute 1894-1900.

632 *Landscape* p.197

CANALETTO (1697-1768)
Giovanni Antonio Canal, view painter; b. Venice, where he practised save for probable visits to Rome c.1719 and c.1740 and documented visits to England 1746-50 and 1751-55; his English patronage was considerable, and was led from 1730 by Joseph Smith, British Consul in Venice, the majority of whose purchases are now in the Royal Collection at Windsor; d. Venice.

600 *A View of Walton Bridge* p.197

The following will appear in the Italian volume of the Dulwich catalogue:

599 *The Bucintoro at the Molo on Ascension Day*

CASTRO, LORENZO A. (fl. 1672-95)
Marine and portrait painter, probably of Portuguese-Jewish descent and probably trained in Antwerp, where Laureys A. Castro was Master of the St Luke's Guild 1664-65; it has also been supposed that a Sebastiano D. Castro, marine painter of Antwerp (by whom three undated works are in the National Maritime Museum) was Lorenzo's father. Lorenzo A. Castro was in England by 1672 when he dated the *Battle of Actium* (National Maritime Museum); in 1680 he painted the portraits of *Sir Robert Clayton*, Lord Mayor of London, and his wife (sold Christie's, 23 June 1950, lots 31, 32) and the Dulwich pictures are dateable between 1672 and 1686. Three genre scenes by L. Castro, a *Toper*, a *Ballad Singer* and a *Friar and Lady* were engraved by J. Smith. A Lawrence Castro was living in the parish of St Giles, Cripplegate in 1695 with his wife and son.

A large Castro, *Sea Port in Spain or Portugal*, was in the Yates Thompson sale, Sotheby's, 2 July 1941, lot 189 (*Cat. of Pictures and Portraits now at 19 Portman Square*, 1921, pl.xxix).

359 *A Galley of Malta* p.78
361 *Ships in Rough Water off a Mediterranean Port* p.78
428 *A Sea Fight with Barbary Corsairs* p.79
436 *A Calm* p.80
437 *A Dutch East-Indiaman off Hoorn* p.80
517 *Dutch Levanters in a Rough Sea* p.81
518 *A Storm at Sea* p.81

The following paintings listed in the Cartwright Inventory of 1686 are now untraced:

217 *a prity Long Seascift of a barge full of passingers & 2 wharfs with men on Them in a gilt frame Castros. £3*

222 *a Large seascifte of tenn foot hie & nine foot broud with with shipps & a man of warr under sayle, a Ruffe water, a whayle & a Long bot with 4 men in it rowing, & a wharfe with seuerall figers on it. £34. Castro.*

223 *a Large seascift of 2 yards Long, & a yard & quarter deep, in it 4 Long bots, a great hie gate, a wharfe, & Ladys & gentellmen going into one of ye Long bots, & a galley with passengers ye Cullers of galley are greene red & whit, a Calme watter, in a gilte frame. Castro £10*

226 *A sea-scift of 2 shipps a galley full of soulders a bot with 4 men in it, a wharfe, a Large hous &Church, painted on a Clouth a yard & 3 quarters Longe, & a yard deepe. Castro. £6*

235 *sea scift of 3 quarters cloth in a black frame dun by Castro*

COLONIA, ADAM (1634-85)
Landscape painter; b. Rotterdam, third generation of a family of painters: s. of Isaac Colonia (1611-63), gr. s. of Adam Louisz Colonia (1574-1651); soon after 1670 he settled in London; with his wife a member of the Dutch church of Austin Friars in 1675; 'especially eminent for his small figures in rural pieces, for his cattle, country wakes, fire-pieces, &c.' (Buckeridge); d.1685 and buried in St Martin's-in-the-Fields. There are works by him at Bolton and Maidstone.

371 *Sheep Shearing* p.82
431 *The Flight into Egypt* p.83

CONSTABLE, JOHN (1776-1837)
Landscape painter; b. East Bergholt, Suffolk; studied at the RA schools from 1800; settled in London 1819; ARA 1819; RA 1829; exhibited RA 1802-1837, BI 1808-1836, and at the Paris salon 1824, 1827; his outstanding ability was only gradually appreciated, despite the deep admiration of his friends, of whom one recalled how 'at all times of the day, at night, and in all seasons of the year, Constable had inexpressible delight in viewing the works of nature'.

657 *Landscape with Windmills, after Jacob van Ruisdael* p.232

COPE, SIR ARTHUR STOCKDALE (1857-1940)
Society portrait painter; b. London; studied at the RA schools 1874; exhibited RA 1876-1935; ARA 1899, RA 1910; Kt. 1917; KCVO 1927; d. Treniffee, Cornwall.

442 *The Rev William Rogers* p.243

CRADOCK, MARMADUKE (d. 1716)
Animal and bird painter (*caveat* the Rev. John Cradock, father of Mary Beale, q.v.) from Somerset; largely self-taught, he worked independently 'for persons that pay'd him p.diem, or that dealt in pictures' (Vertue); buried St Mary, Whitechapel, 24 March 1716; an example of his work in the Tate Gallery (T06488) is signed *M. Cradocke*; two sheets of bird studies by him are in the British Museum and two of his paintings were in Sir Robert Walpole's collection.

519 *Mallards on a Pond*, attributed p.200

DE CRITZ, JOHN, the elder (c.1551/2-1642)
Portrait painter; b. probably in Antwerp and brought to England in 1568, he was serving his apprenticeship under Lucas de Heere in London in 1571; in 1582 he was travelling in France under the patronage of Sir Francis Walsingham; appointed Serjeant-Painter to the King on 11 May 1605 and paid for a whole length of the King in August 1606 and a second portrait in 1607; in 1611 Marcus Gheeraerts the younger, his brother-in-law, was described as Painter to the King.

548 *James VI and I*, attributed p.200

Cruikshank, George (1792-1878)

Illustrator and caricaturist; b. London; s. of the caricaturist Isaac (1764-1811); by the age of twenty he had acquired a considerable reputation as a political cartoonist; his many illustrations included those for *Life in London* 1820-21, *Oliver Twist* 1839, and Ainsworth's *Tower of London* 1840; much of his work was for the temperance movement; d. London.

D1 *The Duke of Sussex in his Library* p.250

Dahl, Michael (1659?-1743)

Portrait painter; b. Stockholm where he studied under Ehrenstrahl; London 1682; in 1684-89 with Henry Tilson (pupil of Lely) he visited Paris and Rome, where he converted to Catholicism; painted eight full-length 'Beauties' for the Duke of Somerset and was patronized by Prince George of Denmark and Queen Anne, for whom he shared with Kneller the commission to paint 14 Admirals; d. London; 'a man of great modesty and few words' (Vertue).

575 *Portrait of a Lady* p.148
576 *Portrait of a Man* p.149

Dance, George (1741-1825),

Architect and draughtsman; studied in Italy 1759-64; a pioneer of neo-classical architecture in England; clerk of works to the City of London 1768, but most of his buildings have now disappeared; founder member of the RA 1769, professor of architecture 1798 (resigned 1806); from 1793 he made a series of portrait drawings of his contemporaries, many of which were engraved by William Daniell.

D2 *Sir Francis Bourgeois*, after p.250

Daniell, William (1769-1837)

Landscape painter and engraver, nephew of Thomas Daniell (1749-1840), with whom he travelled to India 1786-93; studied at the RA schools 1799; ARA 1807, RA 1822; apart from engraving many volumes of landscape views, in 1802 he started to engrave the profile portrait drawings by George Dance, 72 of which were published in two volumes in 1808-14; a further 142 appeared posthumously in 1854.

D2 *Sir Francis Bourgeois, after G. Dance* p.250

de Critz, John, the elder, *see* Critz

De Loutherbourg, *see* Loutherbourg

Denning, Stephen Poyntz (1792/5-1864)

Painter and Curator of Dulwich Gallery 1821-64; there is some confusion over his date of birth: *The Athenaeum*, 1864, p.842, stated he died aged 72 (i.e. b. 1792); Redgrave, *Dictionary of Artists*, 1874, stated he was b.1795, and this was repeated in Bryan's *Dictionary* (1886 ed.); started life as a beggar, and was apprenticed for seven years colouring prints, after which he visited Italy; 'his whole progress' being 'extraordinary' (Farington); exhibited RA 1814-52 and BI 1844, exhibiting from the London address of the miniature painter J.W. Wright 1814-17; a posthumous sale of his work was held at Christie's, 17 August 1864. A copy by him in oils from a Teniers at Dulwich (DPG31) was sold Christie's, 19 November 1992, lot 241.

304 *Princess Victoria aged Four* p.202
655 *A Woodman* p.204

Dobson, William (1611-46)

Portrait painter; b. London, his parents of some social standing; studied in London under William Peake and Francis Cleyn, becoming well-acquainted with works in the Royal Collection by Titian and Van Dyck, of whom Dobson was regarded as the natural successor; by 1643 at the latest he was with the Court at Oxford where he painted the King, his family and courtiers; after the fall of Oxford in May 1646 Dobson returned to London, being nominated Steward of the Painter-Stainers' Company on 5 August, but he died that October, in his house in St Martin's Lane, allegedly very poor; 'had his *Education* been but answerable to his *Genius*, *England* might justly have been as proud of her *Dobson*, as *Venice* of her *Titian*, or *Flanders* of her *Van Dyck*' (Graham).

363 *Richard Lovelace* p.56

Doyle, Richard (1824-83)

Illustrator; b. London, son of the caricaturist John Doyle ('H.B.'); his work combined parody and fantasy, best expressed in his regular contributions to Punch 1843-50 for which he designed the cover; his book *In Fairyland* 1869, with verses by William Allingham, received immediate acclaim and was twice re-issued; d. London.

D3 *Lord John Russell 'at home'* p.251

Dubois, Simon (1632-1708)

Portrait painter; b. Antwerp; studied in Haarlem under Berchem 1646 and Wouwermans 1652-53; in Italy with his brother Edward (1619-96), being recorded in Venice 1657 and Rome 1667; c.1680 he joined his brother in London, where he was much favoured by Lord Somers; in 1706 he married the widowed daughter of Willem van de Velde the younger; 'he painted portraits curiously' thought Vertue, 'tho' not very successfull that way being indeed rather a mannerist than a true imitator of flesh and blood'.

584 *Sir William Jones Kt.* p.150
585 *Elizabeth, Lady Jones* p.151

Dyck, Sir Anthony van (1599-1641)

Portrait and history painter; b. Antwerp, where he studied under Hendrik van Balen 1609; by 1618 an independent master in Rubens's studio; in London 1620-21, receiving a pension from the King; in Italy 1621-27, returning to Antwerp 1628 and later in Brussels and The Hague; settled in London 1632, making short visits to the Netherlands in 1634-5 and in 1640 and 1641 when he returned via Paris; Kt. as Principal Painter to the King (Charles I) 1632; granted denization 1638; d. Blackfriars; 'he was a Person *low* of *Stature*, but *well proportion'd*; very *handsome*, *modest*, and extremely *obliging*' (Graham).

194 *Venetia, Lady Digby, on her Deathbed* p.104
170 *George Digby, 2nd Earl of Bristol* p.106
414 *Charles I*, after p.61
381 *Queen Henrietta Maria*, after p.62
426 *Queen Henrietta Maria*, after p.61
420 *Archbishop Laud*, after p.67
352 *The Infants Christ and St John*, after p.83
405 *Portrait of a Man*, after p.205
201 *Portrait of a Lady*, manner of p.108

Dyck, Sir Anthony van (1599-1641)
The following will appear in the Dutch & Flemish volume of the Dulwich catalogue:
90 *Madonna and Child*
127 *Samson and Delilah*
173 *Emmanuel Philibert of Savoy*
132 *Sunset Landscape with a Shepherd and his Flock*, attributed
81 *Charity*, studio of
73 *A Grey Horse*, manner of

Ellys, John (c.1701-57)
Portrait painter and connoisseur; briefly a pupil of Thornhill and J.R. Schmutz before studying with Vanderbank at St Martin's Lane 1720; with Hogarth established the revived St Martin's Lane Academy 1734, remaining as director until 1747; Principal Painter to the Prince of Wales 1736; a frequenter of the boxing ring, he modelled the thighs and legs for Rysbrack's *Hercules* (Stourhead); acted as dealer/agent for Sir Robert Walpole.
441 *James Allen* p.236
495 *James Allen*, attributed p.237

Fisher, Samuel Melton (1860-1939)
Portrait and genre painter; pupil of Dulwich College; studied at Lambeth school of art and the RA schools 1875, where he was awarded a travelling studentship 1882; studied in France and spent much time in Venice; his work was exhibited RA 1878-1940; ARA 1917, RA 1924; a Governor of Dulwich College 1933-39, where there are several of his portraits; d. Camberley.
497 *The Rev Arthur James Carver* p.240

Fuller, Isaac (1606/20-72)
Portrait and history painter, whose early years are obscure; in Oxford 1641 and said to have studied in France under François Perrier (d. 1650) who was in Italy 1635-45; published a print of Jewish costumes in England 1650 and *Un Libro da Designare* 1654; commissioned to paint a group portrait of the court of assistants by the Painter-Stainers' Company 1657; in Oxford undertook decorative schemes for the College Chapels at All Souls 1663, Magdalen by 1664 and Wadham, and worked at the Sheldonian; in 1669 he was living in the parish of St Giles-in-the-Fields; in London he worked as a scene painter and decorated rooms in the Crown and Mitre Taverns; d. London 17 July 1672, his end hastened by intemperance; 'an English history Painter of good note' with 'a great Genius for Drawing and Designing History, yet which he did not always execute with due Decency' (Buckeridge).
379 *Head of a Girl* p.67
569 *Portrait of a Man*, attributed p.152

Gainsborough, Thomas (1727-88)
Portrait and landscape painter, b. Sudbury, Suffolk; studied in London under Gravelot and worked in Francis Hayman's studio; returned to Sudbury 1748/9 and moved to Ipswich 1752; in 1759 he moved to Bath where he became a successful portrait painter; settled in London 1774; exhibited SA 1761-68, and FS 1774, 1783; foundation member of the RA 1768 where he exhibited 1769-72 and 1777-83; a spirited and witty man, he declared 'he painted portraits for money, landscapes because he loved them, and was a musician because he could not help it'; Bourgeois alleged he 'talked bawdy to the King & morality to the Prince of Wales'.
66 *Philippe-Jacques De Loutherbourg* p.108
140 *Thomas Linley the elder* p.130
302 *Samuel Linley* p.132
320 *Elizabeth and Mary Linley* p.134
331 *Thomas Linley the younger* p.136
588 *A Couple in a Landscape* p.154
316 *Mrs Moody with her sons Samuel and Thomas* p.206

Gheeraerts, Marcus, the younger (1561/2-1636)
Portrait painter; b. Netherlands, came to London 1568 with his Protestant father; m. 1590 Magdalen de Critz, sister of the painter John de Critz the elder and of his stepmother; became the preferred painter of Queen Anne of Denmark (d.1619); granted denization 1619, but was soon supplanted in Royal favour by Paul van Somer and Daniel Mytens and thereafter his sitters came increasingly from outside Court circles; d. London.
389 *Portrait of a Lady* p.68

Green, Madeline (1884-1947)
Figure painter; studied at the Slade; member of the Society of Women Artists 1923; exhibited RA 1912-43, Glasgow Institute of the Fine Arts 1916-46 and RSA 1934; lived in Ealing 1912-1940 and exhibited from addresses in Lincolnshire 1941, Norfolk 1942, Bedfordshire 1943 and Norwich 1946.
618 *Self Portrait* p.208

Greenhill, John (1642-76)
Portrait painter; b. Orchardleigh, Somerset, and grew up in Salisbury; by 1662 a pupil in Lely's studio; William Cartwright's six portraits all date from this time and there are other dated works from 1663 to 1673; he associated with actors (Thomas Betterton owned five pictures by him) who allegedly 'debaucht him from his study'; d. London after a drunken fall (he was then lodging with Parry Walton, q.v., in Lincoln's Fields); 'finely qualify'd by *Nature*, for both the *Sister-Arts* of *Painting* and *Poetry.* But *Death*, taking Advantage of his loose, and unguarded Manner of Living, snatch'd him away betimes' (Graham).
393 *William Cartwright* p.46
387 *'Mrs Cartwright'* p.48
399 *A Lady as a Shepherdess* p.49
416 *James II as Duke of York* p.63
374 *Head of a Bearded Man* p.69
418 *Self portrait* p.70
An album of drawings including several by Greenhill belongs to Dulwich College (see *Mr Cartwright's Pictures* 1987, pp.14-15); it probably includes those listed in the Cartwright Inventory as follows:
17 a creon of a mans head with a beard in a black frame couered with a glass, a clossit pece. £3 by grinhill (vide ante p.69).
18 a creon of pallas head, in a black frame couered with glass, a closit pece. £3 by grinhill
19 a creon of a mans head in a black frame couered with glasse a clossit pece. £2 by grinhill.

Grignion, Charles, the younger (1754-1804)
Portrait and history painter; b. London; studied at the RA schools 1769; exhibited RA 1770-84; in 1781 he went to Italy where he also became a *cicerone* and antiquarian; he lived in Rome until 1799 when he moved to Leghorn, where he died. Described by his friend George Cumberland as 'humane, studious, but slow in his studies, and rather inclined to melancholy'.
595 *Thomas Haines* p.156

HARDING, SYLVESTER (1745-1809)
Artist and publisher; b. Newcastle-under-Lyme, Staffs.; studied at the RA schools 1776; exhibited RA 1776-1802; in 1786 (in partnership with his brother Edward until 1798) he opened a print shop in Fleet Street (it moved to Pall Mall in 1792), where engravings of his drawings were sold; among their main publications were *Shakspeare Illustrated* (30 parts with 150 plates) 1789-93, and the *Biographical Mirrour* 1795; Sylvester published a second volume on his own in 1798 and a third was ready for publication at his death; d. London.

D4 *Edward Alleyn* p.251

HASTAIN, EUGÈNE (b. 1887)
Of Brixton, a pupil at Alleyn's School 1896-99.

553 *The Rev Alfred James Carver* p.240

HAYTER, CHARLES (1761-1835)
Miniaturist; b. London; studied at the RA schools 1786; exhibited RA between 1786 and 1832; professor of drawing and perspective to Charlotte, Princess of Wales; d. London; father of the painter Sir George Hayter.

M1 *Sir Francis Bourgeois, after Beechey* p.247
M2 *Noel Desenfans, after Northcote* p.247

HIGHMORE, JOSEPH (1692-1780)
Portrait painter; b. London; well educated, and self confident (according to Vertue), he had studied law before attending the St Martin's Lane Academy under Kneller c.1714 and Vanderbank 1720; visited the Low Countries 1732 and Paris 1734 (his diary of the latter visit surviving); retired to Canterbury 1761; translated Browne's *De animi immortalitate* 1766; d. Canterbury.

566 *Portrait of a Lady* p.157

HODGKINS, THOMAS FRANCIS (fl.1835, d.1903)
Painter and Curator of Dulwich Gallery 1864-1903; b. Dublin; exhibited SBA 1835-53, RA 1836-39, and BI 1836-54.

446 *The Tribute Money* p.208
492 *Samson and the Lion* p.208
493 *Samson and the Philistines* p.208
D5 *London from Flamsteed Hill, after Jan Looten* p.252

HOGARTH, WILLIAM (1697-1764)
Portrait, history and genre painter and engraver; b. London, apprenticed to the goldsmith Ellis Gamble 1714-c.1720 before studying at St Martin's Lane under Vanderbank from 1720 and at Thornhill's drawing school from 1724; with John Ellys founded the revived St Martin's Lane Academy 1734; married Thornhill's daughter in 1729; apart from his very successful painted and engraved 'modern moral subjects', his portraiture developed from the conversation piece c.1729 to imposing single figures from the late 1730s; visited Paris 1748; published the *Analysis of Beauty* 1753; Serjeant Painter to the King 1757; exhibited SA 1761; d. London.

562 *A Fishing Party* p.158
580 *Portrait of a Man* p.160

HORSLEY, WILLIAM CHARLES (1855-1934)
Portrait and view painter; eldest son of the painter J.C. Horsley; studied at the RA schools 1873; exhibited RA 1875-1911 and SBA 1879-80; travelled in India and Egypt 1875-78; a long-serving member of the Artists Rifles of whom he became an Hon. Colonel.

607 *Old-time Tuition at Dulwich College* p.210

HOSKINS, JOHN (c.1595-1665)
Miniaturist; his early life obscure, but Samuel and Alexander Cooper, his nephews, were 'bred up ... under the Care and Discipline of Mr Hoskins' (Graham), Samuel staying with him until 1641/2; by 1639 the King had acquired eight Hoskins miniatures, two of his Queen from the life, the others copies, and he granted Hoskins an annuity in 1640; it is possible that he retired c.1645 and that his practice was continued by his son, also John Hoskins (c.1617–after 1693); d. London, buried St Paul's, Covent Garden.

M3 *Portrait of a Man* p.248

HUDSON, THOMAS (1701-79)
Portrait painter; b. Devonshire; came to London to study under Jonathan Richardson, whose daughter he married in London in 1725; worked in London and the west country before settling in London in 1740, following the retirement of Richardson; Reynolds (another west countryman) was briefly his pupil 1740-43; in the 1740s he became one of the most fashionable portrait painters (with the assistance of Joseph and Alexander Van Aken as skilled drapery painters); visited France and the Netherlands in 1748 with Hogarth, Hayman, the Van Akens and Henry Cheere, and in 1752 he very briefly visited Rome with Roubiliac; exhibited SA 1761 and 1766; retired from painting in 1767; a noted collector; d. Twickenham.

578 *Portrait of a Lady* p.162
579 *Portrait of a Man* p.163

HUYSMANS, JACOB (c.1633-96)
Portrait and history painter; b. Antwerp where he studied under Frans Wouters 1649-50; before 1660 he was in London where, presumably as a Catholic, he found favour from Queen Catherine of Braganza, whom he painted on several occasions; his elaborate continental Baroque style distinguished him amongst contemporary English painters; d. London.

362 *Portrait of a Lady* p.71

HYSING, HANS (1678-1758)
Portrait painter; b. Stockholm, where he studied under David von Krafft; came to London 1700 and, encouraged by his compatriot Michael Dahl and facilitated by his gentle charm, built up an extensive portrait practice, his sitters including the eldest daughters of George II and Sir Robert Walpole; in 1752 he witnessed Dahl's daughter's will; d. London; 'a Vertuous & valuable example of the present age' (Vertue).

604 *John Dive*, circle of p.164

JERVAS, CHARLES (c.1675-1739)
Portrait painter; b. Shinrone, King's Co., Ireland; a pupil of Kneller 1694-95, he then studied in Paris 1699 and Rome 1700-09 (when he told Addison he pitied poor Titian); succeeded Kneller as Principal Painter to the King 1723 but 'had no success in their Majesties pictures & from thence he lost much favour & Interest at Court' (Vertue); m. 1726 Penelope Hume, a very rich widow; he was in Italy 1738-39 buying pictures for the Royal collection and seeking a cure for poor health; a friend of Swift and Pope and the translator of *Don Quijote* (published posthumously in 1742); d. London, six months after his return from Italy.

567 *Dorothy, Viscountess Townshend* p.165

Johnson, Cornelius (1593-1661)
[Cornelius Jonson (or Janssen) van Ceulen] Portrait painter; b. London of a Flemish/German immigrant family; appointed one of the King's Painters 1632 and still in the King's service in 1641; returned to the Netherlands in 1643, settling in 1652 in Utrecht where he d.. His son (b. 1634) of the same name was also a portrait painter; his portrait of a Dutch Gentleman (DPG564), signed *Cornelius Jonson/ van Ceulen/ fecit/ 1657*, will appear in the Dutch catalogue.

Kettle, Tilly (1734-86)
Portrait painter; b. London; studied at Shipley's Academy and probably St Martin's Lane and the Duke of Richmond's Academy; exhibited FS 1761, SA 1765-76 and RA 1777 and 1781-83; the first professional English portrait painter to go to India, he arrived in Madras in June 1769 and returned to London in November 1776; set out overland for India in 1786, but died in the desert near Aleppo.

Knapton, George (1698-1778)
Portrait painter in oil and pastel; b. London, nephew of the bookseller James Knapton; studied under Jonathan Richardson 1715-22 and at the St Martin's Lane Academy; in Italy 1725-32; painter to the Society of Dilettanti 1736; retired from painting c.1755; appointed Surveyor and Keeper of the King's Pictures 1765; d. London.

Kneller, Sir Godfrey (1646-1723)
(Gottfried Kniller) Portrait painter; b. Lübeck; studied under Ferdinand Bol in Holland; travelled in Italy and France before settling in London in 1676; letters of denization 1683; Principal Painter to William and Mary 1688 (jointly with Riley who d.1791) and thereafter to Queen Anne and George I; Kt. 1692; first governor of the Kneller Academy at Great Queen Street 1711; Bt. 1715; d. London, having 'always lived in the greatest esteem & reputation' (Buckeridge).

Landseer, Sir Edwin (1802-73)
Animalier and portrait painter; b. London; studied at the RA schools 1816; ARA 1826; RA 1831; exhibited RA 1815-73 (animal subjects considerably outweighing portraiture); Kt. 1850; elected PRA 1866 but declined the post due to ill health; d. London.

Lane, Samuel (1780-1859)
Portrait painter; b. King's Lynn; pupil of Farington and Lawrence, whose chief studio assistant he became, overcoming the disadvantages of deafness and partial dumbness; exhibited RA 1804-57, BI 1819 and SBA 1832; retired in 1853 to Ipswich where he died.

Lawrence, Sir Thomas (1769-1830)
Portrait painter; b. Devizes, Wilts.; an infant prodigy, by October 1780 he was in Bath, where he stayed six years taking pastel portraits; by the spring of 1787 he was in London; studied at the RA schools 1787; exhibited RA from 1787; appointed Painter-in-Ordinary to the King 1792; ARA 1791; RA 1794; Kt. 1815; PRA 1820.

Lely, Sir Peter (1618-80)
Pieter van der Faes, known as Peter Lely, portrait and history painter; b. Soest, Westphalia, of Dutch parents; studied in Haarlem under F.P. de Grebber and became a master of the Haarlem Guild 1637; came to England c.1641; Principal Painter to Charles II 1660; Kt. 1680; 'it is hard to determine whether he was the more compleat Painter or Gentleman' (Buckeridge).

Lonsdale, James (1777-1839)
Portrait painter; b. Lancaster; studied in London under Romney and at the RA schools from 1801; exhibited RA 1802-38; active in the formation of the Society of British Artists with whom he exhibited 1824-37; portrait painter to Queen Charlotte.

Loutherbourg, Philip Jacques De (1740-1812)
Landscape painter; b. Strasbourg; trained in Paris under Carl van Loo and Francesco Casanova; elected to the *académie* 1767 when appointed *peintre du roi*; came to London 1771; exhibited RA 1772-1812; RA 1780; a noted scenic painter for Sheridan's Drury Lane theatre and inventor of the popular Eidophosiukon, a dramatic peep show, 'an imitation of Natural Phenomena, represented by Moving Pictures'.

Monamy, Peter (1681-1749)
Marine painter; b. London, s. of a Guernsey merchant; studied under a house-painter 1696-1703; freeman of the Painter-Stainers' Company 1704; modeling his style on that of Willem van de Velde (d. 1707), he became 'much esteem'd among sea-faring people, officers and other marchants etc' (Vertue); d. London; his collection, which was sold on 26 July 1750, included many drawings by Willem van der Velde senior and junior.

Morris, William Bright (1844-1915)
Landscape, portrait and genre painter; studied at Manchester School of Art, South Kensington and the RA schools; exhibited RA 1869-1900 and the Glasgow Institute of the Fine Arts 1897; drawing master of Henry Yates Thompson with whom he travelled in Spain 1876; Yates Thompson commissioned three copies from him c.1901 (and see also DPG304, p.202).

Muller, Robert (1773-c.1800)
Portrait painter; studied at the RA schools 1788; exhibited RA 1789-1800, his sitters including some of George III's children.

Murray, Charles Fairfax (1849-1919)
See p.145.

Nixon, John (c.1750-1818)
A merchant and spirited amateur draughtsman who illustrated his extensive travels in Britain; an amateur actor and convivial host; hon. exhibitor RA 1781-1813; d. Ryde, Isle of Wight (see Christie's sale cats., 4 June 1974, p.14, and 5 November 1974, p.18; K. Sloan, *A Noble Art*, British Museum, 2000, no.142).

Northcote, James (1746-1831)
Portrait and history painter; b. Plymouth; studied at the RA schools 1771; worked in the studio of Reynolds 1771-76; in Italy 1777-80; exhibited RA 1773-1828, BI 1806-31; ARA 1786, RA 1787; an elegant biographer and conversationalist; d. London.

Oliver, Arthur James (1774-1842)
Portrait painter; studied at the RA schools 1790; exhibited RA 1791-1841 and BI 1809-41; from 1830 turned increasingly to still life and historical groups, but failing health curtailed his practice; curator of the RA painting schools 1835.

Opie, John (1761-1807)
Portrait and history painter; b. St Agnes, Cornwall; came to London 1781 and hailed as 'the Cornish wonder'; exhibited RA 1782-1807; ARA 1786, RA 1787; professor of painting at the RA 1805; d. London.

Pether, Abraham (1756-1812)
Landscape and marine painter; b. Chichester where he studied under George Smith; the moonlit water scenes, for which he became best known, first appeared c.1784; exhibited FS 1773-83; SA 1777-80, 1790-91, and RA 1784-1811; d. Southampton.

Prosperi, Christopher (fl.1800-16)
Cristoforo Prosperi, sculptor; in Italy in 1800 when he carved the bust of Sir George Throckmorton after Hewetson (Coughton Court); exhibited (as C. Prosperi) RA 1810-16 from London addresses; an unsuccessful ARA candidate in 1811 and 1814; his *Venus and Cupid* and *Bacchus and Ariadne* of c.1812 are at Stratfield Saye (information from Ingrid Roscoe most gratefully acknowledged).

Reynolds, Sir Joshua (1723-92)
Portrait and history painter; b. Plympton, Devon; studied in London under Thomas Hudson 1740-43; in Italy 1750-52; exhibited SA 1760-68; founder member and first President of the RA 1768, where he exhibited annually until 1790; Kt. 1769; Painter in Ordinary to the King 1784; his extensive portrait business led to an elaborate studio practice amd although his painting technique was not always sound, his fifteen *Discourses* on theory, given at the Royal Academy between 1769 and 1790, became canonical; d. London.

In 1804 Desenfans owned two paintings by Reynolds, each called 'A Little Girl' and each insured for £100 (Desenfans 1804, nos.66 & 67); they did not form part of the Bourgeois Bequest in 1811.

Riley, John (1646-91)
Portrait painter; b. London; pupil of Isaac Fuller and Gerard Soest; on Lely's death he was introduced to Charles II by William Chiffinch (see DPG568) but did not succeed; Freeman of the Painter-Stainers' Company 1682; appointed principal painter toWilliam and Mary with Kneller 1688; worked in partnership with John Closterman (1660-1711) who painted his draperies c.1781-83 and possibly completed pictures Riley left unfinished at his death; d. London; according to Vertue 'a Gentleman extreamly Courteous in his Behaviour, Engaging in his Conversation, & Prudent in all his actions' .

Romney, George (1734-1802)
Portrait painter; b. Beckside, Dalton-in-Furness, Lancashire; studied under Christopher Steele in Lancashire 1755 and practised as a portrait painter in Kendal before coming to London in 1762; visited Paris 1764 and Italy 1773-75; exhibited FS 1763-69 and SA 1770-72; his fashionable portrait practice ended through poor health and he retired to Kendal in 1799.

Russell, John (1745-1806)
Portrait painter in oil and pastel; b. Guildford; following his conversion in 1764 he became an ardent evangelist; studied under Francis Cotes until 1767 and the RA schools 1770; exhibited SA 1768 and RA 1769-1806; published *Elements of Painting with Crayons* 1772; in 1790 appointed Crayon Painter to the King and to the Prince of Wales; d. Hull.

Sandby, Paul (1730-1809)
Draughtsman and topographer; b. Nottingham; worked on a survey of Scotland 1747-52; settled in London 1753; pioneer of aquatint and a popular drawing master; exhibited SA 1760-68; foundation member RA 1768; exhibited RA 1769-1809, BI 1806-08; d. London.

Smart, John I (1756-after 1830)

Portrait, landscape and history painter; b. Ufford, Suffolk; admitted to the RA schools 1 April 1782, aged 27; exhibited RA 1786-1813; c.1787 he settled in Ipswich, where he painted many portraits and several altar-pieces (e.g. the *Christ at Emmaus* at St Nicholas, 1807) and landscapes; exhibited from Ipswich at the SA 1791 and BI 1812-14; living in Ipswich in 1830 (Clarke's *History and Description of Ipswich*, 1830). Whitley (1928a, ii, p.154) refers to John Smart the Ipswich painter observing Reynolds's *modus operandi.*

635 *Self Portrait* p.220
636 *Mrs John Smart I* p.220
637 *Miss Planner* p.221
639 *Self Portrait* p.221

Smart, John II (fl.1822-50)

Portrait painter, son of John Smart I; exhibited RA 1833 and 1850, from London and Ipswich addresses respectively; perhaps the John Smart who exhibited history pieces at the BI 1822-33 from London addresses.

634 *Charles and George Smart, sons of John Smart II* p.222
638 *Mrs John Smart II* p.222
640 *Portrait of a Lady* p.223

Soest, Gerard (1602-81)

(R.H. Merley, *ODNB*, suggests his first name was Gilbert, not Gerard) Portrait painter; of Dutch parentage, he came to London in the 1640s, as shown by the so-called *Sir Thomas and Lady Fairfax* in the National Portrait Gallery (754); by 1657 he was living in Lincoln's Inn Fields, later moving to Cursiters Court where he died; according to Vertue 'his ruff humour' did not please his lady sitters.

573 *Aubrey de Vere, 20th Earl of Oxford* p.182
592 *Sir Henry Vane the younger Kt.* p.184

Soldi, Andrea (c.1703-1771)

Portrait painter; b. Florence; from c.1733 worked profitably in the Levant painting English merchants, before settling in London 1736; his extravagance led to brief imprisonment for debt in 1744; in Scotland c.1756-58; exhibited SA 1760-66, being elected a Fellow 1765, and at the Free Society 1769; he applied to the Royal Academy for charity in 1771, in which year his funeral in London was paid for by Sir Joshua Reynolds.

603 *Louis-François Roubiliac* p.185

Spanton, H. Margaret (1874-1934)

Daughter of the artist and writer William Silas Spanton (1845-1930) and a pupil of Charles Fairfax Murray, her father's close friend; exhibited from Barnet at the New English Art Club 1901-05; bequeathed five pictures to Dulwich in 1934 (see also attributed to Beale DPG611, by Murray DPG612 and British School DPG613); three of her works are in the Brighton and Hove Museum (one dated 1913), presented by Miss J.K. Tarrant in 1935.

641 *Female Nude* p.223
642 *Portrait of a Lady* p.224

Spencer, Gervase (fl.1740-63)

Miniaturist in watercolour and enamel; according to Vertue he was self-taught, having been a footman; dated examples range between 1745 and 1761.

M5 *Portrait of a Lady*, attributed p.249

Stoppelaer, Charles (fl.1703-57)

Portrait painter and actor; a quarter brother of the Guild of St Luke, Dublin, in 1703, made free in 1708; he played on the Irish Stage; sometime before 1737 he went to London, and there are signed and dated portraits in Norwich of 1756 and 1757.

496 *James Allen* p.237

Streeter, Robert, the elder (1624?-79)

Landscape painter; probably travelled in Italy during the Commonwealth; in London in 1658 and Serjeant Painter by 1660-1, painting and guilding Royal coaches, but was soon acknowledged to be 'the greatest and most universal painter that England ever bred', excelling in 'history, architecture and perspective' and a 'very good historian' (Buckeridge); Charles II owned a copy by him after Titian and James II had four of his landscapes; Evelyn described him as 'a very civil little man and lame, but lives very handsomely.' His son Robert succeeded him as Serjeant Painter and d. 'a prosperous gentleman in St Martins-in-the-Fields' in 1711, when his father's books, drawings, casts and prints were sold.

376 *Landscape* p.85

Thornhill, Sir James (1675-1734)

Decorative painter; b. in Dorset; apprenticed to Thomas Highmore in London 1689; first practised as a scenery painter 1705; a director of the Kneller Academy in 1711 and Governor 1716-20; visited the Low Countries 1711 and Paris 1717; in 1718 made History Painter to the King, Sergeant Painter (resigned 1732), Master of the Painter-Stainers' Company and Kt.; MP for Weymouth 1722; FRS 1723; his greatest surviving decorative scheme (1708-27) is at Greenwich Hospital; d. Thornhill Park, Dorset.

D10 *A Group of Connoisseurs* p.254

Vanderbank, John (1694-1739)

Portrait and history painter; b. London, s. of the tapestry weaver John Vanderbank; studied at the Kneller Academy 1711, in 1720 he succeeded Thornhill as governor and (with Chéron) moved the Academy to St Martin's Lane; a gifted, fluent painter and draughtsman whom only intemperance, according to Vertue, prevented from achieving the highest reputation; d. London.

581 *Portrait of a Lady* p.186

Van Dyck, *see* Dyck

Walton, Henry (1745/6-1813)

Genre and portrait painter, b. Dickleburgh, near Diss, Norfolk; went to London 1765; studied under Zoffany c.1770; exhibited SA 1771-3 and 1776, becoming a director in 1772; exhibited RA 1777-79.

589 *Portrait of a Man*, attributed p.187

Walton, Parry (d. 1702)

Still life painter; according to Buckeridge he studied under Robert Walker (1599-1658), painted still life 'very well' and became known for his connoisseurship; shared rooms with Greenhill in Lincoln's Inn Fields (Greenhill died in his home); Surveyor or Repairer of the King's Pictures under William III, in which office he was succeeded by his son Peter (who d. c.1745 aged 'about 80'); buried in St Giles-in-the-Fields.

429 *Still Life* p.86

CHANGES OF ATTRIBUTION SINCE 1998

DPG	*page*	*1998 attribution*	*current attribution*
363	56	attributed to Dobson	Dobson
384	31	after de Critz	British School
396		*British School*	*Netherlandish School (i.e. not in the present catalogue)*
405	205	British School	after Van Dyck
417	32	after Isaac Oliver	British School
488	103	attributed to Bourgeois	Bourgeois
496	237	British School	Stoppelaer
503	127	Unknown	British School
561	190	attributed to Hoare	British School
569	152	British School	attributed to Fuller
573	182	attributed to Soest	Soest
589	187	British School	attributed to Henry Walton
595	156	attributed to Grignion	Grignion
596	170	Hudson	attributed to Knapton
604	164	British School	circle of Hysing
624	215	British School	attributed to Abraham Pether
636	220	British School	Smart I
640	223	British School	Smart I
642	224	British School	Spanton

PREVIOUS OWNERS AND SALES

PREVIOUS OWNERS

NUMERICAL INDEX

CONCORDANCE WITH PREVIOUS CATALOGUES

KEY

DPG
Present picture number. From 1858 until 1890 the pictures were numbered differently.

1858
S.P. Denning assisted by his son the Rev Stephen Denning, 'Catalogue of Pictures', 1858 (ms, Dulwich Picture Gallery archive; unfoliated, listed in order of the old picture numbers up to no.366)

1859
S.P. Denning, 'Catalogue of Pictures', 1859 (ms, Dulwich Picture Gallery archive; unfoliated, listed in order of the old picture numbers up to no.202)

1876
J.C.L. Sparkes, *A Descriptive Catalogue of the Pictures in the Dulwich College Gallery*, 1876 'the first printed catalogue to be more than a list of names' (Bourgeois Bequest alone; alphabetically by artist)

1880
J.P. Richter & J.C.L. Sparkes, *Catalogue of the Pictures in the Dulwich College Gallery*, 1880 (a revision of the 1876 catalogue; Bourgeois Bequest alone, alphabetically by artist)

1890
J.C.L. Sparkes and A.J. Carver, *Catalogue of the Cartwright Collection and other Pictures and Portraits at Dulwich College* (numbered consecutively by groups – portraits, subject pictures, landscapes and sea-pieces, animals etc., Kings and Queens, Sibyls and Virtues)

1892
J.P. Richter & J.C.L. Sparkes, *Catalogue of the Pictures in the Gallery of Alleyn's College of God's Gift at Dulwich*, 1892 (combining the 1880 and 1890 catalogues; alphabetically by artist, a separate sequence listing pictures not exhibited)

1905
Catalogue of the Pictures in the gallery of Alleyn's College of God's Gift at Dulwich, 1905 (revised 4th edition of the 1892 catalogue, without authors' names)

1914
Sir Edward Cook, *Catalogue of the Pictures in the gallery of Alleyn's College of God's Gift at Dulwich*, 1914 (nos. 1-593 listed in order of accession number)

1926
Sir Edward Cook, *Catalogue of the Pictures in the gallery of Alleyn's College of God's Gift at Dulwich*, 1914, revised 1926 (nos. 1-608 listed in order of accession number)

1980
P. Murray, *The Dulwich Picture Gallery, A Catalogue*, 1980 (listed alphabetically by artist, divided into Exhibited and Non-Exhibited Paintings, the latter summarily listed pp.299-305)

1998
R.B. Beresford, *Dulwich Picture Gallery, Complete Illustrated Catalogue*, 1998

2008
the present catalogue

In the table below the given picture number is followed by the page number; thus 6/299 means that DPG6 appears on p.299 (in the 1980 Dulwich catalogue). As noted above, from 1858 until 1890 the pictures were numbered differently.

In the 1858 and 1859 MSS catalogues there is no foliation; picture numbers alone are given.

DPG	1858	1859	1876	1880	1890	1892	1905	1914	1926	1980	1998	2008
6	88	88	88/19	88/20	—	6/2	6/2	6/7	6/7	6/299	6/48	6/92
17	356	—	356/8	356/7	—	17/5	17/5	17/11	17/11	17/26	17/36	17/194
17A	356	—	356/138	356/131	—	356/5	17/5	17/11	17/11	17 /103	17 /196	17 /215
28	338	—	338/108	338/107	—	28/7	28/7	28/17	28/17	28/ 87	28/169	28/114
66	111	111	111/68	111/69	—	66/17	66/17	66/37	66/36	66/59	66/106	66/108
80	122	122	122/187	122/84	—	80/20	80/20	80/44	80/43	80/299	80/139	80/110
89	134	134	134/188	134/84	—	89/23	89/23	89/50	89/53	89/299	89/139	89/110
94	3	3	3/112	3/110	—	94/24	94/24	94/55	94/52	94/299	94/173	94/116
100	127	127	127/20	127/21	—	100/25	100/25	100/56	100/56	100/299	100/48	100/92
102	143	143	143/138	143/131	—	102/26	102/26	102/57	102/60	102/103	102/196	102/116
104	146	146	146/138	146/131	—	104/26	104/26	104/62	104/59	104/103	104/198	104/119
111	153	153	153/7	153/6	—	111/28	111/28	111/66	111/62	111/27	111/36	111/88
135	59	59	59/18	59/20	—	135/34	135/34	135/81	135/76	135/299	135/48	135/93
140	358	—	358/66	358/69	—	140/35	140/35	140/83	140/79	140/59	140/107	130/140
149	—	—	371/20	371/21	—	149/38	149/38	149/89	149/84	149/299	149/48	149/93
150	51	51	51/155	51/147	—	150/39	150/39	150/89	150/84	150/299	150/264	150/124
151	353	—	353/81	353/71	—	151/39	151/39	151/89	151/84	151/299	151/274	151/125
169	97	97	97/7	97/6	—	169/44	169/44	169/104	169/98	169/27	169/ 36	169/90
170	214	—	214/189	214/52	—	170/44	170/44	170/104	170/98	170/54	170/ 98	170/106
171	215	—	215/207	215/188	—	171/45	171/45	171/105	171/99	171/139	171/262	171/122
172	183	183	183/108	183/106	—	172/45	172/45	172/107	172/101	172/87	172/170	172/115
178	359	—-	359/89	359/89	—	178/47	178/47	178/112	178/105	178/76	178/146	178/138
194	242	—-	242/190	242/53	—	194/51	194/51	194/123	194/115	194/55	194/99	194/104
200	213	—-	213/188	213/54	—	200/54	200/54	200/126	200/119	200/300	200/274	200/126
201	250	—-	250/190	250/53	—	201/54	201/54	201/126	201/119	201/300	201/101	201/108
223	285	—-	285/139	285/132	—	223/60	223/60	223/138	223/130	223/104	223/199	223/117
291	—-	—-	—-	—-	53/32	291/80	291/80	291/180	291/168	291/32	291/55	291/196
294	4	4	4/17	4/18	—	294/80	294/80	294/182	294/170	294/301	294/49	294/94
297	55	55	55/94	55/94	—	297/81	297/81	297/183	297/171	297/80	297/155	297/111
298	92	92	92/100	92/98	—	298/81	298/81	298/185	298/173	298/301	298/158	298/113
301	82	82	82/19	82/20	—	301/82	301/82	301/186	301/174	301/301	301/49	301/94
302	361	—-	361/69	361/69	—	302/82	302/82	302/187	302/174	302/60	302/107	302/132
304	—	—	—	—	—	304/82	304/82	304/187	304/175	302/50	302/87	304/202
308	—	—	370/20	370/21	—	308/83	308/83	308/189	308/177	308/301	308/49	308/95
310	20	20	20/17	20/19	—	310/83	310/83	310/190	310/177	310/301	310/49	310/95
311	24	24	24/18	24/19	—	311/84	311/84	311/190	311/177	311/301	311/50	311/95
316	—	—	366/69	366/70	—	316/85	316/85	316/191	316/179	316/ 60	316/108	316/206
318	340	—	340/139	340/132	—	318/85	318/85	318/192	318/180	318/104	318/197	318/120
320	1	1	1/66	1/67	—	320/87	320/87	320/196	320/183	320/60	320/108	320/134
325	38	38	38/18	38/19	—	325/91	325/91	325/200	325/187	325/301	325/50	325/96
331	362	—	362/69	362/70	—	331/92	331/92	331/203	331/189	331/61	331/110	331/136
333	138	138	138/137	138/131	—	333/93	333/93	333/204	333/190	333/105	333/198	333/118
335	23	23	23/17	23/19	—	335/93	335/93	335/204	335/190	335/301	335/50	335/97
339	89	89	89/94	89/94	—	339/94	339/94	339/205	339/191	339/80	339/155	339/112
342	25	25	25/18	25/19	—	342/95	342/95	342/206	342/192	342/301	342/50	342/98

DPG	1858	1859	1876	1880	1890	1892	1905	1914	1926	1980	1998	2008
344	95	95	95/19	95/21	—	344/95	344/95	344/207	344/193	344/301	344/51	344/98
346	—	—	—	—	—	346/95	346/95	346/207	346/193	346/301	346/262	346/224
352	—	—	—	—	81/39	352/97	352/97	352/210	352/195	352/301	352/100	352/83
354	—	—	—	—	62/34	354/97	354/97	354/210	354/196	354/301	354/274	354/72
359	—	—	—	—	113/45	359/99	359/99	359/212	359/198	359/42	359/67	359/78
360	—	—	—	—	112/44	360/99	360/99	360/213	360/198	360/29	360/42	360/76
361	— —	—	—	—	118/45	361/100	361/100	361/213	361/198	361/42	361/67	361/78
362	—	—	—	—	67/36	362/100	362/100	362/213	362/100	362/301	362/136	362/71
363	—	—	—	—	18/14	363/100	363/100	363/214	363/199	363/301	363/88	363/56
364	—	—	—	—	16/13	364/101	364/101	364/216	364/201	364/301	364/275	364/54
365	—	—	—	—	17/14	365/101	365/101	365/216	365/201	365/301	365/275	365/56
367	—	—	—	—	15/13	367/101	367/101	367/216	367/201	367/301	367/275	367/54
368	—	—	—	—	23/15	368/101	368/101	368/217	368/202	368/302	368/275	368/40
369	—	—	—	—	25/16	369/102	369/102	369/217	369/202	369/302	369/276	369/41
370	—	—	—	—	22/15	370/102	370/102	370/218	370/203	370/302	370/276	370/41
371	—	—	—	—	108/43	371/102	371/102	371/218	371/203	371/45	371/ 74	371/82
372	—	—	—	—	14/13	372/103	372/103	372/218	372/203	372/302	372/276	372/53
373	—	—	—	—	20/15	373/103	373/103	373/219	373/203	373/302	373/276	373/59
374	—	—	—	—	65/36	374/103	374/103	374/219	374/204	374/ 62	374/116	374/69
375	—	—	—	—	4/9	375/103	375/103	375/220	375/205	375/32	375/277	375/74
376	—	—	—	—	109/44	376/104	376/104	376/220	376/205	376/122	376/226	376/85
377	—	—	—	—	66/36	377/104	377/104	377/221	377/206	376/302	377/277	377/74
378	—	—	—	—	19/14	378/104	378/104	378/221	378/206	378/302	378/277	378/58
379	—	—	—	—	69/36	379/104	379/104	379/222	379/206	379/302	379/105	379/67
381	—	—	—	—	13/12	381/105	381/105	381/224	381/209	381/302	381/101	381/62
384	—	—	—	—	6/10	384/105	384/105	384/225	384/210	384/302	384/ 79	384/31
385	—	—	—	—	50/30	385/106	385/106	385/225	385/210	385/33	385/207	385/64
387	—	—	—	—	33/20	387/107	387/107	387/227	387/211	387/62	387/116	387/48
388	—	—	—	—	34/20	388/107	388/107	388/227	388/211	388/302	388/278	388/51
389	—	—	—	—	63/35	389/107	389/107	389/227	389/211	389/302	389/113	389/68
390	—	—	—	—	52/32	390/108	390/108	390/228	390/212	390/33	390/278	390/65
391	—	—	—	—	49/29	391/108	391/108	391/228	391/212	391/33	391/278	391/65
392	—	—	—	—	10/11	392/109	392/109	392/229	392/213	392/302	392/278	392/60
393	—	—	—	—	29/18	393/109	393/109	393/230	393/214	393/63	393/116	393/46
395	—	—	—	—	48/27	395/111	395/111	395/232	395/216	395/33	395/279	395/66
399	—	—	—	—	32/20	399/113	399/113	399/233	399/216	399/63	399/117	399/49
400	—	—	—	—	30/19	400/113	4 00/113	400/233	400/216	400/34	400/279	400/50
405	—	—	—	—	64/35	405/114	405/114	405/234	405/218	405/302	405/279	405/205
408	—	—	—	—	87/40	408/115	408/115	408/235	408/218	408/302	408/152	408/84
411	—	—	—	—	31/19	411/115	411/115	411/236	411/219	411/34	411/280	411/52
414	—	—	—	—	8/11	414/116	414/116	414/236	414/220	414/302	414/101	414/61
415	—	—	—	—	74/38	415/116	415/116	415/237	415/220	415/302	415/280	415/244
416	—	—	—	—	12/12	416/116	416/116	416/237	416/220	416/64	416/118	416/63
417	—	—	—	—	7/10	417/117	417/117	417/237	417/220	417/302	417/172	417/32
418	—	—	—	—	27/17	418/117	418/117	418/238	418/221	418/64	418/118	418/70

DPG	1858	1859	1876	1880	1890	1892	1905	1914	1926	1980	1998	2008
419	—	—	—	—	24/16	419/117	419/117	419/238	419/222	419/302	419/280	419/42
420	—	—	—	—	26/17	420/118	420/118	420/239	420/222	420/302	420/101	420/67
421	—	—	—	—	21/15	421/118	421/118	421/239	421/222	421/302	421/280	421/42
423	—	—	—	—	51/31	423/118	423/118	423/239	423/223	423/35	423/281	423/66
424	—	—	—	—	11/12	424/119	424/119	424/240	424/223	424/143	424/270	424/62
426	—	—	—	—	9/11	426/119	426/119	426/241	426/224	426/302	426/101	426/61
427	—	—	—	—	60/34	427/120	427/119	427/241	427/224	427/302	427/281	427/43
428	—	—	—	—	115/45	428/120	428/120	428/241	428/224	428/42	428/67	428/79
429	—	—	—	—	124/46	429/120	429/120	429/241	429/224	429/302	429/254	429/86
430	—	—	—	—	5/10	430/120	430/120	430/242	430/225	430/35	430/281	430/75
431	—	—	—	—	78/38	431/121	431/121	431/242	431/225	431/46	431/74	431/83
436	—	—	—	—	116/45	436/121	436/121	436/243	436/226	436/42	436/67	436/80
437	—	—	—	—	119/46	437/122	437/122	437/243	437/226	437/42	437/67	437/80
438	—	—	—	—	43/26	43/137	438/122	438/244	438/227	438/302	438/281	438/241
439	—	—	—	—	46/26	46/138	439/122	439/244	439/227	439/302	439/282	439/241
440	—	—	—	—	39/23	39/135	440/122	440/244	440/227	440/109	440/204	440/238
441	—	—	—	—	37/22	37/134	441/123	441/246	441/228	441/302	441/102	441/236
442	—	—	—	—	—	—	442/123	442/246	442/229	442/302	442/76	442/243
443	—	—	—	—	1/7	1/131	443/123	443/247	443/230	443/35	443/282	443/20
444	—	—	—	—	35/21	35/133	444/125	444/249	444/231	444/35	444/282	444/22
445	—	—	—	367/196	—	367/129	445/125	445/249	445/232	445/36	445/282	445/228
446	—	—	—	—	—	—	446/126	446/250	446/233	446/302	446/126	446/208
447	—	—	—	—	40/24	40/135	447/126	447/251	447/233	447/302	447/143	447/258
448	—	—	—	—	42/25	42/137	448/127	448/252	448/235	448/302	448/283	448/243
449	—	—	—	—	54/32	54/138	449/128	449/253	449/235	449/74	449/144	449/211
453	—	—	—	—	—	—	453/129	453/255	453/237	453/303	453/263	453/226
454	—	—	—	—	—	—	454/129	454/255	454/237	454/303	454/263	454/227
456	—	—	—	—	47/26	47/138	456/129	456/255	456/237	456/80	456/154	456/142
459	57	57	57/1	57/19	—	57/123	57/131	459/258	459/239	459/303	459/51	459/98
460	74	74	74/18	74/20	—	74/123	74/131	460/258	460/240	460/303	460/51	460/99
461	91	91	91/19	91/20	—	91/123	91/131	461/258	461/240	461/303	461/51	461/99
462	96	96	96/19	96/21	—	96/124	96/132	462/258	462/240	462/303	462/52	462/100
463	109	109	109/19	109/21	—	109/124	109/132	463/259	463/240	463/303	463/52	463/100
464	—	—	368/20	368/21	—	368/124	368/132	464/259	464/240	464/303	464/52	464/195
465	—	—	372/20	372/21	—	372/124	372/132	465/259	465/241	465/303	465/52	465/101
466	—	—	373/20	373/21	—	373/124	373/132	466/259	466/241	466/26	466/52	466/101
467	—	—	374/20	374/22	—	374/124	374/132	467/259	467/241	467/303	467/53	467/102
474	357	357	357/88	357/89	—	357/125	357/133	474/261	474/243	474/76	474/147	474/141
475	360	—	360/89	360/90	—	360/126	360/134	475/262	475/244	475/76	475/147	475/140
476	—	—	369/115	369/113	—	369/126	369/134	476/263	476/244	476/88	476/172	476/143
483	254	—	254/138	254/131	—	254/127	254/135	483/265	483/246	483/303	483/198	483/259
486	321	—	321/217	321/195	—	321/129	321/136	486/267	486/248	486/303	486/283	486/126
488	—	—	377/219	377/196	—	377/130	377/136	488/268	488/248	488/303	488/53	488/103
491	—	—	—	—	—	384/145	384/138	491/270	491/251	491/303	491/53	491/257
492	—	—	—	—	—	385/145	385/138	492/270	492/251	492/303	492/126	492/208

DPG	1858	1859	1876	1880	1890	1892	1905	1914	1926	1980	1998	2008
493	—	—	—	—	—	386/145	386/138	493/270	493/251	493/303	493/126	493/208
494	—	—	—	—	28/17	28/132	28/139	494/271	494/252	494/303	494/283	494/229
495	—	—	—	—	36/22	36/133	36/139	495/271	495/252	495/303	495/284	495/237
496	—	—	—	—	38/23	38/134	38/139	496/271	496/252	496/303	496/284	496/237
497	—	—	—	—	41/24	41/136	41/140	497/272	497/253	497/303	497/102	497/240
498	—	—	—	—	44/26	44/137	44/140	498/273	498/253	498/303	498/284	498/242
499	—	—	—	—	45/26	45/138	45/140	499/273	499/254	499/303	499/55	499/242
500	—	—	—	—	55/33	55/139	55/141	500/273	500/254	500/303	500/144	500/212
502	—	—	—	—	72/37	72/139	72/141	502/274	502/254	502/303	502/310	502/260
503	— —	—	—	—	73/37	73/139	73/141	503/274	503/254	503/303	503/310	503/127
504	—	—	—	—	75/38	75/140	75/142	504/275	504/255	504/303	504/284	504/244
517	—	—	—	—	114/45	114/142	114/144	517/277	517/258	517/42	517/67	517/81
518	—	—	—	—	117/45	117/142	117/144	518/278	518/258	518/303	518/68	518/8
519	—	—	—	—	120/46	120/142	120/144	519/278	519/258	519/303	519/78	519/200
521	—	—	—	—	130/48	130/142	130/144	521/278	521/259	521/303	521/285	521/23
522	—	—	—	—	131/48	131/142	131/144	522/278	522/259	522/304	522/285	522/24
523	—	—	—	—	132/48	132/142	132/144	523/278	523/259	523/304	523/285	523/24
524	—	—	—	—	133/48	133/142	133/144	524/279	524/259	524/304	524/285	524/24
525	—	—	—	—	134/48	134/142	134/144	525/279	525/259	525/304	525/286	525/25
526	—	—	—	—	135/48	135/143	135/145	526/279	526/259	526/304	526/286	526/26
527	—	—	—	—	136/48	136/143	136/145	527/279	527/259	527/304	527/286	527/26
528	—	—	—	—	137/48	137/143	137/145	528/279	528/259	528/304	528/286	528/27
529	—	—	—	—	138/48	138/143	138/148	529/279	529/259	529/304	529/287	529/28
530	—	—	—	—	139/48	139/143	139/145	530/279	530/259	530/304	530/287	530/27
531	—	—	—	—	140/48	140/143	140/145	531/279	531/259	531/304	531/287	531/28
532	—	—	—	—	141/49	141/143	141/145	532/279	532/259	532/304	532/287	532/29
533	—	—	—	—	142/49	142/143	142/145	533/279	533/259	533/304	533/288	533/29
534	—	—	—	—	143/49	143/143	143/145	534/279	534/259	534/304	534/288	534/30
535	—	—	—	—	144/49	144/143	144/145	535/279	535/259	535/304	535/288	535/30
536	—	—	—	—	145/49	145/143	145/145	536/279	536/259	536/304	536/288	536/31
537	—	—	—	—	146/49	146/143	146/145	537/279	537/259	537/304	537/289	537/34
538	—	—	—	—	147/49	147/143	147/145	538/279	538/259	538/304	538/289	538/35
539	—	—	—	—	148/49	148/143	148/145	539/279	539/259	539/304	539/289	539/35
540	—	—	—	—	149/49	149/143	149/145	540/279	540/259	540/304	540/289	540/36
541	—	—	—	—	150/49	150/143	150/145	541/279	541/259	541/304	541/290	541/36
542	—	—	—	—	151/50	151/144	151/146	542/279	542/259	542/304	542/290	542/37
543	—	—	—	—	152/50	152/144	152/146	543/279	543/259	543/304	543/290	543/37
544	—	—	—	—	153/50	153/144	153/146	544/279	544/259	544/304	544/290	544/38
545	—	—	—	—	154/50	154/144	154/146	545279	545/259	545/304	545/291	545/38
546	—	—	—	—	155/50	155/144	155/146	546/280	546/260	546/304	546/291	546/39
547	—	—	—	—	156/50	156/144	155/146	547/280	547/260	547/304	547/291	547/39
548	—	—	—	—	—	—	—	548/281	548/260	548/46	548/79	548/200
549	—	—	—	—	—	—	—	549/281	549/261	549/304	549/160	549/239
550	—	—	—	—	—	—	—	550/282	550/261	550/304	550/29	550/257
551	—	—	—	—	—	—	—	551/282	551/262	551/304	551/160	551/239

DPG	1858	1859	1876	1880	1890	1892	1905	1914	1926	1980	1998	2008
552	—	—	—	—	—	—	—	552/282	552/262	552/304	552/259	552/244
553	—	—	—	—	—	—	—	553/282	553/262	553/304	553/122	553/240
554	—	—	—	—	—	—	—	554/283	554/262	554/304	554/317	554/249
555	—	—	—	—	—	—	—	555/283	555/263	555/78	555/150	555/172
559	—	—	—	—	—	—	—	559/285	559/265	559/78	559/152	559/174
560	—	—	—	—	—	—	—	560/286	560/265	560/78	560/152	560/175
561	—	—	—	—	—	—	—	561/286	561/266	561/138	561/124	561/190
562	—	—	—	—	—	—	—	562/286	562/266	562/68	562/128	562/158
563	—	—	—	—	—	—	—	563/287	563/267	563/79	563/151	563/176
565	—	—	—	—	—	—	—	565/288	565/268	565/108	565/202	565/179
566	—	—	—	—	—	—	—	566/289	566/268	566/304	566/124	566/157
567	—	—	—	—	—	—	—	567/289	567/269	567/71	567/315	567/165
568	—	—	—	—	—	—	—	568/290	568/270	568/109	568/203	568/180
569	—	—	—	—	—	—	—	569/291	569/270	569/36	569/292	569/152
570	—	—	—	—	—	—	—	570/292	570/271	570/73	570/143	570/171
573	—	—	—	—	—	—	—	573/294	573/273	573/119	573/223	573/182
574	—	—	—	—	—	—	—	574/295	574/274	574/26	574/35	574/147
575	—	—	—	—	—	—	—	575/296	575/275	575/49	575/85	575/148
576	—	—	—	—	—	—	—	576/296	576/275	576/49	576/85	576/149
578	—	—	—	—	—	—	—	578/297	578/276	578/70	578/135	578/162
579	—	—	—	—	—	—	—	579/298	579/276	579/70	579/134	579/163
580	—	—	—	—	—	—	—	580/299	580/277	580/68	580/129	580/160
581	—	—	—	—	—	—	—	581/299	581/277	581/130	581/243	581/186
582	—	—	—	—	—	—	—	582/299	582/277	582/304	582/142	582/167
583	—	—	—	—	—	—	—	583/300	583/278	583/304	583/142	583/168
584	—	—	—	—	—	—	—	584/300	584/278	584/29	584/81	584/150
585	—	—	—	—	—	—	—	585/301	585/279	585/29	585/81	585/151
586	—	—	—	—	—	—	—	586/301	586/279	586/138	586/259	586/188
587	—	—	—	—	—	—	—	587/302	587/280	587/84	587/161	587/178
588	—	—	—	—	—	—	—	588/302	588/280	588/61	588/110	588/154
589	—	—	—	—	—	—	—	589/303	589/281	589/69	589/293	589/187
590	—	—	—	—	—	—	—	590/303	590/281	590/109	590/204	590/181
591	—	—	—	—	—	—	—	591/304	591/282	591/304	591/35	591/146
592	—	—	—	—	—	—	—	592/304	592/282	592/119	592/224	592/184
593	—	—	—	—	—	—	—	593/305	593/283	593/304	593/261	593/189
595	—	—	—	—	—	—	—	—	595/284	595/304	595/118	595/156
596	—	—	—	—	—	—	—	—	596/284	596/98	596/136	596/170
598	—	—	—	—	—	—	—	—	598/285	598/105	598/198	598/216
600	—	—	—	—	—	—	—	—	600/286	600/40	600/61	600/197
601	—	—	—	—	—	—	—	—	601/286	601/304	601/218	601/219
603	—	—	—	—	—	—	—	—	603/287	603/120	603/224	603/185
604	—	—	—	—	—	—	—	—	604/287	604/37	604/293	604/164
606	— —	—	—	—	—	—	—	—	606/288	606/72	606/143	606/168
607	—	—	—	—	—	—	—	—	607/288	611/304	611/132	607/210
611	—	—	—	—	—	—	—	—	—	611/45	611/3	611/192

DPG	1858	1859	1876	1880	1890	1892	1905	1914	1926	1980	1998	2008
612	—	—	—	—	—	—	—	—	—	612/304	612/166	612/214
613	—	—	—	—	—	—	—	—	—	613/304	613/294	613/229
618	—	—	—	—	—	—	—	—	—	618/304	618/115	618/208
624	—	—	—	—	—	—	—	—	—	624/305	624/294	624/215
627	—	—	—	—	—	—	—	—	—	627/105	627/199	627/218
631	—	—	—	—	—	—	—	—	—	631/305	631/254	631/260
632	—	—	—	—	—	—	—	—	—	632/305	632/55	632/197
634	—	—	—	—	—	—	—	—	—	634/305	634/222	634/222
635	—	—	—	—	—	—	—	—	—	635/305	635/222	635/220
636	—	—	—	—	—	—	—	—	—	636/305	636/294	636/220
637	—	—	—	—	—	—	—	—	—	637/305	637/222	637/221
638	—	—	—	—	—	—	—	—	—	638/305	638/222	638/222
639	—	—	—	—	—	—	—	—	—	639/305	639/222	639/221
640	—	—	—	—	—	—	—	—	—	640/305	640/294	640/223
641	—	—	—	—	—	—	—	—	—	641/305	641/294	641/223
642	—	—	—	—	—	—	—	—	—	642/305	642/294	642/224
645	—	—	—	—	—	—	—	—	—	645/305	645/317	645/254
646	—	—	—	—	—	—	—	—	—	646/305	646/317	646/230
647	—	—	—	—	—	—	—	—	—	647/305	647/317	647/230
648	—	—	—	—	—	—	—	—	—	648/305	648/144	648/213
650	—	—	—	—	—	—	—	—	—	650/305	650/263	650/228
653	—	—	—	—	—	—	—	—	—	—	653/317	653/247
654	—	—	—	—	—	—	—	—	—	—	654/317	654/247
655	—	—	—	—	—	—	—	—	—	—	655/87	655/204
657	—	—	—	—	—	—	—	—	—	—	—	657/232
658	—	—	—	—	—	—	—	—	—	—	—	658/248
659	—	—	—	—	—	—	—	—	—	—	—	659/248
660	—	—	—	—	—	—	—	—	—	—	—	660/249